Young People Transitioning from Out-of-Home Care

Philip Mendes • Pamela Snow
Editors

Young People Transitioning from Out-of-Home Care

International Research, Policy and Practice

Editors
Philip Mendes
Monash University
Victoria, Australia

Pamela Snow
Rural Health School
La Trobe University
Bendigo, Australia

ISBN 978-1-349-71762-0   ISBN 978-1-137-55639-4   (eBook)
DOI 10.1057/978-1-137-55639-4

Library of Congress Control Number: 2016951217
© The Editor(s) (if applicable) and The Author(s) 2016
Softcover reprint of the hardcover 1st edition 2016 978-1-137-55638-7
The author(s) has/have asserted their right(s) to be identified as the author(s) of this work in accordance with the Copyright, Designs and Patents Act 1988.
This work is subject to copyright. All rights are solely and exclusively licensed by the Publisher, whether the whole or part of the material is concerned, specifically the rights of translation, reprinting, reuse of illustrations, recitation, broadcasting, reproduction on microfilms or in any other physical way, and trans-mission or information storage and retrieval, electronic adaptation, computer software, or by similar or dissimilar methodology now known or hereafter developed.
The use of general descriptive names, registered names, , trademarks, service marks, etc. in this publica-tion does not imply, even in the absence of a specific statement, that such names are exempt from the relevant protective laws and regulations and therefore free for general use
The publisher, the authors and the editors are safe to assume that the advice and information in this book are believed to be true and accurate at the date of publication. Neither the publisher nor the authors or the editors give a warranty, express or implied, with respect to the material contained herein or for any errors or omissions that may have been made.

Cover illustration © Tetra Images / Alamy Stock Photo

Printed on acid-free paper

Foreword

This book makes an important contribution to one of the most significant challenges facing all those responsible for child welfare—how to improve the lives of young people moving on from care.

A body of international research has shown that outcomes for children living in care are poor in comparison to those of other children, and this often casts a long shadow on their adult lives. Those making the journey from care to adulthood have more accelerated and compressed transitions than their peers, and are more likely to be disadvantaged in respect to their main pathways to adulthood: education, training and employment, accommodation and health and well-being.

It was these findings, which, in 2003, led to the setting up of the International Research Network on Transitions to Adulthood from Care (INTRAC), bringing together, for the first time, researchers from Europe, the Middle East, Australia, Canada and the USA. This resulted in an initial mapping exercise, which included 16 countries, and later, further comparative research by INTRAC members. This book builds on this foundation. The contributors from 15 countries explore the diverse policy, practice, legal and research contexts, adding to our understanding of four key areas.

First, earlier research has identified specific groups of vulnerable care leavers whose needs may result in them requiring additional support. In part one, the authors explore in depth two groups: care leavers in the criminal justice system, and the needs of young people with developmental disabilities. The four chapters, taken together, show the importance of adopting a wider life-course approach, recognizing the relationship between individual development and policy context

Second, the chapters contained within part two, both echo and build on the findings of earlier research in identifying both the barriers and the policy reforms needed to improve the educational attainment of care leavers. Recommendations include raising aspirations, better financial and personal support, involving carers and birth families, better information and closer cooperation between teachers and social workers. It is a depressing finding that in countries where such reforms have been introduced, it has led to very little change in outcomes. Perhaps, we need to refocus the debate from using normative outcomes alone, to measuring young people's progress from entry to care, to well into adulthood, not just at the time of leaving.

Third, research shows a notable gap in comparative work on legal and policy frameworks and their implications for leaving care practice as distinct from work arising in specific jurisdictions. The contributions in part three aim to progress comparative narratives—on leaving care law, policy and practice in the UK and Scandinavia, on peer research in England, Northern Ireland and Argentina—an extension of young people's participatory rights, and on research ethics in Switzerland, Germany, Israel and China. The first contribution reminds the reader of the complexity of the comparative task: making comparisons between the 'residual liberal welfare' regime of the UK and the progressive 'social democratic welfare' regime of Scandinavian countries, in how care leavers are supported, shows that whereas the former prioritized care leavers within a strong legal framework, the latter resulted in less consistent support, by more discretionary approaches.

The final part of the book contributes to a greater understanding of leaving care policy and practice in different jurisdictions. This includes chapters from Australia on the gaps between legal and policy frameworks and discretionary practice, and the success and limitations of CREATE, an advocacy project supporting young people leaving care—another contribution extending the narrative of participatory rights. Research from both the USA and England shows the benefits for young people in both 'staying put' in placements where they are settled and receiving ongoing support into adulthood. But, as the chapter from New Zealand shows, ending support at just 17 years of age has negative implications, especially for the cultural identity of Maori young people who are over-represented in care. The chapters on Vietnam, Romania and Russia provide opportunities to compare the strengths and weaknesses of informal networks, including peer support, with the continuation of statist institutional care. Contributions from South Africa and Jordan remind the reader of the significance of wider economic and cultural contexts, respectively, including how poverty and patriarchy impact care leavers' lives.

When INTRAC was formed in 2003, it was inspired by a belief that reaching beyond a parochial understanding of young people's transitions from care to adulthood has the potential to contribute to improved outcomes for this highly vulnerable group of young people. This book represents an important contribution in furthering that belief by introducing original empirical work, discussing current problems faced by care leavers and exploring the many challenges for policy and practice in improving their lives.

Mike Stein
Emeritus Professor
Social Policy Research Unit
University of York

Preface

Young people transitioning from care are universally a vulnerable group. But there are vast differences in their experiences of out-of-home care and transitions from care, and their shorter- and longer-term outcomes. Equally, there are significant differences between jurisdictions in terms of the legislative, policy and practice supports and opportunities made available to them.

This is the first text to challenge and revise existing ways of thinking about leaving care policy, practice and research at regional, national and international levels.

Forty-three contributors from fifteen countries cover a range of topical policy and practice themes and issues presented within national, international or comparative contexts including the experiences of particularly vulnerable groups of care leavers such as those with a disability and those involved in the youth justice system, pathways to educational success and the impact of vastly different care systems and varied socio-economic and cultural contexts on care leaver opportunities and aspirations.

Globally, there appears to be limited and inadequate support for care leavers. Governments and other authorities have taken on the moral and legal obligations associated with a formal *in loco parentis* role, but have too often failed to devote sufficient resources to ensure that the outcomes for those children are better than if they had remained with their family of origin. Policy makers have not displayed the same duty of care they would demand for their own children in terms of ensuring their access to core social, community and economic opportunities and connections.

Our findings highlight the importance of action to lift the visibility of care leavers, to give them a louder voice in defining their needs at a practice and policy level and to address the systemic and structural inequities that deny them the same life chances as their non-care peers.

Acknowledgements

Philip and Pamela are both grateful to the following persons:

- Mike Stein from the University of York for kindly contributing the foreword;
- A number of anonymous reviewers from the International Research Network on Transitions to Adulthood from Care (known as INTRAC) who generously reviewed the book proposal and/or reviewed one of the contributed chapters.
- The individual chapter contributors for their hard work and good humour as we herded them through multiple drafts.
- Kerryn Bagley from LaTrobe University for her conscientious proofing of the manuscript;
- Philippa Grand and Judith Allan from Palgrave for their pleasant and effective collaboration throughout the writing process.

Philip would like to particularly thank the following people: his co-editor Pamela Snow for her reliable and energetic partnership on this project and her valued friendship throughout a number of leaving care research collaborations, and others who have helped considerably along the research journey including Jacky Buchbinder, Ray Carroll, John Chesterman, Bernie Geary, Sue Grigg, Ingrid Hojer, Amanda Jones, Ilan Katz, Paul McDonald, Jade Purtell, Jan Storo, Deb Tsorbaris, Marilyn Webster and numerous colleagues and students from within the Monash

University Social Work Department. He is always grateful to his loving wife Tamar, his children Miranda and Lucas who inspire him on a daily basis and his mother Mary who is always there to listen.

Pamela would like to thank her co-editor Philip Mendes, for his collegiality and energy as a research and writing collaborator (and for luring her over from youth justice to leaving care). She is deeply grateful for the love and support of her husband Stuart, and their family, Alli and Rob, Katie and Josh, and her new grandson Freddie. Seeing Freddie flourish in a safe, loving home is a daily reminder of why we do this work.

Contents

Part I	**Particularly Vulnerable Groups of Care Leavers**	1
1	**The Double-Bind: Looked After Children, Care Leavers and Criminal Justice** Nicola Carr and Siobhán McAlister	3
2	**Young People Transitioning from Out-of-Home Care in Victoria, Australia: Strengthening Support Services for Dual Clients of Child Protection and Youth Justice** Philip Mendes, Pamela C. Snow, and Susan Baidawi	23
3	**Supporting Young People with an Intellectual Disability Transitioning from Out-of-Home Care to Adult Life in Queensland, Australia** Sarah MacDonald, Kathy Ellem, and Jill Wilson	45
4	**A Comparison of Young People with a Disability Transitioning from Out-of-Home Care in Australia and Northern Ireland** Pamela Snow, Berni Kelly, Philip Mendes, and Delia O'Donohue	71

| Part II | Pathways to Educational Success | 91 |

5 Towards a National Policy Framework for Care Leavers in Australian Higher Education — 93
Andrew Harvey, Patricia McNamara, and Lisa Andrewartha

6 I Want to Be Someone, I Want to Make a Difference: Young Care Leavers Preparing for the Future in South Australia — 115
Dee Michell and Claudine Scalzi

7 Muddling Upwards: The Unexpected, Unpredictable and Strange on the Path from Care to High Achievement in Victoria, Australia — 135
Jacqueline Z. Wilson and Frank Golding

8 The Contribution of a Key Scenario to Care Leavers' Transition to Higher Education — 155
Yifat Mor-Salwo and Anat Zeira

9 The Drawback of Getting By—Implicit Imbalances in the Educational Support of Young People in and Leaving Care in Germany — 173
Stefan Köngeter, Wolfgang Schröer, and Maren Zeller

| Part III | Comparative Policy and Practice in Different Jurisdictions | 197 |

10 Leaving Care in the UK and Scandinavia: Is It All That Different in Contrasting Welfare Regimes? — 199
Emily R. Munro, Anne-Kirstine Mølholt, and Katie Hollingworth

11 Peer Research with Young People Leaving Care: Reflections from Research in England, Northern Ireland and Argentina 221
Berni Kelly, Jo Dixon, and Mariana Incarnato

12 Researching Care Leavers in an Ethical Manner in Switzerland, Germany, Israel and China 241
Samuel Keller, Benjamin Strahl, Tehila Refaeli, and Claire (Ting) Zhao

Part IV An Analysis of Policy and Practice in Specific Jurisdictions 263

13 Young People Transitioning from Care in Australia: A Critical But Neglected Area of Policy Development 265
Toni Beauchamp

14 CREATE's Advocacy for Young People Transitioning from Care in Australia 285
Joseph J. McDowall

15 Journeys of Exclusion: Unpacking the Experience of Adolescent Care Leavers in New Zealand 309
Nicola Atwool

16 Youth Leaving Care in Developing Countries: Observations from Vietnam 329
Mary Elizabeth Collins and Bùi Thị Thanh Tuyền

17 Young People Transitioning from Residential Care in South Africa: Welfare Contexts, Resilience, Research and Practice 349
Adrian D van Breda and Lisa Dickens

Contents

**18 Improving Institutional Care to Enhance Outcomes
     for Care Leavers in Russia**   367
Evgenia Stepanova and Simon Hackett

**19 Cast Out and Punished: The Experiences of Care
     Leavers in Jordan**   389
Rawan W. Ibrahim

**20 The Role of Informal Leaving Care Peer Support
     Networks in Romania**   409
Gabriela Dima and John Pinkerton

Index   427

Editors and Contributors

Editors

Philip Mendes is Director of the Social Inclusion and Social Policy Research Unit (SISPRU) in the Department of Social Work at Monash University in Victoria, Australia. He has been undertaking research on young people transitioning from care for nearly 20 years, and has completed major projects pertaining to indigenous care leavers, youth justice, disability, employment and mentoring programmes and other practice and policy supports. He is the author or co-author of ten books including *Young People Leaving State Out-of-Home Care: Australian Policy and Practice* (2011) and a third edition of *Australia's Welfare Wars* (forthcoming late 2016).

Pamela C. Snow is Head of the Rural Health School at La Trobe University in Victoria, Australia. She is a registered psychologist, having qualified originally in speech pathology. Her research is concerned with vulnerable young people, whether in the context of state care, youth justice and/or education. She has published more than 85 papers in refereed journals, and has authored or co-authored 11 book chapters and one book. She is co-authoring a book on controversial interventions for children with neurodevelopmental disorders, *Making Sense of Interventions for Children's Development Disabilities*, to be published in early 2017.

Contributors

Lisa Andrewartha is Research Officer in the Access and Achievement Research Unit at La Trobe University. She has a Bachelor of Applied Science in Psychology (Honours). Andrewartha's recent research publications have focused on improving the access and achievement levels of students who are under-represented in higher education.

Nicola Atwool is Associate Professor in the Department of Sociology, Gender and Social Work at the University of Otago, New Zealand. She returned to academia following six years as a Principal Advisor in the Office of the Children's Commissioner. Prior to that, she was Senior Lecturer in Social Work at the University of Otago and worked with the Children's Issues Centre. Atwool came to academia with nearly 20 years' experience as a practitioner employed by Child, Youth and Family.

Susan Baidawi is a Ph.D. Candidate and Research Officer in the Department of Social Work at Monash University, Australia. Her research interests include young people transitioning from state out-of-home care and older people in prison.

Toni Beauchamp is Principal Policy Officer at Uniting Centre for Research, Innovation and Advocacy in New South Wales. She has a Bachelor of Arts/Social Work and a Masters in Applied Social Policy and Research. Beauchamp has a particular interest in improving support for young people transitioning from care and has published several policy papers on this issue.

Nicola Carr is Lecturer in Criminology in Queen's University Belfast. Her main research focuses on the sociology of punishment in the areas of youth justice, community sanctions, prisons and parole. Her interests include the intersections between institutions of governance such as child protection and welfare and criminal justice, and she has written and researched in this area.

Mary Elizabeth Collins is Associate Dean for Academic Affairs and Professor of Social Welfare Policy at Boston University School of Social Work. Her research focuses on child welfare policy and supports for vulnerable youth. She has most recently published *Macro Perspectives on Youth Aging Out of Foster Care*.

Lisa Dickens is a doctoral graduate in social work at the University of Johannesburg and a senior researcher at Girls and Boys Town South Africa, an NGO that provides child and family services.

Gabriela Dima is an associate professor at Transilvania University of Brasov, Romania, with work experience as a psychologist and social worker. She received her Ph.D. from Queen's University Belfast, School of Sociology, Social Policy and Social Work. She is President of the SCUT Association of Social Services Brasov, a non-governmental organization running programmes for young people leaving care and after care.

Jo Dixon is Research Fellow in the Department of Social Policy and Social Work, University of York. She has conducted several studies of young people in, and leaving, care in the UK. Her current research includes evaluating housing co-operatives for care leavers, and studies of preventative approaches for families and young people on the edge of care.

Kathy Ellem is Lecturer at the School of Public Health and Social Work, Queensland University of Technology. Her research interests include the life experiences of people with intellectual disability (including those people who find themselves in the criminal justice system), disability advocacy and social work with families who have a member with a disability. She has many years of practice experience as a social worker in the disability sector.

Frank Golding is an independent scholar specializing in welfare history, social justice and human rights. His childhood as a ward of the state of Victoria, Australia, in the 'care' of foster mothers and institutions underpins his involvement in care leaver issues as an advocate and lobbyist. After a career as a teacher and school principal including a multi-site English language centre for refugees, he taught in, and managed curriculum and equity programmes in, state education departments and universities. He is the author of 12 published books including a memoir, *An Orphan's Escape: Memories of a Lost Childhood*.

Simon Hackett is Professor of Applied Social Sciences and Principal of St Mary's College, Durham University, UK. His research focuses on the nature and impact of child maltreatment and on professional interventions for children and families.

Andrew Harvey is Director of the Access and Achievement Research Unit at La Trobe University. He has a Bachelor of Arts (Honours) and Ph.D. in Politics. Harvey has published widely on student equity in higher education, including issues of access for care leavers and other under-represented students.

Katie E. Hollingworth is a researcher at the Thomas Coram Research Unit, Institute of Education, University College London. Her particular area of interest is research with children and young people in public care and leaving care. She has worked on a number of studies in this area including a five-country, cross-national study on the post-compulsory educational pathways of young people leaving care (YiPPEE).

Rawan W. Ibrahim is a researcher and practitioner in child and youth alternative care settings. She has been supporting the Jordanian government to embark on the process of deinstitutionalizing children through developing foster care. In addition to implementation science and the development of community-based programmes, her research interests include preparation and post-care support of youth transitioning from substitute care to adulthood. Of particular interest are subgroups such as those separated from families at birth and at-risk young women.

Mariana Incarnato is Executive Director of Doncel, a civil association based in Argentina, which works for the rights of children and adolescents. Incarnato holds a Bachelor of Psychology from the University of Buenos Aires and is a specialist in working with vulnerable groups. She is a former member of the adoption team at the Carolina Tobar Garcia Hospital for children.

Samuel Keller is Research Assistant, Social pedagogue (M.A.), Institute for Childhood, Youth and Family, Zurich University of Applied Sciences, School of Social Work, and a member of the Ph.D. group of the International Research Network on Transitions to Adulthood from Care (INTRAC). His research interests include the well-being and growing up of children, child and youth care and transitions to adulthood.

Berni Kelly is Senior Lecturer in Social Work and Co-chair of the Disability Research Network at Queen's University Belfast. Her main research interests are participatory child and youth disability studies and transitions from care to adult life. She is currently working on two studies of disabled children and young people living in, and leaving, public care in Northern Ireland.

Stefan Köngeter is Professor of Social Pedagogy at the Department for Education at Trier University, Germany. After completing his Ph.D. in 2008, he was a postdoctoral research fellow at the University of Hildesheim, Germany, and at the University of Toronto, Canada. His research interests comprise a broad range of topics in social pedagogy, social work and sociology. He has published extensively on the professionalization of social pedagogy, particularly on relational practices between children, parents and social workers, and on young people leaving care.

Siobhán McAlister is Lecturer in Criminology in Queen's University Belfast. Her research interests are in youth transitions, youth, conflict and marginalization and the intersection between social justice and criminal justice. She is also interested in qualitative research methods and practices with marginalized groups.

Sarah MacDonald is Social Worker and Ph.D. Candidate at the University of Queensland, School of Nursing, Midwifery and Social Work. Her doctoral research is concerned with the experiences of people with intellectual disability transitioning from out-of-home care to adult life. She has worked in direct practice, in research and in governance roles alongside people with intellectual disability for more than 15 years.

Joseph J. McDowall has lectured at both Queensland and Griffith Universities, and since 2002, has conducted consultancies in out-of-home care for governments and NGOs. As Executive Director (Research) at CREATE, he has authored four major national reports, all presenting the voices of young people transitioning from care. He is currently a Visiting Fellow at Queensland University of Technology, and is a Fellow of the Queensland Academy of Arts and Sciences.

Patricia McNamara is Adjunct Senior Lecturer—Social Work in the Department of Clinical and Community Allied Health at La Trobe University. She holds qualifications in education and family therapy, and a Ph.D. in Social Work. McNamara's current research activities focus on education during and post out-of-home care, therapeutic residential programmes and the needs of Forgotten Australians.

Dee Michell spent 15 years in foster care as a ward of the South Australian State. She is Senior Lecturer in the Department of Gender Studies & Social Analysis at the University of Adelaide, where she conducts social research in the areas of widening participation in Higher Education and the history of foster care in Australia.

Anne-Kirstine Mølholt is a Ph.D. student at the Aalborg University, Denmark. Her research topic is the experiences of young people who have left care. She is a board member of both the Danish and Nordic Sociological Associations. Her publications include 'Keeping You Close at a Distance: Ethical Challenges when following Young People in Vulnerable Life Situations' (with Tea Torbenfeldt Bengtsson 2016).

Yifat Mor-Salwo is a doctoral candidate at the School of Social Work and Social Welfare at the Hebrew University of Jerusalem, where she also earned a Bachelor of Social Work and Master of Social Work. With her previous experience as a clinical social worker in residential care, her Ph.D. thesis focuses on the integration of care leavers into higher education.

Emily R. Munro is Professor of Social Work Research and Director of the Tilda Goldberg Centre at the University of Bedfordshire. She is a coordinator of the International Research Network on Transitions to Adulthood from Care, and co-edited *Young People's Transitions from Care to Adulthood: International Research and Practice* (Stein and Munro 2008).

Delia O'Donohue has a Bachelor of Arts, Bachelor of Social Work and Master of Social Work. She is currently working as a consultant undertaking research projects for non-government organizations, group supervision and sessional teaching in the Masters and Bachelor of Social Work programmes at RMIT University. She has extensive direct practice experience managing programmes for disadvantaged young people, and was previously employed as a lecturer in social work at Monash University.

John Pinkerton is Professor of Child and Family Social Work at Queen's University Belfast, UK. He has been involved in researching and writing on leaving care since the early 1990s when he undertook a baseline study in Northern Ireland. He is interested in comparative work, in particular South Africa. He has supervised doctoral research on the Ukraine, Romania, Ghana and China.

Tehila Refaeli is a post-doctoral fellow in the school of Social Work at the Hebrew University, Israel, and an adjunct lecturer at Bar Ilan University. Her research interests include youth at risk during transition to adulthood, and, in particular, transition from care, educational achievements in care and after care and programmes of civic-national service for youth at risk.

Claudine Scalzi has worked as a Youth Worker for the past 12 years, and in a variety of organizations and roles. She is currently State Coordinator of the CREATE Foundation in South Australia, a National organization, which represents the voices of children in out-of-home care.

Wolfgang Schröer is Professor at the School of Social Pedagogy and Organization Studies, University of Hildesheim, Germany. His writings and research activities range from contributions on transnational social support, child and youth care, to writings about citizenship and social policy. He has co-edited special issues on "Children's lives away from home" (2015) within *Transnational Social Review*, and also co-edited the second edition of the German handbook on child and youth care (2016).

Evgenia Stepanova is a Research Associate in the School of Applied Social Sciences, Durham University, UK. She holds a Ph.D. from Durham University, exploring the nature of institutional care for children and young people in Russia.

Benjamin Strahl is Research Assistant, Social Pedagogue (Dipl.), Institute for Social Pedagogy and Organization Studies, University of Hildesheim; and a member of the Ph.D. group of the International Research Network on Transitions to Adulthood from Care (INTRAC). His research interests includes child and youth care, education and care and transitions to adulthood.

Bùi Thị Thanh Tuyền is a Ph.D. student at the School of Social Work, University of Illinois at Urbana-Champaign. She is the former Department Head and Lecturer, Faculty of Social Work, College of Social Sciences and Humanities, Vietnam National University-Ho Chi Minh City, Vietnam. Her research interests include homeless children and adolescents, students with disabilities and gender issues.

Adrian D van Breda is Associate Professor of Social Work and Head of Department at the University of Johannesburg, South Africa. His research interests centre on resilience and youth transitions (particularly care-leaving) using both qualitative and quantitative methods.

Jacqueline Z. Wilson is Associate Professor at the School of Arts at Federation University Australia. Her current research and publications focus on historical sites of incarceration and institutionalization and their role in the formalization and emergence of welfare and justice systems. Wilson is a former ward of the state of Victoria, Australia, and as a child experienced foster care and orphanage placements, periods in youth hostels and homelessness. This underpins her research into care leavers, with a particular interest in archival histories and inclusive record keeping. She has authored more than 40 scholarly publications, including four books, with a research focus on the intersections between public history, incarceration and sites of suffering and trauma.

Jill Wilson has a Bachelor of Social Studies, Master of Social Work and Ph.D., and has worked in the social work programme at the University of Queensland over a lengthy period. She has taught in field education and social work practice, and researched pre-dominantly in the areas of cognitive impairment across age groups, and ageing. Jill has had a long association with Uniting Care Queensland and in the development of human services.

Anat Zeira is Professor at the School of Social Work and Social Welfare at the Hebrew University of Jerusalem, and Head of Research and Evaluation at the Haruv Institute. Her research on the transition to adulthood and independent living of care leavers has been published widely in professional journals and presented at numerous international conferences.

Maren Zeller is Assistant Professor of Social Pedagogy at the Department for Education, Trier University, Germany. She holds a Ph.D. in Education from Hildesheim University. Her recent research focuses on child and youth welfare and on refugee studies. Recently, she has co-edited a special issue on 'Children's lives away from home' (2015) within Transnational Social Review, and co-authored the first German monograph on care leavers (2015).

Claire (Ting) Zhao is a Ph.D. Student in the School of Sociology, Social Policy and Social Work, Queen's University Belfast, and a member of the Ph.D. group of the International Research Network on Transitions to Adulthood from Care (INTRAC). She is interested in youth transition from State care in the context of mainland China.

Abbreviations

AAYPIC	Australian Association of Young People in Care
ABC	Australian Broadcasting Corporation
ACWA	Association of Children's Welfare Agencies, Australia
ADHD	Attention Deficit Hyperactivity Disorder
ARCs	Area Research Coordinators, England
CA	Construyendo Autonomia/Building Independence Study, Argentina
CP	Corporate Parenting Study, England
CHE	Centre for Higher Education Development, Germany
CYCCs	Child and Youth Care Centres, South Africa
CYF	Child, Youth and Family, New Zealand
CYP	Children and Young People in Care
EPIC	Empowering People in Care, Republic of Ireland
FaHCSIA	Department of Families, Housing, Community Services and Indigenous Affairs, Australia
FLACSO	Faculty of Social Sciences, Argentina
GBT	Girls and Boys Town, South Africa
GHQ	General Health Questionnaire, Northern Ireland
GYOW	Go Your Own Way leaving-care kits
HE	Higher Education, Australia
INTRAC	International Research Network on Transitions to Adulthood from Care
IPA	Interpretative Phenomenological Analysis
MOLISA	Ministry of Labour, Invalids and Social Affairs, Vietnam

NCAS	National Care Advisory Service
NEET	Not in Employment, Education or Training
NGOs	Non-Governmental Organizations
NLCBF	National Leaving Care Benchmarking Forum, England
OCC	Office of the Children's Commissioner, New Zealand
OECD	Organisation for Economic Cooperation and Development
OHC	Out-of-Home Care
PR	Peer Research
RFPP	Risk Factor Prevention Paradigm
SA-YES	South African Youth Education for Sustainability
SPSS	Statistical Package for the Social Sciences
UNCRC	United Nations Convention on the Rights of the Child
UNCRPD	United Nations Convention on the Rights of People with Disabilities
VOYPIC	Voice of Young People in Care, Northern Ireland
YiPPEE	Young People from a Public Care Background: Pathways to Education in Europe
YOLO	You Only Leave Once? Study, Northern Ireland

List of Figures

Fig. 10.1	Pinkerton's three-domain model for international comparison (Pinkerton 2008, p. 249)	201
Fig. 12.1	Ethically relevant dimensions in research design and process	244
Fig. 14.1	Organizational structure of the CREATE Foundation as on October 2015	289
Fig. 20.1	Psychosocial phases of transition adapted to leaving care	412
Fig. 20.2	Social ecology of leaving care	413

List of Tables

Table 5.1	Survey responses by university group	96
Table 9.1	Importance of higher education	187
Table 9.2	Support in school	188
Table 18.1	Personal characteristics and institutional experiences of members of staff	376

Introduction

Philip Mendes, Pamela C. Snow

Young people transitioning from out-of-home care (often called care leavers) are universally a vulnerable group whose needs have been neglected not only by their biological parents, but also by their substitute parent, the State. Leaving care is formally defined as the cessation of legal responsibility by the state for young people living in out-of-home care, which generally occurs at no later than 18 years of age. In practice, however, leaving care is a major life transformation, and a process that involves transitioning from dependence on state accommodation and supports (notwithstanding their inherent and considerable limitations) to so-called independence and self-reliance (Cashmore and Mendes 2015). Care leavers often face significant barriers to accessing educational, employment, housing and other development and transitional opportunities that are readily available to their non-care peers (Mendes et al. 2014).

Historically, most countries have provided only limited leaving care support services. However, over the past two decades, there has been grow-

P. Mendes (✉)
Monash University, Melbourne, VIC, Australia

P.C. Snow
Rural Health School, La Trobe University, Bendigo, VIC, Australia

ing international awareness of the needs of care leavers. Consequently, most of the Organisation for Economic Cooperation and Development (OECD) countries and many other jurisdictions have introduced new legislation or expanded existing laws, policies or programmes to assist this group of disadvantaged young people (Mendes et al. 2011). Nevertheless, there is still much more that needs to be done to improve their life chances. In practice, many care leavers still do not receive the ongoing and holistic supports they require to transition successfully into adult life, even though these may be embedded in written policy documents.

To be sure, their experiences vary significantly between and even within national jurisdictions. Indigenous young people form a disproportionate component of care leaver cohorts in anglophone countries such as Australia, Canada, the USA and New Zealand, and struggle to retain their cultural identity and connections (Mendes et al. 2016). The number of care leavers is far greater and their needs more acute in many African, Asian, South American and some former Soviet Bloc countries compared to, say, Western Europe and the English-speaking countries. Equally, there are significant differences between jurisdictions in terms of the legislative, policy and practice supports and opportunities made available to care leavers. Most young people leaving care in the Western world transition from smaller children's homes and foster care or kinship care placements, which are judged to be more effective in facilitating stability and emotional security. In contrast, those living in non-Western countries are still more likely to be placed in large institutions, which can significantly harm children's emotional, cognitive and language development, although the United Nations is actively encouraging a shift towards smaller-scale living arrangements (Stein 2014).

Care leavers are not a homogeneous group, and have varied backgrounds and experiences in terms of the structure and capacity of their families, the type and extent of abuse or neglect, the age at which they enter care, their cultural and ethnic backgrounds, their in-care experiences, their developmental stage and needs when exiting care, the presence of special needs such as developmental disability or mental illness and the quantity and quality of supports available to them.

The leading UK researcher Mike Stein (2012) has broadly classified care leavers into three categories. The first he terms the 'moving-on group'. Young people in this group are likely to have experienced secure and stable placements, be highly resilient, welcome independence and be able to make effective use of leaving and aftercare supports. The second group he terms 'survivors'. They have experienced significant instability and discontinuity. Outcomes for this group tend to reflect the effectiveness of post-care supports provided. The 'strugglers' are the third group. They are likely to have had the most negative pre-care experiences, and are most likely to experience significant social and emotional deficits. Aftercare support is unlikely to alleviate these problems, but is still viewed as important by them. It is important to remember that outcomes for care leavers are fluid, and some may have poor initial transitions and fall into the survivor or struggler group, but later, when they mature (and with the availability of ongoing supports at 20 or 21 years of age), they will be able to 'move on' into the mainstream. They need to be able to access second or third chances, just as ordinary parents in the community stand by their own children as they test limits and learn from their mistakes.

The reasons for the vulnerability of care leavers are arguably threefold. Firstly, many come from highly chaotic and disadvantaged families characterized by poverty, relationship breakdown, substance abuse, violence, disability and mental illness. For example, a study of 170 care leavers aged 18–24 years from five European countries found that almost all came from dysfunctional families in which serious neglect and physical, sexual and/or emotional abuse were prevalent. Most of their parents had low levels of education and were reliant on income security payments. Few of the young people seem to have had parents who supported and prioritized their educational participation and development (Cameron et al. 2012; Jackson and Cameron 2014).

Such pre-care experiences of abuse and neglect often causes long-term trauma that contributes to global and chronic developmental delays. Many children enter care with significant emotional and behavioural problems and physical health deficits. Additionally, the sudden separation from birth parents, extended family and often siblings that occurs on entry to care can be highly debilitating (McDowall 2015).

Secondly, some young people experience inadequacies in State care including poor quality caregivers, and constant shifts of placement, carers, schools and workers. In Australia, the most disadvantaged group of adolescents in care, who are not deemed suitable for foster or kinship placements, are mostly placed in residential care facilities, which operate on a rostered worker model. Residential care workers are generally low-paid and poorly trained, and may lack the skills to understand behavioural manifestations of trauma exposure and to engage and support the young people. Nevertheless, many children and young people in out-of-home care experience supportive and stable placements, including an ongoing positive relationship with carers and workers, which enable them to overcome adversities resulting from their pre-care experiences. Researchers such as Stein (2006) and Wade et al. (2010) remind us that the State care system has produced positive outcomes for many young people despite their earlier deprivation.

Thirdly, many care leavers can call on little, if any, direct family support or other community networks to ease their transition into independent living. They may not have access to the human capital and broader social connections that other young people use to attain part-time work, to develop pathways into further and higher education, to access shared and affordable housing and to form supportive relationships.

In addition to these major disadvantages, care leavers currently experience an abrupt end at 16–18 years of age to the formal support networks of State care, including the funding of their core housing, education or training and health needs. That is, the state as corporate parent fails to provide the ongoing financial, social and emotional support and nurturing offered by most families. Most other young people, at least in countries such as Australia, now live at home until 21 or even 25 years of age (Australian Bureau of Statistics 2009), and even those who leave home may still call on their families for ongoing financial, practical and emotional assistance. In contrast, care leavers, who, as a result of their background experiences, are the group least likely to be developmentally ready for independence at 18 years of age, are expected to almost instantaneously transform into self-sufficient adults without any safety net.

So why is there such universal tardiness in improving supports for care leavers? One factor seems to be that children who grow up in out-of-home care are still stigmatized as an 'undeserving' group. For much of the twentieth century, a similar stigma was attached to children born to single mothers, who were labelled bastards and illegitimate, and hence not deserving of equal life chances (Handler and Hasenfeld 2007; Reekie 1998). Thankfully, legal and moral prejudices against unmarried mothers and their children have significantly declined. But care leavers seem to remain a group apart who are judged to be unworthy of the same opportunities as their non-care peers (Michell 2015; Michell et al. 2015). Policy makers continue to focus on their perceived individual failings, rather than on the significant structural barriers to their successful transition into adult life. The limited resources devoted to their welfare seems to almost represent an implicit warning to the societal mainstream of the negative consequences for those citizens who fail to conform to expected standards of parenting and family values and functioning.

Another factor influencing the abandonment of substitute parental duties at 18 years is that state care is costly and a serious drain on public finances at a time of global financial austerity (Cronin 2013). For example, Australia currently spends $AUD2.2 billion nationally on out-of-home care (Productivity Commission 2015). However, caring for any children is expensive, and the birth parents of non-care young people generally do not abrogate their financial responsibilities when their child attains 18 years of age. Yet, most jurisdictions only spend a tiny amount of their overall out-of-home care budget on leaving care and post-care supports. This is despite the fact that a number of cost–benefit analyses suggest that greater social investment in care leavers in the short to medium term would reduce the degree of welfare dependency and related government costs in the longer term by much greater levels (Raman et al. 2005; Peters et al. 2009; Hannon et al. 2010). But governments remain reluctant parents, and seem to be unwilling to spend this extra money, even if it will produce large savings in the longer term for those in their care.

In this text, our 43 contributors from 15 different countries address a range of key debates pertaining to leaving care policy and practice within national and international contexts. Part one explores the experiences of particularly vulnerable groups of care leavers such as those who are involved in the youth justice system (and often later, the adult criminal justice system), and those who have a significant disability. For example, Nicola Carr and Siobham McAlister from Northern Ireland examine some of the oft-used theoretical explanations for the over-representation of care leavers in the criminal justice system. They suggest that a complex interplay of individual characteristics and social environments impacts the identity and behaviour of young people, and determines whether there is a capacity for desistance from offending. Philip Mendes and colleagues from Australia present the findings of a three-year study of the views of service providers and care leavers as to policies and practices that might reduce this over-representation. They recommend a range of reforms including particularly a trauma-informed approach that could enable young people to overcome the adverse developmental impacts of horrendous childhood experiences.

Similarly, two chapters explore the particular challenges and needs of young people with a developmental disability who are over-represented in out-of-home care systems, and whose outcomes tend to be poor. Sarah McDonald and her colleagues from Queensland, Australia, document the complex disadvantage and poor outcomes experienced by a small group of care leavers with an intellectual disability. They argue for policy and practice responses that address the intersecting experiences of intellectual disability, relationships and service systems in order to deliver holistic whole-of-life services and supports. Pamela Snow and her colleagues compare and contrast the findings of two recent studies of care leavers with a disability in Australia and Northern Ireland. They argue that significant policy and practice reforms are required, providing for ongoing specialist support, greater participation by care leavers, more transparent definitions of disability and clearer eligibility criteria for access to youth and adult support services. Even the definition of 'disability' remains contested, and so is a barrier to serious policy and practice reform.

Part two analyses the stories of care leavers who have successfully entered higher education, and the policies and practices that either enhance, or alternatively inhibit, such access. Andrew Harvey and colleagues present the findings of a study that critically examined strategies for raising university access by care leavers in Australia. They recommend a number of reforms to improve education pathways including the collection of nationally consistent data, identification of care leavers as an under-represented group within the higher education system and improved assistance from a range of child welfare and educational stakeholders. Dee Michel and Claudine Scalzi discuss the findings from a study of care leavers with experience of further and higher education. Their findings concur with those of Harvey et al. in emphasizing the need for carers, workers and teachers to provide encouragement to children in care to achieve educational success.

Jacqueline Wilson and Frank Golding dissect their own challenging pathways from care to educational achievement. They highlight the many barriers and inequities confronting care leavers, and urge policy makers to provide financial and personal support to enable the educational aspirations of those leaving care. Yifat Mor-Salwo and Anat Zeira present the findings of a study of young people who successfully progressed from residential care to higher education in Israel. They highlight the importance of both carers and birth families supporting the value of education. Stefan Kongeter and his colleagues examine the educational pathways of older adolescents in, and leaving, care in Germany. They found that nearly half their participants were interested in progressing to further or higher education, but that their aspirations were often not shared by care system staff, resulting in limited support. They argue that greater financial and social assistance is required to facilitate greater access to higher education.

Part three presents comparisons of policy and practice in different countries or jurisdictions. Emily Munro and her colleagues examine similarities and differences in legislation, policy and practice in the UK and Scandinavia. They debunk the widespread assumption that the social democratic welfare regime in Scandinavia would offer more generous assistance to care leavers than the residual liberal welfare regime in the UK. On the contrary, the social investment focus in the UK, which is concerned with both the social and economic costs of disadvantage, has driven greater aftercare support by local authorities, whereas aftercare assistance in Scandinavia has remained reliant on local discretion. Nevertheless, the message from both jurisdictions is that regulation needs to be accompanied by adequate resourcing and supportive relationships with professional and non-professional networks to facilitate improved outcomes.

Berni Kelly and colleagues assess the benefits and challenges of using peer research (PR) methods in England, Northern Ireland and Argentina. They conclude that PR enhances recruitment, reduces attrition and facilitates rapport and empathy with participants. But they also document challenges such as the need for greater time and additional resources, and ongoing training and support for peer researchers. They recommend that clear pathways be established to ensure co-production of data collection, analysis and dissemination.

Samuel Keller and his colleagues explore the ethical challenges of leaving care research in four different countries: China, Germany, Israel and

Switzerland. They highlight four chronological dimensions based on the research field work experience: entering the field, completing the interview, leaving the field and reflecting on cultural factors in ethical decision-making.

Part four provides an overview of policy, practice and legislation in specific jurisdictions. Toni Beauchamp and Joseph McDowall both discuss the Australian context. Beauchamp notes that most states and territories, and even the Commonwealth, have introduced policies and legislation assisting care leavers, but, in practice, access to aftercare support tends to be limited and discretionary. She argues in favour of the introduction of a legal duty of support that proscribes mandatory assistance until 25 years backed up by satisfactory budget allocation. McDowall, in contrast, analyses the advocacy activities of the CREATE Foundation, which supports children and young people in, and leaving, care. He discusses their key lobbying strategies such as collaborations with government, biennial conferences, media actions and policy submissions, and argues that the Foundation has been effective in providing a voice for care leavers in policy debates and contributing to improved support for transitions from care. But he also acknowledges some constraints on their work such as limited funding, and the barriers placed by government that limit their access to the OHC population.

Nicola Atwool provides a case study of New Zealand, and notes the inadequacy of existing supports, which cease at the tender age of 17 years. This is of particular concern given the high proportion of indigenous Maori children in care, and their struggles to retain their cultural identity when leaving care. She recommends extension of the leaving care age until at least 18 years of age, and urges the introduction of ongoing transition services in order to overcome the social exclusion of care leavers.

Mary Collins and Bui Tuyen analyse the informal systems of care offered by non-government and voluntary agencies in Vietnam. They argue that despite the absence of a formal child welfare system, the existing leaving care supports have a number of strengths including flexibility around age of departure, the teaching of life skills and a broader cultural context of communal social solidarity. Evgenia Stepanova and Simon Hackett critically examine the child welfare system in Russia, which is still dominated by old-style institutional care. Drawing on an empirical study of care leavers and caregivers, they propose a number of specific policy and practice reforms including greater professional training for caregivers, and staffing approaches that facilitate supportive and ongoing relationships between caregivers and care leavers.

Adrian D van Breda and Lisa Dickens argue that the developmental social welfare approach in South Africa, whilst intended to address the high prevalence of general poverty and inequality, particularly amongst the youth population, has tended to neglect the specific needs of care leavers. Noting limited research on care leavers in South Africa, to date, they argue for the development of enhanced support models that teach independent living skills and provide opportunities for positive education and employment outcomes.

Rawan Ibrahim critically examines the adverse impact of patriarchal culture and associated stigmatization on care leavers in Jordan. These cultural factors exacerbate their existing social disadvantage by creating additional barriers to accessing housing, employment and social relationships. She argues for the inclusion of a cultural component within international models of leaving care.

Finally, Dima and Pinkerton explore the role of informal peer networks in assisting care leavers. Drawing on three sets of data from Romania, they argue that peer networks can facilitate access to key resources such as housing, money, food, jobs and emotional support. However, there are negatives as well as benefits, and peer networks may reinforce negative behaviours and a 'care identity' that blocks them from moving into the societal mainstream.

Our contributors cover no fewer than 15 different jurisdictions, but their narratives present a commonality of limited and inadequate support for care leavers. Governments and other authorities that have taken on the moral and legal obligations associated with a formal *in loco parentis* role have too often failed to devote sufficient resources to ensure that the outcomes for those children are better than if they had remained with their family of origin. Policy makers have not displayed the same duty of care they would demand for their own children in terms of ensuring their access to education, training, employment, housing, health care and other core social, community and economic opportunities and connections.

These commonalities remain despite the fact that our authors cover vastly different socio-economic contexts and welfare regimes. Their studies also incorporate contrasts between formal government and voluntary non-government child welfare systems, foster or kinship versus institutional care, large numbers of children and young people in care as opposed to much smaller numbers, different factors such as poverty and migration in Vietnam contrasted with legally assessed child abuse and neglect in Western countries driving entry into care and major differences in cultural attitudes towards care populations. Yet, similar concerns around exclusion from the social and economic mainstream prevail.

Clearly, much more needs to be done across the globe to raise the visibility of care leavers, to give them a louder voice in defining their needs at a practice and policy level and to address the systemic and structural inequities that deny them the same life chances as their non-care peers.

References

Australian Bureau of Statistics. (2009). *Home and away: The living arrangements of young people.* Canberra: ABS.

Cameron, C., Jackson, S., Hauari, H., & Hollingworth, K. (2012). Continuing educational participation among children in care in five countries: Some issues of social class. *Journal of Education Policy, 27*(3), 387–399.

Cashmore, J., & Mendes, P. (2015). Children and young people leaving care. In A. Smith (Ed.), *Enhancing children's rights: Connecting research, policy and practice* (pp. 140–150). Houndmills: Palgrave Macmillan.

Cronin, M. (2013). Care leavers. In G. Brotherton & M. Cronin (Eds.), *Working with vulnerable children, young people and families* (pp. 85–105). Hoboken: Taylor and Francis.

Handler, J., & Hasenfeld, Y. (2007). *Blame welfare, ignore poverty and inequality.* Cambridge: Cambridge University Press.

Hannon, C., Wood, C., & Bazalgette, L. (2010). *In loco parentis.* London: Demos.

Jackson, S., & Cameron, C. (2014). *Improving access to further and higher education for young people in public care.* London: Jessica Kingsley Publishers.

McDowall, J. (2015). *Sibling placement and contact in out-of-home care.* Sydney: CREATE Foundation.

Mendes, P., Johnson, G., & Moslehuddin, B. (2011). *Young people leaving state out-of-home care: A research-based study of Australian policy and practice.* Melbourne: Australian Scholarly Publishing Press.

Mendes, P., Pinkerton, J., & Munro, E. (2014). Guest editorial: Young people transitioning from out-of-home care: An issue of social justice. *Australian Social Work, 67*(1), 1–4.

Mendes, P., Saunders, B., & Baidawi, S. (2016). *Indigenous care leavers in Victoria: Final report.* Melbourne: Monash University Department of Social Work.

Michell, D. (2015). Foster care, stigma and the sturdy, unkillable children of the very poor. *Continuum: Journal of Media & Cultural Studies, 29*(4), 663–676.

Michell, D., Jackson, D., & Tonkin, C. (Eds.) (2015). *Against the odds: Care leavers at university.* Elizabeth: People's Voice Publishing.

Peters, C. M., Dworsky, A., Courtney, M., & Pollack, H. (2009). *Extending foster care to age 21: Weighing the costs to government against the benefits to youth.* Chicago: Chapin Hall.

Productivity Commission. (2015). *Report on government services.* Canberra: Productivity Commission.

Raman, S., Inder, B., & Forbes, C. (2005). *Investing for success: The economics of supporting young people leaving care.* Melbourne: Centre for Excellence in Child and Family Welfare.

Reekie, G. (1998). *Measuring immorality: Social inquiry and the problem of illegitimacy.* Cambridge: Cambridge University Press.

Stein, M. (2006). Wrong turn. *The Guardian*, 6 December.

Stein, M. (2012). *Young people leaving care.* London: Jessica Kingsley Publishers.

Stein, M. (2014). How does care leaver support in the UK compare with the rest of the world?. *Community Care*, http://communitycare.co.uk/2014/10/23/care-leaver-support-uk-compare-rest-world/

Wade, J., Biehal, N., Farrelly, N., & Sinclair, I. (2010). *Maltreated children in the looked after system: A comparison of outcomes for those who go home and those who do not.* London: Department for Education.

Part I

Particularly Vulnerable Groups of Care Leavers

1

The Double-Bind: Looked After Children, Care Leavers and Criminal Justice

Nicola Carr and Siobhán McAlister

Research consistently shows that young people from out-of-home care (OHC) are over-represented in criminal justice systems. The disproportionate numbers of people with a care history within the youth justice system and adult prisons have led some to pose the question as to whether OHC is simply a stepping stone to custody (Blades et al. 2011). Concerns regarding over-representation while in care, among young people transitioning from care and ex-care leavers, have been reported in a wide range of contexts including England and Wales (Barn and Tan 2012; Darker et al. 2008), Northern Ireland (Youth Justice Review Team 2011), Australia (Malvaso and Delfabbro 2015; Mendes et al. 2014; Mendes et al. in this volume), and the USA (Cusick and Courtney 2007; Jonson-Reid and Barth 2000; Vaughn et al. 2008). Findings from the research literature on why young people transitioning from care may be more vulnerable to becoming involved in the criminal justice system can be distilled into three main themes. Firstly,

N. Carr (✉) • S. McAlister
School of Sociology, Social Policy and Social Work, Belfast, UK

many young people in care have experienced a range of adversities that place them at higher risk of offending. Secondly, the care experience may in itself be 'criminogenic' (i.e. a factor leading to an increased likelihood of offending). Thirdly (and linked to the first two points), the transition to adulthood for young people leaving care is often compressed and accelerated, placing them at increased vulnerability to a range of negative outcomes.

This chapter charts these three themes by considering the research on care leavers coming into contact with youth or adult justice systems. We note the application of criminological theory in a small number of studies, and argue that the findings from research on desistance, while focused on the reasons why people cease offending, may provide a useful framework for considering future areas of research and implications for practice. This is because it holds potential for an examination and understanding of the interplay of agency, structure and the importance of identity in young people's lives and in transitions.

Risk Factors

Much of the research on the over-representation of young people in care and care leavers within the criminal justice system has been influenced by 'risk factor' research, which seeks to establish and quantify a range of characteristics that place young people at risk of offending (Farrington 1996, 2007). This broad body of research, sometimes referred to as the 'Risk Factor Prevention Paradigm' (RFPP) (Haines and Case 2008), is premised on identifying precursors to personal and socially harmful behaviours in order to intervene to reduce risk and harm (Haines and Case 2008; O'Mahony 2009). It has been particularly influential in the sphere of youth justice, but has also permeated other areas of social policy relating to families, communities, child and youth development and education and health (Armstrong 2004; Kemshall 2002; Turnbull and Spence 2011).

RFPP is derived from longitudinal research such as the Cambridge Delinquency Study (Farrington 2007), which followed a group of young people over the life course and sought to retrospectively identify factors that led some to become involved with offending in order to develop predictive tools that would enable earlier intervention. This work and further developments have led to the identification of a range of putative risk factors focusing on the characteristics of the individuals and their immediate environment. Individual factors include hyperactivity, low self-control, low IQ, poor ability to delay gratification and poor school performance. Environmental risk factors include lack of parental supervision, disrupted families, low family income and living in poor, high-crime areas (see Farrington 1996, 2007).

There are numerous critiques of risk factor research and its applications. Some question its predictive utility, arguing that it lacks explanatory power by virtue of its conflating of correlations and causality (O'Mahony 2009). Others have observed that the narrow conceptions of what constitutes risk (i.e. those focusing on the characteristics of individuals) do not sufficiently account for wider structural influences such as levels of inequality and the extent of social welfare provision (France 2008; MacDonald et al. 2005). Linked to this are observations that the focus on the level of the individual is associated with neo-liberal strategies of 'responsibilization' whereby the target of intervention (i.e. the risk-bearing subject) bears both the burden of these risks and the responsibility for effecting change (Phoenix and Kelly 2013).

Given the orientation of the RFPP, it is therefore unsurprising that research regularly points to an overlap between the backgrounds of those with experiences of care and the risks associated with offending (Darker et al. 2008; Hayden 2010; Schofield et al. 2012). Similar risk factors, which are said to increase a young person's propensity to offend, are extensively reported in studies of care populations, for example, poor caregiver attachments, lack of parental supervision and experiences of maltreatment (Smith and Thornberry 1995; Stewart et al. 2008). Some studies, therefore, seek to explain the over-representation of young people from state care in the criminal justice system by reference to the fact that they are more likely to score highly in many risk factor domains (Schofield et al. 2012; Schofield et al. 2015; Vaughn et al. 2008).

While identification of risks can add to our understanding and potentially help to target services and interventions, the application of the RFPP lens (particularly in relation to individual risk) is potentially tautological. And even where attention is paid to wider factors, such as family composition and community context, these tend to be narrowly constructed in that they preclude consideration of wider important structural factors, such as levels of inequality or social welfare provision. In an attempt to widen this lens, an emerging body of work has sought to integrate a consideration of individual factors alongside the characteristics of the care system. This research has focused on systemic issues within the care system and provision of supports (or the absence of these) for young people leaving care (Fitzpatrick 2014; Mendes et al. 2014).

Criminogenic Care?

The type and quality of care placement may have an impact on whether a young person becomes involved in offending and/or comes to the attention of authorities for criminal behaviour (Darker et al. 2008; Hayden 2010; Taylor 2006). In particular, problematic issues have been identified regarding residential care placements when compared with foster care placements. Residential care is often considered a placement of 'last resort' (Hayden 2010; Shaw 2014). In many instances, young people in residential care have experienced multiple previous placements. Residential care may also be used for older teenagers who are considered 'too difficult' to place in foster care. This positioning of residential care means that young people with multiple and complex difficulties are placed together in an environment that is ill-equipped to meet their complex developmental needs (Littlechild 2011; Shaw 2014). Within this context, peer influences may be particularly significant (Ashford and Morgan 2004; Taylor 2006; Shaw 2014). Furthermore, policies in residential units may lead to the criminalization of young people. Examples include calling the police for relatively minor infractions, which, in a non-care context, would be dealt with by parents or other adults without recourse to authorities (Darker et al. 2008; Hayden 2010; Fitzpatrick 2014). Other policies may also lead to young people in residential care coming to the attention of the police, and therefore increasing their likelihood of being charged with incidental offences

(Hayden 2010). For example, within the UK, there are policies in place requiring residential units to report a young person as missing if they fail to return home at a particular time. In some instances, this can lead to young people incurring criminal charges (e.g. being found in possession of a drug when they are located), and early contact with the police can impact on future contact. This issue has garnered recent policy attention in the context of reviews focusing on child sexual exploitation and the particular vulnerabilities of young people who go missing from care (Jay 2014). Here, it has been noted that, in some instances, young people are treated as potential offenders and that, within this context, the fact that they have been the victims of crime may not be recognized (Fitzpatrick 2014; Jay 2014). Further still, wider research shows that young people who have had prior negative experiences of police contact may be reluctant to make reports when they have been the victim of crime themselves, thereby compounding this negative effect (McAlister and Carr 2014).

The criminalization of young people in care is an issue that intersects with other areas of social policy and the extent to which boundaries between child welfare and youth justice systems are delineated. One of the obvious differences that impacts on this is the fact that the minimum age of criminal responsibility varies widely across countries. In Europe alone, it ranges from 10 (England, Wales, Northern Ireland, Switzerland) to 18 (Belgium), in the USA it varies from 6 to 14, in Australia it is 10 (although *doli incapax* provisions also apply) (Cipriani 2009; Cuneen et al. 2011; Dunkel 2015). *Doli incapax* refers to a presumption that a child is incapable of a crime because he/she does not have sufficient understanding of right and wrong. This can be used as a rebuttable presumption, that is, it must be taken as true by the court unless proven otherwise. In Australia, this applies to children aged 10–14. In some countries (e.g. England, Northern Ireland, Republic of Ireland), *doli incapax* provisions previously existed in legislation, but have been repealed. In places where the age of criminal responsibility is lower, there are clearly higher risks of young people being officially processed through the criminal justice system and, as a consequence, acquiring a criminal record (Carr et al. 2015). If, as the research evidence cited above suggests, young people from care are more likely to come into contact with the criminal justice system by virtue of the fact that they are on the radar of the child welfare system, then this may have a long-reaching effect. The impact of system contact and the potential for young people to be 'recycled' through the criminal justice system are supported by findings from the *Edinburgh Study of Youth Transitions and Crime* (a longitudinal study on pathways into, and out of, offending of a large cohort of young people who started secondary school in 1998). In this research, McAra and McVie (2007, p. 319) found that 'selection effects in the youth justice process mean that certain categories of young people – the "usual suspects" – become propelled into a repeat cycle of referral into the system'. Given the issues highlighted regarding the disproportionate contact that looked after children may have with criminal justice agencies, it is not hard to see how they too may be construed as 'usual suspects'. Moreover, the further a young person progresses through the system, the greater the difficulty in desisting from offending. This has led McAra and McVie (2007, p. 315) to conclude that 'the key to reducing offending lies in minimal intervention and maximum diversion'.

Placement stability also emerges as a key area in relation to explorations of the link between care environments and involvement with the criminal justice system, both within care and for young people who have left care (Barn and Tan 2012; Cusick et al. 2012; Ryan and Testa 2005). Placement instability is typically associated with a range of more negative outcomes for care leavers (Cashmore and Paxman 2006; Stein 2006a). However, disentangling whether placement instability is a causal or correlational factor in subsequent negative outcomes is difficult, particularly in light of the fact that placements break down for a range of reasons, including young people's behaviour, their dissatisfaction with a placement, their age at placement, placement type, supports provided and the capacity of carers to cope (Koh et al. 2014; Leathers 2006; Sallnas et al. 2004; Vinnerljung et al. 2014). For example, in a recent US study, Koh et al. (2014) found that factors associated with placement stability included the absence of a mental health diagnosis (clinically determined) for the young person and placement with relative caregivers. Similar results were reported in a Swedish study, which also found that a young person's 'anti-social behaviour' was a significant risk factor for placement breakdown (Sallnas et al. 2004).

In a study specifically considering the impact of placement instability on juvenile delinquency, Ryan and Testa (2005) found that young people who had experienced maltreatment and been placed in substitute care had higher rates of delinquency than similar children who had not been removed from their family. Placement instability increased the risk of delinquency for male foster children, but not for females (Ryan and Testa 2005). This differential is probably explained by the fact that females generally have much lower levels of involvement in delinquency. In this study, the authors employ the concepts of social capital and social control to explain their findings, noting that:

> …multiple placements after entering substitute care further depletes a child's stock of social capital, which weakens social attachments and social controls and increases the probability of delinquency. (Ryan and Testa 2005, p. 245)

Transitions from Care and Criminal Justice Involvement

The processes associated with transitioning from care have been the focus of a growing body of research in recent years. Set alongside a broader focus on youth transitions in the context of changing social, institutional and demographic patterns, literature in this area has explored the variable patterns of transition for young people who experience multiple disadvantages and social exclusion (e.g. MacDonald et al. 2005; Thomson et al. 2002). Numerous empirical studies in a range of countries attest to the challenges faced by young people transitioning from care, particularly when these transitions are fractured, accelerated, and poorly supported (Courtney et al. 2010; Mendes and Moslehuddin 2006; Stein 2006a). While official data suggest an over-representation of people with care experience in the criminal justice system, the links between the difficulties faced in this transitional period and involvement with the criminal justice system have only been explored in a small range of studies to date.

Findings from the Midwest Study identify significantly higher rates of self-reported offending among young people transitioning from care at age 17–18 compared to the general population (Cusick and Courtney

2007). However, as the study progressed, two years later, at age 19, fewer differences in self-reported offending rates were found between the two populations; that said, young care leavers reported higher rates of certain types of offending, including damage to property and engagement in violent offences (Cusick and Courtney 2007). Notably, while differences in self-reported rates of offending between the two groups declined over time, a significantly higher proportion of care leavers reported having been arrested by age 19. The report authors comment that this finding may reflect the higher engagement in serious offending by youth in OHC, *or* it could be because care leavers face higher levels of scrutiny by both child welfare systems and the police (Cusick and Courtney 2007).

Another US-based study conducted in Missouri explored the characteristics associated with a heightened risk of involvement with the criminal justice system for young people transitioning from care (Vaughn et al. 2008). In this research, 20 per cent of young people (n = 404) reported an arrest experience over a three-year period (from ages 17–19). Notably, most young people (69 per cent of the sample) were classified as presenting a 'low-risk' of criminal involvement. Exploring a range of variables including experiences of maltreatment as children, neighbourhood characteristics, levels of family supports, mental health difficulties and substance misuse, this research generated typologies indicating factors most associated with risk of criminal justice involvement.

Young people at 'low-risk' of legal involvement were more likely to be female, 'of colour' and less likely to associate with deviant peers or to live in socially disorganized neighbourhoods. While the difference between genders is not surprising given the differential rates at which men and women are processed through the criminal justice system, the lower rates of contact for young people 'of colour' (an aggregate group of 'non-white' young people) is surprising, particularly in light of a wide body of research noting disproportionate minority contact with the criminal justice system. The authors posit that this finding may reflect the fact that white young people may be less likely to be placed in care, but that when they are, they may present with more complex needs.

Having employment and family supports also reduced the risk of legal involvement (Vaughn et al. 2008). Conversely, young people at 'high risk' of involvement in offending were more likely to have a diagnosis of Attention-

Deficit Hyperactivity Disorder (ADHD) or a conduct disorder. They were also more likely to live in socially disorganized neighbourhoods and associate with delinquent peers. Further, they experienced higher levels of prior physical abuse compared to other young people in the sample. The range of factors identified in this study focus more on the individual characteristics of young people rather than on the nature of the care system, although one variable included the number of caseworkers a young person had experienced during their time in care. Young people in the higher risk group had a greater number of caseworkers throughout their time in care, although this was not found to be statistically significant (Vaughn et al. 2008).

Theoretical Explanations

Earlier findings from the Midwest Study cited above (Cusick and Courtney 2007) and Vaughn et al.'s (2008) research suggest that an interplay between individual characteristics and a young person's environment may place young people at risk of offending in the period during which they transition from care. Importantly also, Cusick and Courtney note that young people who are in receipt of services may be subject to greater surveillance, leading to quicker escalation into the criminal justice system. In further studies on this topic, criminological theory, exploring the relevance of social bonds and the impact of 'strain', has been employed to help explain why some young people transitioning from care may be at heightened risk of involvement in the criminal justice system.

Additional analysis of the Midwest data set by Cusick et al. (2012) following young people's arrest rates up to age 24, employed Hirschi's (1969) 'social bond' theory to explore the factors that place youth transitioning from foster care at greater risk of criminal justice involvement. Social bond theory posits that individuals bonded to social groups (e.g. family, church, schools) are less likely to engage in delinquency (Hirschi 1969). Sampson and Laub's (1990) elaboration of this theory integrates a life-course perspective in considering these mechanisms of social control and their variable influence over various life stages. This perspective may have particular salience given that placement in the care system is likely to have an effect on social bonds. Placement in care may enable young people to form alternative social bonds (Cusick et al. 2012), and/or it may disrupt existing social bonds (for good or ill). Movement from the care system may also mark a point of disruption in social ties and links to institutions.

Analysis of the Midwest data shows that for young people transitioning from care, social bonds in the interpersonal domain (i.e. attachment to birth parents or substitute caregivers) did not have a significant effect on likelihood of arrest. The one notable exception to this was where young people reported not having a biological mother. Foster youth without a living mother experienced a 64 per cent increase in the risk of arrest; however, bonds to education and employment were associated with a lower risk of arrest (Cusick et al. 2012). With regard to the characteristics of care placements, young people who were in residential care at the time of the baseline interview faced a significantly higher risk of arrest compared to young people in non-relative foster care. Multiple placement moves were also associated with higher risks of arrest (Cusick et al. 2012). Further analysis of this data highlights important gender differences in regard to criminal justice involvement for young people transitioning from care (Lee et al. 2012, 2014). For young women who had become parents and had their child residing with them, there was a lower risk of arrest. However, a similar effect was not found for young men. Drawing on wider research on the impact of motherhood as a mechanism of informal social control for women from poorer backgrounds, Lee et al. (2014) note that further research is required into the longer-term impact of social exclusion for young women who become parents at an early age.

Another study of young people leaving care in England explored whether they experienced particular strains that made them more vulnerable to offending (Barn and Tan 2012). This drew on Agnew's (1992, 2001) concept of 'General Strain Theory' (GST) which argues that strains or stressors increase the likelihood of negative reactions, such as criminal behaviour. According to Agnew, there are several possible categories of 'strain'. These include loss of positive stimuli (e.g. end of a relationship), the presence of negative stimuli (e.g. experiencing abuse) and 'goal blockage' (e.g. failure to achieve just goals) (Agnew 2001, p. 319). This research explored whether strains such as experiences of victimization, unemployment, school exclusion or homelessness placed young care leavers at risk of offending. Significantly, many young people were themselves victims of crime (40.7 per cent), and young women reported high rates of serious victimization such as rape, attempted rape and domestic violence. Perhaps unsurprisingly, young people who experienced a range of these strains were more likely to engage in criminal activity, while those who acquired higher education and employment skills were less likely to do so (Barn and Tan 2012).

Expanding the Gaze

The need to develop theoretical perspectives in relation to a growing body of empirical literature on the challenges facing young people leaving care has been noted (Stein 2006b). As we have observed at the outset of this chapter, the literature on the over-representation of young people from care in criminal justice systems has predominantly focused on three main domains: individual risk factors, the nature of the care system and the difficulties facing young people as they transition from care. Some of the literature has integrated these elements. The application of criminological theory to analysis of this issue has so far focused on the strains that young people experience and their social bonds. Both of these perspectives provide useful insights; however, we argue there is a need to look more broadly at the intersection of structural and individual factors, and at how a young person's sense of identity is bound within this intersection.

Findings from research on desistance from crime may provide a useful framework, both for research and practice. This body of work focuses on the reasons why people stop offending, but, through this lens, we can gain insights into onset of offending, and what causes people to cease offending over time. While different emphases are placed on the relative importance of structure and agency in desistance literature (e.g. Giordano et al. 2002; Healy 2014; LeBel et al. 2008), more recent syntheses note the importance of the interplay between structure and agency in the process of desistance (Farrall et al. 2011; LeBel et al. 2008; McNeill et al. 2012). Also, the need to pay adequate attention to both *objective* (e.g. employment) and *subjective* (e.g. motivation or self-beliefs) dimensions of the desistance process is emphasized (Laub and Sampson 2001; LeBel et al. 2008).

Summaries on this topic identify three main domains in the research literature: maturational reform, social bonds and subjective narratives (McNeill et al. 2012). Maturational reform encompasses both age-related changes in patterns of offending behaviour (best illustrated by the age-crime curve, which shows peak rates of offending in the late teens/early 20s and a decline in offending over time) and age-related life transitions (Kazemian 2007). Research on social bonds demonstrates that desistance from offending is linked to informal social controls as a result of stronger links between an individual and society (e.g. through employment or parenthood) (Sampson and Laub 1990). Important subjective level themes include feelings of hope and self-efficacy, shame and remorse, the extent to which stigma is felt and internalized and the capacity of a person to envisage and build an 'alternative identity' (see Giordano et al. 2002; LeBel et al. 2008; Maruna 2001). Underscoring the relationship between subjective narratives and life transitions that are often associated with maturation, the types of 'alternative identities' identified in research on this topic include 'being a good parent' or a 'family man' (LeBel et al. 2008).

Further important contributions of desistance research note the importance of both social and human capital in desisting from crime (McNeill et al. 2012). Advocates of desistance-based approaches argue that this perspective provides a useful counter-balance (if not a corrective) to deficit models that view individuals as risk subjects to be managed (McNeill et al. 2012). Importantly, there is also recognition of the capacity of individuals to change. It is worth noting that there are resonances between the strengths-based perspective of desistance scholarship and research on resilience, particularly its later iterations, which have focused on wider social domains (Fitzpatrick 2011). Although, for an overall critique of the manner in which the concept of resilience has been deployed in social work, see Garrett (2015).

Some of the key themes of desistance research such as maturational reform, social bonds and subjective narratives have clear resonance with the over-representation of young people leaving care in the criminal justice system. Focusing attention towards social bonds underscores the need to develop strategies to support young people in their transition from care. That some research suggests an association between desistance from crime and 'the opportunities … afforded in the transition to adulthood' (Barry 2010, p. 165) further emphasizes the need for support during this period. Further to this, greater recognition of the importance of subjective narratives underlines the degree to which identity is bound up in interaction with systems that have the power to inscribe labels.

Conclusion

Integrative approaches to the study of desistance (i.e. those that aim to capture the interplay of agency and structure) and the importance of reflexivity and personal identity (e.g. Farrall et al. 2010; Weaver 2012) provide a useful framework for research and practice in this area. Of course, the interplay between structure and agency and debates about the relative significance of each is not new (e.g. Giddens 1984); however, in our reading of the research on the intersection of looked after populations and criminal justice systems, we note that insufficient attention is paid to both macro- (such as social security provisions) and micro-level factors (such as young people's sense of identity) and the interactions between these domains. With an over-emphasis on individual risk factors, there has been limited attempt to bridge the divide between structure and agency. Even where structure is explored, this has tended to be at the cursory level of system characteristics (e.g. placement types and number of placement moves). This occludes attention towards the wider social policy context in which the care system operates, where comparative analysis highlights significant variation, for example, in the rates of children in care and the range of welfare entitlements and supports available to families (Carr 2014; Munro et al. 2005; Stein and Munro 2008; Stein 2014). Of course, a similar point can be made in respect of demographic patterns in criminal justice systems (Cavadino and Dignan 2005).

Similarly, attention has focused on the characteristics of young people in identifying risk factors that may increase their likelihood of becoming involved in offending. Within this body of work, limited attention has been paid to young people's subjective accounts—that is, the manner in which they interpret, navigate and make sense of their situations.

Given that identity is a core issue for young people in care (Fransson and Storø 2011; Lee and Berrick 2014), the question of identity in relation to the transition from care and involvement in the criminal justice system would seem to be an important area to focus attention, not least because both systems (i.e. care and criminal justice) potentially shape identity in profound ways. Findings from research on desistance provide a useful bridge across some of these areas, directing attention towards the individual in context, a young person's journey through the care system, questions of identity, transitions from care and the wider social context of support and opportunities.

References

Agnew, R. (1992). Foundation for a general strain theory of crime and delinquency. *Criminology, 30*(1), 47–87.

Agnew, R. (2001). Building on the foundation of general strain theory: Specifying the types of strain most likely to lead to delinquency. *Journal of Research in Crime and Delinquency, 38*(4), 319–361.

Armstrong, D. (2004). A risky business? Research policy, governmentality and youth offending. *Youth Justice, 4*(2), 100–117.

Ashford, B., & Morgan, R. (2004). Criminalising looked-after children. *Criminal Justice Matters, 57*(1), 8–38.

Barn, R., & Tan, J. (2012). Foster youth and crime: Employing general strain theory to promote understanding. *Journal of Criminal Justice, 40*(3), 212–220.

Barry, M. (2010). Promoting desistance among young people. In W. Taylor, R. Earle, & R. Hester (Eds.), *Youth justice handbook: Theory, policy and practice* (pp. 158–167). Cullompton: Willan Publishing.

Blades, R., Hart, D., Lea, J., & Wilmott, N. (2011). *Care – A stepping stone to custody?* (London: Prison Reform Trust). Available at:http://www.prisonreformtrust.org.uk/Portals/0/Documents/careasteppingstonetocustody.pdf

Carr, N. (2014). Invisible from view: Leaving and aftercare provision in the Republic of Ireland. *Australian Social Work, 67*(1), 88–101.

Carr, N., Dwyer, C., & Larrauri, E. (2015). *Young people, criminal records and employment barriers*. Belfast: NIACRO.

Cashmore, J., & Paxman, M. (2006). Predicting aftercare outcomes: The importance of 'felt' security. *Child and Family Social Work, 11*(3), 232–241.

Cavadino, M., & Dignan, J. (2005). *Penal systems. A comparative approach*. London: Sage.

Cipriani, D. (2009). *Children's rights and the minimum age of criminal responsibility*. Farnham: Ashgate.

Courtney, M. E., Hook, J. L., & Lee, J. S. (2010). *Distinct subgroups of former foster youth during young adulthood: Implications for policy and practice*. Chicago: Chapin Hall Center for Children at the University of Chicago.

Cuneen, C., White, R., & Richards, K. (2011). *Juvenile justice: Youth and crime in Australia*. Melbourne: Oxford University Press.

Cusick, G. R., & Courtney, M. E. (2007). *Offending during late adolescence. How do youth aging out of care compare with their peers? Issue brief*. Chicago: Chapin Hall Publications.

Cusick, G. R., Havlicek, J. R., & Courtney, M. E. (2012). Risk for arrest: The role of social bonds in protecting foster youth making the transition to adulthood. *American Journal of Orthopsychiatry, 82*(1), 19–31.

Darker, I., Ward, H., & Caulfield, L. (2008). An analysis of offending by young people looked after by local authorities. *Youth Justice, 8*(2), 134–148.

Dunkel, F. (2015). Juvenile justice and crime policy in Europe. In F. E. Zimring, M. Langer, & D. S. Tannehaus (Eds.), *Juvenile justice in global perspective* (pp. 9–62). New York: New York University Press.

Farrall, S., Bottoms, A., & Shapland, J. (2010). Social structures and desistance from crime. *European Journal of Criminology, 7*(6), 546–570.

Farrall, S., Sharpe, G., Hunter, B., & Calverley, A. (2011). Theorising structural and individual level processes in desistance and persistence: Outlining an integrated perspective. *Australian and New Zealand Journal of Criminology, 44*(2), 218–234.

Farrington, D. (1996). *Understanding and preventing youth crime*. York: JRF.

Farrington, D. P. (2007). Childhood risk factors and risk-focused prevention. In M. Maguire, R. Morgan, & R. Reiner (Eds.), *The oxford handbook of criminology* (pp. 602–640). Oxford: Oxford University Press.

Fitzpatrick, C. (2011). What is the difference between 'desistance' and 'resilience'? Exploring the relationship between two key concepts. *Youth Justice, 11*(3), 221–234.

Fitzpatrick, C. (2014). *Achieving justice for children in care and care leavers. Howard league what is justice? Working papers 14/2014*. Available at: https://d19ylpo4aovc7m.cloudfront.net/fileadmin/howard_league/user/pdf/Research/What_is_Justice/HLWP_14_2014.pdf

France, A. (2008). Risk factor analysis and the youth question. *Journal of Youth Studies, 11*(1), 1–15.

Fransson, E., & Storo, J. (2011). Dealing with the past in the transition from care. A post-structural analysis of young people's accounts. *Children and Youth Services Review, 33*(12), 2519–2525.

Garrett, P. M. (2015). Questioning tales of 'ordinary magic': 'Resilience' and neo-liberal reasoning. *British Journal of Social Work*. doi:10.1093/bjsw/bcv017.

Giddens, A. (1984). *The constitution of society*. Cambridge: Polity Press.

Giordano, P., Cernkovich, S., & Rudolph, J. (2002). Gender, crime and desistance: Toward a theory of cognitive transformation. *American Journal of Sociology, 107*, 990–1064.

Haines, K., & Case, S. (2008). The rhetoric and reality of the 'Risk Factor Prevention Paradigm' approach to preventing and reducing youth offending. *Youth Justice, 8*(1), 5–20.

Hayden, C. (2010). Offending behavior in care: Is children's residential care a criminogenic environment? *Child and Family Social Work, 15*(4), 461–472.

Healy, D. (2014). Becoming a desister. Exploring the role of agency, coping and imagination in the construction of a new self. *British Journal of Criminology, 54*(5), 873–891.

Hirschi, T. (1969). *A general theory of crime*. Stanford: Stanford University Press.

Jay, A. (2014). *Independent inquiry into child sexual exploitation in rotherham 1997–2013*. Available at: http://www.rotherham.gov.uk/downloads/file/1407/independent_inquiry_cse_in_rotherham

Jonson-Reid, M., & Barth, R. P. (2000). From placement to prison: The path to adolescent incarceration from child welfare supervised foster or group care. *Children and Youth Services Review, 22*(7), 493–516.

Kazemian, L. (2007). Desistance from crime: Theoretical, empirical, methodological and policy considerations. *Journal of Contemporary Criminal Justice, 23*(1), 5–27.

Kemshall, H. (2002). *Risk, social policy and welfare*. Buckingham: Open University Press.

Koh, E., Rolock, N., Cross, T. P., & Eblen-Manning, J. (2014). What explains instability in foster care? Comparison of a matched sample of children with stable and unstable placements. *Children and Youth Services Review, 37*, 36–45.

Laub, J. H., & Sampson, R. J. (2001). Understanding desistance from crime. In M. Tonry (Ed.), *Crime and justice* (Vol. 28, pp. 1–69). Chicago: University of Chicago Press.

Leathers, S. J. (2006). Placement disruption and negative placement outcomes among adolescents in long-term foster care: The role of behavior problems. *Child Abuse and Neglect, 30*(3), 307–324.

LeBel, T., Burnett, R., Maruna, S., & Bushway, S. (2008). The 'chicken and egg' of subjective and social factors in desistance from crime. *European Journal of Criminology, 5*(2), 131–159.

Lee, C., & Berrick, J. D. (2014). Experiences of youth who transition to adulthood out of care: Developing a theoretical framework. *Children and Youth Services Review, 46,* 78–84.

Lee, J. S., Courtney, M. E., & Hook, J. L. (2012). Formal bonds during the transition to adulthood: Extended foster care support and criminal/legal involvement. *Journal of Public Child Welfare, 6*(3), 255–279.

Lee, J. S., Courtney, M. E., & Tajima, E. (2014). Extended foster care support during the transition to adulthood. Effect on the risk of arrest. *Children and Youth Services Review, 42,* 34–42.

Littlechild, B. (2011). Conflict resolution, restorative justice approaches and bullying in young people's residential units. *Children and Society, 25*(1), 47–58.

MacDonald, R., Shildrick, T., Webster, C., & Simpson, D. (2005). Growing up in poor neighbourhoods: The significance of class and place in the extended transitions of 'socially excluded' young adults. *Sociology, 39*(5), 873–891.

Malvaso, C. G., & Delfabbro, P. (2015). Offending behavior among young people with complex needs in the Australian out-of-home care system. *Journal of Child and Family Studies, 24,* 3561–3569 doi:10.1007/s10826-015-0157-z.

Maruna, S. (2001). *Making good: How ex-convicts reform and rebuild their lives.* Washington, DC: American Psychological Association.

McAlister, S., & Carr, N. (2014). Experiences of youth justice: Youth justice discourses and their multiple effects. *Youth Justice, 14*(3), 241–254.

McAra, L., & McVie, S. (2007). Youth justice? The impact of system contact on patterns of desistance and offending. *European Journal of Criminology, 4*(3), 315–345.

McNeill, F., Farrall, S., Lightowler, C., & Maruna, S. (2012). *How and why people stop offending: Discovering desistance* (Institute for Research and Innovation in the Social Sciences). Available at: http://www.iriss.org.uk/sites/default/files/iriss-insight-15.pdf

Mendes, P., & Moslehuddin, B. (2006). From dependence to interdependence: Towards better outcomes for young people leaving state care. *Child Abuse Review, 15*(2), 110–126.

Mendes, P., Snow, P., & Baidawi, S. (2014). Young people transitioning from out-of-home care in Victoria: Strengthening support services for dual clients of child protection and youth justice. *Australian Social Work, 67*(1), 6–23.

Munro, E. R., Stein, M., & Ward, H. (2005). Comparing how different social, political and legal frameworks support or inhibit transitions from public care to independence in Europe, Israel, Canada and the United States. *International Journal of Child and Family Welfare, 8*(4), 191–202.

O'Mahony, P. (2009). The risk factors prevention paradigm and the causes of youth crime: A deceptively useful analysis? *Youth Justice, 9*(2), 99–114.

Phoenix, J., & Kelly, L. (2013). You have to do it yourself' responsibilization in youth justice and young people's situated knowledge of youth justice practice. *British Journal of Criminology, 53*(3), 419–437.

Ryan, J. P., & Testa, M. F. (2005). Child maltreatment and juvenile delinquency. Investigating the role of placement and placement instability. *Children and Youth Services Review, 27*(3), 227–249.

Sallnas, M., Vinnerljung, B., & Westermark, P. K. (2004). Breakdown of teenage placements in Swedish residential and foster care. *Child and Family Social Work, 9*(2), 141–152.

Sampson, R. J., & Laub, J. H. (1990). Crime and deviance over the life course: The salience of adult social bonds. *American Sociological Review, 55*, 609–627.

Schofield, G., Ward, E., Biggart, L., Scaife, V., Dodsworth, J., Larsson, B., et al. (2012). *Looked after children and offending: Reducing risk and promoting resilience*. Norwich: University of East Anglia.

Schofield, G., Biggart, L., Ward, E., & Larsson, B. (2015). Looked after children and offending: An exploration of risk, resilience and the role of social cognition. *Children and Youth Services Review, 51*, 125–133.

Shaw, J. (2014). Why do young people offend in children's homes? Research, theory and practice. *British Journal of Social Work, 44*(7), 1823–1839.

Smith, C., & Thornberry, T. (1995). The relationship between childhood maltreatment and adolescent involvement in delinquency. *Criminology, 33*(4), 451–481.

Stein, M. (2006a). Research review: Young people leaving care. *Child and Family Social Work, 11*(3), 273–279.

Stein, M. (2006b). Young people ageing out of care: The poverty of theory. *Children and Youth Services Review, 28*(4), 422–434.

Stein, M. (2014). Young people's transitions from care to adulthood in European and Postcommunist Eastern European and Central Asian Societies. *Australian Social Work, 67*(1), 24–38.

Stein, M., & Munro, E. (2008). *Young people's transitions from care to adulthood: International research and practice*. London: Jessica Kingsley Publishers.

Stewart, A., Livingston, M., & Dennison, S. (2008). Transitions and turning points: Examining the links between child maltreatment and juvenile offending. *Child Abuse and Neglect, 32*(1), 51–66.

Taylor, C. (2006). *Young people in care and criminal behaviour*. London: Jessica Kingsley Publishers.

Thomson, R., Bell, R., Holland, J., Henderson, S., McGrellis, S., & Sharpe, S. (2002). Critical moments: Choice, chance and opportunity in young people's narratives of transitions. *Sociology, 36*(2), 335–354.

Turnbull, V., & Spence, J. (2011). What's at risk? The proliferation of risk across child and youth policy in England. *Journal of Youth Studies, 14*(8), 939–959.

Vaughn, M. G., Shook, J. J., & McMillen, J. C. (2008). Aging out of foster care and legal involvement: Toward a typology of risk. *Social Service Review, 82*(3), 419–446.

Vinnerljung, B., Sallnas, M., & Berlin, M. (2014). Placement breakdowns in long-term foster care – A regional Swedish study. *Child and Family Social Work*, (pp. 1–11). doi:10.1111/cfs.12189.

Weaver, B. (2012). The relational context of desistance: Some implications and opportunities for social policy. *Social Policy and Administration, 46*(4), 395–412.

Youth Justice Review Team (2011). *A review of the youth justice system in Northern Ireland*. Belfast: Youth Justice Unit, Department of Justice.

2

Young People Transitioning from Out-of-Home Care in Victoria, Australia: Strengthening Support Services for Dual Clients of Child Protection and Youth Justice

Philip Mendes, Pamela C. Snow, and Susan Baidawi

Introduction

A significant proportion of young people transitioning from out-of-home care (OHC) experience involvement with the Youth Justice system, exposing them to further risks and reducing their likelihood of full social and economic engagement in mainstream society. However, little is known about the experiences of this vulnerable dual order client group as they transition from care. This chapter reviews the findings of a research project based on a partnership between Monash University and seven non-government child and youth welfare agencies in Victoria, Australia, and

P. Mendes (✉)
Monash University, Melbourne, VIC, Australia

P.C. Snow
Rural Health School, La Trobe University, Bendigo, VIC, Australia

S. Baidawi
Monash University, Melbourne, VIC, Australia

© The Author(s) 2016
P. Mendes, P. Snow (eds.), *Young People Transitioning from Out-of-Home Care*, DOI 10.1057/978-1-137-55639-4_2

identifies practices and policies that could reduce the over-representation of young people leaving OHC via the Youth Justice system.

The project involved three phases: (1) Interviews and focus groups with 77 key stakeholders from the OHC system, Youth Justice system and youth drug and alcohol services and legal services; (2) interviews with a group of 15 care leavers (aged 18–26 years) in Victoria, who had also experienced involvement with the Youth Justice system; and (3) consultations with the research partners to develop a best-practice model. Findings and recommendations are considered in the light of international research and policy initiatives in this area.

International evidence shows an over-representation of children and young people who have been subject to child protection notifications or placed in OHC among those who come before the Youth Justice system, including both police contact and court involvement (Blades et al. 2011; Cusick et al. 2010; Darker et al. 2008; Fitzpatrick and Williams 2014; Hart 2006; Jacobson et al. 2010; Summerfield 2011; Taylor 2006; West and Farrington 1973).

A number of Australian studies have also found a significant link between experiences of OHC and criminal behaviour, both during and directly after leaving care (McFarlane 2010; Raman et al. 2005; Wood 2008). For example, two national surveys by McDowall for the CREATE Foundation (2008, 2009) found that high proportions of care leavers surveyed (19.2 per cent and 27.8 per cent, respectively) had experienced involvement with the Youth Justice system. Surveys of Youth Justice populations also suggest strong links between the two, pointing to a need for both the statutory child protection and youth justice agencies to consider the needs of this specific group. For example, evidence from three separate studies in New South Wales indicates that 21–28 per cent of males and 36–39 per cent of females on community-based (Wood 2008) or custodial (Murphy et al. 2010) Youth Justice orders had a history of OHC placement. Similarly, the latest Victorian Youth Parole and Youth Residential Board annual report estimated that 43 per cent of young people in custody had previous child protection involvement, and 19 per cent had a current child protection order (Youth Parole Board and Youth Residential Board Victoria 2015). A number of factors have been shown to contribute to this association, as detailed in the following sections.

Child Maltreatment, Youth Offending and OHC

Research indicates that young people who have experienced maltreatment are more likely to have subsequent offending records (AIHW 2012; Stewart et al. 2002); of these, those placed in OHC were twice as likely to have subsequently offended than those who were never placed in OHC (Ryan and Testa 2005; Stewart et al. 2002). In correlational studies such as these, it is not possible to determine causality; however, it has been proposed that OHC placement 'is likely to be indicative of the seriousness of the maltreatment' (Stewart et al. 2002, p. 5), potentially placing these groups at elevated risk of poor psychosocial outcomes, including affiliation with socially marginalized peers and offending behaviour.

Children whose first OHC placement occurs at an older age or who continue to experience maltreatment into adolescence are more likely to offend (Jonson-Reid 2002; Jonson-Reid and Barth 2000b; Malvaso and Delfabbro 2015; Ryan and Testa 2005; Smith et al. 2005; Stewart et al. 2008). Additionally, studies suggest that offending is more likely among young people who have experienced greater placement instability (Barn and Tan 2012; Cusick et al. 2010; Johnson-Reid and Barth 2000b; Ryan and Testa 2005; Taylor 2006; Widom 1991) or who have had placements in group homes or residential care settings (Ryan et al. 2008; Taylor 2006; Wise and Egger 2008). While some research suggests that offending behaviour occurs subsequent to placement instability (Ryan and Testa 2005), the inverse may also be true in some cases (Darker et al. 2008). Not surprisingly, there is also evidence that young people entering care as a result of behavioural problems are more likely to offend than those placed solely due to maltreatment (Coleman and Jenson 2000; Jonson-Reid and Barth 2000a; Widom 1991).

Studies of dual order young people have reported that males offend at higher rates than females (as is the case across the board with youth offending), and that the risk of offending increases throughout adolescence, and then declines in the approach to early adulthood (Cusick et al. 2010; Darker et al. 2008; Ryan et al. 2008, 2010; Stewart et al. 2002). Dual order client populations also display other attributes associated with youth offending, including higher levels of criminality amongst family members, educational exclusion or disengagement, substance abuse and mental health issues (Darker et al. 2008; Halemba et al. 2004).

Youth Offending and Leaving Care

Some studies have examined youth offending during the transition from care. Care leavers in the USA were found to be twice as likely to engage in offending from age 16 to 17, and more likely to report being arrested between 18 and 19 years of age compared to their peers in the general population (Cusick and Courtney 2007). However, by age 21–22, there were fewer differences between the offending of care leavers and the general population (Cusick et al. 2010). A UK study of 39 care leavers identified that only one of eight young people who had left care aged 18 or over had served a custodial sentence, compared to 13 of the 20 who had been discharged by the age of 16, indicating that age of discharge may impact upon post-care offending (Taylor 2006). A more recent study by Lee et al. (2012) also suggested that remaining in care past the age of 18 years reduced the likelihood of criminal justice system involvement for females.

To date, no Australian study has specifically examined youth offending and contact with Youth Justice systems amongst state wards during the period of leaving care (i.e. during late adolescence). This is a significant time for three key reasons. Firstly, involvement with both the Child Protection and Youth Justice sectors signifies particular vulnerability to poor post-care outcomes, including involvement in the adult criminal justice system (Culhane et al. 2011; Kalb and Williams 2002; Lynch et al. 2003). Secondly, research indicates that, in general, it is during the leaving care period (i.e. between 18 and 21) that offending increases (Farrington 1986; Hirschi and Gottfredson 1983). Thirdly, offending behaviour during this time is likely to impact adversely upon the success of the transition from state care.

Currently there are over 43,000 children and young people living in OHC in Australia (Australian Institute of Health and Welfare 2015). It is estimated that 3124 young people aged between 15 and 17 years were discharged from OHC in 2013–14, including 806 in Victoria

(AIHW 2015). In recognition of the need to provide ongoing assistance to young people being discharged from state care, Victoria legislated, via the *Children, Youth and Families Act 2005*, for the provision of leaving care and after-care services for young people up to 21 years of age (Department of Human Services 2015a). But these supports remain discretionary rather than mandatory.

At a national level, the Out of Home Care Standards introduced in December 2010 require all young people to have a *Transition from Care Plan* commencing at 15 years of age, detailing proposed assistance with housing, health, education and training, employment and income support (Department of Families, Housing, Community Services and Indigenous Affairs 2011). However, neither the Act nor the National Standards make any specific reference to support for young people involved with Youth Justice during their transition from care; nor does the updated Victorian protocol between Child Protection and Youth Justice services (DHS 2013).

Study Aims and Methodology

The aims of this study were to gain an in-depth understanding of the views and experiences of key stakeholders pertaining to the over-representation of care leavers in the youth justice system and to develop best-practice guidelines to inform future policy in this area.

This study stemmed from a long-standing concern voiced by a number of Victorian welfare and legal agencies that young people in, or leaving, care in Victoria were disproportionately involved in the youth justice system. An associated concern was that child protection appeared to provide little or no support to care leavers when they were released from custody. Youth Justice in Victoria refers to systems 'responsible for the statutory supervision of young people in the criminal justice system'. Youth Justice orders in Victoria comprise community-based and custodial tariffs (including remand) for young people aged 10–20 years, with a strong diversionary focus where possible (DHS 2015b).

The Victorian Child Safety Commissioner convened a public forum in March 2011 to canvass potential interest and involvement in the project.

This forum was attended by about 40 representatives from the government and non-government sectors pertaining to child protection, youth justice and legal services. As a result of this forum, a partnership was developed with seven agencies to conduct the project: The Office of the Child Safety Commissioner (later renamed the Victorian Commission for Children and Young People) and a consortium of non-government organizations delivering services in the OHC and Youth Justice systems in Victoria (Berry Street, Jesuit Social Services, OzChild, the Salvation Army Westcare, the Youth Support and Advocacy Service, and Whitelion). The study was funded by a grant from the Helen McPherson Smith Trust, together with cash and in-kind contributions from the seven partner agencies. The study was approved by the Monash University Human Research Ethics Committee.

The research was overseen by an Advisory Committee comprised of representatives from the partner organizations together with those from the Department of Human Services (OHC and Youth Justice branches), and the Centre for Excellence in Child and Family Welfare. The Advisory Committee oversaw all three phases of the research process, including having input into, and providing feedback concerning data collection procedures and data collection instruments, as well as interim and final reports. However, it should be noted that the study did not receive permission from the Victorian Government to speak with current Child Protection or Youth Justice staff. The following sections outline the three major phases of the project.

Phase One: Key Stakeholder Consultations

Phase One of the study aimed to access the perspectives of key stakeholders to generate an in-depth understanding of: why care leavers are over-represented in the youth justice system; ongoing support provided by child protection services to dual order care leavers; the role of leaving care plans in addressing involvement with youth justice; the nature of collaboration and consultations between child protection and youth justice services during the leaving care period; actions taken by youth justice organizations to address the needs of care leavers and best-practice social and educational programmes for this sub-group of care leavers.

The study was advertised to partner agencies who invited staff contributions to the research by way of individual interviews or focus groups. Participants were self-selecting (i.e. a non-probability sample) members from the project partner agencies and other organizations. In some instances, individuals were approached directly based on their expertise in the study area, or as a result of snowball sampling from previous participants. A total of 77 individuals participated in interviews or focus groups in this initial phase of the study.

Semi-structured focus groups and interviews were conducted with the key stakeholders. Data were gathered around six key issues identified in the aforementioned aims. These topics were developed based on a review of the existing literature and consultation with policy and practice experts. Focus groups have been established as an effective method for qualitative data collection in social work research (Linhorst 2002). This methodology was aimed at stimulating discussion between agency staff around the key issues, in order to generate responses which may not have been previously considered by individual participants (Alston and Bowles 2003). Where focus groups were impractical, individual interviews were conducted, generating in-depth reflections and case examples from respondents regarding their experiences and views around the key issues. The use of multi-method approaches is also widely accepted in social work research (Linhorst 2002). Combining focus group and individual interview methods allows for the uncovering of both broad macro-level concepts and micro-level individual experiences, generating a more complete understanding of the issues being examined.

All interviews and focus groups were audio-taped and transcribed and the data was then entered into NVivo9 for coding. Thematic analysis was conducted by categorizing recurring ideas within the transcript data (specifically where a response or concept was raised on three or more occasions) in order to identify the key findings. Multiple coding of a selection of transcripts by two members of the research team was utilized to check inter-rater reliability of the coded themes. This method has been suggested as useful for enhancing rigour in qualitative data analysis (Barbour 2001; Mays and Pope 1995).

Findings

Phase One consultations primarily focused upon the factors that appeared to contribute to offending among young people in and leaving care; the factors or responses which promoted positive outcomes in relation to offending among this group; and community or systemic factors which may impede or assist in addressing the risks of offending behaviour among young people in, and leaving, OHC.

A more detailed outline of the findings is contained in earlier publications (Mendes et al. 2012, 2014a). Consistent with other research, the respondents framed offending behaviour as a 'trauma-related outcome'. In particular, it was argued that young peoples' adverse childhood experiences generated difficulties in physical, mental, emotional and behavioural regulation, which in turn created barriers to establishing and maintaining supportive relationships and connections (e.g. with family, carers, peers and schools). Delayed maturity resulting from the impact of trauma upon young peoples' development was seen to result in impaired decision-making, limited consequential thinking, low emotional maturity and high levels of impulsivity and risk-taking behaviour.

Three key mediators between maltreatment and offending among young people in OHC were identified including educational disengagement, substance use and association with antisocial peers. A number of other factors which appeared to increase the potential for offending behaviour were also identified, including the involvement of the young person's family in the criminal justice system and exposure to further traumatic experiences (e.g. resulting from attempts at reunification, bullying or exposure to violence, and abuse or neglect from peers, caregivers or others).

Relationships and positive social connections with peers and the wider community were understood to be critical for reducing the problematic impacts of previous adverse experiences and enhancing resilience among young people in OHC. Yet, respondents explained the great difficulties faced in attempting to provide young people with the safety and stability required for positive attachments to occur and for therapeutic processes to be implemented.

Some identified examples of barriers to promoting stability and other positive outcomes included: multiple placement breakdowns which prevent the formation of relationships necessary to address trauma and other risks; the difficulty in accessing specialist supports which specifically address trauma, mental health issues and learning difficulties; some children and young people being exposed to further trauma after entering the OHC and Youth Justice systems; and the co-location of young people in both residential care and Youth Justice environments, which potentially raises their exposure to behaviour and attitudes (e.g. substance use, offending, educational disengagement) that increase the likelihood of offending behaviour emerging or escalating. Additionally, the legislated end of OHC at 18 years is problematic. While some care leavers may be ready for independence at 18 years, many are not developmentally mature enough to cope on their own with limited resources. This abrupt end to state care may lead to an escalation or emergence of offending behaviour.

Some aspects of the Youth Justice system were also seen to be unsuited to meeting the needs of young people in OHC. They included: lengthy times for court processes; limited court support, for example, to assist with understanding and emotional support; limited state-wide diversion options; variable understanding of community and custodial Youth Justice staff concerning the impacts of complex trauma and attachment difficulties and how to effectively engage with care leavers; limited trauma-specific therapeutic interventions available in custodial Youth Justice settings and the potential for re-traumatization through exposure to violence, bullying and strip-searching.

Overall, respondents identified the need for addressing offending behaviour and its underlying drivers; however, there were concurrent concerns regarding the need to avoid criminalizing young peoples' behaviour and entrenching their involvement in the justice system.

Phase Two: Interviews with Dual Order Care Leavers

Phase Two of this study aimed to access the perspectives of young care leavers to generate an in-depth understanding of: the reasons why some young people who have been in OHC become involved in the Youth Justice system; how Child Protection and Youth Justice work together, particularly in understanding what happens when a young person who is involved in Youth Justice leaves OHC; the backgrounds of care leavers in the Youth Justice system, and what happens to them after they leave OHC; and social or educational programmes seen as having helped, or could help, this group of young people.

The study was advertised to the partner agencies, and agency staff identified young people who met the following eligibility criteria, and who were currently or previously accessing the agency: aged 18 to 26 years; had previous involvement in OHC (at least six months in kinship care, foster care or residential care placements); and had previous involvement in the Youth Justice system (either community-based or custodial youth justice involvement).

Convenience (non-probability) sampling was utilized given the difficulty of locating young people within the target group. Interview location and time was arranged by either the agency staff or by the research assistant contacting the young person. Semi-structured, in-depth interviews were conducted with the young people covering a range of topics, including OHC history and experiences, education history and experience, leaving care experience, post-care experience, early offending and Youth Justice history and experience. Young people also completed a short demographic questionnaire with the interviewer at the conclusion of the interview. All interviews were audio-recorded and transcribed. Thematic analysis was then conducted using the data from interview transcripts with NVivo9 software. Quantitative data was entered into SPSS software for basic descriptive analysis.

The final sample comprised 15 young people aged 18–26 years (average age = 20.4 years) who were interviewed between February 2012 and May 2013. Interviews ranged in length from 20 to 98 minutes (mean = 44 minutes). During the interviews, visual timelines for each person were created using paper and pencil to track events such as entry into care, changes in placement and schools, as well as leaving care and youth justice involvement. The young people were able to refer to the timeline to describe temporal relationships between events.

Findings

The young people in the study sample presented with similar characteristics of social disadvantage as have been documented among both leaving care and Youth Justice custodial populations more broadly, including high rates of school exclusion, impaired mental health, issues with intellectual functioning, substance abuse problems and early parenthood (Courtney and Dworsky 2006; Indig et al. 2011; Mendes et al. 2011; Summerfield 2011; Youth Parole Board and Youth Residential Board Victoria 2015).

A brief summary of findings is presented; however, more detail is available in the Phase Two final report (Mendes et al. 2013). The findings suggest that offending behaviour among young people in OHC can be usefully conceptualized as a trauma-related outcome, which followed four main themes: young people displayed challenging behaviours which constitute criminal offending, such as assault and property destruction; young people sought to self-medicate symptoms of complex trauma through the use of alcohol and other drugs which led to offending through lowered thresholds for challenging behaviour or offending to fund substance use; young people were exposed to offending behaviour in others, not only through family and social relationships, but also through placement in residential care units and in youth justice custodial environments, which may contribute to offending behaviour; and limited supports and resources in the post-care period appeared to be associated with increased offending behaviour.

The young people reported having entered care for diverse reasons and at various ages. Around half had entered care in adolescence due to behavioural issues (specifically violence and substance abuse problems), family conflict or running away from home, rather than as a direct result of abuse and neglect. This is consistent with previous research, which has noted that young people entering care as a result of behavioural issues are at heightened risk for involvement in offending behaviour (Ryan 2012). All of the young people had eventually experienced placements in residential care, echoing previous research which has identified this group being at a higher risk for offending (Ryan et al. 2008).

The transitions from care for this group tended to be chaotic, and were often associated with escalating substance use and/or offending behaviour immediately preceding, during or soon after the transition from care. This finding accords with key stakeholder consultations, which indicated that there was great difficulty in engaging high-risk young people in leaving care processes. Overall, there were fairly negative outcomes in relation to many life domains—over half of the young people had experienced homelessness since leaving care, few had experiences of ongoing involvement in education or employment, two were pregnant at the time of the interview and four young people had one or more children of their own.

The respondents' educational experiences were broadly reflective of the OHC and Youth Justice populations (Cashmore and Paxman 2007). None of the young people had completed high school, one third had described specific learning difficulties and/or intellectual disabilities and more than three quarters of the young people had experiences of school suspension and/or expulsion. Young people often regretted their loss of educational attainment; many blamed themselves for these unrealized goals, while others expressed disappointment in the care system which they believed had allowed them to disengage from education too easily (Cashmore and Paxman 2007; Jackson 2001; Mendes et al. 2011; Taylor 2006). Additionally, as has been noted in previous Australian research (Stewart et al. 2008), the transition from primary to secondary education appeared to be a high-risk time for educational exclusion and/or disengagement, as did the time of entry into residential care.

A number of issues were seen by young people as contributing to their eventual educational disengagement, including bullying, interpersonal conflicts with peers, teachers and principals, learning difficulties, substance use, offending and accommodation transience associated with placement changes and detention in Youth Justice custody. The importance of educational disengagement as a predictor of future offending among care leavers has been identified in previous international research, which suggested that education appeared more significant than substance abuse issues as a factor associated with post-care offending among males (Ryan et al. 2007). Encouragingly, around half of the young people managed to re-engage in education via alternative pathways with the support of workers, and the majority had engaged in education courses and/or training programmes at the time of the interview. At the same time, translating training and education into employment opportunities proved difficult for this group, and only a minority of the young people reported having had any work experience.

For nearly two thirds of the young people, offending behaviour commenced at the age of 12–13 years. Assault, theft, substance use and property damage were the main types of initial offences described; however, most described multiple offence types emerging fairly simultaneously. The three main social contexts described in relation to young peoples' initial offending included socially-based offending (with friends, peers in residential care and partners; lone offending (generally consisting of thefts or offending in residential care contexts e.g. assaults and property destruction); and family-based offending (with immediate or extended family members).

There was consistency between the factors which young people described as being associated with their offending, and those described in the Phase One key stakeholder consultations, namely, substance use, including being substance-affected at the time of committing offences as well as a minority of respondents who reported offending to fund substance use; and social pressure, which came from peers in residential care, friends outside of the care system, partners and family members.

Involvement in the OHC system tended to precede involvement in the Youth Justice system, which occurred at an average age of 14 years (between 10 and 16 years). One of the most noteworthy themes was the general lack of knowledge and recall by many young people concerning the precise reasons they were involved with Youth Justice, or the orders to which they were subject. It is likely that the chaotic nature of the young peoples' lives and offending resulted in difficulties in connecting their own behaviour and the various judicial consequences experienced. Both positive and negative appraisals of Youth Justice community and custodial programmes were described; however, many young people believed these interventions made little difference to their offending behaviour.

Nearly half of the young people had also experienced involvement with the adult criminal justice system. All of these participants were male; six had spent time in adult custody since leaving care, and four had further charges pending. These participants tended to have entered care at a later age (after 10 years), either due to behavioural issues or family conflict. Post-care factors, which were more common among the young people who proceeded to the adult justice system, included having no support from a post-care worker at the time of leaving care, experiencing homelessness since leaving care and having no non-professional post-care supports or networks (i.e. only being connected to voluntary or involuntary services or workers since leaving care).

Encouragingly, two thirds of the young people had either desisted or greatly reduced their offending behaviour by the time of the interview. Becoming a parent, attaining affordable housing and dealing with substance abuse issues were each described as key factors or 'turning points' (Johnson and Mendes 2014), which precipitated a reduction in offending behaviour. Some young people who had reduced their offending frequency and/or severity described a shift in their attitudes based on a level of care for themselves and others, which had not previously dominated their decision-making, including wanting a better life, not wanting to lose children and realizing the negative impact of their offending on their lives.

The four young people who continued offending at the time of the interview were all males aged between 19 and 25 years, who were currently on adult criminal justice orders (bail or parole). Three of these young people had further court cases pending. Extensive family involvement in the criminal justice system, later age of entry to care, problematic alcohol use and estrangement from family characterized this group of young people. Additionally, these young people appeared to have no significant connection to adults in their lives other than various agency workers.

Phase Three: Development of Good Practice Recommendations

Phase Three of this study aimed to develop good-practice recommendations for reducing the over-representation of care leavers in the youth justice system. An outline of the recommendations was drafted, which incorporated findings from Phases One and Two of the present study together with previous research. The outline was presented to representatives of partner agencies for feedback regarding content and structure, in both individual agency consultations and at the level of the project Advisory Committee. This feedback then informed a draft final report, which was subsequently presented to the project Advisory Committee for further feedback prior to finalization.

The findings, which are outlined in greater detail in our Phase Three report (Mendes et al. 2014b), point to the utility of a trauma-informed approach for preventing and addressing the over-representation of young people in and leaving care in the Youth Justice system. Such an approach is consistent with the understanding that experiences of complex trauma are pervasive in the lives of dual order young people, and seeks to minimize the potential for re-traumatization and further disconnection, as well as promoting opportunities for connection and healing.

The approach suggested, therefore, emphasizes the need for a common understanding of the nature of complex trauma and its impacts, accompanied by policies and practices which are congruent with this growing body of knowledge. Additionally, it suggests the need for a shared responsibility across government and the broader community in working towards the healing and social inclusion of children and young people in and leaving OHC, including those who are involved with the Youth Justice system.

The recommendations provided are underpinned by key principles relating to recovery from complex trauma, including:

- Safety: The maintenance of physical safety across all environments;
- Stability: Stability in living environment and relationships, reducing the need for relocation and disconnection from networks;
- Connection: Supportive direct care and other family, peer and social connections as key tools for addressing trauma;
- Understanding: An understanding of trauma and its impact across all service systems (including universal services), and concurrent support for young people to understand their own experiences, needs and strengths;
- Healing: Access to evidence-supported therapeutic interventions, particularly those addressing the impact of complex trauma;
- Continuous improvement: Ongoing evaluation of outcomes of interventions and services, and adjustment of policies and practices accordingly.

The recommended strategies aim to both prevent and address offending behaviour and Youth Justice system involvement among young people in, and leaving, care. These strategies are focused on the various sectors or services which are commonly involved in the lives of dual order care leavers, including child and family welfare services and youth justice services, but also education, mental health and youth drug and alcohol services.

The dual order Child Protection and Youth Justice client group often presents with complex needs which cannot be adequately addressed within a single service sector or at a single point in the life of a young person. The recommendations emphasize the growing evidence base concerning more effective approaches with children and young people who are survivors of complex trauma. Such approaches should inform future policy and practice towards reducing the over-representation of young people leaving care via the youth justice system.

Conclusion

Our findings are consistent with previous research, confirming that dual order care leavers are a particularly vulnerable group. They appear to be for the most part male, have a later age of entry into care, have come into contact with residential care environments, have disengaged from education and other support systems and lack formal and informal support at the time of leaving care. There seems to be limited effective collaboration between services delivering support to these young people at the time of leaving care, including child protection, youth justice, the non-government OHC sector, and leaving care and post-care services.

Key proposals for policy and practice reform include improved availability of family-based interventions for young people with offending behaviours either prior to entering care, during leaving care planning or within Youth Justice interventions; therapeutic care options; the need for trauma-informed approaches in OHC, education and youth justice systems; flexible strategies for supporting education retention; a range of accessible substance abuse and mental health treatment options; and post-care accommodation and support including affordable housing. The state obligation to support care leavers beyond 18 years appears to be doubly important for the dual order group of young people. They are not likely to conform to normative patterns of maturation and developmental timing, and will almost certainly require ongoing and extensive support and second or even third chances if they are to overcome the adverse developmental impacts of earlier traumatic experiences.

This study has various limitations. Firstly, it is based primarily on data which was largely qualitative in nature. In the key stakeholder consultations, certain sectors were over-represented among the respondents (namely, the non-government OHC sector and the youth alcohol and other drugs sector), while others were under-represented (the education, mental health and statutory Child Protection and Youth Justice sectors).

In the second phase of the study (interviews with care leavers), again the data collected was largely qualitative in nature. It was neither possible to gain a larger sample of care leavers, nor to ascertain the representativeness of the sample, given the lack of aggregate state-wide data concerning dual order care leavers. Additionally, the sample of care leavers was aged 18–26 years at the time of the interviews; therefore, some experiences described may not necessarily reflect recent policy and practice. Owing to the use of agencies as a sampling frame for locating care leavers, the results are likely to be more reflective of the experiences of young people who remain connected to services and supports after leaving care.

This may under-represent certain groups of care leavers, particularly the most disadvantaged subgroups, including those who may have remained involved with Youth Justice and/or were detained in the adult custodial justice system at the time of the study. Conversely, young people who may have had previous involvement with Youth Justice services, but successfully moved on and were no longer connected to services post-care, may also be under-represented in the findings. In the case of dual order care leavers, the study findings relied on retrospective self-report. Such recollections are subject to issues concerning participant recall and bias, as well as the impact of trauma upon memory storage and retrieval (Anda et al. 2006). As Taylor (2006, pp. 69–70) explained, 'the memories of care leavers may be further complicated by the often traumatic nature of their earlier experiences and by the fragmented picture that they may have as a result of movement and change'.

Finally, this study adopted a generic approach which effectively considered dual order care leavers as a homogenous group. It is acknowledged that such an approach does not have the scope to consider the specific needs of particular subgroups of dual order care leavers, including: those who identify as Aboriginal and Torres Strait Islanders (AIHW 2014);

dual order female care leavers; dual order care leavers from culturally and linguistically diverse backgrounds; dual order care leavers who also present with a disability; dual order care leavers who are young parents; and dual order care leavers residing in non-metropolitan areas. While it is envisaged that the major points covered by the recommendations will also be pertinent to these groups, further consideration should be given to identifying and addressing their specific needs, in terms of prevention, intervention and supports.

References

Alston, M., & Bowles, W. (2003). *Research for social workers: An introduction to methods* (2 ed.). London: Routledge.

Anda, R. F., Felitti, V. J., Bremner, J. D., Walker, J. D., Whitfield, C., Perry, B. D., et al. (2006). The enduring effects of abuse and related adverse experiences in childhood – A convergence of evidence from neurobiology and epidemiology. *European Archives of Psychiatry and Clinical Neuroscience, 256*, 174–186.

Australian Institute of Health and Welfare (2012). *Child protection Australia 2010–11*. Canberra: Australian Government.

Australian Institute of Health and Welfare (2014). *Indigenous child safety*. Canberra: Australian Institute of Health and Welfare.

Australian Institute of Health and Welfare (2015). *Child protection Australia 2013–14*. Canberra: Australian Government.

Barbour, R. S. (2001). Checklists for improving rigour in qualitative research: A case of the tail wagging the dog? *BMJ, 322*(7294), 1115–1117.

Barn, R., & Tan, J. (2012). Foster youth and crime: Employing general strain theory to promote understanding. *Journal of Criminal Justice, 40*, 212–220.

Blades, R., Hart, D., Lea, J., & Wilmott, N. (2011). *Care – A stepping stone to custody? The views of children in care on the links between care, offending and custody*. London: Prison Reform Trust.

Cashmore, J., & Paxman, M. (2007). *Longitudinal study of wards leaving care: Four to five years on*. Sydney: Social Policy Research Centre.

Coleman, H., & Jenson, J. M. (2000). A longitudinal investigation of delinquency among abused and behaviour problem youth following participation in a family preservation program. *Journal of Offender Rehabilitation, 31*(1–2), 143–162.

Courtney, M., & Dworsky, A. (2006). Early outcomes for young adults transitioning from out-of-home care in the USA. *Child and Family Social Work, 11*, 209–219.

Culhane, D., Byrne, T., Metraux, S., Moreno, M., Toros, H., & Stevens, M. (2011). *Young adult outcomes of youth exiting dependent or delinquent care in Los Angeles County*. Los Angeles: Conrad N. Hilton Foundation.

Cusick, G., & Courtney, M. (2007). *Offending during late adolescence: How do youth aging out of care compare with their peers?* Chicago: Chapin Hall Center for Children.

Cusick, G., Courtney, M., Havlicek, J., & Hess, N. (2010). *Crime during transition to adulthood: How youth fare as they leave out-of-home care*. Washington, DC: National Institute of Justice.

Darker, I., Ward, H., & Caulfield, L. (2008). An analysis of offending by young people looked after by local authorities. *Youth Justice, 8*(2), 134–148.

Department of Families, Housing, Community Services and Indigenous Affairs (2011). *An outline of national standards for out-of-home care*. Canberra: Australian Government.

Department of Human Services (2013). *Protocol between child protection and youth justice*. Melbourne: State Government Victoria.

Department of Human Services (2015a). *Young care leavers: For young people who are leaving or have left out-of-home care in Victoria*. Melbourne: Victorian Government.

Department of Human Services (2015b). *Youth justice*. Melbourne: Victorian Government.

Farrington, D. (Ed.) (1986). *Age and crime* (Vol. 7). Chicago: The University of Chicago Press.

Fitzpatrick, C., & Williams, P. (2014). *Examining 'clear approach': An intervention for care leavers on an intensive alternative to custody order*. Lancaster: Lancaster University and Manchester Metropolitan University.

Halemba, G., Siegel, G., Lord, R., & Zawacki, S. (2004). *Arizona dual jurisdiction study: Final report*. Pittsburgh: National Center for Juvenile Justice.

Hart, D. (2006). *Tell them not to forget about us – A guide to practice with looked after children in custody*. London: National Children's Bureau.

Hirschi, T., & Gottfredson, M. (1983). Age and the explanation of crime. *American Journal of Sociology, 89*(3), 552–584.

Indig, D., Vecchiato, C., Haysom, L., Beilby, R., Carter, J., Champion, U., et al. (2011). *2009 NSW young people in custody health survey: Full report*. Sydney: Justice Health and Juvenile Justice.

Jackson, S. (2001). *Nobody ever told us school mattered: Raising the educational attainments of children in care*. London: British Agencies for Adoption and Fostering.

Jacobson, J., Bhardwa, B., Gyateng, T., Hunter, G., & Hough, M. (2010). *Punishing disadvantage – A profile of children in custody*. London: Prison Reform Trust.

Johnson, G., & Mendes, P. (2014). 'Taking control and 'moving on': How young people turn around problematic transitions from out-of-home care. *Social Work and Society, 12*(1), 1–15.

Jonson-Reid, M. (2002). Exploring the relationship between child welfare intervention and juvenile corrections involvement'. *American Journal of Orthopsychiatry, 72*(4), 559–576.

Jonson-Reid, M., & Barth, R. P. (2000a). From maltreatment to juvenile incarceration: Uncovering the role of child welfare services. *Child Abuse & Neglect, 24*, 505–520.

Jonson-Reid, M., & Barth, R. P. (2000b). From placement to prison: The path to adolescent incarceration from child welfare supervised foster or group care. *Children and Youth Services Review, 22*(7), 493–516.

Kalb, G., & Williams, J. (2002). *The relationship between juvenile and adult crime*. Melbourne: Melbourne Institute of Applied Economic and Social Research.

Lee, J., Courtney, M., & Hook, J. (2012). Formal bonds during the transition to adulthood: Extended foster support and criminal/legal involvement. *Journal of Public Child Welfare, 6*(3), 255–279.

Linhorst, D. (2002). A review of the use and potential of focus groups in social work research. *Qualitative Social work, 1*(2), 208–228.

Lynch, M., Buckman, J., & Krenske, L. (2003). *Youth justice: Criminal trajectories*. Canberra: Australian Institute of Criminology.

Malvaso, G. G., & Delfabbro, P. (2015). Offending behaviour among young people with complex needs in the Australian out-of-home care system. *Journal of Child and Family Studies*. doi:10.1007/s10826-015-0157-z.

Mays, N., & Pope, C. (1995). Rigour and qualitative research. *British Medical Journal, 311*, 109–112.

McDowall, J. (2008). *CREATE report card 2008: Transitioning from care*. Sydney: CREATE Foundation.

McDowall, J. (2009). *CREATE report card 2009: Transitioning from care: Tracking progress*. Sydney: CREATE Foundation.

McFarlane, K. (2010). From care to custody: Young women in out-of-home care in the criminal justice system. *Current issues in criminal justice, 22*(2), 345–353.

Mendes, P., Johnson, G., & Moslehuddin, B. (2011). *Young people leaving state out-of-home care: A research-based study of Australian policy and practice.* Melbourne: Australian Scholarly Publishing Press.

Mendes, P., Snow, P. C., & Baidawi, S. (2012). *Young people transitioning from out-of-home care in Victoria: Strengthening support services for dual clients of child protection and youth justice.* Melbourne: Monash University.

Mendes, P., Snow, P. C., & Baidawi, S. (2013). *Young people transitioning from out of home care in Victoria: Strengthening support services for dual clients of child protection and youth justice: Phase two report.* Melbourne: Monash University.

Mendes, P., Baidawi, S., & Snow, P. C. (2014a). Young people transitioning from out-of-home care in Victoria: Strengthening support services for dual clients of child protection and youth justice. *Australian Social Work, 67*(1), 6–23.

Mendes, P., Baidawi, S., & Snow, P. C. (2014b). *Good practice in reducing the over-representation of care leavers in the youth justice system. Leaving care and youth justice – Phase three report.* Melbourne: Monash University.

Murphy, P., McGinness, A., Balmaks, A., McDermott, T., & Corriea, M. (2010). *A strategic review of the new South Wales Juvenile Justice System.* Canberra: Noetic Solutions Pty Ltd.

Raman, S., Inder, B., & Forbes, C. (2005). *Investing for success: The economics of supporting young people leaving care.* Melbourne: Centre for Excellence in Child and Family Welfare.

Ryan, J. P. (2012). Substitute care in child welfare and the risk of arrest: Does the reason for placement matter? *Child Maltreatment, 17*(2), 164–171.

Ryan, J., & Testa, M. (2005). Child maltreatment and juvenile delinquency: Investigating the role of placement and placement instability. *Children and Youth Services Review, 27*(3), 227–249.

Ryan, J., Hernandez, P., & Herz, D. (2007). Developmental trajectories of offending for male adolescents leaving foster care. *Social Work Research, 31*(2), 83–93.

Ryan, J., Marshall, J., Herz, D., & Hernandez, P. (2008). Juvenile delinquency in child welfare: Investigating group home effects. *Children and Youth Services Review, 30*, 1088–1099.

Ryan, J., Hong, J., Herz, D., & Hernandez, P. (2010). Kinship foster care and the risk of juvenile delinquency. *Children and Youth Services Review, 32*, 1823–1830.

Smith, C., Ireland, T., & Thornberry, T. (2005). Adolescent maltreatment and its impact on young adult antisocial behavior. *Child Abuse and Neglect, 29*(10), 1099–1119.

Stewart, A., Dennison, S., & Waterson, E. (2002). Pathways from child maltreatment to juvenile offending. *Trends & Issues in Crime and Criminal Justice, 241*, 1–6.

Stewart, A., Livingstone, M., & Dennison, S. (2008). Transitions and turning points: Examining the links between child maltreatment and juvenile offending. *Child Abuse & Neglect, 32*, 51–66.

Summerfield, A. (2011). *Children and young people in custody 2010–11 – An analysis of the experiences of 15–18 year olds in prison*. London: HM Inspectorate of Prisons and the Youth Justice Board.

Taylor, C. (2006). *Young people in care and criminal behaviour*. London: Jessica Kingsley Publishers.

West, D. J., & Farrington, D. P. (1973). *Who becomes delinquent?* London: Heinemann.

Widom, C. (1991). The role of placement experiences in mediating the criminal consequences of early childhood victimization. *American Journal of Orthopsychiatry, 61*(2), 195–209.

Wise, S., & Egger, S. (2008). *The looking after children outcomes data project*. Melbourne: Australian Institute of Family Studies.

Wood, J. (2008). *Report of the special commission of inquiry into child protection services in NSW* (Vol. 1). Sydney: State of New South Wales.

Youth Parole Board & Youth Residential Board Victoria (2015) *Annual report 2014–15*. Melbourne: Victorian Government.

3

Supporting Young People with an Intellectual Disability Transitioning from Out-of-Home Care to Adult Life in Queensland, Australia

Sarah MacDonald, Kathy Ellem, and Jill Wilson

Introduction

Young people with mild or borderline intellectual disability transitioning from out-of-home care (OHC) to adult life are particularly vulnerable to the poor adult life outcomes experienced by many care leavers. Little is known about their lived experience of transitioning from OHC to adult life, limiting effective policy and practice responses to this group. This chapter reviews the findings of a

---

S. MacDonald
School of Nursing Midwifery and Social Work, Chamberlain Building, University of Queensland, St Lucia, Qld, Australia

K. Ellem (✉)
School of Public Health and Social Work, Faculty of Health, Queensland University of Technology, Kelvin Grove Campus, Qld, Australia

J. Wilson
School of Nursing Midwifery and Social Work, Chamberlain Building, University of Queensland, St Lucia, Qld, Australia

© The Author(s) 2016
P. Mendes, P. Snow (eds.), *Young People Transitioning from Out-of-Home Care*, DOI 10.1057/978-1-137-55639-4_3

Queensland study involving six young adults with mild or borderline intellectual disability making this transition and considers recommendations for improved policy and practice responses targeted to these experiences.

Mild or Borderline Intellectual Disability

Intellectual disability is characterized by impairments in intellectual and adaptive functioning across conceptual, social and practical domains or skill sets, which have their onset before the age of 18 (American Psychiatric Association 2013). Contemporary diagnostic schema emphasize adaptive functioning as a more useful indicator of individual ability than measures of intellectual functioning such as IQ testing (APA 2013). The functional effects of intellectual impairment in this group relate primarily to cognitive and communication abilities (Gillberg and Soderstrom 2003). People with mild or borderline intellectual disability (hereafter referred to as people with intellectual disability) may have difficulty making themselves understood and understanding others; they may take longer to learn new things and may have difficulty transferring knowledge to different social contexts; they may find it challenging to understand and apply abstract concepts such as numbers, time and money; and they may struggle to recognize and/or articulate emotions in themselves and others. They often require support to manage daily living tasks and to navigate social barriers that constrain their life opportunities (Fernell and Ek 2010; Hebblethwaite et al. 2011; Snell et al. 2009).

Whilst the labels 'mild' and 'borderline' intellectual disability are the conventional terminology used in the Australian context to specify the disability experience of the young people in this research, this is not the preferred language of many people who experience this type of impairment (Atkinson 1997). This language is seen by some to reflect a medicalized diagnostic approach (Oliver 2009) and risks misrepresenting their experience (e.g., as 'mild'), thus obscuring the significant social, legal, political and economic disadvantages such people face (Finlay and Lyons 2005; Rioux and Bach 1994).

Intellectual Disability, Child Maltreatment and OHC

It is well established that children with disabilities are at increased risk of child maltreatment compared with non-disabled children, with estimates indicating they are 1.7–3.4 times more likely to experience abuse (Hershkowitz et al. 2007; Sullivan 2009). They are more likely to enter OHC, experience extended stays in-care and placement disruptions and are less likely to be reunified with birth parents than non-disabled children (Brown and Rodger 2009; Bruhn 2004; Slayter and Springer 2011).

Little research specifically considers the experience of children and young people with intellectual disability in OHC (Sainero et al. 2013), and poor identification of this group within OHC populations is a noted barrier to targeted responses, nationally and internationally (Mendes and Snow 2014; Slayter and Springer 2011). It is not known how many children and young people with an intellectual disability are in OHC in Australia; however, a number of studies attest to their likely over-representation (e.g., Raman et al. 2005). Seventeen per cent of children in foster care in Queensland identify themselves as having a disability, with cognitive and learning disorders commonly identified disability types (Commission for Children Young People and Child Guardian 2010).

Intellectual Disability and the Transition from OHC to Adult Life

The transition to adult life is a particularly challenging time for young care leavers with an intellectual disability. Whilst little is empirically known about their experiences, a small, but emerging, body of research indicates they are likely to experience homelessness, unemployment, mental health issues, involvement in the criminal justice system, early pregnancy, exploitation and abuse, addiction and financial debt (Edwards 2010; Fudge Schormans and Rooke 2008; Jackson et al. 2006; Mendes and Snow 2014).

Like all care leavers, they must negotiate the effects of trauma associated with pre-care abuse or neglect and inadequate and/or abusive in-care experiences, where these occur (Courtney and Dworsky 2006; Mendes 2009). They are impacted by limited informal support networks (Cashmore and Paxman 2006) and inadequate post-care support (Mendes and Moslehuddin 2003). Systemic issues impeding targeted responses to care leavers with intellectual disability include poor quality transition planning; a lack of coordination between systems involved with care leavers with a disability (Hill 2009); and limited appropriate post-care accommodation options for people with a disability (Fudge Schormans and Rooke 2008). It has been noted that care leavers with a disability often experience a 'vacuum of support' from both mainstream after-care services and adult disability services (Mendes et al. 2011, p. 32).

This population of care leavers experiences additional challenges such as difficulty acquiring skills and managing day-to-day tasks (Geenan et al. 2007; Hill et al. 2010; Osgood et al. 2007). They may experience difficulty assuming normative adult roles (Myklebust 2012); reduced social inclusion (Gray et al. 2014), restricted intimate partner relationships (McGuire and Bayley 2011); and increased external controls on decision-making, assumption of responsibility, and financial independence (Suto et al. 2005; Wehmeyer and Abery 2013). Those who become parents may face prejudicial attitudes about their capacity to learn to parent. They often receive inadequate support to build parenting skills and are more likely to have their children removed from their care (Llewellyn 2013).

Study Aims and Methodology

This study aimed to build knowledge of the lived experience of young adults with a mild or borderline intellectual disability who are making the transition from OHC to adult life, and to consider the implications of this for improved policy and practice responses to this group.

Six young people (four women and two men) aged 18–27 were recruited over a period of 15 months. Recruitment occurred through human service agencies to identify eligible young people who were aged

18–30; identified as having a mild or borderline intellectual disability; and who had 'aged out' of non-kinship OHC. Recruitment via agencies also ensured appropriate support could be provided to research participants if needed. Service providers distributed recruitment information and consent forms written in easy English to eligible young people whom they determined had capacity to give consent and to participate in interviews. The researcher (a social worker experienced in direct practice with people with intellectual disability) used her professional judgement to confirm young people's capacity at an initial contact meeting prior to their participation in the research, and monitored this during the research interviews.

Recruitment of young people was difficult, despite intensive efforts. The involvement of gatekeeper service providers was crucial for identifying eligible young people; however, many agencies were not able to offer this assistance due to gaps in service provider knowledge of clients' OHC histories (in the case of adult services) or loss of contact with clients when they exited OHC (in the case of child services). These gaps reflect systemic issues noted by many researchers as negatively impacting care leavers (e.g., Malvaso and Delfabbro 2015). Other recruitment challenges included lack of interest from young people in research participation and lack of the support needed to enable their participation. Given the small sample of young people who were recruited, theoretical saturation did not occur, and a second phase of data collection was conducted with ten human service providers experienced in supporting this population (findings from this phase will be reported elsewhere).

Young people participated in between two and six in-depth interviews about their experiences *before*, *in*, *exiting* and *after care*, and their *hopes and dreams for the future*. Multiple interviews supported young people's communication needs, with some young people requiring more interviews than others. Interviews were conducted using a topical life story approach (Ellem et al. 2008; Plummer 2001) and were guided by a brief interview protocol structured around the aforementioned life periods. Life maps were developed to document, order and check young people's stories (Gray and Ridden 1999), and provided additional structure to support communication. Written life story narratives were developed for each young person and member-checked for accuracy. Interview transcripts were coded using NVivo, and a thematic analysis of interview data was conducted. Ethics approvals were obtained from the University of Queensland and two non-government human research ethics committees, and executive approval to recruit service users was obtained from a third non-government agency. Participants have been assigned pseudonyms in this chapter.

Findings

The thematic analysis of young people's interviews identified themes relating to their early and adult lives. This chapter will outline the four themes relating to young people's adult life experiences. The first theme (*Adult Life After Care*) concerns the practical reality of young people's adult lives, while the three other themes (*Living with Intellectual Difference*, *The Light and Dark of Relationships*, *and The Double Edge of Service Support*) relate to the intersecting experiences that shape young people's experience of adult life after OHC.

Adult Life After Care

All young people said adult life began at their exit from care. All anticipated that in adult life they would have increased personal freedom to make their own choices and/or be free from control by others. The majority expected increased responsibility for themselves, and some expected increased responsibility for others (e.g., parenting children),

> You can go wherever you want, do whatever you want, no-one can tell you what to do unless you are in a pub or something. You've got to pay your bills. You've got to pay your phone bills and stuff. (Steven)
>
> Look after your kids, look after your place, do your housework. (Monica)

Young people discussed conventional aspirations for adult life. All said they wanted to live in their own home and get a job. The majority wanted to travel on public transport independently (two young people wanted to get a driver's license and a car). Many young people wanted to have a partner and/or children, and to go on holidays.

At the same time, the majority of young people expressed concern about their ability to manage increased personal responsibility '…I was used to all of having someone there to, like, cook, clean, do everything for me that I was worried about how was I supposed to cope doing everything' (Sarah-Jane).

Having Difficulty

In practice, all young people had difficulty achieving their aspirations for adult life.

Housing and Housing Instability

Young people's accommodation experiences in adult life were mixed. Most young people said they were supported by Child Safety Officers (CSO) to locate and move to new accommodation on their exit from care, including public housing, adult disability supported accommodation and a private boarding arrangement. One young person was supported to remain living with her foster carer in an arrangement brokered by a disability service provider: 'Child Safety were going to put me in a home – one of those homeless facilities. And Aunty Bernadette knew I wouldn't survive really well in that. So I stayed here…' (Maria).

Since exiting care, two young people had lived in the same accommodation, and one had moved once in seven years. Three young women had experienced housing instability, moving between nine and eleven times and living in a range of settings, including supported accommodation; temporary accommodation with family or friends; and crisis accommodation. Two women had lived in male hostels (with a partner), one had lived on the streets (when she was six months pregnant) and another had lived in a notorious caravan park: 'Dangerous place that is, because they've got speed heads and junkies and drugs and shootings, stabbings and kidnappings, all that going on there' (Missy).

Employment and Meaningful Activity

Four young people had been employed since exiting care, while one young person was in paid employment at the time of the research. Two had quit jobs (one after becoming homeless and another following conflict with the boss) and one young person was fired: 'I lost this job because I had too many injuries and accidents, and I was really rude to the boss' (Adam).

Many young people said they experienced a lack of meaningful activity in adult life, after leaving the daily routine provided by school. Three young people received support to participate in post-school employment training and two to engage in voluntary work, though none secured paid employment from this. Two young people had not engaged in any paid work since their exit from care, and two others had spent long periods of time looking for work,

Interviewer:	So once you finished the Cert II in Engineering, you had about six months, you said, where you weren't doing anything.
Steven:	Yeah, I was, like, dead. I didn't know what I was doing. I freaked out. That's when I was going in and out of the pub a lot.

Parenting and Removal of Children

Two women were parents at the time of the research, and one became pregnant. All three women became pregnant within two years of exiting care. Neither of the young men expressed a desire to have children, with one clear he did not want to be a parent. One young woman said she wanted to get married before having children.

Young people's parenting experiences were complicated by the removal of their own children into OHC. One woman had one of her three children removed from her care, while another had both of her children removed from her care.

Interviewer:	So when you were at the hospital, did Child Safety come there?
Sarah-Jane:	Yep.
Interviewer:	And what did they say to you?
Sarah-Jane:	They told me – well, they told us that they were taking him, all just because already had Peter in their care.
Interviewer:	And how old was Billy when they came?
Sarah-Jane:	He was only a couple of hours old.
Interviewer:	A couple of hours old. And what was that like for you?
Sarah-Jane:	Hard, heart-breaking.

Despite these experiences, parenting remained a significant daily life activity. One woman had multiple weekly contact visits with her two children, while another had monthly contact visits with her child in OHC and shared the care of the two children living with her and her partner – '…it feels like since I've got two toddlers, it feels like that Oscar [partner] and I are like a childcare worker. It feels like childcare' (Monica).

Gaps in Living Skills

All young people discussed difficulties with daily living tasks, including reading, cooking, budgeting and independent travel,

Interviewer:	What things are hard?
Sarah-Jane:	Making your way to a place with someone or, like, making your way to a certain place where you're supposed to meet this worker or something.

Other difficulties were suggested in young people's stories, but either not acknowledged or discussed in detail by young people themselves. For example, all young people were subject to adult guardianship and/or financial administration, but few said why this occurred. Some young people told stories that suggested they had difficulty problem-solving and anticipating likely consequences, but did not explicitly identify having these difficulties themselves,

Interviewer:	Why did they say that they'd taken him [child] to Child Safety?
Sarah-Jane:	All they said then was that it was because I didn't went to the daycare and pick him up…
Interviewer:	And did you tell them that you'd asked the worker to pick him up.
Sarah-Jane:	Yes.
Interviewer:	And what did they say?
Sarah-Jane:	They then said that it wasn't their responsibility to pick him up, that it was mine. I then told them that I couldn't, because I had a cold, I didn't want to give it to no one else, and to be blamed for it.

The Legacy of Trauma

Many young people said they experienced psychological and emotional difficulties in adult life, including depression, anxiety, difficulty trusting others and anger issues.

> If someone says a wrong thing about me, my angriness will come out and then my aggressive will come out. So I'm on mood stabilize tablets and they control me not to go that way. (Monica)

Others made comments that suggested they may have undiagnosed mental health conditions,

Interviewer:	And why did you need Tony [partner] with you at all times?
Sarah-Jane:	Because I got scared on the inside.
Interviewer:	What were you scared of?
Sarah-Jane:	I don't know. But I knew I was scared of something.
Interviewer:	And was that a new thing?

Sarah-Jane: I have always felt like that in my whole life.

Some young people told stories that suggested they experienced difficulty regulating emotions, but did not acknowledge these themselves. For example, one young person said he/she was fired for being rude to the boss, while another was subject to a domestic violence order,

> I decided one night to go out drinking with a few friends and got really smashed, and told her [Mum] I have a lot of hard feelings about her and, yeah, so she got a DVO put against me. (Missy)

Some young people attributed mental health problems in adult life to early life experiences of abuse: 'I probably had the anxiety and the fear problem, probably when I got molested at four' (Monica). Others attributed mental health problems to their experiences in OHC: 'I needed counseling because of the place I was living at, from all the youth workers. And I said that to them' (Steven). Others said adult life experiences negatively impacted their mental health. For example, two young people said they experienced depression following the removal of their children into OHC; and one young person was diagnosed with post-traumatic stress disorder after escaping a violent relationship.

Young people's capacity to achieve their aspirations for adult life was constrained by gaps in personal and social resources arising in the context of high levels of trauma and instability in early and adult life relationships. Difficulty in learning and different treatment as a result of intellectual disability were also identified as constraints. To bridge these gaps, young people were reliant on support from others; however, that was not always available and/or accessible.

Getting Support

All young people were engaged with support services in adult life, as per the recruitment design. The majority of service supports to young people in adult life were provided by specialist disability services, including disability lifestyle support, disability supported accommodation and disability employment services. Some young people accessed generalist services including public housing, intensive parenting residential facilities, counselling and legal services; however, with the exception of public housing, these services were short-term.

Most young people experienced an abrupt end to support from OHC service providers and caregivers at their exit from care. However, two young people maintained a degree of familiar support when they moved to adult disability accommodation provided by the same agency as their OHC placements, although their relationships with support workers ended because adult services were staffed by different workers than those in child services.

The majority of young people reported receiving practical support from significant others in adult life. These included accommodation, cooking lessons and meal preparation, parenting support, and assistance with budgeting, reading and transport. In some cases, this support was temporary and assisted young people in crisis (often when service supports had broken down). For example, one young person 'self-placed' with various friends and family members from the time she left care at age 16 until she secured public housing at age 18. For some young people, this support was ongoing and assisted positive outcomes. One young person was able to live with and parent her two youngest children with the support of her partner who was assessed by Child Safety as the primary caregiver (despite her eldest child being in OHC); another continued living with a foster carer after her exit from care and completed a Technical and Further Education (TAFE) qualification, before moving out-of-home at age 20.

Some young people received assistance from significant others to manage emotional and psychological difficulties. One young person said her partner assisted her when she was unwell with depression: 'he grabs all the knives and takes them, he hides them so I don't use any stuff in the house. And it works' (Missy). Another person felt her sister understood how she was feeling when her child was removed from her care:

> Well, I know that I texted May, like, three days after it happened, and no-one had informed her about it, so she was angry. But at the same time she was hurt, because she knew I was hurting. And that she knew that I

wasn't really looking after myself, because she knew that I was hurting so much. (Sarah-Jane)

Living with Intellectual Difference

Young people had difficulty achieving their aspirations for adult life as a result of difficulty learning, and differential treatment in society that they attributed to their experience of intellectual disability.

Learning Differently

Many young people described their experience of intellectual disability in terms of difficulty learning, for example, 'I have a learning thing' (Missy). Some young people said they had a different learning pace, 'Because my disability classifies as slow learning, so I process things a bit slowly than most' (Maria); and others a different learning style. 'How I learnt is I like to have it step by step. Either with writing or with pictures, and that's how I learn' (Monica).

Many young people said they had difficulty learning practical living skills in adult life, including using public transport, cooking and reading. Some said they learnt new skills with support, for example, one young person was accompanied by her support worker on the bus to and from TAFE (a vocational training college) until she could travel independently; others said they were embarrassed to ask for the support they needed 'Cause I don't want the teachers from the college to think that I'm stupid or think that I can't do the work, or think that I can't answer the question' (Sarah-Jane).

Treated Differently

Some young people said they were subject to different treatment on account of their intellectual disability, including discrimination in employment. 'It's hard enough trying to get in the [mechanic] industry. People saying don't do it. And people won't accept me because I have a disability' (Steven). Two people used non-disclosure as a strategy to avoid different treatment by others, 'I don't tell them [students at TAFE] that I have a learning thing because, then, they kind of treat me different' (Maria). For many young people, the underlying meaning of being treated differently (and, in turn, of having an intellectual disability) was that they were not capable,

Interviewer:		Okay. And what did the [Family Court] judge say?
Sarah-Jane:		That he [child] could go home, but someone has to be the guardian of him, 'cause the judge reckoned that neither me or Tony [partner] are capable.
Interviewer:		Yeah. And why, why did the judge reckon that?
Sarah-Jane:		Cause I had an adult guardian and that he saw that Tony had a disability.

It is not surprising that most young people did not use the term 'intellectual disability' to describe themselves. One young person did not directly discuss having an intellectual impairment after the recruitment phase, while another used a different disability label. 'It's Aspergers. Aspergers is spectrum syndrome. It stuffs up your brain majorly' (Steven).

The Light and Dark of Relationships

Relationships with significant others are important to young people as they make the transition from OHC to adult life; however, the dark side of many relationships is continuing maltreatment.

Connection

All young people were supported to maintain contact with family when they were in OHC, and the majority reconnected with family members at their exit from care (most commonly mothers and siblings, with only one young person reconnecting with their father). As discussed, many young people received practical and emotional support in these relationships. Some young people formed intimate partner relationships following their exit from care, which provided them with connection and support in adult life. For example, two young women met and moved in with new partners when they were homeless, while two young women invited a new partner to live with them following the removal of a child into OHC.

In contrast, young people's relationships with caregivers and service providers in OHC settings generally ended at their exit from care, when they were referred to new services for support in adult life. Similarly, whilst a number of young people discussed positive relationships with teachers and school friends, most of these ended when they left school. Two exceptions highlighted the supportive potential of service relationships continuing from early to adult life: one young person was supported by a school guidance officer to move to a boarding arrangement with a teacher aide, and another was supported to remain living with her foster carer until age 20.

Abuse

The dark side of relationships with significant others in adult life were ongoing experiences of abuse, and most young people discussed experiences of sexual, financial and/or emotional abuse in these relationships. For example, one young person was sexually assaulted by her mother's partner, and rejected by her mother when she reported this to the police; two young people reported domestic violence in intimate partner relationships.

The Double Edge of Service Support

The service support young people received at their transition from OHC to adult life often had a 'double edge' in that this support was often linked to continuing regulation in adult life.

Regulation

Many young people discussed ongoing decision-making control by service providers in adult life. Transition from care planning was managed by service providers and focused on securing material resources and linking young people with adult services (primarily accommodation and employment/training). There was little evidence that transition from care planning processes was tailored to support young people's participation. One young person agitated to be involved; three appeared to accept a 'recipient' role; and one evidenced a lack of engagement. 'Pretty boring, even though it's about me' (Maria). One young person left care at age 16 before planning had commenced. Some young people discussed transition from care plans that were implemented seamlessly by service providers (with no involvement from young people themselves); for example, two young people moved from OHC accommodation to adult disability supported accommodation provided by the same agency, while others discussed poor and/or last minute planning processes they had little control over, that contributed to feelings of worry and fear at their transition from care.

> Well, what happened was the Department are supposed to do a transitioning from care but that didn't happen with me. Aunty Bernadette kept telling the Department … what I'm going to do because – you know. And then it got tricky because we were getting – when it was getting to my birthday, we were getting all this paperwork, like, Centrelink and Housing and it got like Aunty Bernadette didn't know really what to do. (Maria)

All young people were subject to statutory regulation in adult life, including Adult Guardian, Public Trustee, Child Protection and Domestic Violence orders. Whilst a small number of young people said they received benefits from these services, for example, 'I wanted to get my money managed a bit easier. It's going pretty good' (Adam); others rejected them as invasive controls.

> Steven: They [Public Trustee] would never get hold of my bank accounts 'cause I'd go off at them.
> Interviewer: Yeah, so they manage your money do they?
> Steven: No they don't, I wouldn't let them.

Some young people discussed their fear of being subject to control in future adult lives; '…fearing the fact that if I ever have kids the Department will put that against me, being in care' (Maria).

Receiving Services

As care leavers with intellectual disability, young people reported receiving a range of resources and services at their exit from care that were additional to that provided to care leavers in general. All young people received the Disability Support Pension and/or Youth Allowance Disability Supplement, paid at a higher rate than Youth Allowance payments received by care leavers without a disability; and the majority were supported by CSOs to transition from OHC services to adult disability services, except for one young person, who exited care at age 16 to live with a friend (however, a CSO facilitated her engagement with a disability outreach service in her first year OHC).

Despite high levels of engagement with services in adult life, young people indicated that they did not always receive the support they needed to achieve benefits from these. For example, whilst four young people reported support to obtain paid employment, only one reported assistance to maintain this. Three people who received no ongoing support subsequently quit or were fired from their jobs. Similarly, no support was provided to the young person who moved in with her former teacher aide, and this relationship (and accommodation) broke down after the young person travelled interstate without telling her landlady, who reported her as a missing person to the police.

Young people also discussed gaps in support available to them. For example, only one received professional mental health treatment as an adult, although most said they received medication or counselling treatment for mental health and/or behaviour issues in OHC and continued to experience these issues in adult life. Similarly, one young person attended hospital antenatal appointments when she was pregnant, but did not receive any parenting skills training prior to the birth of her first child, who was removed from her care.

Discussion

This study contributes to the knowledge and understanding of the experiences of young people with mild or borderline intellectual disability making the transition from OHC to adult life by documenting the experiences of six young people currently engaged in this transition, and considering the implications of this for policy and practice. This is an exploratory study with a small sample size, and therefore the findings cannot be generalized. The timing of young people's transitions also took place at different times and in different policy and practice contexts in Queensland. Despite these limitations, several conclusions can be drawn from the study findings.

Young people reported multiple adversities in the context of overlapping experiences of intellectual difference, maltreatment in relationships and regulation in service systems that constrained the personal and social resources available to them in their transition from OHC to adult life. They experienced gaps in adult living skills, restricted support networks and discrimination. Their experiences are consistent with research on people with intellectual disability with complex needs (e.g., Dowse et al. 2014).

In common with the general population of care leavers, these young people entered adult life abruptly, with restricted informal support networks and with gaps in adult life skills, and many experienced mental health issues (Cashmore and Paxman 2006; Mendes 2009; Mendes and Moslehuddin 2003; Stein 2008). They reported negative impacts of poor OHC experiences of placement instability, ongoing experiences of abuse, restricted decision-making control and limited development of skills for adult life. In early adult life, they reported multiple forms of social disadvantage, including housing instability, unemployment, early parenting and removal of children into OHC and abuse in relationships. Like many people with intellectual disability, they experienced constrained access to adult roles and regulation of adult responsibilities (Myklebust 2012; Suto et al. 2005; Wehmeyer and Abery 2013). They had high levels of contact with service systems, but received inadequate assistance to develop practical skills for social participation and to exercise personal choice and control (Ellem et al. 2013).

Young people varied in the degree to which they discussed adult life difficulties, and how they understood these experiences. They were more likely to identify external constraints in service systems and relationships as causing difficulties in adult life, than their experience of intellectual impairment. Similarly, they were more willing to discuss the impact of trauma and disruption in family and OHC than that of intellectual impairment. Young people's limited acknowledgement of the impact of intellectual impairment on their experiences may indicate this held greater stigma for them, and/or may reflect reduced personal insight, as discussed later in this chapter.

Young people relied on support from services and significant relationships to assist them in the transition from OHC to adult life. In comparison to most care leavers, they received additional resources and service support that assisted them in their transition from care to early adulthood, including higher income support as recipients of the Disability Support Pension, and support to engage with adult disability support services at, or soon after, their transition from care. Some young people reported positive caregiver relationships and maintained these into adult life; some formed new supportive adult life relationships, or received holistic and ongoing service support and were more able to develop skills for adult life, maintain adult roles and manage crises.

All young people reported negative impacts of a lack of available accessible, and/or reliable support. Service supports often addressed single needs, rather than a coordinated suite of supports to respond to multiple needs, and some needs were unmet, such as support to develop daily living or parenting skills. Many service supports provided young people with material resources, but few developed their personal skills and relationship networks. Furthermore, many of the services and resources young people were engaged with at transition from care and in adult life broke down due to a lack of ongoing support to maintain these engagements through inevitable life challenges. Young people were often reliant on relationships with significant others when this occurred.

As with most care leavers, participants reported a limited number of supportive adult connections, as a result of disrupted relationships with their family of origin, including contexts of abuse and neglect and an abrupt end to relationships at their exit from service systems. Whilst the majority reconnected with family in adult life, and many formed new relationships with intimate partners, most continued to experience exploitation and abuse in these relationships. Young people often had difficulty protecting themselves or extricating themselves from these relationships, because they relied on them for resources, support and belonging.

As noted, all young people demonstrated some degree of restricted insight and/or willingness to acknowledge their difficulties and support needs (e.g., factors impacting their capacity to care for children and/or manage their finances). Many disputed statutory support and/or regulation as unwarranted (e.g., guardianship and administration; removal of their children) with limited insight into why these occurred. Support from services and significant relationships did not remove structural barriers to social participation (e.g., high rates of unemployment) impacting on people with intellectual disability, including the effects of discrimination and stigma.

Implications for Policy and Practice

This study contributes knowledge of the lived experience of the transition from OHC to adult life of young people with intellectual disability, notably absent to date in research on care leavers and young adults with intellectual disability. Whilst the sample of young people is small and the findings cannot be generalized beyond the six participants, some useful insights for policy and practice with this population are suggested.

Despite being a relatively well-resourced group of care leavers and receiving higher levels of income and service support in adult life than care leavers in general, the six young people experienced significant difficulties making the transition from OHC to adult life. These difficulties reflected intersecting experiences of intellectual disability, personal relationships and service systems. Policy and practice responses to this group must engage with the complexity of their experiences and build the capacity of young people, their significant others, and service systems. Key recommendations are as follows:

- Early intervention and intensive outreach support to families experiencing complex disadvantage to build parenting capacity and address presenting needs (e.g., intellectual disability [parent and/or child]; mental illness; intergenerational abuse, neglect and child protection involvement; domestic violence; drug and alcohol abuse; homelessness; and unemployment).

- Training for child protection officers, residential workers and foster carers to build expertise in recognizing and responding to intellectual disability and trauma.
- Recruitment and training of specialist foster carers to provide placements responsive to complex needs of young people with intellectual disability who have experienced trauma, including small caring loads; commitment to long-term engagement; and funding and resources to support placement stability.
- Targeted responses to young people with intellectual disability transitioning from care to adult life, including extended transition planning (early and regular planning meetings; inclusive planning and making processes; and supportive communication practices); extended care orders and/or tailored transitional accommodation and support; and extended post-care support (holistic, flexible and responsive to crisis), including support to manage and/or build significant relationships, address gaps in personal skills and resources and access and sustain valued adult roles.

The study findings suggest some key principles of effective practice with this population of care leavers, including their need for *ongoing assistance* into adult life; *persistence* from service providers in engaging and maintaining engagement, especially in times of crisis; *flexible* support to meet changing needs; and *inclusive practice* responsive to needs presented by experiences of intellectual disability, trauma and service/system histories. These principles are consistent with extant research on marginalized adults with intellectual disability (Ellem et al. 2013) and care leavers with complex needs (Malvaso and Delfabbro 2015).

Intensive relationship-based support is recognized as the foundation of effective practice with this group (Ellem et al. 2012). Effective practitioners reach out to young people, their families and caregivers, and they work developmentally to build a network of committed relationships with deep knowledge of the young person, their needs, hopes and dreams. Key dimensions of holistic support to young people with intellectual disability in OHC and during their transition from OHC to adult life include:

- *Therapeutic support* responsive to the needs of intellectual disability, to recover from experiences of maltreatment and loss; to understand experiences of intellectual impairment and disability; to plan goals for adult life.
- *Learning support* to build personal skills and knowledge for meaningful participation in adult life roles, relationships and achievement of personal goals.
- *Relationship support* to build and sustain supportive relationships with family, caregivers and community members for long-term connection and belonging; and to manage and/or end difficult or abusive relationships.
- *Inclusion support* to participate in community life, including access to opportunities (e.g., participation in meaningful roles and decision-making) and resources (e.g., material, services and relationships).

Young people with intellectual disability making the transition from OHC to adult life are particularly vulnerable to poor adult life outcomes. This vulnerability occurs in the context of intersecting experiences of intellectual disability and complexity in relationships and service systems. Effective policy and practice responses to this group will mirror this complexity by delivering holistic and developmental services and support responsive to young people's experiences of trauma, disrupted relationships and intellectual disability. Only then will young people with mild or borderline intellectual disability have a better chance at good outcomes following the transition from OHC to adult life.

The researcher gratefully acknowledges the contribution of Professor Jill Wilson (Principal Advisor) and Dr Kathy Ellem (Associate Advisor) to the doctoral study on which this chapter reports.

References

American Psychiatric Association (2013). *Intellectual disability*. Arlington: American Psychiatric Association.

Atkinson, D. (1997). *An auto/biographical approach to learning disability research*. Aldershot: Ashgate.

Brown, J. D., & Rodger, S. (2009). Children with disabilities: Problems faced by foster parents. *Children and Youth Services Review, 31*, 40–46.

Bruhn, C. M. (2004). Children with disabilities. *Journal of Aggression, Maltreatment & Trauma, 8*(1), 173–203.

Cashmore, J., & Paxman, M. (2006). Predicting after-care outcomes: The importance of 'felt' security. *Child and Family Social Work, 11*, 232–241.

Commission for Children, Young People & Child Guardian (2010). *Views of children and young people in foster care, Queensland, 2010*. Brisbane: Commission for Children, Young People & Child Guardian.

Courtney, M. E., & Dworsky, A. (2006). Early outcomes for young adults transitioning from out of home care in the USA. *Child and Family Social Work, 11*, 209–219.

Dowse, L., Cumming, T. M., Strnodova, I., Lee, J.-S., & Trofimovs, J. (2014). Young people with complex needs in the criminal justice system. *Research and Practice in Intellectual and Developmental Disabilities, 1*(2), 174–185.

Edwards, R. (2010). Nobody knows: Young people with disability leaving care. *Parity, 23*(5), 20–21.

Ellem, K., Wilson, J., Chui, W. H., & Knox, M. (2008). Ethical challenges of life story research with ex-prisoners with intellectual disability. *Disability & Society, 23*(5), 497–509.

Ellem, K., Wilson, J., O'Connor, M., & MacDonald, S. (2012). Supporting young people with mild/borderline intellectual disability exiting state out-of-home care: Directions for practice. *Developing Practice, 32*, 53–65.

Ellem, K., O'Connor, M., Wilson, J., & Williams, S. (2013). Social work with marginalized people who have a mild or borderline intellectual disability: Practicing gentleness and encouraging hope. *Australian Social Work, 66*(1), 56–71.

Fernell, E., & Ek, U. (2010). Borderline intellectual functioning in children and adolescents – Insufficiently recognized difficulties. *Acta Paediatrica, 99*, 748–753.

Finlay, W. M. L., & Lyons, E. (2005). Rejecting the label: A social constructionist analysis. *Mental Retardation, 43*(2), 120–134.

Fudge Schormans, A., & Rooke, J. (2008). When there are no choices: The consequences of a lack of adult living placements for young adults with intellectual and/or developmental disabilities leaving child welfare care. *Journal on Developmental Disabilities, 14*(1), 107–126.

Geenan, S., Powers, L. E., Hogansen, J. M., & Pittman, J. O. (2007). Youth with disabilities in foster care: Developing self-determination within a context of struggle and disempowerment. *Exceptionality, 15*(1), 17–30.

Gillberg, C., & Soderstrom, H. (2003). Learning disability. *The Lancet, 362*, 811–821.

Gray, B., & Ridden, G. (1999). *Life maps of people with learning disabilities*. London: Jessica Kingsley.

Gray, K. M., Piccinin, A., Keating, C. M., Taffe, J., Parmenter, T. R., Hofer, S., et al. (2014). Outcomes in young adulthood: Are we achieving community participation and inclusion? *Journal of Intellectual Disability Research, 58*(8), 734–745.

Hebblethwaite, A., Jahoda, A., & Dagnan, D. (2011). Talking about real-life events: An investigation into the ability of people with intellectual disabilities to make links between their beliefs and emotions within dialogue. *Journal of Applied Research in Intellectual Disabilities, 24*(6), 543–553.

Hershkowitz, I., Lamb, M. E., & Horowitz, D. (2007). Victimization of children with disabilities. *American Journal of Orthopsychiatry, 77*(4), 629–635.

Hill, K. (2009). Individuals with Disabilities Act of 2004 and the John H. Chafee Foster Care Independence Act of 1999: What are the policy implications for youth with disabilities transitioning from foster care. *Child Welfare, 8*(2), 5–23.

Hill, K., Lightfoot, E., & Kimball, E. (2010). Foster care transition services for youth with disabilities: Findings from a survey of county service providers. *Child Welfare, 89*(6), 63–81.

Jackson, R., O'Connor, M., & Chenoweth, L. (2006). *Journeys of exclusion*. Brisbane: Community Living Association.

Llewellyn, G. (2013). Parents with intellectual disability and their children: Advances in policy and practice. *Journal of Policy and Practice in Intellectual Disabilities, 10*(2), 82–85.

Malvaso, C., & Delfabbro, P. (2015). Young people with complex needs leaving out-of-home care: Service issues and the need to enhance practice and policy. *Children Australia, December*: 1–11.

McGuire, B. E., & Bayley, A. A. (2011). Relationships, sexuality and decision-making capacity in people with an intellectual disability. *Current Opinion in Psychiatry, 24*, 398–402.

Mendes, P. (2009). Young people transitioning from out-of-home care: A critical analysis of Australian and international policy and practice. *Australian Social Work, 62*(3), 388–402.

Mendes, P., & Moslehuddin, B. (2003). Graduating from the Child Welfare System. *Youth Studies Australia, 22*(4), 37–43.

Mendes, P., & Snow, P. (2014). The needs and experiences of young people with a disability transitioning from out-of-home care: The views of practitioners in Victoria, Australia. *Child and Youth Services Review, 36*, 115–123.

Mendes, P., Johnson, G., & Moslehuddin, B. (2011). *Young people leaving state out-of-home care: Australian policy and practice*. Melbourne: Australian Scholarly Publishing.

Myklebust, J. O. (2012). The transition to adulthood for vulnerable youth. *Scandinavian Journal of Disability Research, 14*(4), 1–17.

Oliver, M. (2009). *Understanding disability: From theory to practice* (2 ed.). Houndsmill: Palgrave Macmillan.

Osgood, D. W., Foster, E. M., Flanagan, C., & Ruth, G. R. (2007). Introduction: Why focus on the transition to adulthood for vulnerable populations? In W. D. Osgood, E. M. Foster, C. Flanagan, & G. R. Ruth (Eds.), *On your own without a net: The transition to adulthood for vulnerable populations* (pp. 1–26). Chicago: The University of Chicago Press.

Plummer, K. (2001). *Documents of life 2: An invitation to critical humanism*. London: Sage.

Raman, S., Inder, B., & Forbes, C. (2005). *Investing for success: The economics of supporting young people leaving care*. Melbourne: Centre for Excellence in Child and Family Welfare.

Rioux, M. H., & Bach, M. (1994). Foreword. In M. H. Rioux & M. Bach (Eds.), *Disability is not measles: New research paradigms in disability* (pp. vii–xii). Toronto: Roeher Institute.

Sainero, A., del Valle, J. F., Lopez, M., & Bravo, A. (2013). Exploring the specific needs of an understudied group: Children with intellectual disability in residential child care. *Children and Youth Services Review, 35*, 1393–1399.

Slayter, E., & Springer, C. (2011). Child welfare-involved youth with intellectual disabilities: Pathways into and placements in foster care. *Intellectual and Developmental Disabilities, 49*(1), 1–13.

Snell, M. E., Luckasson, R., Borthwick-Duffy, S., Bradley, V., Buntinx, W. H. E., Coulter, D. L., et al. (2009). Characteristics and needs of people with intellectual disability who have higher IQs. *Intellectual and Developmental Disabilities, 47*(3), 220–233.

Stein, M. (2008). Resilience and young people leaving care. *Child Care in Practice, 14*(1), 35–44.

Sullivan, P. M. (2009). Violence exposure among children with disabilities. *Clinical Child and Family Psychology Review, 12*, 196–216.

Suto, W. M. I., Clare, I. C. H., Holland, A. J., & Watson, P. C. (2005). Capacity to make financial decisions among people with mild intellectual disabilities. *Journal of Intellectual Disability Research, 49*(3), 199–209.

Wehmeyer, M. L., & Abery, B. H. (2013). Self-determination and choice. *Intellectual and Developmental Disabilities, 51*(5), 399–411.

4

A Comparison of Young People with a Disability Transitioning from Out-of-Home Care in Australia and Northern Ireland

Pamela Snow, Berni Kelly, Philip Mendes, and Delia O'Donohue

Readers of this text will be only too familiar with the overarching vulnerability of children and adolescents in the state care system. Their young lives have been punctuated by experiences of unstable housing, parental mental health and/or substance abuse problems, parental absence, maltreatment (abuse and/or neglect) of various forms and often a profound lack of capital of all kinds, including financial, social and human (Arnau Sabates and Gilligan 2015; Stein and Munro 2008;

P. Snow (✉)
Rural Health School, La Trobe University, Bendigo, Australia

B. Kelly
School of Sociology, Social Policy and Social Work, Queen's University Belfast, Belfast, Ireland

P. Mendes
Monash University, Clayton, Australia

D. O'Donohue
School of Global Urban and Social Studies, RMIT University, Melbourne, Australia

Mendes et al. 2011). Compounding this risk trajectory is the fact that the state as a 'parent' fails to provide the practical, financial, social and emotional scaffolding that other families offer well into a young person's 20s and even beyond. Other chapters in this text describe these vulnerabilities in detail, and outline the fragmented policy and practice frameworks that are typically in place for such young people. In this chapter, however, we focus on those young people who experience the double disadvantage of disability in addition to the experience of living in state care. Disabilities can be easily overlooked or misconstrued, such that specialist services are not sought. Disabilities of various forms also increase the likelihood of maltreatment, due to the strain they can place on early attachment processes and the capacity of primary carers to bond with their infant (Snow 2009).

Being in the state care system in, and of, itself flags developmental concerns for young people. The experience of emotional neglect, for example, is not at all benign. Rather, it deprives the young person of opportunities to engage in social and emotional learning in the interpersonal space; such learning encompasses detecting and understanding affective cues in others, responding empathically to the feeling states of others and receiving emotional and social warmth from others (Perry 2006). All of these skills are fundamental to the capacity to form and maintain close relationships, which, in turn, is foundational to mental health across the lifespan. Even in the absence of disability, neglect conspires against the optimal development of social and emotional skills, and can leave the young person with a severely constricted repertoire of interpersonal and social problem-solving skills. Young people with limited cognitive, linguistic, academic and vocational resources as a result of maltreatment are simply not in a position to find their way in the world at the age of 18. Add to this already complex mix a disability diagnosis, and we have a young person at high risk of long-term social and economic exclusion and a life on the margins.

In this chapter, we seek to untangle some of the complex and sometimes contradictory terminology surrounding notions of disability, and review the limited evidence dealing with the interface between disability and leaving care. We will focus on two key jurisdictions: the Australian state of Victoria and Northern Ireland (NI), in order to identify key issues as well as flagging some possible policy and practice directions that hold promise. First, however, we must grapple with the contested terminology space around what constitutes 'disability'.

Disability: Terminology, Classification and Diagnosis

Traditionally, health practitioners have thought about disability as being something that is either *congenital* (present at birth, though sometimes not diagnosed until a later developmental period, for example, autism spectrum disorder [ASD]) or *acquired* (e.g. traumatic brain injury). If we adopt a biomedical approach to disability classification and terminology, we can refer to tomes such as the Diagnostic and Statistical Manual of the American Psychiatric Association (5th edition; DSM-5; American Psychiatric Association 2013) for criteria to meet a diagnostic threshold. Diagnostic criteria, such as those included in the DSM-5, are particularly important in circumstances where a disorder lacks objective markers. However, many developmental disabilities are not easy to measure and classify. For example, one clinician may decide that a particular child has an ASD, while another will determine that the same child's difficulties are better accounted for by a label such as social-pragmatic communication disorder. Unfortunately, in many instances, diagnostic decisions are unduly influenced by the availability of clinical services for children with some clinical conditions, but not for others. In Victoria, for example, it has been possible in recent years for children with a diagnosis of ASD to access a reasonably generous package of government-funded allied health services. This is likely to have influenced clinical decision-making for children who might more accurately be characterized by the diagnostic label *reactive attachment disorder* due to carer neglect, but who would not be eligible for intervention services with such a diagnostic label. These factors mean that it is very difficult to ascertain accurate epidemiological data about prevalence and incidence rates of disability, so service planning is, in many cases, inadequate, and is characterized by significant expertise gaps, both clinically and geographically. Further, some developmental disabilities are likely to be over-represented in care populations (e.g. foetal alcohol spectrum disorder), yet equally likely to go undiagnosed, due to the absence of an objective criterion-referenced 'test' that rules in or out a diagnosis.

There is no consistent definition of disability in Australia. The Australian Bureau of Statistics defines disability as 'Any limitation, restriction or impairment, which has lasted, or is likely to last, for at least six months and restricts everyday activities' (ABS 2012). As may be seen, this definition is quite broad, in line with the Commonwealth and State Disability Agreement (CSDA 1998), which defines people with a disability as those who have: '…an intellectual, psychiatric, sensory, physical or neurological impairment or acquired brain injury (ABI) (or some combination of these), which is likely to be permanent and results in substantially reduced capacity in either self-care management, mobility and/or communication' (Australian Institute of Health and Welfare 2003, p. 13). Notably, although this definition includes psychiatric conditions, the current Victorian Disability Act, which is used to define eligibility for disability services, does not include psychiatric illness in its definition of disability (Department of Human Services 2006). It defines disability as:

- a sensory, physical or neurological impairment or acquired brain injury or any combination thereof, which is, or is likely to be, permanent; and
  - causes a substantially reduced capacity in at least one of the areas of self-care, self-management, mobility or communication; and
  - requires significant ongoing or long-term episodic support; and is not related to ageing; or
- an intellectual disability; or
- a developmental delay.

Similarly, there are varied definitions of disability in use in Northern Irish policy and practice, with ongoing inconsistencies in how service providers define disability across child and adult services. Indeed, Health and Social Care Trusts in NI have yet to deliver on their duty under Schedule 2 (3) under the Children (NI) Order (1995) to open and maintain a register of disabled children, mostly due to a lack of agreement on how to define disability in childhood linked to concerns about the impact of widening eligibility criteria for access to services.

The NI Disability Discrimination Act (1995) defines disability as '…a physical or mental impairment which has a substantial and long-term adverse effect on a person's ability to carry out normal day-to-day activities' (p. 8). The Act has since been extended, by the Disability Discrimination Order (DDO; NI, 2006) and the Autism Act (2011), which strengthens the coverage of the 1995 Act to include social and communication impairments related to autistic spectrum conditions and also removes the requirement for people with mental ill health to prove that their condition is 'clinically well-recognized' (DDO; NI, 2006, p. 39). Whilst this discrimination legislation offers an inclusive definition of disability, eligibility for services is primarily guided by child and disability law, which focuses more on permanent conditions, and makes less reference to the impact on daily activities. In relation to disability services, practice is still guided by the Chronically Sick and Disabled Persons (NI) Act (1978), which defines disabled people as: '…blind, deaf or dumb, and other persons who are substantially handicapped by illness, injury or congenital deformity and whose handicap is of a permanent or lasting nature or are suffering from a mental disorder' (p. 2). Similarly, under Article 2 (2) of the Children NI Order (1995), children are disabled if they are, '…blind, deaf or dumb or suffering from mental disorder of any kind or substantially and permanently handicapped by illness, injury or congenital deformity or such other disability as may be prescribed'.

It is important to note that such definitions contrast with the United Nations Convention on the Rights of People with Disabilities (UNCRPD), to which both Australia and NI are signatories. Article 1 of the UNCRPD defines disabled people as 'those who have long-term physical, mental, intellectual or sensory impairments which in interaction with various barriers may hinder their full and effective participation in society on an equal basis with others'. This definition not only acknowledges the impact and experience of impairment but also, importantly, highlights disabling barriers in society, which may lead to social inequality and exclusion. One of the five Health and Social Care Trusts in NI developed good practice guidance on transition planning for disabled care leavers; this used a similar definition of disability that acknowledged the need for services to address disadvantage and inequalities: 'A child or young person has a disability if he/she has a significant impairment, and, without the provision of additional assistance, resources or information, would be disadvantaged/restricted in or prevented from participating in the life of the community, both in the manner which might reasonably be expected and in comparison to other children of similar age, respecting individual culture and circumstances' (WHSCT 2010, p. 4). This guidance document also explicitly included young people who did not meet eligibility thresholds for adult disability services but have ongoing disability-related needs. Unfortunately, however, this is only practice guidance from one Trust, and this definition has not been widely adopted across the region.

In this chapter, the term disability will encompass physical, sensory and neurodevelopmental conditions (e.g. intellectual disability, ASD, language disorder) that may be present irrespective of maltreatment, as well as psychiatric conditions that are more likely to occur in the context of maltreatment and trauma exposure (e.g. reactive attachment disorder, anxiety, depression, conduct disorder, attention disorders). It is noted that disabilities in the latter category may, of course, occur in the absence of substantiated maltreatment; however, their over-representation in care populations cannot be overlooked. Including psychiatric conditions in the definition of disability for this population reflects the body of evidence concerning the long-term psychosocial harms associated with childhood maltreatment (Springer et al. 2003), as well as reflecting critical disability theory, which considers functional activity limitations and inequalities that go beyond the need to overcome physical barriers to inclusion (Shakespeare 2013).

The lack of a consistent definition of disability and accurate data is a problem, both nationally and internationally. In a federal system such as Australia, we must contend with up to eight different disability definitions, rendering impossible the task of undertaking state-based comparisons. In writing about OHC in the UK, Cousins observed that disabled children are '…scandalously invisible. So much time has been spent arguing about definitions of disability that serious and comprehensive data collection has been abandoned. Even less is known about disabled children in public care, except that they are over-represented in comparison with their not-disabled peers, even if they mainly enter care for reasons unconnected to disability' (2009, p. 60). Similarly, in consideration of the number of disabled children in OHC across the UK's four nations,

Hill et al. (2015) concluded that the lack of attention to the prevalence and experience of disabled children living in, and leaving, state care indicates that this group of children is persistently overlooked, which has a detrimental impact on the development of services to effectively meet their needs.

Inconsistent approaches to assessing disability across agencies providing OHC and support services to young people with a disability are also an issue, nationally and internationally. Cousins suggested that both a child's circumstances *and* an organization's perceptions and requirements conspire to determine whether a child is defined as disabled (Cousins 2006 in Wyber 2012). This is compounded by the fact that specialist knowledge is often required in order to identify and understand behavioural phenomena that might easily be misconstrued and potentially responded to in ways that are punitive and counter-productive. A young person with an undiagnosed language impairment may, for example, fail to understand two-stage instructions delivered verbally by staff against background noise, and so not comply with an apparently simple request. This may result in workers interpreting non-compliance as a sign of challenging behaviour or low motivation to engage.

Some studies suggest that professionals in the child welfare field lack knowledge and skills in relation to disability, particularly assessment skills, and this contributes to under-identification of disabilities in the OHC population. Ellem et al. (2012) observed that child welfare professionals struggle to identify and work with young people who have an intellectual disability, and often fail to recognize that challenging behaviours that have developed as a result of the stress and trauma of being in care can mimic behaviours seen in the context of intellectual disability. They also report that often people with mild or borderline intellectual disability are not eligible for disability services and, thus, become an invisible group who are significantly disadvantaged on most measures.

Research suggests that whilst in care, children with disabilities experience more placement breakdowns than their non-disabled peers, fewer family reunifications, and remain in care longer (Baker 2011; Kelly et al. 2015; Wyber 2012). However, there is a notable absence of empirical research on disabled children living in, and leaving, care. In a review of research literature on disabled care leavers, Kelly et al. (2014a) found a small number of previous studies of disabled care leavers, which were mainly small-scale, qualitative and focused on young people with intellectual disabilities. In contrast, a larger body of research is available on the mental health needs of care leavers; this is mainly quantitative and larger scale, employing diagnostic measures of mental health and disorder. From the research that is available, it is clear that disabled care leavers are more likely to experience poorer outcomes, including engagement with criminal justice, social isolation, homelessness and abuse or exploitation (Courtney et al. 2007; Edwards 2010; Fudge Shormans and Rooke 2008; Goldblatt et al. 2010). For those who fall through the service net in terms of borderline and undiagnosed disabilities, the outcomes are even poorer (Ellem et al. 2012; Rabiee et al. 2001). It is within this context that the authors undertook studies in Australia and NI to investigate the experiences of disabled care leavers and enhance understanding of how best to develop policy and practice to more effectively meet their transitional support needs.

Disabled Care Leavers in Victoria, Australia

The State of Victoria legislated via the *Children, Youth and Families Act 2005* for the provision of leaving care and aftercare services for young people up to 21 years of age. The *Children, Youth and Families Act 2005* appears to oblige the government to assist care leavers with finances, housing, education and training, employment, legal advice, access to health and community services and counselling and support depending on the assessed level of need, and to consider the specific needs of Aboriginal young people. The government has established mentoring programmes, post-care support and placement services, specific supports for Aboriginal young people, specialist programmes known as Springboard for young people leaving residential care and housing supports for young people transitioning from care. In 2013–14, the overall funding for Victorians leaving care and post-care services totalled just over 11 million Australian dollars (Victorian Government 2013).

In principle, these services are intended to meet the needs of all Victorian care leavers, but, in practice, they remain discretionary rather than mandatory, and many care leavers experience difficult transitions in key areas such as housing, health, education and employment. A few of these services target young people with a disability, but there is no specific reference to their needs within the overall service framework (Cummins et al. 2012). The newly introduced National Disability Insurance Scheme may eventually provide discrete supports to all young people with a disability, including care leavers, but the full range of services is yet to be confirmed.

In 2014, Snow, Mendes and O'Donohue reported on a study conducted across more than ten non-government agencies in Victoria, Australia, providing services to young people with disabilities exiting state care. This study built on the findings of a prior investigation (Mendes and Snow 2014) that employed in-depth interviews with leaving care workers, and identified a range of key concerns, many of which might be said to be equally true of young people without a disability, for example, the lack of planned transitions from care and absence of aftercare services; poorly planned transitions; crisis-driven system; challenges associated with engaging young people in the leaving care planning process; and problems associated with lack of inter-agency collaboration. Other difficulties were not unique to young people with disabilities, but posed particular threats in the context of disability, for example, being exited from care and soon-after being homeless or in prison, and the risk of abuse and exploitation after leaving care. Finally, workers identified a range of risks that particularly faced care leavers with disabilities of various forms, for example, young people receiving a reduced level of support on transitioning to adult disability services; young people with disabilities being transitioned into aged care facilities or rooming/boarding houses; young people with borderline disabilities, undiagnosed disabilities and mental illness not receiving the accommodation and services they need; and young people with disabilities (whether or not diagnosed) being deemed unsuitable for mainstream accommodation because they are seen as being 'too high needs'. Workers also observed that the most common type of disability seen in the leaving care population is mental illness, and yet, such diagnoses are not deemed eligible for disability services. Finally, it was observed that difficulties are further exacerbated because most young people with a borderline intellectual disability, undiagnosed disability and/or mental illness are simply not developmentally ready to progress to independence, and would not be ready even in the absence of trauma exposure.

In their subsequent study, Snow et al. (2014) investigated the experiences of care leavers themselves. To this end, 15 young adults (aged 18–26) took part in in-depth interviews concerning their experiences of having a disability and exiting the state care system. Self-identified disabilities represented in the sample included ASD, intellectual disability, anxiety, depression, attention-deficit hyperactivity disorder and physical disability, with all, but one, participant identifying more than one condition. In addition, more than half identified serious behavioural difficulties, and three quarters identified substance abuse issues.

The themes that emerged from these in-depth interviews closely mirrored the issues identified by leaving care workers in the Mendes and Snow (2014) study described above. In particular, young people described chronically unstable accommodation arrangements and the breakdown of accommodation placements whilst in care for a range of psychosocial reasons (e.g. staff not being willing or able to manage the young person's unpredictable and often dysregulated behaviour). Young people described a dearth of independent living skills (e.g. budgeting, cooking) and said that these were addressed in only a very cursory fashion, if at all, in the context of care planning. In fact, very few (three) had any recollection of being involved in formal leaving care planning. Respondents universally described negative experiences of school, both academically and socially. Eight respondents had attended alternative school settings, and the remaining seven described various experiences of extra support in mainstream settings. Changes of school were common, with eight participants attending more than five schools. Post-school training and employment were the exception, rather than the norm, and a lack of basic literacy and numeracy skills further reduced the likelihood of secure employment. This situation is further exacerbated by the fact that more than half of the sample participants did not receive any funding support on leaving care. Factors that made the system almost un-navigable for such young people included a lack of involvement in planning for leaving care; multiple changes of worker; lack of access to information about services to which they were eligible; the experience of further abuse in foster-care settings, and being totally unprepared for the demands of so-called 'independent living'.

Disabled Care Leavers in NI

Current disability and child care policy in NI emphasizes a whole child, multi-agency and outcomes-focused approach with a combination of preventive universal support services and specialist provision targeted at subgroups of the population. However, disabled care leavers are often not clearly identified as a group requiring targeted interventions (Kelly et al. 2014b). The Children (Leaving Care) Act (NI) 2002 created new duties on Trusts to prevent early discharges from care and improve transition services to support care leavers, including financial assistance. Duties extend until the young person is 21 years, or up to 25 if the Trust is supporting their further education and training. However, the Act does not highlight the specific additional support, which may be required by disabled care leavers. Departmental guidance and regulations on leaving care does have a dedicated section on the additional needs of disabled care leavers (DHSSPSNI 2005); however, the subsequently published Standards for Leaving Care Services in NI (DHSSPSNI 2012) makes minimal reference to the additional needs of disabled care leavers.

Within this policy context, Kelly led a collaborative three-year research project on the transitional experiences of care leavers with intellectual disabilities and mental health needs in NI, commencing in 2012. The study involved building a profile of disabled care leavers based on demographic data provided by social workers across the region, followed by case studies of 31 care leavers. For the first stage of building a profile of disabled care leavers, social workers in the five Health and Social Care Trusts in NI completed a survey for each disabled young person leaving care on their caseloads. These young people were identified from the bi-annual statistical return on the population of care leavers that Trusts made to their funder in September 2013. Trusts kept a record of all care leavers (16–25-year olds who were leaving/had left care) returned under the category of disability or mental health need (with diagnosed impairment/disorder or receiving/referred to disability or mental health services). Individual social workers for these young people then completed an online survey, which captured demographic data on each young person (such as age, disability, gender and family background) and information on their care experience, needs and access to services.

A total of 314 completed surveys were returned, mostly about young people aged 16–18 (69.1 per cent) or 19–20 (28.7 per cent). Only 2.2 per cent were about young people aged 21 and none pertained to care leavers over the age of 21, indicating that disabled care leavers are exiting care services by the age of 20. More than half of the sample were in the mental health category (57.3 per cent), just over a fifth (21 per cent) had intellectual disabilities and 12.1 per cent had ASD. Reflecting the findings from the Australian study, just over one-fifth of those in the intellectual disability category also had co-existing mental health needs, and just over two-thirds of those with ASD had co-existing mental health and/or intellectual disability (a further 5.7 per cent had more multiple forms of impairment).

Just over half (52.2 per cent) of the study sample was male; however, females outnumbered males in the mental health category (55 per cent), and males with ASD far exceeded females (86.8 per cent male). Most young people had been in care for over five years (51 per cent), or 3–5 years (25 per cent). Of those in care for shorter periods, the majority were in the mental health category and aged 17–18. Reflecting previous research on care experience for disabled children, almost half had three or more placement changes during their time in care. Although almost a fifth (19 per cent) were still in school, almost a third (30.9 per cent) were not in any education, training or employment. Only 10.5 per cent were employed, and of these, only half were in paid employment. Following similar trends for the general care leaver population, 12.1 per cent were parents (most with one child), and 5.1 per cent were pregnant. More than half of the parents (52.6 per cent) were not living with their children.

Social workers reported that more than one in five of the sample had attempted suicide in the 12 months prior to the survey, and almost half of these had attempted suicide more than once. Despite these concerns, just over a quarter of the overall sample was in receipt of child/adolescent mental health services, and only a third was receiving adult mental health services. Social workers reported high levels of ongoing risks of suicide, sexual exploitation and substance misuse. A considerable number had received a police caution (40.8 per cent), and almost a third (mostly males with mental health needs) had a conviction, which was usually incurred after their entry to care.

Most young people were in receipt of aftercare services, with access to either a social worker or personal adviser. However, contact with these professionals varied. For example, a fifth of those with a personal adviser had no contact with them. Those who were older and with an intellectual disability or ASD were less likely to have access to aftercare services. It could be argued that this decline in use of aftercare services as young people age out of care is appropriate. However, cessation of these aftercare services is concerning given the ongoing support needs of the population and their limited access to adult services. Only 13 per cent were accessing adult disability services and a fifth were accessing adult mental health services. There were also some notable differences in the demographics of those accessing adult services. For example, the majority of those accessing adult disability services had an intellectual disability, with very low numbers of young people with ASD accessing adult disability services. In addition, just over half of those with an assessed mental illness were in receipt of child or adult mental health services, and females far outnumbered males in adult mental health services (60 per cent).

Social workers reported concerns for those who refuse assessment or services, particularly those with substance misuse problems who may disengage or be refused access. The main barriers to accessing adult services were lengthy waiting lists for diagnostic assessments, disengagement from the young person, and higher thresholds for eligibility for adult services. Many young people not engaged in adult services were reported to present with ongoing high levels of vulnerability in the community and low levels of independent living skills. Social workers also reported concerns about the lack of supported accommodation options and adult foster placements for this population of care leavers. This left some young people without necessary support and increased their vulnerability in the community, and disengagement from education, training or employment.

The case study stage of the research involved semi-structured interviews with a purposive sample of 31 care leavers with intellectual disabilities and/or mental health needs across the region. This group included young people with ASD, with 'severe' to 'borderline' intellectual disabilities, and with a range of mental health needs (including depression, anxiety, personality disorder and suicidal ideation). Interviews with care leavers were led by specially trained peer researchers (for further details on this methodology, please see the chapter by Kelly, Dixon and Incarnato in this text). The case studies also involved semi-structured interviews with the young person's social worker and/or personal adviser and, where appropriate, their carer and birth parent. Finally, with permission, the young person's case file was accessed. As these case studies yielded a rich range of qualitative data, which cannot be fully reported in this chapter, the main themes from the perspective of the young people are highlighted.

Some of the key priorities for this group of care leavers mirror those for any care leaver group: moving into safe accommodation, managing finances, pursuing education/training or getting a job and becoming independent. However, disabled care leavers also encountered challenges in their efforts to enjoy positive outcomes across these domains. Some of these difficulties were structural due to limited access to information about social security benefits, and unclear or high-level eligibility criteria for access to financial and practical support with housing, education/training or employment. In addition, often due to the withdrawal of services and the lack of alternative adult placements, some young people returned home to their birth families where there were ongoing concerns about how well their needs would be met, or risk of exploitation. In addition to practical support, disabled care leavers also highlighted the importance of ongoing support from carers, friends or birth-family members. These social relationships provided much needed support and guidance for some care leavers; however, for others, managing the dynamics of social and family relationships was challenging. Experiences of leaving care were also often described as a time when disabled young people were re-negotiating their disability, family relationships, care and adult identities. In the context of changing services and re-assessments of disability, this could create much confusion and uncertainty. These emotional and relational aspects of their care leaving experience were least likely to be adequately addressed by formal services, which focused on more practical outcomes. Some study participants reported positive relationships with individual workers who understood their impairment-related needs, advocated on their behalf and dedicated much time and resources to their relationship. However, others described feeling isolated, with limited access to formal services and low levels of social inclusion. In addition, some young people reported feeling unsafe in their area and had experienced exploitation in their personal relationships and peer networks. A final key theme emphasized by young people was the importance of being involved in choices about their futures. Some disabled care leavers felt their views were not taken seriously or that limited efforts were made to involve them in pathway planning. Some young people also emphasized the need for more time to make decisions and engage in post-care activities. A number of young people had withdrawn from services when they initially left care, but were not permitted to re-engage with services when their circumstances had later changed.

Common Themes

From the findings from both studies, it is possible to identify core common themes in relation to the disabled care leavers.

- Poor outcomes in terms of education/training, employment, housing and crime are evident across both jurisdictions, particularly for those with mental health needs.
- Case closure at 21 years (in NI) and at 18 years (in Australia) is often inappropriate for care leavers with mental health needs/disabilities who are still in transition, often awaiting assessment for adult services or still planning to leave former care arrangements.
- Post-care services provide some practical assistance up to the age of 18 (in Australia) or 21 (in NI), but not all care leavers are aware of the range of services available. In addition, services may not adequately meet the needs of care leavers with disabilities or ongoing mental health needs.
- There is a shared concern for those with borderline and undiagnosed impairments falling through the gaps in services.
- Complex service systems, limited trans-disciplinary working and high thresholds for adult services are reported in both studies.
- Shortages in appropriate supported living options lead some care leavers to move to unsafe post-care housing options, aged care facilities or to a risk of homelessness.

- Concerns about risks of abuse and exploitation post-care need urgent attention. Many of these young people are considered to be vulnerable adults, and despite ongoing corporate parenting duties, their cases in aftercare services were often closed regardless of whether or not adult services were engaged.

It is interesting to note these strong common themes emerging from both studies. Although Victoria and NI have differing service structures and policies, many of the findings from professional and care leavers' perspectives are similar. However, a few interesting differences can be identified, which are likely to reflect the differing methods employed across studies and some differences in the population of young people interviewed. Firstly, in the NI study, in addition to structural outcomes-focused challenges, young people emphasized the relational aspects of their care leaving experiences, including family dynamics, peer relations, neighbourhood safety and personal relationships. Secondly, identity issues were often at the forefront of their reflections on their care leaving experience as they continued to navigate their sense of self and their place in the society. As the NI study involved repeated interviews with young people over the course of a year and involved peer researchers as interviewers, there may have been more opportunity to explore these relational and identity experiences. Finally, whilst there was much variance in the individual experience of care leavers across both studies, the heterogeneity of the population of disabled care leavers in terms of cultural background was particularly evident in the Australian study, which identified added disadvantages for those living in rural areas.

Policy Implications

The findings from both studies indicate that current policy and practice is not adequately directed at the complex needs of disabled care leavers. Both studies clearly show that disabled care leavers are a distinct and particularly vulnerable group requiring ongoing specialist support and targeted investment and interventions. As a starting point, a clear definition of disability in policy and practice guidance would improve identification of this group of care leavers and service planning to meet their needs. The UNCRPD provides the basis for a shared understanding of disability, with an inclusive definition that acknowledges bodily impairment and disabling barriers in society. Aligned with the need for a clear definition of disability, eligibility criteria for access to aftercare services and adult disability or mental health services should be transparent and address barriers in access to services for those with borderline or moderate levels of disability, for whom social workers have ongoing concerns about vulnerability in emerging adulthood.

The findings from both studies provide further evidence of poorer outcomes for some disabled care leavers, which must be addressed in future policy and practice developments. Explicit identification and inclusion of disabled young people across child and family and disability and mental health policy would raise awareness of their increased risk of negative post-care outcomes and clarify obligations for multi-agency working to address their needs. Linked to this, regulations and procedural guidance for service providers need to clearly specify longer-term and wide-ranging responsibilities for this group of care leavers. There are also serious ongoing safeguarding concerns for many of the disabled care leavers in both studies, highlighting the need to further develop adult protection policy and advocacy services. Commissioners of services should carefully monitor the implementation of policy and fulfilment of the roles and responsibilities of all agencies.

Finally, disabled care leavers should be at the centre of all decisions relating to their transition to adult life to facilitate meaningful, self-determined life choices. Information about their rights, eligibility for services and post-care options must be accessible and person-centred; pathway planning should be undertaken well in advance of leaving care to facilitate self-determined choices, meaningful supports for post-care lives and clear pathways to specialist support. This emphasis on participation also applies to the social experiences of disabled care leavers and further efforts to provide increased opportunities for social inclusion and participation in policy and practice developments.

Future Research Directions

Whilst the two studies featuring in this chapter contribute to our understanding of their profile and the experiences of disabled care leavers across two jurisdictions, there is a clear need for further empirical research in this area. Both studies show the importance of attention to the diversity of this population in future research in relation to experiences of impairment, cultural contexts and family, peer or community systems of support. It is also crucial that future research incorporates the views of disabled care leavers at various stages of the care leaving journey to ensure the consideration of their perspectives and priorities. Longitudinal studies tracking disabled care leavers would also enhance our understanding of their continued needs as they move into young adult lives and longer-term outcomes. Building knowledge and understanding of the needs and experiences of disabled care leavers in these ways should help ensure their transitional support needs are further prioritized and more comprehensively addressed in future policy and service developments.

References

American Psychiatric Association (2013). *Diagnostic and statistical manual of the American Psychiatric Association* (5 ed.). Washington, DC: American Psychiatric Association.

Arnau Sabates, L., & Gilligan, R. (2015). What helps young care leavers to enter the world of work? Possible lessons learned from an exploratory study in Ireland and Catalonia. *Children and Youth Services Review, 53*, 185–191.

Australian Bureau of Statistics (2012). *Australian social trends, March Quarter 2012*. www.abs.gov.au/AUSSTATS/abs@.nsf/Lookup/4102.0Main+Features40March+Quarter+2012#end8. Accessed 24 July 2015.

Australian Institute of Health and Welfare (2003). *Disability prevalence and trends*. Canberra: AIHW. www.aihw.gov.au/WorkArea/DownloadAsset.aspx?id=6442455759. Accessed 24 July 2015.

Baker, C. (2011). *Permanence and stability for disabled looked after children*. Glasgow: Institute for Research and Innovation in Social Services. www.iriss.org.uk/sites/default/files/iriss_insight11.pdf. Accessed 21 Sep 2015.

Courtney, M., Dworsky, A., Ruth, G., Havlicek, J., & Perez, A. (2007). *Midwest evaluation of the adult functioning of former foster youth: Outcomes at age 21*. Chicago: Chapin Hall Center for Children at the University of Chicago.

Cousins, J. (2006). *Every child is special: placing disabled children for permanence*. London: British Association for Adoption and Fostering.

Cousins, J. (2009). Disability: Still taboo in family placement? *Adoption and Fostering, 33*(2), 54–65.

Cummins, P., Scott, D., & Scales, B. (2012). *Report of the protecting Victoria's vulnerable children inquiry*. Melbourne: Department of Premier and Cabinet.

Commonwealth and State Disability Agreements (1998). https://www.dss.gov.au/our-responsibilities/disabilityand-carers/program-services/government-international/commonwealth-state-and-territory-disability-agreements. Accessed August 8, 2016.

Department of Human Services (2006). *A guide for disability service practitioners*. Melbourne: State Government Victoria.

DHSSPSNI (2005). *Leaving and after care–Guidance and regulations: Volume 8*. London: Stationery Office.

DHSSPSNI (2012). *Standards for Leaving Care Services in NI*. Belfast: DHSSPSNI.

Edwards, R. (2010). Nobody knows: Young people with disability leaving care. *Parity, 23*(5), 20–21.

Ellem, K., Wilson, J., O'Connor, M., & Macdonald, S. (2012). Supporting young people with mild/borderline intellectual disability exiting state out-of-home care: Directions for practice. *Developing Practice, 32*, 53–65.

Fudge Schormans, A., & Rooke, J. (2008). When there are no choices: The consequences of a lack of adult living placements for young adults with intellectual and/or developmental disabilities leaving child welfare care. *Journal on Developmental Disabilities, 14*(1), 107–126.

Goldblatt, B., Edwards, R., McHugh, M., Katz, I., Abello, D., Eastman, C., et al. (2010). *Evaluation of the leaving care programme. Report for ageing, disability and home care department of human services*. Sydney: University of New South Wales.

Hill, L., Baker, C., Kelly, B., & Dowling, S. (2015). Being counted? Examining the prevalence of looked-after disabled children and young people across the UK. *Child and Family Social Work*, June; (pp. 1–9). doi:10.1111/cfs.12239

Kelly, B., McShane, T., Davidson, G., & Pinkerton, J. (2014a). *A review of literature on disabled care leavers and care leavers with mental health needs*. Belfast: Queen's University Belfast.

Kelly, B., Hanna-Trainor, L., Davidson, G., & Pinkerton, J. (2014b). *A review of policy and legislation relating to care leavers with learning disabilities and/or mental health needs in Northern Ireland*. Belfast: Queen's University Belfast.

Kelly, B., Dowling, S., & Winter, K. (2015). *The views and experiences of looked after disabled children and young people in care in Northern Ireland*. Belfast: OFMDFM and Queen's University Belfast.

Mendes, P., & Snow, P. (2014). The needs and experiences of young people with a disability transitioning from out-of-home care: The views of practitioners in Victoria, Australia. *Children and Youth Services Review, 36*, 115–123.

Mendes, P., Johnson, G., & Moslehuddin, B. (2011). *Young people leaving state out-of-home care: A research-based study of Australian policy and practice*. North Melbourne: Australian Scholarly Publishing.

Perry, B. L. (2006). Understanding social network disruption: The case of youth in foster care. *Social Problems, 53*(3), 371–391.

Rabiee, P., Priestley, M., & Knowles, J. (2001). *Whatever next? Young disabled people leaving care*. Leeds: First Key Ltd.

Shakespeare, T. (2013). The social model of disability. In L. J. Davis (Ed.), *The disability studies reader* (pp. 216–221). London: Routledge.

Snow, P. C. (2009). Child maltreatment, mental health and oral language competence: Inviting speech language pathology to the prevention table. *International Journal of Speech Language Pathology, 11*(12), 95–103.

Snow, P. C., Mendes, P., & O'Donohue, D. (2014). *Young people with a disability leaving state care – Phase two report*. Melbourne: Monash University.

Springer, K. W., Sheridan, J., Kuo, D., & Carnes, M. (2003). Long-term health outcomes of childhood abuse. *Journal of General Internal Medicine, 18*, 864–870.

Stein, M., & Munro, E. (Eds.) (2008). *Young people's transitions from care to adulthood: International research and practice*. London: Jessica Kingsley.

Victorian Government (2013). *Planning for leaving care, child protection manual, Advice no. 1418*. Retrieved 1 Apr 2013, from http://www.dhs.vic.gov.au/cpmanual/out-of-home-care/care-and-placement-planning/?a=660199

Western Health and Social Care Trust (WHSCT) (2010). *Good practice guidance on transition planning for young people leaving care with a disability*. Derry: WHSCT.

Wyber, J. (2012) What are the risk factors in the abuse and treatment of children with disabilities?. *Master of health science dissertation*. Auckland: Auckland University of Technology.

Part II

Pathways to Educational Success

5

Towards a National Policy Framework for Care Leavers in Australian Higher Education

Andrew Harvey, Patricia McNamara, and Lisa Andrewartha

Introduction

Around 40,000 children live in out-of-home care (OHC) in Australia, and this number has risen every year over the past decade (Australian Institute of Health and Welfare (AIHW) 2015). OHC may include relative/kinship care, foster care, residential care, family group homes and independent living. Approximately 93 per cent of children are in OHC on care and protection orders issued by a statutory authority or court (AIHW 2015). Once a child has been placed in care, the state government acts as a corporate parent and assumes responsibility for decision-making and care arrangements. Typically, children in care confront specific educational challenges and disruptions from an early age, and

---

A. Harvey (✉) • L. Andrewartha
Access & Achievement Research Unit, La Trobe University, Melbourne, VIC, Australia

P. McNamara
Melbourne, VIC, Australia

many face compounding disadvantage. A substantial proportion of these children come from low socio-economic status, regional and/or indigenous backgrounds (State Government of Victoria 2012).

People who spent time in OHC before the age of 18 are subsequently referred to as care leavers when they transition out of the system. Post-transition outcomes are not well-documented, and there is a particular paucity of Australian research into the transition of care leavers to tertiary education. In Australia, tertiary education includes both vocational education and training and higher education. Vocational education and training is generally provided by state-funded Tertiary and Further Education (TAFE) institutions or private institutions, and higher education is generally provided by Commonwealth-funded universities. The limited available evidence suggests that care leavers are particularly under-represented in higher education (Mendes et al. 2014; Murray and Goddard 2014). This situation is concerning, as higher education is linked to lifetime advantages, such as improved employment opportunities and earning potential (Lomax-Smith et al. 2011; Norton 2012). It is, therefore, important to examine the progression of this group into higher education, nationally, and the factors that might increase aspirations, access and success at university.

Study Aims and Methodology

The study aimed to develop a strategy for raising university access among care leavers by exploring the nature, causes and extent of under-representation, and by recommending policy reform within both the education and community service sectors. The project was led by La Trobe University and included MacKillop Family Services and Berry Street as formal partners. MacKillop Family Services is a leading provider of services for children, young people and families in Victoria, New South Wales and Western Australia. Berry Street is the largest independent child and family welfare organization in Victoria. The research was overseen by a Reference Group comprising local and international academic experts and Australian stakeholders, and was funded by the National Centre for Student Equity in Higher Education at Curtin University. Ethics approval was granted by the La Trobe University Education Faculty Human Research Ethics Committee. The full results and recommendations of this project are presented in the final report titled 'Out of care, into university' (Harvey et al. 2015b).

There were four key stages of the project. Stage One involved a review of international and national research on the educational needs and outcomes of care leavers. The focus of the review was major research reports published from the year 2000 and associated policy documents. Stage Two involved an examination of the landscape of educational data collection. Within this analysis, we specifically compared the limited amount of national data on the higher education outcomes of care leavers with the well-established model of data collection that occurs in the UK.

Stage Three involved a survey of universities about institutional policies and strategies for supporting care leavers. The survey was designed using the Qualtrics online survey tool, and senior equity staff at all 37 Australian public universities were invited to participate. A total of 28 universities responded to the survey, representing a 76 per cent response rate. Survey responses were obtained from at least one university located within each of the six Australian states and two territories of Australia. Survey responses also covered a range of university types, including technology-focused; research-intensive (known as the 'Group of Eight' or Go8), innovative research; and regional universities. See Table 5.1 for survey responses by university group.

Stage Four involved interviews with 11 senior representatives from community service organizations across Australia. Major service providers were identified through an Internet search of government and agency websites. A mix of national, multi-state and single-state agencies was selected to ensure national coverage. Most organizations offered foster care and residential and kinship care programmes. The interviews were semi-structured and covered data collection in relation to educational progress and outcomes; expectations for university study; perceived facilitators and barriers for higher education; and case studies. Interviews were digitally recorded, transcribed and analysed for content and themes using NVivo 10 software (QSR International 2012). An interpretative phenomenological approach was applied to the analysis (Smith et al. 2009).

Table 5.1 Survey responses by university group

University group	Responded to survey	Did not respond to survey	Total
Non-aligned universities	9	3	12
Group of Eight (Go8)	7	1	8
Innovative Research Universities (IRU)	6	0	6
Regional Universities Network (RUN)	4	2	6
Australian Technology Network (ATN)	2	3	5
Total	28	9	37

Findings, Stage One: Review of the Literature

The UK

In the UK, the first major research project to examine the experiences of care leavers in higher education was the *By Degrees* project (Jackson et al. 2005). The project followed 50 university care leaver students per year for three years. Care leavers reported a lack of information and advice about universities and courses, and uncertainty about the financial and accommodation support available. Living independently or in OHC families without higher education experience made it particularly difficult for this group to obtain adequate information and advice. Educational opportunities for those in care were typically limited, and university staff regularly underestimated the academic potential of care leavers. At the time, only one university in the UK had a comprehensive policy relating to care leavers. The *By Degrees* report recommended that 'All higher education institutions should have a comprehensive policy for recruitment, retention and support of students from a care background' (p. xiv).

Substantial progress has been made within the UK university sector since the *By Degrees* report. Care leavers are formally recognized as an underrepresented group in higher education, and their participation is closely monitored in England, Northern Ireland, Scotland and Wales. From 2006, Buttle UK (a trust which supports children and young people in need) began awarding a 'Quality Mark' to higher education providers who demonstrate commitment to young people in care and leaving care. The Quality Mark is now being phased out, with a view to embedding practice into mainstream provision (Buttle UK 2014). England has had a particularly strong focus on the higher education participation of care leavers for a number of years. In 2006, England's Office of Fair Access (OFFA) wrote to all institutions with access agreements to encourage them to consider the needs of care leavers in their access agreements. From 2014, care leaver data have been collected at enrolment by the Higher Education Statistics Agency.

Since the year 2000, there have also been several additions to the legislation on the education of care leavers in England and Wales. The *Children (Leaving Care) Act 2000* introduced the first statutory requirement for local authorities to support young people aged 16–24 years in education. The *Children and Young Persons Act 2008* brought forward a statutory £2,000 local authority bursary for young care leavers at university. From April 2011, *The Children Act 1989 Guidance and Regulations Volume 3: Planning Transition to Adulthood for Care Leavers* implemented a suite of regulations and guidance around strengthening the planning of educational transitions (All-Party Parliamentary Group for Looked After Children and Care Leavers 2012).

The increased policy and legislative focus on care leavers has encouraged higher education institutions to provide more support for this group, particularly through bursaries, accommodation, outreach, admissions policies and dedicated positions. These measures have increased the proportion of care leavers continuing to higher education in England, from approximately 1 per cent of 19-year-old care leavers in 2003 (Department for Business Innovation and Skills 2014) to 6–7 per cent of 19–21-year-old care leavers in 2014 (Department of Education 2014). This figure remains well below the 40 per cent higher education participation rate of young people in the general population, but it is, nonetheless, a significant improvement (The Centre for Social Justice 2015).

Continental Europe

Following the *By Degrees* research, the YiPPEE research project (*Young people from a public care background: pathways to education in Europe*) examined the education pathways of care leavers across England, Denmark, Sweden, Hungary and Spain. This project found that people from public care had similar experiences of severe educational disadvantage across all five countries. For example, young people from care were '…under pressure to opt for short-cycle occupational training in order to become economically independent as soon as possible rather than higher level academic or vocational options with the potential to lead to more satisfying careers in the longer run' (Jackson and Cameron 2012, p. 8). Success in education was facilitated by stability of placement and schooling, being placed with carers who gave priority to education and having sufficient financial support and suitable accommodation (Jackson and Cameron 2012). The research also highlighted that 'reliable statistical information is an essential basis for improving the educational opportunities of young people who have been in care' (Jackson and Cameron 2012, p. 10). Jackson and Cameron (2014) published a comprehensive account of their cross-nation findings in their subsequent book, *Improving Access to Further and Higher Education for Young People in Public Care*.

The USA

There has been a considerable amount of research into the college experiences of people from foster care in the USA. Wolanin (2005) reported that only about 50 per cent of young people in foster care complete high school compared to 70 per cent of their peers. Of those who complete high school, and are therefore potentially college qualified, only about 20 per cent enrol in higher education compared to 60 per cent of their peers. Access to college is mitigated by inability to meet admission standards, a belief that college is 'not for people like me', and financial constraints. People from foster care who do access college also have very high rates of attrition. Success at college is impeded by inadequate information; lack of family support; no stable home base; and inadequate support through financial aid, student services and counselling. Two large-scale projects led by Professor Peter Pecora further highlighted the low college completion rates for people from foster care (Pecora et al. 2003, 2005).

In 2008, three significant federal laws were passed that were designed to increase college access for people from foster care: the *Fostering Connections*

Act; *College Cost Reduction Act*; and the *Higher Education Opportunity Act* (Legal Center for Foster Care and Education 2008). Some US states have extended foster care beyond 18 years of age, and this change has been associated with increased participation in higher education (Courtney and Dworsky 2005). However, national college completion rates for this group have remained low. Only 4 per cent of students from foster care complete a four-year college degree by the age of 26, compared to 36 per cent of the general population (Courtney et al. 2011).

Australia

Australian research has consistently documented the poor overall school achievement and completion rates of young people in OHC. Major barriers to school success include placement instability and frequent school changes; trauma associated with past abuse and neglect; mental health and substance abuse issues; behavioural issues, including involvement in the criminal justice system; absenteeism; bullying; and lack of family support (CREATE Foundation 2006; Fernandez 2008; Frederick and Goddard 2010; McFarlane 2010; Townsend 2012). Students in care may also have lower aspirations for education and lower expectations placed on them to succeed (Creed et al. 2011).

To date, there has been no national-level data collection of school outcomes of people in care. However, two large-scale studies by the Australian Institute of Health and Welfare (AIHW) matched educational achievement data and community service data across multiple jurisdictions (AIHW 2007, 2011). Results showed that children on guardianship or custody orders, many of whom were in OHC, had poorer reading and numeracy test scores compared with their peers.

Australians from OHC face another set of barriers to educational success at post-school level. At 18 years of age, legal protection and formal assistance from the State decreases dramatically (Creed et al. 2011), and the risk of homelessness, unemployment and poor educational outcomes increases (Johnson et al. 2010; Thoresen and Liddiard 2011). The sudden reduction in support contrasts with the experience of most young people in the general population who stay in the parental home receiving continuous support into their early-to-mid 20s (Australian Bureau of Statistics 2013). In recent years, most states and territories have introduced legislation or policy to assist care leavers beyond 18 years of age (Mendes 2014). However, there are differences across jurisdictions in the types of support provided and the upper age limit for this support (Department of Social Services 2014). Under the *National Framework for Protecting Australia's Children 2009–2020*, governments have commenced the process of establishing a nationally consistent approach to supporting care leavers (Department of Social Services 2014).

Fee waivers have recently been introduced in South Australia, Victoria and Western Australia for care leavers wishing to pursue vocational education and training at TAFE institutes (Beauchamp 2014). TAFE institutes provide a wide range of vocational tertiary education courses and are largely funded by state/territory governments. The TAFE fee waivers for care leavers, however, do not extend to all states and territories, and there are no equivalent initiatives for higher education. In contrast to England, care leavers do not constitute a distinct equity group in Australia, and, as a result, no data are collected to monitor their higher education access, participation or retention rates. The six equity groups in Australian higher education are people from socio-economically disadvantaged backgrounds; Aboriginal and Torres Strait Islander people; women in non-traditional courses and postgraduate study; people from non-English speaking backgrounds; people with disabilities; and people from rural and isolated areas (Department of Education Employment and Training (DEET) 1990). While a significant number of care leavers fall within the established equity groups, especially students from low socio-economic status, rural and indigenous backgrounds, care leavers are not monitored separately (Harvey et al. 2015a; Mendes et al. 2014).

Few Australian studies have focused on care leavers and higher education. As Mendes et al. (2014) noted in a review of existing literature, 'we know strikingly little about the experiences of care leavers who enter higher education in Australia' (p. 249). A 2009 report by the CREATE Foundation detailed the results of a survey of 471 young people who were in care or had left care. Of those who had left care, only 35 per cent had completed Year 12. At the time of the study, only 11 per cent were studying at TAFE, and 2.8 per cent were studying at university (McDowall

2009). Cashmore et al. (2007) examined the employment and educational outcomes of 47 care leavers in New South Wales. Care leavers were less likely to have completed secondary school compared with same-age counterparts in the general population. They were also much less likely to be in full-time work or education four to five years after leaving care. More positive outcomes were associated with staying in the same placement after care and receiving social support after leaving care.

More recently, there have been a number of small, qualitative studies in Australia. Jurczyszyn and Tilbury (2012) interviewed 13 young people who were in care or leaving care in Queensland. They found that interest in higher or further education was influenced by having someone to encourage educational aspirations and explore careers and university life; advocacy to overcome practical barriers; and high expectations from carers, workers and teachers. Mendis et al. (2014) interviewed 18 university-educated women who had spent time in OHC. They found that educational experiences differed based on factors such as personality, resilience and individual care circumstances, confirming the need for a tailored and responsive approach to improving the educational outcomes of care leavers. Michell et al. (2015) also published the stories of 14 care leavers who had transitioned to higher education. Each care leaver described their experience of overcoming major obstacles in order to succeed 'against the odds'.

Stage Two: Analysis of National and State Data Sources

National data on the education of Australians in OHC are limited. Data are typically held at state or territory level, within human services departments, and only for minors (up to the age of 18 at best). The Australian Bureau of Statistics collects a limited amount of national data on the educational outcomes of children in OHC through the National Census. There are, however, two major limitations to these data. First, data are only collected on foster care and not the other types of OHC. Second, individuals under the age of 15 are regarded as foster children in the Census, while individuals over the age of 15 are only counted as foster children if they are living with a foster parent at the time of the Census (Australian Bureau of Statistics 2012).

Despite these limitations, the Census data set does allow examination of a subset of people who have spent time in state care—individuals who are living with their foster parent after 18 years of age. The educational outcomes for this group are relatively poor. Only 45 per cent of the foster care group aged 18–30 completes Year 12, compared to 77 per cent of the same age group nationally. Only 2 per cent of the foster care group aged 18–30 completes a higher education qualification, compared with the national rate of 20 per cent (Australian Bureau of Statistics 2011).

In 2013, the AIHW proposed a national method for linking education and child protection data for children aged 0–17 years (AIHW 2013). The first phase of this project involved linking with National Assessment Program – Literacy and Numeracy (NAPLAN) data (collected at Years 3, 5, 7 and 9) and the Child Protection National Minimum Data Set (CPNMDS). The CPNMDS includes the following key statistics for the national OHC group up to 17 years of age: age and sex profile; Aboriginal and Torres Strait Islander status; state; and OHC placement type. While this national linkage project will allow monitoring of school-level achievement, there are no existing plans to continue monitoring educational outcomes beyond 17 years of age. The absence of post-17 monitoring is problematic, particularly given the rising importance of post-secondary qualifications to economic success.

In contrast to Australia, reliable data on the educational outcomes of care leavers are publicly available in the UK. Since the Buttle UK Quality Mark programme was launched in 2006, higher education institutions have been asked to submit statistics on care leaver enrolments each year. The final annual statistics report pertained to the 2013–14 academic year and included data on care leaver enrolments from 59 higher education institutions and 26 further education colleges. A total of 1229 care leavers were identified in the sector. These data allowed for cross-sectional analysis to be conducted by various demographic variables, institution type and mode and field of study (Buttle UK 2015). The publication of reliable data has allowed the higher education outcomes of care leavers to be accurately monitored and has propelled targeted policy implementation and action.

An evaluation of the Quality Mark programme found that it had been an effective driver in the development of comprehensive care leaver strategies. Before the programme commenced, only a single higher education provider had a dedicated care leaver policy. By 2013, 56 per cent of higher education institutions had developed specific policies and strategies aimed at care leavers (Starks 2013). While only one institution offered a care leaver bursary as part of its access agreement in 2006, this number rose to 31 institutions in 2011–12, and 52 institutions in the agreements for 2014–15. In addition, 39 institutions have set targets for care leavers, and 49 have specified outreach activity for care leavers in the 2014–15 agreements (Department for Business Innovation and Skills 2014).

While the data collected by Buttle UK have proven useful, only students enrolled within a higher education institution are included. There is a gap in the data that limits the ability to measure the proportion of care leavers transitioning to higher education. This issue is overcome by data collected by the Department of Education in England. Each year, the department releases a publicly available data pack detailing the outcomes of all care leavers at 19–21 years of age. The data are collected through a dedicated data return, which utilizes a standardized methodology, which all local authorities must return to the Department for Education (2014). From 2014, data on care leavers are collected from all higher education institutions by the Higher Education Statistics Agency using a care leaver identifier, which will allow for improved analysis, research and evaluation (Department for Business Innovation and Skills 2014).

Stage Three: Survey of University Policies and Practices

Our research involved a survey of senior equity representatives across Australian public universities. The survey was designed to determine the types of policies, support structures and procedures universities currently have in place that specifically target care leavers, and how universities can increase higher education access and support for care leavers. Invitations to complete the online survey were emailed to senior equity representatives at the 37 Australian public universities. A total of 28 universities responded to the survey, representing a 76 per cent response rate.

The survey results showed that universities have few policies, support structures or procedures specifically targeted at care leavers. Of the 28 universities that responded to the survey, only 11 reported having any initiatives specifically targeted at care leavers (39 per cent). Those 11 universities covered all five university groups (Go8, IRU, RUN, ATN and non-aligned) and spanned four of the eight states and territories of Australia. Four universities had multiple initiatives in place for care leavers, while seven had only one type of initiative in place.

The most frequent types of initiatives for care leavers were specific admission policies (five universities), relationships with OHC service providers (five universities) and outreach programmes (four universities). Two universities had recruitment policies or guidelines for care leavers. Only one university offered scholarships targeted at care leavers; one university collected data about care leaver status; and one university tracked the progress of care leavers. None of the surveyed universities reported providing accommodation support for care leavers.

While it was rare for universities to have many support programmes specifically targeted at care leavers, it was common for respondents to describe general equity policies and procedures that may cater to this group indirectly. Two universities had also taken recent steps to better support care leavers—one had advertised for a care coordinator, and another had established a working group to explore the needs of care leavers.

Respondents were asked what higher education institutions could do to increase access for care leavers. The most frequently made suggestions were to offer targeted scholarships and financial support, build partnerships with OHC service providers and work closely with secondary schools to support students in OHC. Respondents were asked what higher education institutions could do to better support care leavers while they are studying. The most frequently made suggestions were to provide scholarships and financial support, to provide accommodation support, to ensure care leavers are linked to student support services and to create institutional awareness and recognition of the group in equity policies and initiatives.

Stage Four: Interviews with Key Representatives from the Community Service Sector

The investigators conducted 11 interviews with representatives from community service organizations. The interviews confirmed that these community service organizations do not systematically track individual educational progress and do not collect aggregated data on the educational outcomes of young people in care. Despite the lack of data collection, all, but one, interviewee described their organization as prioritizing education of the young people in their care. About half of the organizations appear to have education policies manifest in annual or more frequent reviews of school progress. According to interviewees, higher education opportunities for care leavers were created by long-term, stable placements, which lead to continuity of primary and secondary schooling, committed advocates and caseworkers, financial support, housing support and being able to remain in a long-term foster home. As one interviewee stated:

> …going to tertiary education is quite strongly dependent on their care experience, in the same way that children who grow up with their birth families would have the aspirations determined by their parents as well.

Interviewees described several barriers to higher education transition including lack of confidence of care leavers, premature expectations of adult responsibility, mental health issues, early pregnancy, drug and alcohol misuse and family conflict. Trauma and early attachment disruption clearly impact brain development and can manifest in problems with concentration, memory and learning (Perry and Szalavitz 2006; van der Kolk 2005). Placement discontinuity and school disruption, learning difficulties and inadequate supports to address classroom behaviour appear to be associated with low academic aspirations. For example, one interviewee commented:

> If you've gone year after year where you're gradually getting further and further behind, because a lot of days you don't go to school because of what's happen-

ing at home, or you do go to school and you're sitting inside the Principal's office, or you're sent home because of your behaviours, you naturally fall behind academically, even though you've got absolutely the potential.

Raising Aspirations and Higher Education Preparedness

Interviewees reported that children in OHC sometimes aspire to attend university, but this aspiration often diminishes during adolescence. Notably, it was felt that when carers themselves had received a higher education, they appeared to be more aspirational for the young people in their care. By contrast, where birth parent and caregivers had been educationally disadvantaged, they were less likely to hold higher education aspirations for their children. One interviewee explained that:

> We have a high percentage of carers that have low education (achievement) and they've had low aspirations themselves. And we know the impact that that has on the kids that they have in their home.

The number of young people from OHC participating in tertiary education was estimated at between 1 per cent and 20 per cent, with about 90 per cent of that group attending TAFE or undertaking apprenticeships rather than directly transitioning to university. A number of interviewees observed that young people leaving care are often unprepared to transition to higher education when they are 18 years old. The phenomenon of young people returning to study in their late 20s or early 30s was mentioned by several interviewees.

Major barriers to higher education were identified as placements ending at 18 years, housing issues, financial issues, lack of interdepartmental collaboration, lack of carer educational training, lack of birth parent support for ongoing education and lack of on-campus mentorship and support. Interviewees described the most useful interventions to support transition into higher education as trauma/mental health responses, behaviour management strategies, mentoring, carer training, enhancement of birth parent engagement and aspirations and academic tutoring. A team approach to welfare and educational case management was also stressed, along with the importance of building trust through continuity of supportive relationships. Funding young people to remain in care, especially in long-term foster or kinship care placements, was also considered vital. Suggestions for university/government policy and programmatic improvements included waiving university and TAFE fees for care leavers, offering financial and housing support, providing mentorship and social support on campus and transitional programmes to develop academic skills. As one interviewee stated:

> I really think scrapping [university] fees for kids who have been in care needs to happen so that they've got some incentive to keep on going… For young people who can't live at home, maybe if there's some allocation within the residential colleges on university campuses for kids who have been in care to have a scholarship access to those residential units might help as well, as that would provide them with living support, emotional support, mentoring and good people around them that are motivated to help them keep going.

Indigenous Pathways to Higher Education

The number of indigenous care leavers transitioning to higher education is extremely small. One interviewee representing an indigenous-controlled provider of child and family welfare services reported that in over ten years of managing OHC, she could not recall one young person from her programme transitioning directly to university. A number of young people had, however, commenced TAFE study, including several who had started a TAFE course in their 20s when their lives had stabilized.

It was estimated that approximately 50 per cent of caregivers employed by one indigenous-controlled organization have experienced tertiary education themselves; as with non-indigenous caregivers, this experience appears to impact positively on carers' educational aspirations and advocacy for the children in their care. However, indigenous young people in care also experience some unique barriers to successful secondary education completion and higher education transition. There may be intergenerational trauma such as Stolen Generation experience in the family—a legacy of past policies of assimilation and institutionalization, which included the forcible separation of indigenous children from their parents into non-indigenous care (Human Rights and Equal Opportunity Commission 1997). Many young people also need to attend to cultural responsibilities; this is especially true of those from remote communities. As a result, this group may not be ready to transition into higher education until later in life. One interviewee explained:

> So for Aboriginal kids in out of home care they want to revisit (their country and family), and be part of something that they've sort of missed out on along the way perhaps. They may be ready for tertiary education in their later 20s when maybe they're starting to form other relationships themselves and get a bit more stability in their lives.

Conclusions

Our findings identify major reforms that are required to improve the access and achievement of care leavers in higher education. The collection of nationally consistent data on higher education access and outcomes is essential as is knowing the specific outcomes for indigenous care leavers. The AIHW (2013) is linking child protection data with school-level educational data, but extending this project to post-secondary level would help to build the evidence base.

There is an urgent need for greater recognition of care leavers as an under-represented group within the higher education sector. The absence of higher education data collection at national level is partly related to the nature of the national student equity framework, which was established in 1990. Since the framework identified six disadvantaged groups in higher education, university equity policies and national equity funding have been targeted to these six groups. While care leavers are often subsumed within and across the six groups, we believe that the extent and nature of their disadvantage require tailored policies and specific data collection. In the short-term, given the low number of care leavers in higher education, data on care leaver status could be collected by universities themselves, and by the statewide tertiary admissions centres that enable prospective students to apply for special entry access schemes. Notably, from 2015, the Victorian Tertiary Admissions Centre is enabling scholarship applicants to self-identify explicitly as care leavers. Additionally, universities need to provide stronger and more transparent support to raise university aspirations and increase the recruitment, access and achievement of care leavers.

Further policy and legislative reform is also required within the community service sector. In particular, there is a need for greater support for care leavers beyond the age of 18. While most states and territories have legislation that provides support beyond 18 years, that provision is discretionary, not mandatory. Lasting change will depend on collaboration among care leavers, carers, education institutions, caseworkers and community service organizations. The authors are now undertaking a project, funded by the Sidney Myer Foundation, which employs strategic cross-sectoral collaboration to develop supported education pathways for care leavers.

Finally, there is a need for broad cultural change. Our findings reveal care leavers to be a group consistently underestimated and overlooked by others. Care leavers deserve better access to the highest, and most financially rewarding, level of education and the economic prosperity that flows from this education. A national agenda for care leavers in higher education requires legislative, policy and cultural reforms, within both the higher education and community service sectors.

Acknowledgement This chapter is based on research funded through an external research grant provided by the National Centre for Student Equity in Higher Education at Curtin University.

References

All-Party Parliamentary Group for Looked after Children and Care Leavers (2012). *Education matters in care: A report by the independent cross-party inquiry into the educational attainment of looked after children in England.* London: Who Cares Trust.
Australian Bureau of Statistics. (2011). Australian census of population and housing. Retrieved 20 June 2014 from ABS TableBuilder Pro.
Australian Bureau of Statistics. (2012). Statement – Child Type, from http://www.abs.gov.au/websitedbs/censushome.nsf/home/statementspersonctpp?opendocument&navpos=430. Accessed 20 June 2014.

Australian Bureau of Statistics. (2013). *Young adults: Then and now*. Retrieved June 12, 2014, fromhttp://www.abs.gov.au/AUSSTATS/abs@.nsf/Lookup/4102.0Main+Features40April+2013#livingar

Australian Institute of Health and Welfare (AIHW) (2007). *Educational outcomes of children on guardianship or custody orders: A pilot study, Child welfare series no. 42. Cat. No. CWS 30*. Canberra: Australian Government.

Australian Institute of Health and Welfare (AIHW) (2011). *Educational outcomes of children on guardianship or custody orders: A pilot study, Stage 2, Child welfare series no. 49. Cat. No. CWS 37*. Canberra: Australian Government.

Australian Institute of Health and Welfare (AIHW) (2013). *Development of an ongoing national data collection on the educational outcomes of children in child protection services: A working paper, Child welfare series no. 56. Cat. No. CWS 46*. Canberra: Australian Government.

Australian Institute of Health and Welfare (AIHW) (2015). *Child protection Australia 2013–14, Child welfare series no.61. Cat. No. CWS 52*. Canberra: Australian Government.

Beauchamp, T. (2014). *A strong future for young people leaving out-of-home care: UnitingCare children young people and families position paper on leaving care and aftercare*. New South Wales: UnitingCare Children, Young People and Families.

Buttle UK (2014) Buttle UK to phase out its Quality Mark, as the education sector states its commitment to care-leavers. Retrieved June 23, 2014, from http://www.buttleuk.org/pages/announcement.html

Buttle UK (2015). *Quality mark annual statistical report, academic year 2013–14*. London: Buttle UK.

Cashmore, J., Paxman, M., & Townsend, M. (2007). The educational outcomes of young people 4–5 years after leaving care: An Australian perspective. *Adoption & Fostering, 31*(1), 50–61. doi:10.1177/030857590703100109.

Courtney, M., & Dworsky, A. (2005). *Midwest evaluation of the adult functioning of former foster youth: Outcomes at age 19*. Chicago: Chapin Hall Center for Children at the University of Chicago.

Courtney, M., Dworsky, A., Brown, A., Cary, C., Love, K., & Vorhies, V. (2011). *Midwest evaluation of the adult functioning of former foster youth: Outcomes at ages 26*. Chicago: Chapin Hall at the University of Chicago.

CREATE Foundation (2006). *Report card on education 2006*. Sydney: CREATE Foundation.

Creed, P., Tilbury, C., Buys, N., & Crawford, M. (2011). The career aspirations and action behaviours of Australian adolescents in out-of-home-care. *Children and Youth Services Review, 33*, 1720–1729. doi:10.1016/j.childyouth.2011.04.033.

Department for Business Innovation and Skills (2014). *National strategy for access and student success in higher education*. London: Department for Business Innovation and Skills.

Department for Education. (2014). *Children looked after by local authorities in England: Guide to the SSDA903 collection 1 April 2014 to 31 March 2015*.

Department of Education. (2014). 2012 Appendix 5 – Equity performance data. http://docs.education.gov.au/node/34993

Department of Education Employment and Training (DEET) (1990). *A fair chance for all: National and institutional planning for equity in higher education*. Canberra: Australian Government Publishing Service.

Department of Social Services. (2014). Transitioning to independence from out of home care: Discussion paper. Retrieved June 11, 2014, from http://www.dss.gov.au/our-responsibilities/families-and-children/publications-articles/transitioning-to-independence-from-out-of-home-care-discussion-paper?HTML

Fernandez, E. (2008). Unravelling emotional, behavioural and educational outcomes in a longitudinal study of children in foster-care. *British Journal of Social Work, 38*, 1283–1301. doi:10.1093/bjsw/bcm028.

Frederick, J., & Goddard, C. (2010). School was just a nightmare: Childhood abuse and neglect and school experiences. *Child and Family Social Work, 15*, 22–30. doi:10.1111/j.1365-2206.2009.00634.x.

Harvey, A., Andrewartha, L., & McNamara, P. (2015a). A forgotten cohort? Including people from out-of-home care in Australian higher education policy. *Australian Journal of Education, 59*(2). doi:10.1177/0004944115587529.

Harvey, A., McNamara, P., Andrewartha, L., & Luckman, M. (2015b). *Out of care, into university: Raising higher education access and achievement of care leavers* (National Centre for Student Equity in Higher Education (NCSEHE), Curtin University). Retrieved June 29, 2015, fromhttps://www.ncsehe.edu.au/research/research-reports/

Human Rights and Equal Opportunity Commission (1997). *Bringing them home: Report of the national inquiry into the separation of Aboriginal and Torres Strait Islander children from their families*. Sydney: Human Rights and Equal Opportunity Commission.

Jackson, S., & Cameron, C. (2012). *Final report of the YiPPEE project. Young people from a public care background: Pathways to further and higher education in five European countries*. London: Thomas Coram Research Unit, University of London.

Jackson, S., & Cameron, C. (2014). *Improving access to further and higher education for young people in public care: European policy and practice*. London: Jessica Kingsley Publishers.

Jackson, S., Ajayi, S., & Quigley, M. (2005). *By degrees: Going to university from care*. London: Institute of Education, University of London.

Johnson, G., Natalier, K., Mendes, P., Liddiard, M., Thoresen, S., Hollows, A., et al. (2010). *Pathways from out-of-home care*. Melbourne: Australian Housing and Urban Research Unit.

Jurczyszyn, R., & Tilbury, C. (2012). Higher and further education for care leavers: A road less travelled. *Developing Practice: The Child, Youth and Family Work Journal, 33*, 10–22.

Legal Center for Foster Care and Education (2008). *Foster care & education Q & A. Federal laws that increase educational opportunities for older youth in out-of-home care*. Chicago: American Bar Association and Casey Family Programs.

Lomax-Smith, J., Watson, L., & Webster, B. (2011). *Higher education base funding review*. Canberra: Department of Education, Employment and Workplace Relations.

McDowall, J. J. (2009). *CREATE Report card 2009. Transitioning from care: Tracking progress*. Sydney: CREATE Foundation.

McFarlane, K. (2010). From care to custody: Young women in out-of-home care in the criminal justice system. *Current Issues in Criminal Justice, 22*(2), 345–353.

Mendes, P. (2014). Leaving care, or left alone? How not to fail young people transitioning from out-of-home care. Retrieved June 11, 2014, fromhttp://www.abc.net.au/religion/articles/2014/02/13/3944328.htm

Mendes, P., Michell, D., & Wilson, J. Z. (2014). Young people transitioning from out-of-home care and access to higher education: A critical review of the literature. *Children Australia, 39*(4), 243–252.

Mendis, K., Gardner, F., & Lehmann, J. (2014). The education of children in out-of-home care. *Australian Social Work, 68*(4), 483–496. doi:10.1080/0312407X.2014.963134.

Michell, D., Jackson, D., & Tonkin, C. (Eds.) (2015). *Against the odds: Care leavers at university*. Elizabeth: People's Voice Publishing.

Murray, S., & Goddard, J. (2014). Life after growing up in care: Informing policy and practice through research. *Australian Social Work, 67*(1), 102–117. doi:10.1080/0312407X.2013.868010.

Norton, A. (2012). *Graduate winners: Assessing the public and private benefits of higher education*. Melbourne: Grattan Institute.

Pecora, P., Williams, J., Kessler, R. J., Downs, A. C., O'Brien, K., Hiripi, E., et al. (2003). *Assessing the effects of foster care: Early results from the Casey National Alumni Study*. Seattle: Casey Family Programs.

Pecora, P., Kessler, R. C., Williams, J., O'Brien, K., Downs, A. C., English, D., et al. (2005). *Improving family foster care: Findings from the Northwest Foster Care Alumni Study*. Seattle: Casey Family Programs.

Perry, B., & Szalavitz, M. (2006). *The boy who was raised as a dog and other stories from the child psychiatrist's notebook: What traumatised children can teach us about loss, love and healing*. New York: Basic Books.

QSR International (2012). *NVivo qualitative data analysis software, Version 10*. Melbourne: QSR International.

Smith, J. A., Flowers, P., & Larkin, M. (2009). *Interpretative phenomenological analysis: Theory, method, research*. London: Sage.

Starks, L. (2013). *Assessing the impact of the Buttle UK quaility mark in higher education*. Leeds, Buttle UK.

State Government of Victoria (2012). *Report of the protecting victoria's vulnerable children inquiry*. Melbourne: Department of Premier and Cabinet.

The Centre for Social Justice (2015). *Finding their feet: Equipping care leavers to reach their full potential*. London: The Centre for Social Justice.

Thoresen, S. H., & Liddiard, M. (2011). Failure of care in state care: In-case abuse and postcare homelessness. *Children Australia, 36*(1), 4–11. doi:10.1375/jcas.36.1.4.

Townsend, M. (2012). *Are we making the grade? The education of children and young people in out-of-home care*. Ashfield: Department of Family and Community Services.

van der Kolk, B. (2005). Developmental trauma disorder: Toward a rational diagnosis for children with complex trauma disorders. *Psychiatric Annals, 35*(5), 401–408.

Wolanin, T. R. (2005). *Higher education opportunities for foster youth: A primer for policymakers*. Washington, DC: Institute for Higher Education Policy.

6

I Want to Be Someone, I Want to Make a Difference: Young Care Leavers Preparing for the Future in South Australia

Dee Michell and Claudine Scalzi

Introduction

> There is no greater indictment of the fostercare system when a news website's go-to-option for an article on growing up in fostercare is me, an overweight middling comedian with jokes about wanking and pies. Couldn't get a doctor? An accountant? (Corey White 2015)

Corey White's recent success at the Melbourne International Comedy and Edinburgh Fringe Festivals no doubt prompted *News.Com*'s invitation. But his self-deprecating question about who is asked to speak on the Australian foster care system is insightful and troubling. Are there no professionals in Australia, such as doctors and accountants, who experienced

---

D. Michell (✉)
Gender Studies and Social Analysis, School of Social Sciences,
Faculty of Arts, The University of Adelaide, Adelaide, SA, Australia

C. Scalzi
CREATE Foundation, Adelaide, SA, Australia

© The Author(s) 2016
P. Mendes, P. Snow (eds.), *Young People Transitioning from Out-of-Home Care*, DOI 10.1057/978-1-137-55639-4_6

foster care as children? Or, do those who extend invitations to speak on the system not expect to find professionals amongst foster care alumni? Either way, and as Corey[1] says, it is an indictment on the system if it does not produce university-educated professionals, or that the Australian community does not expect it to.

This twofold problem—the under-representation of care leavers with university qualifications and what Harvey et al. (2015b, p. 6) call the '…omnipresent soft bigotry of low expectations' of children and young people in care—has only recently attracted sustained attention in Australia. In 2000, the CREATE Foundation (see Chap. 14 by Joseph McDowall in this volume) launched the first of their subversive Report Card series, evaluating and challenging governments and their agents on the provision of education and other services to the children and young people (CYP) in their care, from the perspective of the CYP, the previously silenced group (Nicholson et al. 2015). Social work academics like Philip Mendes have, for a decade, been advocating for improved transition plans to reduce the structural disadvantages young people face when they 'age out' of the system, including access and support for further education (Mendes et al. 2011, 2014). Others have commenced a focus on academic achievements (Cashmore and Paxman 1996; Michell 2012; Mendes et al. 2014), and show that care leavers *do go to university*, but suggest more could if they were encouraged to do so.

Evidence-based advocacy necessarily focuses on the over-representation of care leavers amongst the vulnerable and disadvantaged (Bromfield and Osborn 2007). Complicating and unsettling this narrative of vulnerability and disadvantage, which risks feeding into a deficit discourse perpetuating stereotypical views of care leavers as 'losers', is the increasing presence of university-educated care leavers, the once-dismissed and derided, now challenging the systemic oppression of CYP in Australia's child protection system (e.g. Penglase 2005; Wilson 2013 and Golding 2015, and their chapter in this text). Lanai Vasek/Scarr's 2010 'coming out' story in the national newspaper, *The Australian*, Corey White's success and Karise Eden, winner of the inaugural *The Voice Australia* series, mentored by British care leaver Seal, contribute to this narrative disturbance, as does the presence of three prominent Australians in Season 6 of *Who Do You*

Think You Are, whose parents were in care: Jackie Weaver, Dave Hughes and Adam Goodes. Finally, recent projects such as CREATE's 2014 *The Power Within*—involving 21 successful adult care leavers, nine with university qualifications—encourage CYP in care to resist stigma and refuse to be defined by their care experience.

Our contribution to addressing the widespread low valuation of CYP with a care background and their under-representation at university is to report on a small qualitative research project we conducted in 2013. Inspired by the above examples and research overseas (e.g. that of Sonia Jackson, described below), we chose to explore young people's experiences of university in the state of South Australia. We wanted to know if, while in care, they were expected or encouraged to further their education at university, what contact they had with professionals and whether they were currently engaged in tertiary, particularly university study. What we found was that CYP in care, just like any other CYP, require continual encouragement and support to inspire and sustain their drive to succeed in education. For many of the young people who participated in this project, such support was either lacking or inconsistent. What we also found was an exciting group of thoughtful, resilient and creative young people determined to carve out successful futures, regardless of difficult starts in life and the ongoing stigma of having been in care.

Care Leavers at University

The story of Australian care leavers at university is inextricably linked to the expansion of universities in the twentieth century. Each time a structural opening has occurred to enable others besides the middle and upper classes, to attend, the name of a care leaver who managed to slip in and change the trajectory of his/her life can be found. One example is esteemed academic and art historian, Bernard Smith (1916–2011), who was in formal foster care at a time when such boys went into labouring jobs at age 14 (and girls into domestic service). Yet, and with the support of his foster mother, he finished high school, and eventually went to university because the University of Sydney in 1945 removed Latin as a prerequisite for admission (Smith 2002).

Despite this initiative by the country's oldest university, and a number of Australian Federal Government attempts during the twentieth century to create opportunities for 'non-traditional' students to attend university, HE has largely been regarded as a rite of passage for those from the middle and upper classes, and as exceptional for others. However, findings of the *Review of Australian Higher Education* (Bradley et al. 2008) that three equity groups—Indigenous Australians, those from low socio-economic status (SES) backgrounds and students from rural and regional areas—remained under-represented in Australian universities, prompted the Federal Labor Government in 2009, to set ambitious targets for increasing enrolments of these 'non-traditional' students from less than 15 per cent to 20 per cent by 2020. Such targets follow on from comparable international policies from the late twentieth century and are seen as a way to simultaneously address possible future skills shortages *and* patterns of under-representation of people from disadvantaged and/or low SES backgrounds (Forsyth 2015).

Care leavers are not well represented in the current widening participation agenda, which broadly continues with the current Federal Coalition Government. Although the need for improved educational outcomes for CYP in care is widely acknowledged and provided for in the 2011 National Standards for out-of-home care (FahCSIA 2011), this education framework only applies to the age of 18. When it comes to HE access, care leavers are not seen as a specific equity group despite the likelihood that only 1 per cent of care leavers enter university (based on international figures). Therefore, their access to, and participation at, university is not tracked, and specific programmes have not been developed to improve access, participation and retention (Harvey et al. 2015a, b).

Care leavers are also under-represented in the abundance of research resulting from the Australian Government enrolment targets and subsequent financial incentives. There is limited research that precedes the Bradley Review: Cashmore and Paxman (2007) emphasized stability in care and at school as factors in academic success, and Tilbury et al. (2009) concluded young people need encouragement to consider HE, both during and after secondary schooling. The sparse post-Bradley research includes Mendis' study, which shows the diverse paths, including mature-age entry, many academically successful women have taken to university (Mendis

2012; Mendis et al. 2014). Reeny Jurczyszyn, motivated to explore the topic because of her own experience in care, stresses that young people in care need more assistance than their peers in the form of advocacy and mentoring in order to access HE (Jurczyszyn and Tilbury 2012; Jurczyszyn 2015). These studies have been supplemented with autobiographical accounts from care leavers, which highlight a variety of experiences, from Gregory Smith's recent mid-life journey to Technical and Further Education (TAFE) while homeless, and subsequent undergraduate and then postgraduate studies, to the benefits Jacqueline Wilson (2013; see also her chapter in this volume) experienced in attending an 'alternative' community school during her late adolescence.[2]

The plight of care leavers is a global phenomenon, but there are some jurisdictions where attention has been more seriously focused on increasing their access to university. For example, the ongoing research and advocacy since 1987 by education academic Sonia Jackson has led to significant studies in the UK and Europe (e.g. Jackson et al. 2005; Jackson and McParlin 2006; Jackson and Cameron 2012). Moreover, Jackson's work has contributed to changes in policy and practice; amongst other initiatives, the successful *Staying Put* programme allows young people to remain in foster care beyond age 18 (Munro et al. 2012). Additionally, a number of universities now have overt care leaver specific support in place, including scholarships such as that provided by Huddersfield in the name of care leaver, poet, and Chancellor of the University of Manchester, Lemn Sissay. Activity in the USA to support care leavers includes the Federal Fostering Connections to Success and Increasing Adoptions Act of 2008 and the College Cost Reduction legislation of 2009 (Day et al. 2011); provisions at state level includes the extension of the age of leaving care to 25 years in California (Nance 2008); and programmes such as the 2001 Chafee Education and Training Voucher (ETV) package provides financial assistance for both HE and other training (Hernandez 2012).

Although Australia is lagging behind the UK, Europe and the USA in progress to increase the representation of care leavers in HE, the current widening participation agenda has at least—and at last—provided an environment conducive to the conversation. The aim of the study described here was to explore whether young people had been encouraged towards HE goals during their time in South Australian State care.

Methodology

Our theoretical framework for the project was Strengths Perspective (Saleeby 1996, 2006). This perspective assumes people are intelligent, capable and experts in their own lives. It identifies and values resistance and survival strategies, is focused on hope and possibilities rather than problems and offsets the socio-cultural devaluation of marginalized groups (Guo and Tsui 2010; Roche 1999; Whitehouse and Colvin 2001). It is an apposite perspective for a group of people often seen as 'damaged goods' but who '…deserve to be approached as strong, capable survivors who should not be defined by the deficits of their pasts' (Watt et al. 2013, p. 1410).

A qualitative methodological approach using focus groups was chosen as a good fit between the care leaver University of Adelaide researcher and the CREATE Foundation objectives. The latter include ensuring that all CYP in care are respected, listened to and active participants in decisions that affect their lives. Focus group research can shift the power imbalance between researcher and participants, reduce the possibility of intimidation by the researcher and increase the likelihood that participants will collectively shape the conversation (Smithson 2008). Other advantages of this methodology are a sense of safety in numbers, inclusivity of people who have difficulty reading and writing, and it increases the capacity of participants to support and encourage each other to explore stigmatized and wounding experiences. It has also been observed that shared experiences allow shifts from self-blame to exploring structural and systemic barriers, and participants become an active part of the research process (Kitzinger 1994, 2005). There are risks associated with the method, and thus there is a need for skilled facilitators to quickly build trust and rapport, manage potential conflict and ensure all members have an opportunity to speak (Wilkinson 1998; Kitzinger and Barbour 1999). As well, face-to-face group settings are inherently more public than individual interviews or online surveys, making privacy and anonymity harder, if not impossible, to guarantee (Farquhar and Das 1999). Both researchers have extensive experience in conducting focus groups, and we managed the risks by discussing their possibility at the outset and by establishing group norms.

Two focus groups were convened, one in December 2013, and the other in late January 2014, at the CREATE office in Adelaide, a location already familiar to the majority of participants. Participants were identified through the clubCREATE database, a compilation of the contact details for clubCREATE members. CYP with a care experience join clubCREATE to enjoy a range of CREATE publications and opportunities to join in events, programmes and activities with other young people with a care experience. Potential participants were contacted by CREATE; the consultation purpose was explained to them, and they were then invited to participate in the focus groups. Participants were told that CREATE Foundation and the University of Adelaide follow policies and guidelines for dealing with any disclosures of harm (or potential harm) during consultations, consistent with relevant state and territory legislation, and each participant was given a consent form to sign that explained the process (as approved by the University of Adelaide Human Ethics Committee).

There were five young women aged between 18 and 24 in each focus group. Although some young men initially agreed to participate, only women arrived on the day of the focus groups. Of the ten participants, three were in residential care placements and seven were in foster care. Three entered care when they were less than five years of age, four were between five and nine years of age and three were between 10 and 15 years of age when they entered care. Two participants identified as Aboriginal. Before formal commencement of the focus group discussions, confirmation of the young person's consent to participate was obtained. The groups were also informed that the University of Adelaide researcher had a care background. As the discussion commenced, participants were invited to partake of the refreshments provided.

The discussion was led by the authors, and began by posing predetermined questions. These covered earliest memories of school, how/if school was different after entering State care, what participants would like to see changed in the school system, teacher responses to in-care status, education plans, knowledge of tertiary education, hopes and dreams for the future and experiences of university. De-identified responses were handwritten on large sheets of paper in full view of participants. Field notes were also made after each focus group, and the data were analysed considering both structural impediments faced by the young women, as well as the strengths they evinced when discussing their experience in care and plans for the future. In the following section, we elaborate on the stories of five indicative young women, using pseudonyms, and highlight the general lack of support and encouragement afforded to the women in order for them to explore university as an option. Themes also highlight their resourcefulness in carving out futures, and the stigma young people in care continue to face, as well as creative ways in which they negotiate it.

Findings

Most participants said they began thinking about what they might like to do in the future while they were still at school. All but two were aware of care-leavers who held university degrees, and almost all noted carers, particularly their foster mums, among those who talked to them about their futures, with teachers the next likely to discuss this, followed by social workers and youth workers. However, only two young women had experienced any encouragement and guidance in considering tertiary education, one from a teacher and one from a case worker. Others found alternative sources of inspiration, including wanting to do things differently to their birth parents. Two participants were at university, but neither believed that university was the only measure of success; they did, however, want all CYP in care to see university as a viable option.

Support and Encouragement

Jade spent her childhood and youth in the one positive and stable foster care placement, which she entered as a toddler. Although such stability in a long-term home is often a factor in education success for care leavers (Cashmore and Paxman 2007; Cameron 2007; Jackson and Cameron 2012; Jurczsyn and Tilbury 2012), Jade's foster mother did not encourage her to continue her education beyond high school:

> She didn't think I would be able to do university. She seemed to think I was some hurt individual who wasn't capable of much.

It is likely that Jade's foster mum wanted to protect her daughter from possible failure and was unaware of how this could act as discouragement (Walther et al. 2015). In the end, it was a Year 12 teacher who influenced Jade to do a Bachelor of Science. Given her interests as well as the uncertainty she felt about the specifics of a career, this degree was suggested as a broad one, enabling a range of opportunities. Studying for her undergraduate degree was difficult for Jade, harder than she expected, but this is not unusual for young people in care at university (Mayall et al. 2015). Jade was uncomfortable asking for help because, when she was in care, she felt like she 'was always asking for help'. Once Jade had commenced at university, her foster mother became more supportive, including paying for expensive textbooks.

Because she found that, contrary to the advice she had received, 'there actually were not many job opportunities as a Science graduate', twenty-four-year-old Jade subsequently went on to do a Masters in Social Work. Like other women in the group, for her second degree she was motivated by her desire to do a better job than many of the social workers she herself had encountered. Jade experienced problems during her social work placement, as unresolved childhood trauma and grief were triggered, but she was thankful the placement coordinator was helpful and supportive. At the time of the research, Jade was confident of completing her second degree.

Twenty-year-old Sally was the only other person in the sample who had been encouraged to consider a career (as opposed to getting a job), and the only one currently studying at TAFE. Sally went into residential care (a decision she made because she did not want foster parents to replace her parents) as a 15-year-old, something she described as a positive experience. Towards the end of high school, Sally often discussed with her case worker a range of career options, including youth work and nursing. The case worker then obtained all the information and talked over the requirements with Sally. Unsurprisingly, Sally continues to maintain a relationship with this encouraging case worker, but, in the end, she did not do as well at school as she had hoped, something she attributes to the distracting presence of the young man who is now her fiancée.

Sally currently combines working in an aged care facility with studying at TAFE, with an aim to qualify as an enrolled nurse. She also plays netball at State level and lives independently, proudly describing the way she manages all this by being well organized, cooking all her meals in advance and freezing them so she can avoid that task at the end of a tiring day (cooking was a skill Sally learnt at age 12 when she cared for her younger brothers). Sally hastened to assert during the discussion that 'TAFE is further education too!' and to explain that if she liked being an enrolled nurse, she would consider going to university to do a Bachelor of Nursing. However, the most important thing for Sally is to 'be a good parent', reflecting her experience of being inadequately parented in her birth family and the pleasure she took in caring for her brothers, the youngest of whom she 'still looks out for'.

Making Their Own Way

Terri's story illustrates that young people might be inspired by the situation of their birth family to go in a different direction. The other university student in the group, 19-year-old Terri might be described as a member of Mendis et al.'s (2014) 'Determined Group', those who demonstrate considerable agency in the face of adversity. Even though support for university study was absent, Terri was strongly motivated to make a success of her life and had just completed her first year of study towards a Bachelor of Nursing. In contrast to Sally, for whom being a good parent was emphasized, Terri's focus was a career and has been ever since she was motivated as a ten-year-old to become a nurse, after a period in hospital. Terri's decisions have also been shaped by the lack of career in her birth family: 'they only had jobs and often were without work'.

Along with her studies, Terri was gaining practical experience as a volunteer paramedic. Working as a paramedic stimulated her thinking about a possible move from nursing to medicine, and caused her to reflect on earlier low expectations because she was 'not pushed harder at school and at home'. She was also not appropriately advised on the prerequisite courses she could have done in high school to leave open the possibility of applying for medicine at university.

Terri also had another ambition, that of taking her medical training into the army. In this, she is again motivated by her birth family:

> I want to join the army. There is a history of the army in my birth family. Plus I want to wear a uniform so I don't need to think about what to wear every day. I think I'll need to increase my fitness levels first though.

The capable and determined Terri had already undertaken her own research to assess the entry requirements for joining the army and decided she would need to improve her fitness levels before applying.

Ashlie's story is the all too familiar one of disruption caused to education by placement changes, but her story also illustrates that leaving school early is not necessarily the end of formal education. Ashlie had, on the whole, a positive foster care experience until her foster parents separated and she was moved into a new placement. In care since infancy, she had shifted primary school several times, as her foster care family wanted all the children to go to the same school. Despite stability for most of her childhood, no one encouraged Ashlie to proceed to further education. Because of the disturbance in her foster care placement during late adolescence, Ashlie decided she did not want to finish Year 12, and took this up in Education Plan meetings with social workers, carers and teachers, where she, unfortunately, felt her wish to leave was ignored. In the end, Ashlie demonstrated leadership, agency and tenacity as she advocated for herself by taking up the matter with both the school principal and the Chief Executive of the State agency responsible for child protection in South Australia, Families SA.

Although she finished school early, Ashlie was inspired and encouraged by a close friend to continue with her education. She subsequently completed Year 12 at Marden Senior College, a secondary school actively supporting mature-age students. For her compulsory Year 12 research project, Ashlie chose to investigate the foster care system and discovered CREATE. Again inspired by someone she knew, this time a youth worker at CREATE, at the time of the research, Ashlie had recently applied to TAFE to do a Certificate 4 in Youth Work, reflecting what is known about the role of sound relationships between youth workers and their clients (Crawford and Tilbury 2007). She was also in the process of advocating to see her foster brother, an important relationship for her, but one disregarded by authorities when she moved placement. Missing her brother meant that if she had the chance, the one thing Ashlie would want to change about the foster care system 'would be fostering relationships between past foster care siblings when you have moved placement'.

The final case example we have chosen to explore in more detail is that of Christy, a young Aboriginal woman, the quiet one in her group, but ambitious. Christy (aged 18) had an unsettled time at school as she had multiple placements and therefore multiple schools. Despite this, she made friends easily and enjoyed the social aspect of school. At the time of our research, she was completing her secondary education at an Aboriginal Community College and was determined she 'wanted to be someone…she wanted to make a difference' as well as 'to help people' and to 'have a decent job, a house and a car'.

Christy was as emphatic about not having children as she was about transforming her circumstances; like Terri, her focus was career, and she had plans to be a social worker. In this, Christy, like Jade, was inspired to be different from the many 'lazy' social workers she had encountered—'they say they'll do something then they don't, or they take a very long time to do it'—as well as by a social worker she knows who also has a State care experience. Christy believed this latter social worker to be far more empathetic and understanding, particularly about the need for Christy to maintain a connection with her birth family.

Negotiating Stigma

Participants were keenly aware of stereotypes of State children being 'damaged' and 'different' in a way that suggests 'deficient', rather than 'diverse'. These findings are unsurprising given the long history of stigma associated with CYP in Australian State care (Michell 2015); it was also something Tamsin Dancer (2012) found when working at CREATE, where many CYP 'felt on the outer' (p. 90). Women in our study had poignantly wished for adults in their lives to see them as 'a whole and usual person', rather than a 'tainted, discounted one' (Goffman 1963, p.3), as well as provide them with the support and encouragement to succeed. All felt, in different ways, however, that the stigma of being in care had impacted their education: they were often told that they 'would not go anywhere'. Participants reported that most teachers either anticipated or enabled their failure by accepting and/or excusing incomplete tasks and assignments. They also reported that carers and caseworkers were often disinterested. Some reported being bullied by other students, often feeling isolated and alone, and feeling conflicted about whether or not to 'come out' as having been in care (Mayall et al. 2015).

Jade, despite her one stable foster care placement, and generally positive experience, found school a not entirely safe zone. This was because of the fear of being stigmatized and marginalized. She expected to be treated as 'different' and from a young age feared being exposed:

> I kept people from knowing that I was in foster care, I was worried about what people might think.

Jade now attributes her fear to comments made by her foster mother, who was also in foster care. Because she maintained strong connections with her birth family, complications and conflicts arose for Jade during opportunities for sharing school events with both families:

> I found school activities like concerts awkward because I didn't want both sets of parents there because it would give it away that I was in care.

Although Jade would have loved to have both her families at school concerts and other events, she did not want to risk exposure by having to explain her family situation. In the end, she invited only her foster family along.

For Ashlie, who was also in a stable foster care placement for much of her childhood, routine school procedures and curriculum items that focus on normative family arrangements caused her to feel awkward and embarrassed:

> I would like to see teachers being aware of what CYP go through; it can be confronting in a classroom setting to get consent forms filled in and family tree activities [can expose difference].

Sally, too, was concerned about being exposed for fear of being treated differently:

> It was bad enough that payments, forms, everything, all had to be done differently to everyone else…I didn't want to complicate things more.

Sally had no confidence that people who have not been through the system would actually understand what is going on. Instead, she expected they will judge her as deficient in some way because of her background. The only person Sally had confided in was her boyfriend, but she went to some lengths to avoid telling him the reason, by saying her parents had died, and because she maintains contact with her birth mother, she told him that her mother is her step-mother.

Terri talked about how her experience of safety did not change once she was placed in foster care; where previously school had been a sanctuary, home became a safe place too. However, she felt that because of her difficult background, teachers did not push her to succeed. She also told a touching story of trying to enrol her brothers into her school, but was informed the school had already filled their quota of taking State children. This response made Terri think that schools do not want to have children with Guardianship of the Minister orders—'GOM kids', as they are colloquially known in South Australia—in their ranks.

Discussion and Conclusion

The findings from our small qualitative study align with the research of others in Australia and beyond. Young people with a care background can, and do, achieve bachelor and higher-level university degrees. But where the young people want to be seen as capable of reaching educational heights not usually expected of this demographic, those responsible for their care—social workers, teachers and carers—often have difficulty seeing beyond a low birth status and the neglect and/or trauma which precipitated a movement into care. Therefore, young people are often not supported in their ambitions for the future, and important conversations about aspirations and educational goals are missing, even if there are conversations regarding plans for the future (e.g. Jackson and Martin 1998; Jackson et al. 2011; Jackson and Cameron 2012; Jurczyszyn and Tilbury 2012; Mendis 2012).

Because of the general lack of, or inconsistent nature of, the support they received, the women felt responsible for themselves, and saw education as a way to erase or correct the taint of State care (Goffman 1963). They also wanted to make a difference in the child protection system by being better social workers, and to change the trajectory of their family histories by having a career and/or by being better parents. Although their aims could be interpreted as 'modest and normative' (Jackson and Cameron 2012, p. 252), the young women demonstrated considerable agency in keenly resisting the usual low expectations of their demographic, and fit within a typology of 'fighting for dreams' (Walther et al. 2015) by not dismissing disadvantage, but resisting having their futures defined by it.

The findings highlight the issues of most concern for the young people. Carers, workers and teachers all need to be more encouraging to help them achieve in education; the difference in their family situations needs to be respected as further evidence of the diversity in the Australian community, not of deficiency; teachers should have training to enable them to better support and understand CYP with a care experience; and everyone involved with CYP in care should be helping them reach their full potential. Given the impact of ongoing stigma, clearly what is also needed is for the broader Australian community to both understand the impact of care on children and young people while not limiting them to being defined by this experience.

Notes

1. Corey's experience in care, which suggests that the State was no better a Parent than the one he was removed from, needs exploring too, but is beyond the scope of this chapter.
2. Autobiographical accounts are a reminder that not everyone with a care background has been through the State child protection system, as the families of both Pam Petrilli and Stacey Page avoided that by making their own foster and kinship care arrangements. Theirs and Smith's stories are included with Jurczyszyn's in *Against The Odds*.

Acknowledgements We acknowledge the contributions and support of the ten young people who shared their time and expertize. We also thank the Faculty of Arts at the University of Adelaide for the financial support to undertake the project.

References

Bradley, D., Noonan, P., Nugent, H., & Scales, B. (2008). *Review of Australian higher education*. Final report. Retrieved from http://gellen.org.au/wp-content/uploads/2011/04/Higher_Educatio_Review.pdf

Bromfield, L., & Osborn, A. (2007). 'Getting the big picture': A synopsis and critique of Australian out-of-home care research. *Child Abuse Prevention Issues, 26*, 1–39.

Cameron, C. (2007). Education and self reliance among care leavers. *Adoption & Fostering, 31*(1), 39–50.

Cashmore, J., & Paxman, M. (1996). *Wards leaving care: A longitudinal study*. Sydney: NSW Department of Community Services.

Cashmore, J., & Paxman, M. (2007). *Longitudinal study of wards leaving care: Four to five years on*. Sydney: NSW Department of Community Services.

Crawford, M., & Tilbury, C. (2007). Child protection workers' perspectives on the school-to-work transition for young people in care. *Australian Social Work, 60*(3), 308–320.

Dancer, T. (2012). From the outside.... *Developing Practice: The Child, Youth and Family Work Journal, 32*, 87–91.

Day, A., Dworsky, A., Fogarty, K., & Damashek, A. (2011). An examination of post-secondary retention and graduation among fostercare youth. *Children and Youth Services Review, 33*, 2335–2341.

Department of Families, Housing, Community Services and Indigenous Affairs (FaHCSIA). (2011). National standards for out of home care. Available online https://www.dss.gov.au/our-responsibilities/families-and-children/publications-artiCare-leavers/an-outline-of-national-standards-for-out-of-home-care-2011

Farquhar, C., & Das, R. (1999). Are focus groups suitable for 'sensitive' topics? In R. Barbour & J. Kitzinger (Eds.), *Developing focus group research: Politics, theory and practice* (pp. 47–63). London: Sage.

Forsyth, A. (2015). Expanding higher education: Institutional responses in Australia from the post-war era to the 1970s. *Paedagogica Historica: International Journal of the History of Education, 51*(3), 365–380.

Goffman, E. (1963). *Stigma: Notes on the management of spoiled identity*. Englewood Cliffs: Prentice-Hall.

Guo, W., & Tsui, M. (2010). From resilience to resistance: A reconstruction of the strengths perspective in social work practice. *International Social Work, 53*(2), 233–245.

Harvey, A., Andrewartha, L., & McNamara, P. (2015a). A forgotten cohort? Including people from out-of-home care in Australian higher education policy. *Australian Journal of Education, 59*(2), 182–195.

Harvey, A., McNamara, P., Andrewartha, L., & Luckman, M. (2015b). *Out of care, into university: Raising higher education access and achievement of care-leavers.* Final report. Melbourne: La Trobe University.

Hernandez, L. (2012). Promoting higher education for youth leaving fostercare: College preparation and campus based programs. *Developing Practice, 32*, 72–86.

Jackson, S. & Martin, P.Y. (1998). Surviving the care system: Education and resilience. *Journal of Adolescence, 21*, 569–583.

Jackson, S., & Cameron, C. (2012). Leaving care: Looking ahead and aiming higher. *Children and Youth Services Review, 34*(6), 1107–1114.

Jackson, S., & McParlin, P. (2006). The education of children in care. *The Psychologist, 19*(2), 90–93.

Jackson, S., Ajayi, S., & Quigley, M. (2005). *Going to university from care.* London: Institute of Education, University of London.

Jackson, S., Ajayi, S. & Quigley, M. (2011). *Case study on the impact of IOE research into 'Going to University from Care'.* London: Institute of Education, University of London.

Jurczyszyn, R. (2015). Care to university. In D. Michell, D. Jackson, & C. Tonkin (Eds.), *Against the odds: Care leavers at university* (pp. 13–20). Elizabeth: People's Voice Publishing.

Jurczyszyn, R., & Tilbury, C. (2012). Higher and further education for care leavers. *Developing Practice, 33*, 10–22.

Kitzinger, J. (1994). Introducing focus groups. *BMJ, 311*, 299–301.

Kitzinger, J. (2005). Focus group research: Using group dynamics to explore perceptions, experiences and understandings. In I. Holloway (Ed.), *Qualitative research in health care* (pp. 56–69). Maidenhead: Open University Press.

Kitzinger, J., & Barbour, R. (1999). The challenge and promise of focus groups. In R. Barbour & J. Kitzinger (Eds.), *Developing focus group research: Politics, theory and practice* (pp. 1–20). London: Sage.

Mayall, H., O'Neill, T., Worsley, A., Devereux, R., Ward, S., & Lynch, D. (2015). The experiences of care leavers (post-care adults) in social work education. *Social Work Education, 34*(2), 151–164.

Mendes, P., Michell, D., & Wilson, J. (2014a). Young people transitioning from out-of-home care and access to higher education: A critical review of the literature. *Children Australia, 39*(4), 1–10.

Mendes, P., Pinkerton, J., & Munro, E. (2014b). Guest editorial: Young people transitioning from out of home care. *Australian Social Work, 67*(1), 1–4.

Mendes, P., Johnson, G., & Moslehuddin, B. (2011). *Young people leaving state out-of-home care: A research-based study of Australian policy and practice.* Melbourne: Australian Scholarly Publishing.

Mendis, K. (2012). Exploring ways in which to support the education of children in care. *Developing Practice, 33*, 25–34.

Mendis, K., Gardner, F., & Lehmann, J. (2014). The education of children in out-of-home care. *Australian Social Work, 68*(4), 483–496.

Michell, D. (2012). A suddenly desirable demographic? Care leavers in higher education. *Developing Practice, 33*, 44–58.

Michell, D. (2015). Fostercare, stigma and the sturdy, unkillable children of the very poor. *Continuum: Journal of Media & Cultural Studies, 29*(4), 663–676.

Munro, E., Lushey, C., National Care Advisory Service, Maskell-Graham, D., & Ward, H. with Holmes, L. (2012). *Evaluation of the staying put 18+ family placement programme pilot final report.* London: Department for Education.

Nance, M. (2008). Helping foster care youth access college. *Diverse, 10*(January), 12–13.

Nicholson, J., Kurnik, J., Jevgjovikj, M., & Ufoegbune, V. (2015). Deconstructing adults' and children's discourse on children's play: Listening to children's voices to destabilise deficit narratives. *Early Child Development and Care, 185*(10), 1569–1586.

Penglase, J. (2005). *Orphans of the living: Growing up in 'care' in twentieth-century Australia.* Fremantle: Curtin University Books.

Roche, S. (1999). Using a strengths perspective for social work practice with abused women. *Journal of Family Social Work, 3*(2), 23–37.

Saleeby, D. (1996). The strengths perspective in social work practice. *Social Work, 41*(3), 296–305.

Saleeby, D. (2006). *The strengths perspective in social work practice.* London: Pearson/Allyn & Bacon.

Smith, B. (2002). *A pavane for another time.* Melbourne: Macmillan.

Smithson, J. (2008). Focus groups. In P. Alasuutari, L. Bickman, & J. Brannen (Eds.), *The sage handbook of social research methods.* Los Angeles: Sage.

Tilbury, C., Buys, N., & Creed, P. (2009). Perspectives of young people in care about their school-to-work transition. *Australian Social Work, 62*(4), 476–490.

Vasek, L. (2010) 'The secret history of me', The Weekend Australian Magazine, 26–27 June, 15-18.

Walther, A., Warth, A., Ule, M., & du Bois-Reymond, M. (2015). Me, my education and I': Constellations of decision-making in young people's educational trajectories. *International Journal of Qualitative Studies in Education, 28*(3), 349–371.

Watt, T., Norton, C., & Jones, C. (2013). Designing a campus support program for fostercare alumni: Preliminary evidence for a strengths framework. *Children and Youth Services Review, 35*, 1408–1417.

White, C. (2015, October 2015). Calling the fostercare system broken is like saying Agent Orange is a 'bit itchy. *News.com* 1 Available online http://www.news.com.au/lifestyle/real-life/opinion-calling-the-foster-care-system-broken-is-like-saying-agent-orange-is-a-bit-itchy/story-fnu2q5nu-1227550920058

Whitehouse, M., & Colvin, C. (2001). 'Reading' families: Deficit discourse and family literacy. *Theory Into Practice, 40*(3), 212–219.

Wilkinson, S. (1998). Focus groups in feminist research: Power, interaction, and the co-construction of meaning. *Women's Studies International Forum, 21*, 111–125.

Wilson, J. Z. (2013). Education dissonance. In R. Brandenburg & J. Z. Wilson (Eds.), *Pedagogies for the future. Leading quality learning and teaching in higher education* (pp. 125–138). Rotterdam: Sense Publishers.

Wilson, J. Z., & Golding, F. (2015). Latent scrutiny: Personal archives as perpetual mementos of the official gaze. *Archives Science*, first published online October 5, Springer.

7

Muddling Upwards: The Unexpected, Unpredictable and Strange on the Path from Care to High Achievement in Victoria, Australia

Jacqueline Z. Wilson and Frank Golding

It is indisputable that education is a key avenue to personal, social and economic success in Australian society; and that, conversely, its lack can lead to lifelong deprivation and social exclusion. This chapter focuses on the specific educational challenges that confront children in out-of-home care (OHC), and those who have been discharged from care as young adults. It is noted that a very small percentage of care leavers complete education, and some of the core reasons for this are discussed. We are both care leavers, and in this chapter we provide emblematic case studies by recounting our own experiences. We conclude that many of the obstacles we had to surmount were, and are, common to care leavers of our generations and also those currently in OHC. We conclude with a brief summary of policy reforms necessary to ensure educational equity for care leavers.

J.Z. Wilson (✉)
Federation University Australia, Ballarat, VIC, Australia

F. Golding
Kensington, VIC, Australia

© The Author(s) 2016
P. Mendes, P. Snow (eds.), *Young People Transitioning from Out-of-Home Care*, DOI 10.1057/978-1-137-55639-4_7

It is axiomatic that education is good for both the individual and the society. However, contemporary public debates are increasingly shifting towards the instrumental advantages of 'getting an education', meaning acquiring recognized credentials to join the skilled workforce, to raise one's own standard of living as well as raising the nation's productivity (Caro and Bonnor 2012; Lietz 2010). At a time of increasing youth unemployment in many countries (International Labour Organization 2015), school leavers with no credentials or low-level educational qualifications find it increasingly hard to get jobs. Many will carry unemployment or underemployment as a major handicap throughout their lives.

The aim of this chapter is to examine some of the factors that influence the educational outcomes for one of the most vulnerable and 'at risk' groups of young people, that is, those who have been in institutional care. We both have childhood backgrounds in OHC and are both former wards of the State, and both encountered significant obstacles to completing our education; we discuss these obstacles and account, as far as possible, for our eventual respective successes in overcoming these.

There is a vast body of literature on reasons why some students flourish, while others struggle. John Hattie (Hattie 2009; Hattie and Yates 2013) synthesized over 800 meta-analyses of education research, mainly from social and cognitive psychology, and found that a child's achievement is influenced by a multitude of interacting factors such as teacher expertise, teacher personality, teacher–student relationships, parent–teacher relationships, student motivation and cognitive mindset. However, psychological variables alone do not explain the extraordinarily unequal outcomes from schooling globally. The circumstances in which children are located are at least equally important—the socio-economic background of children and their families, the experiences they have before enrolment, what they go home to at the end of each day, the expectations and demands of their teachers, the support systems and communication networks in which the children are enmeshed, and, perhaps most importantly, the resources made available for schooling (Lamb et al. 2010; Teese et al. 2007).

Some children are more unequal than others. Extensive research 'consistently shows that children in residential and foster care fall progressively behind those living with their own families, and leave school with few qualifications, if any' (Jackson 1994, p. 267). This basic finding has been reiterated many times since Jackson's early work (Australian Institute of Health and Welfare 2011; Dill and Flynn 2012; Hojer et al. 2008; Jackson and Cameron 2009; McDowall 2013a; Townsend 2011; Trout et al. 2008). Underachievement among care leavers is a problem internationally. For example, the European Union's YiPPEE (Young people from a public care background pathways to education in Europe) project, which examined data in England, Denmark, Sweden, Spain and Hungary, confirmed that in each country, young people in public care were severely disadvantaged educationally in comparison with others in their age cohort (Jackson and Cameron 2012).

The growing body of research points to clusters of obstacles to school achievement at all the critical points along the educational journey, beginning with conditions prior to State care (Mendes et al. 2011). Poverty, inadequate housing and nutrition and traumatic events in children's lives—physical, emotional and sexual abuse and various forms of neglect—are part of the story. Abrupt separation from family can, of course, result in long-term trauma, exacerbated in many cases when children do not understand the reasons. Some believe they have been abandoned, while others blame themselves. Most are bewildered, angry and confused. Some carry these emotions into school: they 'act out', get offside with teachers, are suspended, miss crucial class time and experience cumulative educational disadvantage (McDowall 2013b).

The care system itself puts additional obstacles in the way of vulnerable young people (Jackson 1994). Despite abundant evidence that stability of relationships with siblings, peers and adults matters a great deal to children while in care, welfare systems move socially vulnerable children from placement to placement, and school to school, often requiring them to make social adjustments at critical points in the education calendar (Allen and Vacca 2010; McDowall 2013a; Tilbury et al. 2009). Moreover, few children find adults who care enough to take a personal interest in them (Townsend 2011). Social and education services' failure to work together results in inadequate support for school progress. In many instances, there are no facilities for homework and tutoring is rare; while education authorities assert that personal planning is important, many children in care say they had never participated in making a plan and are not aware of their education plan even if it exists (McDowall 2013b).

Poor school achievement and early school leaving obviously result in very low rates of care leaver participation in higher education (Courtney et al. 2010; Harvey et al. 2015; Salazar 2011; Wolanin 2005), a problem seen internationally. Findings from the YiPPEE project showed that only around 8 per cent of young people who had been in care as children go on to higher education—about five times fewer than young people overall (Jackson and Cameron 2012, p. 8). This is relatively better than the situation in New Zealand (Abbott 2010; Ward 2001) and in Australia (Australian Institute of Health and Welfare 2011; Cashmore and Paxman 2007; Harvey et al. 2015; McDowall 2013a), and comparable with the Americas (Courtney et al. 2010; Salazar 2011; Wolanin 2005).

Among the features of the child welfare system that play an important part in producing this lamentable outcome, one in particular stands out: the poor standard of corporate parenting of children in care, as indicated by lack of respect for the children and often their families, abysmally low expectations and poor provision of educational opportunities. Research overwhelmingly affirms parents' significant impact on children's educational achievements. One major study from the UK, Ireland, Australia, New Zealand, the USA and Canada concluded that improvement in the quality of parent–child interaction is the factor likely to make the most difference to subsequent achievement (Harris and Goodall 2009). When parents are actively engaged, children are more likely to develop positive self-esteem, be motivated to learn, be positive about school and achieve good grades (Perkins 2014). At secondary school level, students whose parents are engaged in their schooling are also more likely to maintain high aspirations, including for further education and to build a career; longitudinal studies show that they are likely to achieve their goals (Gemici et al. 2014). Students whose parents want them to attend university are four times more likely to complete Year 12 and eleven times more likely to plan to attend university compared with those whose parents expect them to choose a non-university pathway (Gemici et al. 2014). Students whose friends plan to attend university are also significantly more likely to plan to attend university (Gemici et al. 2014). This confirms the importance of being immersed in a family and peer culture of high expectations, and many parents make an effort to ensure their child is placed and kept in such an environment (Gemici et al. 2014). In the face of this abundant evidence about the importance of parent involvement, it is clear that the corporate parenting in many out-of-home settings is woefully inadequate. To make matters worse, many staff members themselves are poorly educated and see no great value in schooling (Townsend 2011). Yet there is clear evidence that caregiver expectations and support are associated with higher levels of academic success for the children in their care (Cheung et al. 2012).

Many social workers, schools and, in a corporate sense, the welfare system itself do not hide their low expectations of young people in care. An inexhaustible supply of anecdotes recount former wards being denigrated, labelled and treated as 'low-grade specimens' from low-grade backgrounds (Care Leavers Australia Network 2011). Over time, through this 'soft bigotry of low expectations' (Harvey et al. 2015, p. 6), many children lose confidence in their abilities, develop poor self-esteem and come to blame themselves for their lack of progress. The body of research on all these matters extends over decades, but many of the issues remain unresolved currently (e.g. as evidenced in Australia in the proceedings of the Royal Commission into Institutional Responses to Child Sexual Abuse, 2013–2017, and the Senate Community Affairs References Committee Inquiry into Out-of-home Care 2015).

This paradigm of contemptuous essentializing has a long history, and its language was given legitimacy from the very top. For example, in 1942, between stints as Prime Minister of Australia, Robert Menzies was confident that middle Australia shared his belief that children should be treated according to the merits or faults of their parents:

> [T]o say that the industrious and intelligent son [sic] of self-sacrificing and saving and forward-looking parents has the same social deserts and even material needs as the dull offspring of stupid and improvident parents is absurd. (Menzies, in Brett 1992, p. 13)

Menzies' views were supported by information that was already decades old. For instance, in 1927, the Victorian Children's Welfare Department's Annual Report included a research paper by Dr. K. S. Cunningham (later, the first Executive Officer of the prestigious Australian Council for Educational

Research). Cunningham tested the intelligence levels of the children at the Receiving Depot and claimed that they fell into four clear groups, with the proportions being Normal (19 per cent); Dull or borderline (46 per cent, 'Can be educated within limits, e.g., often learn to read'); Imbecile (33 per cent, 'Formal education out of the question') and Idiot (2 per cent). Cunningham advised the Children's Welfare Department, it should keep 40 per cent of the inmates in institutions permanently (Cunningham 1928).

Cunningham's methodology and results were markedly crude even by the standards of the day, but remained unchallenged. No one suggested that troubled children ripped away from their parents and thrown into an alienating and punishing environment might be too distressed or traumatized to show their real capabilities. Sweeping claims such as '[i]t is usually discovered that children in institutions are educationally retarded at the point of entry' by a prominent social work academic (Tierney 1963, p. 42) prompted no examination of the reasons they should have fallen behind. Such was the ignorance and contempt exhibited towards institutionalized children and their families that, until the 1970s, medical scientists from prestigious institutes were given ready access to babies and children without the knowledge or consent of their parents (Community Affairs References Committee 2004). As we write, the Australian Royal Commission into Child Sexual Abuse is examining the experimental use of electric shock treatment in 1971 to 'cure' homosexuality (Royal Commission, Transcript 18 August 2015, p. C8495) and the administration of Upjohn's newly developed Depo-Provera as a contraceptive for incarcerated girls in the 1970s—decades before it was approved for mainstream use in Australia (Transcript 24 August 2015, p. C9474). In no cases was parental knowledge and consent deemed necessary, and the children were not of an age to give consent even if they were asked.

The Case Studies

The following case studies draw upon our experiences as children and adolescents in OHC, focusing particularly on the challenges we encountered to accessing and completing our education, and the factors that contributed to our eventual academic successes. As will be apparent, our experiences reflect many of the limitations and injustices built into both policy and practice, then and now.

Case Study 1: Frank Golding

From the age of two during the Second World War until he was 15, Frank Golding was a ward of the State of Victoria along with two older brothers. After placements with three foster families and two other institutions, Frank spent the rest of his childhood in the Ballarat Orphanage. Throughout this time, he was given no information as to the whereabouts of his parents or why he was in institutions. In later life when he gained access to the records, he learnt that his soldier-father had initiated this incarceration as a drunken act of revenge against his non-compliant partner. He also discovered that his reformed father and reconciled mother had made multiple futile attempts to retrieve him and his brothers.

Lack of respect for children in care went hand-in-hand with low expectations to render limited educational provision as the norm. A journalist inspecting the Ballarat Orphanage in the 1880s was well-pleased to find children being prepared for their 'natural' roles in life:

> The girls are taught and practised in all that pertains to labourious housewifery. They have to wash, cook, scrub, mend and make clothes, and at the age of fourteen or fifteen, turn out as useful little domestic help as the Australian house-keeper could desire.
>
> But there is more interest perhaps, at least to the masculine mind, in the education of the boys…It begins with good feeding and discipline. It proceeds to the ordinary state school education, but it goes on thence to teaching in gardening and farming, in various trades—indeed to the laying of the foundations of a sound manhood in the boy. (*The Argus*, Melbourne, 8 June 1889, p.10)

Little changed over the decades. The 1889 training regime was still the standard when in 1943, after short stints in three foster families and two earlier institutions, four-year-old Frank Golding became a long-term inmate of this same Ballarat Orphanage. As in many orphanages of the day, basic schooling was provided on site, up to the legal school leaving age (then 14) to complement the gendered out-of-school training that would prepare the inmates as domestic servants or kitchen hands, farm or town labourers or trade apprentices. The educators' style further exemplified the system's disrespect for their charges. Without parents to complain, classroom teachers could humiliate, abuse and otherwise debase the children in their 'care' with impunity (Golding 2005).

Some, however, saw the merit of providing a broader education for children in care. In 1946, the Education Department advised the Ballarat Orphanage that the children 'should go and mix with other pupils in the suitable post-primary schools of Ballarat'. The Head Teacher replied that none of the 18 children in Grade Six would progress to secondary school because of the 'extra responsibility' involved, and because of 'the prior history of the children' (VPRS, 14514/P/0001, 29/1/1946). Thus, Golding's two older brothers went on to Grades Seven and Eight on-site where they passed the time until they could be sent out to work—neither to a position of their own choosing (VPRS, 14514/P/0001, 11/12/1946).

In 1950, without explanation, Frank and three other children from the Ballarat Orphanage were sent to the High School on the other side of town. Thrust into a 'normal' school, rubbing shoulders with 'normal' teenagers, he, for the first time, came into contact with young people with aspirations for higher education. A vague concept of education beyond school level began to dawn. But that prospect might have remained unattainable, had the Welfare Department had its way. Decades later as an adult accessing his personal file, he was surprised to find this note in response to the question of the day: should the boy be allowed to finish Year 10?

> Undoubtedly, all the boys will return to the mother and Golding [Frank's father] in due course and it is just a question of whether he [Frank] should be retained and given an education at the expense of the State when his future earnings will probably be collected by the mother. (State Ward File 66851, 31.3.1952)

It is barely comprehensible to the modern observer that a Welfare officer should assert that a child's right to education ought to be sacrificed on the grounds that others might also benefit from that education. But his attitude reflected time-worn establishment views on the children of the

State as financial burdens. Seventy years earlier, a Royal Commissioner had given his opinion on what should be done with 12-year-olds who had been sent to school while in the 'care' of the State:

> [U]nder no circumstances ought they, I think, to be given back, as they sometimes now are, to the parents or relatives who have quietly looked on while the State was supporting them, until these have defrayed the whole charges of State maintenance. (Victoria 1878: 159)

Golding's parents had frequently sought the return of their children. Among the purported reasons they were refused custody was their unmarried status, and that their home was not deemed 'a sufficiently reasonable moral environment' (Golding 2005, p. 221). Frank and his brothers were what an earlier generation would term 'the living issues of unlegitimized sexual union' (Kammerer 1918). However, after many refusals, he was suddenly allowed, at age 15, to return to his parents—a matter largely of chance (Golding 2005).

Frank's mother and father had both left school as soon as they were old enough to get a job and had been locked into a life of poorly paid and unfulfilling, unskilled jobs. They had no insights into the formal education system, but they understood the instrumental value of qualifications and credentials. Thus, they were adamant that their son stay at school for as long as he was capable.

By a combination of hard work, his parents' unwavering support, the encouragement of one or two special teachers and a system of teaching bursaries to pay for books and other requisites, Frank successfully negotiated secondary school. Beyond that, his knowledge of career paths was very limited. The only way he knew to proceed further was through teaching scholarships provided by the State to meet an acute shortage of teachers. He did not necessarily want to be a teacher, but it was a respectable career, and he was happy to accept the reliable funding that enabled him to live independently. Success at Teachers' College resulted in a further scholarship to university, making him the first of his family, and certainly among the first State wards, to progress to tertiary education (Golding 2015a).

Several aspects of Frank Golding's post-school experience stand out. One was the continual improvement in academic results that came with successive stages of post-orphanage education. Beginning with solid passes, by the time he reached Master's level, he was routinely achieving high distinctions. This might suggest that many of the features of institutional life described earlier had kept the brakes on his early learning, but with opportunity and experience in the academic world over the years, he was able to find ways of closing the gaps between him and his peers. Alongside that was a burning ambition to prove that he could succeed, when the system had let him know for many years that he was not worthy. When he was young, he had never seen anyone study. Now his children, and their children, have never seen anyone not study.

Case Study 2: Jacqueline Wilson

Jacqueline Wilson was born several generations after Frank Golding, in the mid-1960s. Unlike Frank, her childhood experience of OHC consisted of a series of irregular and temporary placements, totalling nine in all over the course of her primary years, in orphanages, foster care and Salvation Army hostels. These periods in care reflected a dysfunctional and chaotic home life characterized by rampant domestic violence and repeated relocations as her mother tried to escape her abusive ex-husband (Jacqueline's stepfather).

As a consequence of such instability, Jacqueline experienced a radically fragmented primary education, attending a total of 20 different primary schools. This pattern of disruption began early, with several false starts to beginning school, and involved not merely changing schools but lengthy periods of non-attendance. The months at home threw her onto her own resources from a young age, so by the time she began school in earnest, she had already taught herself to read.

Jacqueline's secondary education also began inauspiciously, with a brief period at Heidelberg High, a notoriously 'tough' school serving the public housing estate in which her mother had recently found a degree of domestic stability. Jacqueline, by nature studious and with what might be termed an 'instinctive' sense of the value of education, stood out among many of her fellow students. Thus, her single term at the school was marked by intense teasing and bullying. A teacher who saw her academic potential recommended that she seek out a more scholarly environment.

In the absence of reliable adult mentoring at home, it fell to Jacqueline to hunt out a school that matched her teacher's vision for her and which had a vacancy. Many phone calls later, she found herself accepted into Vaucluse College, a Catholic school for girls several suburbs away (a distance requiring a bus, two trains, and over a kilometre walk). Arriving some months into the school year and with little idea of what was expected of her, she found that the teachers' assumptions regarding students' general knowledge, academic skill levels, cultural capital and overall scholastic mindset—what sociologists term *habitus*—made her acutely aware of the many gaps in her education thus far, and emphasized her 'otherness' in the classroom.

Jacqueline felt socially isolated from the other students due to a profound cultural, geographical and class divide; her socio-economic circumstances were never less than dire. Although the school's fees were at the low end for the Catholic system, they were well beyond her mother's budget, which led to a steady, and fruitless, stream of written reminders openly issued in plain sight of other students, detailing the growing account total. These were followed by equally regular summonses to the principal's office and pointed queries regarding the outstanding debt. Promises to pay were met with increasing scepticism.

Highly visible poverty—and its inevitable stigma—combined with increasingly robust financial demands from the school, eventually led to a loss of hope for Jacqueline's academic future. In Year 9, she was informed that the subjects she had completed furnished no pathway to Year 12. Her alternative would, therefore, be a 'secretarial' career or something similarly limiting. These dispiriting developments at school coincided with an escalation in long simmering domestic strife brought on by her mother's increasingly out-of-control prescription-drug addiction. At age 14, Jacqueline became homeless.

With continued enrolment at Vaucluse unviable, and her living situation parlous, months passed with no school attendance at all. For a young adolescent with a strong sense of the value of education and a conviction that it was the key to escaping poverty, the loss of schooling was extremely distressing. After perhaps six months, a social worker took an interest in the problem and suggested a very different school altogether: Lynal Hall, an alternative community school running a varied programme that enabled students to 'customize' their curriculum and build personal relationships.

The pedagogical style and benefits of alternative settings such as Lynal Hall for a student whose circumstances and background render them as the 'outsider' have been discussed elsewhere (Wilson 2013a). Suffice to say here that the school's ethos and teaching approach were very much what Jacqueline needed at that moment. The teachers and, crucially, the principal proved active, interested mentors prepared to go well out of their way to help students in need of special care. She felt, for the first time, that she fitted in both academically and socially and, to a large extent, was able to disregard her background, at least while at school.

This happy condition was to prove temporary, however, as she was still in dire straits domestically. Over the past decade, police, youth workers and social workers had regularly intervened in her life and that of her family, and those workers now put it to her that her problems would be solved if she were made a ward of the State.

It is a matter of record (Wilson 2013b) that that solution turned out to be a wilfully mendacious and absurdly simplistic forecast. Her caseworkers evinced no discernible sympathy for her academic aspirations. On the contrary, in fact, they had no respect for her as a person. They, and the system they represented, proceeded to put in place a whole new set of obstacles to her education. She found herself very much in a 'Catch-22' situation: the support and resources extended to her as a State ward were manifestly inadequate, effectively making it almost impossible to remain at school; at the same time, she was firmly told that a condition of her wardship—with all its meagre 'benefits'—was her remaining at school. The State, as her legal guardian, imposed on her the condition that she had to house herself, or face indefinite incarceration (Wilson 2013b)—then the system's standard 'solution' to youth homelessness.

So, after almost three years of hand-to-mouth subsistence and consequently patchy school attendance, Jacqueline had no choice but to abandon Lynal Hall. From then on, with her wardship finally behind her (she was discharged just shy of her eighteenth birthday), she drifted from place to place, menial job to menial job, enrolling in a succession of schools as a mature-age student in a continuing effort to complete her education.

Finally, at age 25, Jacqueline completed Year 12. A university offer ensued. Continued difficult circumstances prevailed, however, and a further five years passed before she was able to begin a Bachelor of Arts at La Trobe University. She majored in sociology and history, and threw herself into her studies with all the fervour of a person bent on catching up on everything she had missed, reading as avidly as ever, but now with the intensely focused purpose of the academic high-achiever. As a result, she graduated with first-class Honours and was awarded the University Medal. From there she went on to Monash University, completing her PhD in History four years later. She has since forged a successful academic career—like Frank Golding, one of only a handful of former State wards to achieve this.

Concluding Remarks

Both of the individual cases outlined above exemplify some of the huge and complex barriers and inequities facing care-leavers. In considering what led to ultimate academic success in these cases, however, it is apparent that both share a combination of highly motivated personalities—what Mendis (2012, p. 32) terms 'hopeful thinking'—especially with regard to obtaining an education, fortuitous mentoring from influential adults at crucial moments and simple luck. That these are what it took stands as an indictment of the system. Children in OHC experience their life as quintessential outsiders, and the system did, and does, nothing to reverse that. In fact, it is far more likely to exacerbate it. Both authors experienced, and were almost beaten by, a series of major, and gratuitously imposed, obstacles to achieving goals that mainstream individuals possessing merely ordinary or average aspiration and ability can realistically expect to achieve with minimal hindrance.

It might be thought that the historical cases cited above are relics of a bygone era, but evidence from very recent care-leavers suggests that historic attitudes continue to pervade contemporary OHC. In 2015, a care-leaver from the Youth Movement Initiative in Victoria told an Australian Senate committee that:

> There is such stigma attached to foster kids and to kids who are in care or who have had a care experience. We are automatically seen as people who come from a low socioeconomic status and that we are always going to be in that status; we are not going to get out of it, we are not going to achieve anything. So when we do, there is such surprise—and it is offensive. I never had any doubt that I would go to university, and it is just horrifying that everyone else does. (Community Affairs References Committee 2015, p. 97)

Another young care-leaver submitted that:

> …the fact that I managed to fight to get there and did eventually get in was a shock, because it is so unheard of…The expectation is so low from a community standpoint, from the departmental standpoint, from the agencies and the wider general public. (CARC 2015, p. 97–8)

While there is a continuing need to combat negative assumptions and stigma around expectations and aspirations for young people in care—and to provide resources and support for a greater number to enter and complete university courses—it is inspiring to see care-leavers making it 'against the odds'—the title of a recent collection of such stories (Michell et al. 2015). The 17 stories in that collection do not always have a happy ending, but they are all tales of 'tremendous courage, resilience and determination' (Michell et al. 2015, p. 10). Some of the stories show that it is still possible to get to university, and succeed, even after being forced to leave school at age 15. All the narrators are the first in their family to go to university. There is a strong sense among these university graduates that their stories provide an important message: 'If others can do it so can I; and if I can do it so can others like me. And the message for the care system? You don't think we can do it, but if you give us the chance, with the right support, we'll show you we can'. But it would be wrong to frame this discussion of success as a matter of individual resilience and determination. Opportunity is not often a question of luck. Nor does success come without systemic support and structured resources.

In a submission to the Royal Commission, Golding wrote about educational opportunity as a form of redress:

> Many survivors were not in a position to benefit from whatever educational opportunities were offered during their childhood and youth. Some feel that loss very keenly because their lack of education was not related to their intelligence or general capacity to benefit. In some cases, they feel it is now too late for them to benefit from attending further education classes or undertaking courses in higher education; but they are very keen that their children should have access to these benefits as a form of compensation for the trauma that has blighted their lives. In any event, apart from the instrumental value of educational and training qualifications that enhance employment prospects, there is a great deal to be gained from education that will help with personal and social development and the improvement of general well being. I strongly recommend that the Commission pay close attention to the merits of setting up a trust fund for scholarships and related support for education opportunities as an element of redress and healing. (Golding 2015b, p. 5–6)

We agree with the YiPPEE report that:

> Social workers and professionals tend to focus on the risks and problems in the lives of children and young people in out-of-home care. It is important to recognize the positive features, strengths and competences of these young people and their at times astonishing capacity for resilience. An essential factor to translate this into educational success is access to support and encouragement from at least one significant adult, not necessarily a direct carer, who can give them good advice, focus on the opportunities open to them and help them develop a perception of themselves as competent learners. (Jackson and Cameron 2012, p. 96)

To which we would add the following: support from their corporate parent—the State—which has a duty of care to see that the opportunities for children in care are no less than those given to their children by any 'good enough' parent. In this, and much of the preceding, the needs expressed and the deficiencies suffered are consistent with those identified by Kathy Mendis (2012), who, in her study of academically successful care-leavers, enumerates a series of basic policy imperatives that must be met if care-leavers are to consistently succeed. These include, *inter alia*, continuing and substantial financial support based on the actual needs of students; viable accommodation, once again taking account of real-world educational circumstances; assistance with material educational resources (e.g. computers); and personal mentoring and emotional support. Mendis (2012) notes that many of these conditions are met, or are at least under consideration at policy level, in the UK and parts of the USA. None is systematically provided in any state or territory in Australia. It should be noted, too, that such diverse and robust support mechanisms need to be in place from the earliest move of the child into OHC, and need to be continued *well after care ends for the young adult* (Jurczyszyn and Tilbury 2012). Only with such wholehearted support at government level can the profound educational inequities experienced by care-leavers be eliminated.

References

Abbott, D. (2010). Do supported transitions from Foster Care achieve better outcomes for young people? An evaluation of young people's perspectives and experiences of Dingwall Trust's Launch Care to Independence Service. A research report for Master of Social Work (Applied). Albany: Massey University.

Allen, B., & Vacca, J. S. (2010). Frequent moving has a negative affect on the school achievement of foster children makes the case for reform. *Children and Youth Services Review, 32*, 829–832.

Australian Institute of Health and Welfare. (2011). *Educational outcomes of children on guardianship or custody orders: A pilot study*, Stage 2, Child Welfare Series no. 49, CWS 37. Canberra: AIHW.

Brett, J. (1992). *Robert Menzies' forgotten people*. Sydney: Macmillan.

Caro, J., & Bonnor, C. (2012). *What makes a good school?* Sydney: New South Books.

Cashmore, J., & Paxman, M. (2007). *Longitudinal study of wards leaving care: Four to five years on*. Sydney: Social Policy Research Centre.

Cheung, C., Lwin, K., & Jenkins, J. M. (2012). Helping youth in care succeed: Influence of caregiver involvement on academic achievement. *Children and Youth Services Review, 34*, 1092–1100.

CLAN (Care Leavers Australia Network). (2011). *Struggling to keep it together: A national survey about older care leavers who were in Australia's orphanages, children's homes, foster care and other institutions*. Sydney: CLAN.

Community Affairs References Committee. (2004). *Forgotten Australians: A report on Australians who experienced institutional or out-of-home care as children*. Canberra: Senate of Australia.

Community Affairs References Committee. (2015). *Out of home care*. Canberra: Senate of Australia.

Courtney, M., Dworsky, A., Lee, J., & Raap, M. (2010). *Midwest evaluation of the adult functioning of former foster youth: Outcomes at ages 23 and 24*. Chicago: Chapin Hall, University of Chicago.

Cunningham, K.S. (1928) Report on intellectual status of children under care of Children's Welfare Department. In Children's Welfare Department and Reformatory Schools, *Report for the year 1927*. Melbourne: Government Printer.

Dill, K., & Flynn, R. J. (Eds.) (2012). *Educational interventions, practices, and policies to improve educational outcomes among children and youth in out-of-home care. Children and youth services review*, Special Issue, 34, 6, June.

Gemici, S., Bednarz, A., Karmel, T., & Lim, P. (2014). *The factors affecting the educational and occupational aspirations of young Australians*. Adelaide: NCVER. Retrieved from: www.lsay.edu.au/publications/2711.html. Accessed 12 Aug 2015.

Golding, F. (2005). *An orphan's escape: Memories of a lost childhood*. Melbourne: Lothian Books.

Golding, F. (2015a). Going to the shop. In D. Michell, D. Jackson, & C. Tonkin (Eds.), *Against the odds: Care leavers at university* (pp. 103–109). Adelaide: People's Voice Publishing.

Golding, F. (2015b). A response to Royal Commission. *Consultation paper: Redress and civil litigation*, 28 February.

Harris, A., & Goodall, J. (2009). *Helping families support children's success at school* (Save the Children). At: http://www.savethechildren.org.uk/sites/default/files/docs/Helping_Families_Review_of_Research_Evidence_(5)_1.pdf. Accessed 13 Aug 2015.

Harvey, A., McNamara, P., Andrewartha, L., & Luckman, M. (2015). *Out of care, into university: Raising higher education access and achievement of care leavers* (Access & Achievement Research Unit). Bundoora: LaTrobe University.

Hattie, J. (2009). *Visible learning: A synthesis of over 800 meta-analyses relating to achievement*. Oxford: Routledge.

Hattie, J., & Yates, G. (2013). *Visible learning and the science of how we learn*. Oxford: Routledge.

Hojer, I., Johannson, H., Hill, M., Cameron, C., & Jackson, S. (2008). *State of the art literature review: The educational pathways of young people from a public care background in five EU countries* (Working Paper 2). London: Thomas Coram Research Unit, Institute of Education, University of London.

International Labour Organization (ILO). (2015). *Youth Unemployment*. http://www.ilo.org/global/topics/youth-employment/lang–en/index.htm. Accessed 24 Aug 2015.

Jackson, S. (1994). Educating children in residential and foster care: An overview. *Oxford Review of Education, 20*(3), 267–279.

Jackson, S., & Cameron C. (2009, November). *Unemployment, education and social exclusion: The case for young people of young people from social care*. Paper presented to the YiPPEE research team, Brussels.

Jackson, S., & Cameron, C. (2012). Final report of the YiPPEE project WP12 Young people from a public care background: Pathways to further and higher education in five European countries. London: Thomas Coram Institute. http://tcru.ioe.ac.uk/yippee. Accessed 31 July 2015.

Jurczyszyn, R., & Tilbury, C. (2012). Higher and further education for care leavers: A road less travelled. *Developing Practice, 33*, 9–22.

Kammerer, P. G. (1918). *The unmarried mother: A study of five hundred cases, criminal science monographs, American Institute of Criminal Law and Criminology*. London: Heinemann.

Lamb, S., Markussen, E., Teese, R., Sandberg, N., & Polesel, J. (Eds.) (2010). *School dropout and completion: International comparative studies in theory and policy*. New York: Springer.

Lietz, P. (2010). School quality and student achievement in 21 European countries. In D. Hastedt & M. von Davier (Eds.), *Issues and methodologies in large-scale assessments* (pp. 57–84). Princeton: IEA-ETS Research Institute.

McDowall, J. J. (2013a). *Experiencing out-of-home care in Australia: The views of children and young people* (*CREATE report card 2013*). Sydney: CREATE Foundation.

McDowall, J. J. (2013b). *Young person report card: A national study, CREATE report card 2013 special edition*. Sydney: CREATE Foundation.

Mendes, P., Johnson, G., & Moslehuddin, B. (2011). *Young people leaving state out-of-home care: Australian policy and practice*. Melbourne: Australian Scholarly Publishing.

Mendis, K. (2012). Exploring ways in which to support the education of children in care. *Developing Practice, 33*, 26–34.

Michell, D., Jackson, D., & Tonkin, C. (Eds.) (2015). *Against the odds: Care leavers at university.* Adelaide: People's Voice Publishing.

Perkins, K. (2014). Parents and teachers: Working together to foster children's learning. *The Research Digest*, QCT, No. 10. Retrieved August 11, 2015, http://www.qct.edu.au.

Royal Commission into Institutional Responses to Child Sexual Abuse, Australia. (2015). *Case study 30*: *State run youth training and reception centres.* Melbourne. http://www.childabuseroyalcommission.gov.au/case-study/404f8386-a4de-4a6a-bea3-dd3a850b0b73/case-study-30,-august-2015,-melbourne. Accessed 30 Aug 2015.

Salazar, A. M. (2011). *Investigating the predictors of postsecondary education success and post—College life circumstances of foster care alumni.* Doctoral dissertation, Portland State University, Portland.

State Ward File 66851, Memo Mr Hodgens to Mr Devine, 31.3.1952, held by Department of Human Services & Health, Victoria.

Teese, R., Lamb, S., Duru-Bellat, M. (2007). *International studies in educational inequality, theory and policy.* New York: Springer.

Tierney, L. (1963). *Children who need help: A study of child welfare policy and administration in Victoria.* Melbourne: Melbourne University Press.

Tilbury, C., Buys, N., & Creed, P. (2009). Perspectives of young people in care about their school-to-work transition. *Australian Social Work, 62*(4), 476–490.

Townsend, M. L. (2011). *Are we making the grade? The education of children and young people in out-of-home care.* PhD thesis. Southern Cross University, Lismore.

Trout, A. L., Hagaman, J., Casey, K., Reid, R., & Epstein, M. H. (2008). The academic status of children and youth in out-of-home care: A review of the literature. *Children and Youth Services Review, 30*, 979–994.

Victoria. Royal Commission on Public Education (1877-1878) & Pearson, C. H. 1. (1878). *Public education*: *Royal Commission of Enquiry*: *Report on the state of public education in Victoria and suggestions as to the best means of improving it*, Melbourne: John Ferres, Government Printer.

Victorian Public Records Series (VPRS) 14514/P/0001, Correspondence Files 1946.

Ward, T. (2001). The tyranny of independent living. *Social Work Now, 18*, 19–27.

Wilson, J. Z. (2013a). Educational dissonance: Reconciling a radical upbringing and a conformist career. In R. Brandenburg & J. Wilson (Eds.), *Pedagogies for the future* (pp. 125–138). Rotterdam: Sense.

Wilson, J. Z. (2013b). Redeeming sites of injustice: Human rights and the forgotten Australians. *Public History Review, 20,* 148–152.

Wolanin, T. R. (2005). *Higher education opportunities for foster youth: A primer for policymakers.* Washington, DC: Institute for Higher Education Policy.

8

The Contribution of a Key Scenario to Care Leavers' Transition to Higher Education

Yifat Mor-Salwo and Anat Zeira

Young people leaving care are amongst the most vulnerable in society, facing a rapid and risky transition to adulthood. Care leavers are proportionally underrepresented in higher education, and there has been little research on those who have succeeded in integrating into higher education and on the factors contributing to their success. This chapter reports on a qualitative study that examined the key scenario of care leavers' successful integration into higher education in Israel. Semi-structured, in-depth interviews were conducted with 45 alumni of educational residential settings in Israel who were studying or had completed studies in higher education institutions. The interviews revealed three main narratives: (1) those who stayed at a residential care facility that failed to promote education,

Y. Mor-Salwo (✉)
School of Social Work and Social Welfare, The Hebrew University of Jerusalem, Mt. Scopus, Jerusalem, Israel

A. Zeira
School of Social Work and Social Welfare, The Hebrew University, Mt. Scopus, Jerusalem, Israel

© The Author(s) 2016
P. Mendes, P. Snow (eds.), *Young People Transitioning from Out-of-Home Care*, DOI 10.1057/978-1-137-55639-4_8

but the scenario they brought from home helped them integrate into higher education; (2) those who brought this scenario from home, their stay at a residential care facility promoting education became a tool for realizing it; and (3) those who did not bring this scenario from home, but staying at a residential care facility that promoted education allowed them to revise their scenario to include higher education.

The study results suggest that residential care facilities have the ability to help young people realize their key scenario or revise it in order to support their integration into higher education. Care facilities should make greater efforts to impart the value of education to help care leavers integrate successfully into society.

Care leavers are a vulnerable group of young people experiencing difficulties in various life domains. Many studies describe their transition to adulthood as a challenging and risky period. Research generally shows worryingly low participation rates of care leavers in higher education (Casas and Montserrat 2010; Courtney and Dworsky 2006; Pecora et al. 2006). Specifically, one comprehensive study conducted in several European countries indicates that only 7 per cent of care leavers enter higher education in Spain, and similarly, in Hungary, the proportion is 6 per cent (Casas and Montserrat 2010). In England, Jackson and Cameron (2014) reported an increase in care leaver participation in higher education from 1 per cent in 2003 to 6 per cent in 2010; this is still extremely low compared with the 46 per cent of their peers, who have not been in public care, participating in higher education. Similarly, Mendes and Moslehuddin (2004, 2006) reviewed Australian research and reported lower levels of educational outcomes among care leavers. In the USA, care leavers' Bachelor's completion rate was eight times lower (2.7 per cent versus 24.4 per cent) than that of the general population in a similar age range (Pecora et al. 2006).

A few studies in Israel also demonstrate the disadvantage experienced by these young people compared with their peers in the general population. However, it seems that the educational outcomes of Israeli care leavers are relatively better than those of care leavers in other countries. Zeira and Benbenishty (2008) interviewed 500 graduates of educational care facilities in Israel several years after they left the educational residential setting, and found that 14.8 per cent of graduates were currently enrolled in a recognized university or college, and 8.7 per cent had a Bachelor's degree. Notwithstanding this, a study that investigated the educational outcomes of an entire cohort comparing alumni of educational residential settings with the general population found lower rates of care leavers entering higher education (Zeira et al. 2014).

The difficulties experienced by care leavers in transitioning to higher education are often linked with other problems they have, even before leaving care, and expressed in low educational achievements already at earlier stages. Many care leavers finish their term in public care with significant educational gaps, and therefore their starting point is well behind that of the general population (Casas and Montserrat 2010; Jackson and Cameron 2011). Many young people leave the care system without a high school diploma (Casas and Montserrat 2010). For example, in the USA, one-third of 603 alumni of foster care aged 19 years had no high school diploma, compared to 9.4 per cent in the general population (Courtney and Dworsky 2006). Even care leavers who do achieve a high school diploma perform significantly below the general population (Department for Education 2014), and experience difficulties in transitioning to, and completing, higher education. In fact, many of them who do enter higher education do so many years after their peers in the general population (Casas and Montserrat 2010). This is mainly because care leavers experience pressure to enter the world of work, and to become financially independent much earlier than their peers who can rely on their family's support (Jackson and Cameron 2011). In addition, care leavers are academically underprepared, suffer low aspirations and lack support and guidance for higher education. Therefore, integration into higher education remains an elusive dream for many of them (Jackson et al. 2005; Jackson and Cameron 2014).

Despite the barriers encountered, however, some care leavers do succeed in transitioning to higher education (Martin and Jackson 2002). Only a few studies have examined such care leavers and the factors related to their integration (Hines et al. 2005; Jackson and Cameron 2011, 2014; Jackson and Martin 1998; Jackson et al. 2005). The purpose of this chapter is to examine the factors related to successful transition of alumni of educational residential settings in Israel to higher education as part of their transition to adulthood.

Factors Related to the Integration of Care Leavers into Higher Education

Over the years, there have been some attempts to identify factors that are associated with successful transition to higher education of care leavers. One of the first studies in this area identified factors associated with success in higher education among 38 care leavers in England who received different academic degrees (Jackson and Martin 1998). These factors were care and school stability; having learnt to read and write early and fluently; being with significant others such as a parent or a therapist who encouraged education participation, offered consistent support and served as a potential role model; and having positive relationships outside the care facility with peers, including with others with academic aspirations. Later, Jackson et al. (2005) conducted in-depth interviews with 129 care leavers who studied in universities in England. Similarly, they indicated that successful integration into education involved several factors: the personal characteristics of young people (e.g. motivation to succeed in school and to achieve goals they set for themselves); consistent participation in school and high achievements in school; and a positive attitude to school and support from their environment (e.g. care facility, friends, siblings, school). These factors have been echoed in other studies (e.g. Hines et al. 2005; Merdinger et al. 2005).

Finally, the European research project *Young People in Public Care: Pathways to Education in Europe* (YiPPEE) indicated a broad consensus among young people in different countries about the factors that helped them to successfully enter higher education. The most important factors from the perspective of care leavers were the motivation to have a better life than their parents, care stability and school stability, having caregivers who gave priority to education, feeling that there was somebody who really cared about them and their achievements and financial support and suitable housing so that they could pursue their educational goals (Jackson and Cameron 2011).

In summary, research into successful integration into higher education of care leavers has identified several factors related to their successful transition. Some of the factors are related to the young person, while others were found in external resources such as the biological family or the care facility, and the emotional or practical support that they could provide.

The Key Scenario for Transition to Adulthood in Israel

The key scenario is a concept coined by Ortner (1973) to describe a mode of action appropriate to correct and successful living in a specific culture. Every culture has a number of key scenarios, which formulate appropriate goals and suggest effective action for achieving them. The key scenarios lead the life of the actors in the culture. They formulate local definitions of the 'good life' and success, and also formulate key cultural strategies with which to attain these. The key scenario in the transition to adulthood in industrial societies includes integration into higher education, integration into work and establishing a family (Arnett 2000).

In Israel, the key scenario of transition to adulthood also includes higher education. It encompasses finishing high school, completing military service (two years for girls and three for boys), transition into higher education and subsequently into the workforce and establishing a family (Mayseless 2002). In recent decades, the transition of Israeli young people to adulthood, especially among middle and higher classes, but recently also among lower classes, includes extended overseas travel after military service as well (Maoz 2004). The present study sought to explore the role of the key scenario regarding the integration of alumni of educational residential settings in Israel to higher education.

Methods

Population and Participants

The out-of-home care system in Israel is somewhat different from that of most Western countries (Zeira et al. 2014). With a strong preference towards residential placement (as opposed to placing children in foster families), in 2013, about 75 per cent of the 9,186 welfare placements—due to child maltreatment—were to residential facilities and 25 per cent were to foster families. Additionally, in 2012, a total of 18,005 children were living in educational residential settings or youth villages (National Council for the Child 2014). Placement to these settings is voluntary, and is often seen as an effective and non-stigmatizing response to the unmet educational and personal needs of many children and adolescents from the social and geographical periphery of Israel (Kashti et al. 2000).

The study sample included alumni of educational residential settings in Israel who were studying or had completed studies in a higher education institution. Altogether, 45 participants were recruited (33 females) using convenience sampling combined with snowball sampling. They all aged out of educational residential settings following at least three years. Participants were 25–30 years old; 12 had obtained a Bachelor's degree, 22 were still studying towards this degree, five obtained a Master's degree, five were still studying for Master's degree and one participant was studying in a PhD programme.

Procedure

Because higher education institutions in Israel do not identify students as care leavers, participants were recruited by responding to a published call via social networks and through the universities. Requests were made to the educational residential settings to contact their alumni. Participants were also asked to contact their friends and encourage them to participate in the study, either by directly contacting the researcher, or by passing their contact details to the researcher.

The study utilized a qualitative approach. Semi-structured, in-depth interviews were conducted with participants. The interview guidelines were based on central themes previously identified in the literature and were pilot tested with a small number of care leavers who completed higher education. Each interview had two parts: first, participants were prompted to describe how they entered higher education. This approach gave participants an opportunity to narrate their story without any prior restrictions set by the researchers (Rosenthal 1993). The second part of the interview included researcher's questions to clarify and expand specific themes. At the end of the interview, participants provided background demographic information (e.g. age, number of years in residential care, level of educational training). Each interview lasted between one to two hours. All interviews were audio recorded and transcribed. The names of participants were changed. The study and its entire procedures were reviewed and approved by the Ethics Committee of the Hebrew University.

Analytic Plan

Using Grounded Theory (Strauss and Corbin 1990), we first analysed the data to identify a common factor that is related to the integration of care leavers into higher education, and their capacity to overcome the considerable challenges that they face. Here, the concept of *key scenario* evolved and rose to prominence. We then sifted through all the data again to find sequences, providing information about how the young people acquired this key scenario and what helped them realize it. This analysis yielded three main narratives. All analyses were conducted by the first author, and an additional independent researcher who discussed analyses and reached full consensus on the narratives, as per processes described by Kvale (1996).

Findings

The Israeli key scenario for transition to adulthood includes higher education. The desire to conform to this key scenario played a major role for care leavers in the study in the integration into higher education. They wish to be no different from other young people, and they perceive higher education as a tool for success and progress in life. Lena, one of the care leavers in the study who obtained a Master's degree, observed:

> This is what is acceptable in Israel… Most people I know which are Israeli born graduate high school, serve in the army, fly away usually to India or to South America, returning, going to university, graduate, establish a family, it is some kind of a scheme, some kind of pattern that people follow…you follow this like it's part of the natural life process here, somehow it feels right and natural.

Lena clearly describes the key scenario in transition to adulthood that is accepted in Israel: from graduating high school, through the military service, to extended travel overseas, then higher education and establishing a family. She, like other participants in this study, followed this path to correspond with the key scenario.

Analysis of the interviews revealed three narratives that portray different meanings to the place of the care facility and the family in the successful integration into higher education by acquiring this key scenario: (1) those emancipating from a residential care facility that failed to promote education, but the scenario they brought from home helped them integrate into higher education; (2) those who brought this scenario from home, and their stay at the residential care facility became a tool for acquiring higher education; and (3) those who did not bring this scenario from home, but by prioritizing education, the residential care facility encouraged them to change their scenario to include higher education. These three narratives will be presented in detail below.

Narrative 1: First of All—It's Home

This narrative pertains to the significant place of the key scenario acquired via their birth family. These young people came from families in which the key scenario included higher education as part of the way to progress in life. This key scenario had been clearly transferred to their children, and it acted as a compensatory factor to the stay in a care facility that failed to promote education. Dror, a care leaver from a facility that failed to promote education, stressed in the interview the major place of the key scenario that he brought from home:

> So I think first of all—it's home. What we got at home, even though I wasn't a good student, I knew that studying is something that is very important to my mother, that we will study because… because she passed it on to us that it is the key to… an important key to life.

Dror's words stress the importance of the key scenario he got at home to his integration into higher education. The fact that his mother insisted that education is an important key in life was a significant factor in his integration into higher education. Meir, a care leaver who completed his Master's degree and was about to start his PhD studies at the time of the interview, also describes the importance of the scenario he brought from home to his integration into higher education:

> There was encouragement from parents, I mean, yes, at the end you maximize the goals that people talked about their importance, even if you don't know it at the moment, it seeps… I remember, my father always was telling me… Because it was evident that I really didn't care about studying, and my dad was telling me you should have a high school diploma even if you hang it in the toilet, the main thing is to illustrate that the certificate was not important, but it's some kind of tool…

Meir showed that although he did not care about school while in care, the importance that his birth family gave to education as a tool for progress in life was a major factor in his integration into higher education.

This narrative emphasizes the major role birth families ascribe to education versus the minor role ascribed to this by the care facility. Dror highlighted the little attention that his care facility gave to education: 'I felt that somewhere their goal was not that we'll get good grades in high school... because it did not happen... Their goal was for us to be better people...' He further explained why he believes the care facility didn't emphasize education:

> It was more important for them to keep us on track than our academic success... but I think that's because there was such a diverse population, some had no parents, others were immigrants or had all kinds of economic problems, I don't know what, so, uh... you can't get the attention of everyone. You need some common ground, well... I will not say low, but the common denominator should be relevant to everyone, so... it was clear that education was some kind of a bonus.

Dror explained that the care facilities' failure to promote education results from prioritizing the response to various more basic needs of the young people. It was more important to keep the young people *on track* in terms of their emotional and social behaviour than to promote their education. This approach, as Dror later elaborated, puts him and his friends in an inferior starting point:

> I tell you that a lot of kids from this facility didn't continue to study. I have friends who have not completed twelve years of education. And because of the gaps... So on the one hand, I understand the devotion of the care facility... and on the other hand I know that as an individual you can lose in the way, that you can somewhere stuck a little.

Dror talked about aging-out of the care facility with educational gaps:

> When I finished high school I have no high school diploma. By the way, I think almost all of us had no high school diploma. Like, maybe 10 percent, 15–20 percent, no more than that... but you see as I told you that the standard that they set was relatively low that nobody really gave it much attention.

The involvement of birth families in the education of their children while in care is sometimes the only thing that rescued them from educational failure. Smadar, a care leaver who was completing her Bachelor's degree at the time of the interview, came from a family who was active in enabling their daughter to conform to this scenario. Smadar entered a care facility that failed to emphasize education at the tenth grade. By the end of her first year, she failed in almost all the subjects. She described how her mother's involvement helped her successfully acquire a high school diploma:

> 'Till tenth grade I was fine, average. Then in tenth grade I do not know what happened to me, I freaked out, I decided not to go to school anymore and failed in 11 out of 12 subjects… The truth is that my mother saved the situation there… I really, really wanted to visit Poland, to a journey, so my mom told me you want to go to the journey to Poland, no problem, but you should not fail in eleventh grade… then I said—well okay, I really improved… so I have high school diploma like that: at tenth grade I have no grades, at eleventh grade I completed all tenth grade's subjects—it's amazing, really good grades, and at twelve grade I didn't care, so my grades were fine…

Smadar's story also indicates that even if the care facilities do not promote education, young people bring the key scenario its importance from the birth families. The active practices and values of families that encourage education are, therefore, important factors in the successful integration to higher education.

Narrative 2: The Care Facility Made It Possible

Another narrative describes a care facility that promoted education as a vehicle for realizing the key scenario young people brought from home. Here, families instil in their children the notion that acquiring a higher education is important. However, because families had to cope with various difficulties (e.g. poverty or the challenges of migration), they could not provide their children with tools or resources that are necessary to bring this key scenario into practice. These young people stayed at a care facility that promoted education, thus, their motivation for studying met appropriate conditions that enabled them to accomplish the key scenario derived from their families.

Natalia, a care leaver who obtained a Master's degree, described the integration into higher education as an obvious step in life: 'I always knew I will get higher education... It's impossible without higher education, I was raised on it'. However, Natalia's mother's had difficulties in providing her with the conditions to implement this scenario, and she described the way the care facility enabled her:

> My mother worked very hard, we came to Israel... a single mother, she worked a lot, we went to the care facility because we did not want to be at home, because we were at home alone... Also studying in the care facility was cheaper for mom than if we were going to a regular school. In the care facility you get the books, notebooks, and stationary, you only to come and study. You need private lessons? You will have them... The teachers there really invested... If you wanted to do the matriculation, you could do it. They helped you in everything, just take it, everything is with a silver spoon, just take the spoon...

Natalia described the care facility as a place that provides whatever is necessary to promote education, such as teaching materials and tutoring. The concept of 'with a silver spoon' (i.e. being privileged) emphasizes the abundance she felt. Getting in the care facility with a motivation to study was perceived by Natalia and other young care leavers in this group as an opportunity to fulfil their educational aspirations.

Dana was another care leaver whose family emphasized education, but could not provide her with the appropriate conditions because of their poor economic status. Dana, who at the time of the interview had obtained her Bachelor's degree, describes her entry into the care facility as a result of her desire to access proper resources to progress educationally:

> I went to the care facility ah... because I really, really wanted to... I mean I had the motivation but... I felt in terms of the education, I was not getting enough in town as I can get elsewhere. I had eight fails when I came to the care facility, **eight fails** (emphasis)... I always felt it was not my fault..., cognitive level, that what the environment provided me in the terms of my home didn't match what other students in my class get, for example: computer—I didn't have... tutoring there's nothing to be said, even things

like writing a short essay was too big for me because I did not know how to write, my mom was working late, I did not have anyone to sit with…

Dana described herself as a student with motivation to study, but without the proper resources to succeed: a parent that could help with homework, computer, and so forth. As she describes below, getting into the care facility with the intent to study, in addition to the resources she received there, helped her to progress educationally, and even to achieve excellence:

> And I went to the care facility, my goal was to study, really, I was there to study and I can tell you already in the first semester I had only two fails, that it was an achievement for me. There were things that were hard for me… Huge gap… And the care facility really gave me support, as much tutoring as I wanted, every day they sit with you to do homework… So slowly-slowly I graduated with honors.

Dana's story, like the stories of other care leavers who present their narrative, illustrates the care facility as a factor that enables the attainment of the key scenario that was acquired at home and includes higher education. Care facilities that promote education became a tool for making the key scenario happen, or in Dana's words: 'they made it affordable".

Narrative 3: There It Started, in the Care Facility

The third narrative demonstrates the centrality of the care facility in the integration of the care leavers into higher education. These young people came from families in which higher education was not included in the key scenario of transition to adulthood. Living in the care facility is described as an experience that shaped their identity in various areas, including education. It changed the key scenario of their transition to adulthood by making higher education a target they should strive for.

Nava, one of the care leavers who was the first in her family to acquire higher education and had by the time of the interview obtained her Master's degree, emphasized the central role of the care facility in her integration into higher education:

> Well, I can tell you bluntly that what helped me most integrating into higher education is the care facility... Here you had an option, that even children who live at their parents' home who are millionaire do not receive: individual attention, all the classes you wanted to go, help in studying..., Here you have a library with teachers who come and teach and help you with homework, then it all together, you know, you're getting the help, you learn to believe in yourself and learn to know the strengths you have, so this what helped me most. There it started, in the care facility, there all the staff with all the process I went through here and then I realized I do want to study... Because studying by itself is the key... and... This is a key to open a door... but yes I want to do something with my life, to be **someone** (bold), not to be another one like the parents who works at the factory and barely finish the month...

Nava attributed her integration into higher education to the care facility. Like other care leavers in this group, she described in detail active practices of empowerment that the care facility undertook to promote her education. The care facility that Nava described is a place that facilitated the importing of higher education to her scenario. There she started to realize that she wanted to study, and that studying 'is the key to open a door'.

Also for Lital, a care leaver who was the first in her family who obtained a Bachelor's degree, life in the care facility was a formative experience: 'It just shaped my life in everything'. Being in a place that encouraged education allowed her to revise the key scenario of transition to adulthood in her family and to include higher education:

> If I was at home this (acquiring higher education) wouldn't have happened, **for sure** (emphasis), certainly, certainly, certainly, each time I spoke with them, even when I was at the most stressed time of my exams: Leave it, leave these studies, leave it, why do you need it? My house didn't support studying, do you understand? In my house it was like why are you studying? But it's because her (the mother) life story was hard, she married at age 18, had children and that's all, and she worked only for us, she does not know what is it... if maybe I was in a supportive environment, for sure it would influence... but no, they were not part to the matter at all... I think it is the care facility or that I didn't want to be what I saw in my childhood.

Lital's story, as well as the stories of other care leavers who present this narrative, indicates that by promoting education, the care facility allowed young people to revise their key scenario. Coming from families whose key scenario lacked higher education, they now view it as an important factor in their transition to adulthood.

Conclusions

This study sought to identify factors related to the successful integration of Israeli care leavers into higher education. The findings reveal three narratives confirming the major role played by the key scenario of transition to adulthood, which includes higher education. The first narrative describes care leavers who brought the key scenario from their birth family, and integrated into higher education despite staying at a care facility that failed to prioritize and promote education. The second narrative pertains to care leavers who attributed their integration into higher education to their stay at a care facility that prioritized and promoted education, and thus served as a tool for accomplishing the key scenario they brought from their birth families. The third narrative was presented by care leavers who did not bring from home a key scenario that included higher education, and the care facility granted them an opportunity to revise their key scenario to include higher education. These findings are consistent with previous research that found an association between encouragement to pursue education from significant others (e.g. parents or staff in care) and positive educational outcomes. Prioritizing education and positive attitudes about it are, therefore, significant factors in the successful integration of care leavers into higher education (Jackson and Cameron 2014; Jackson and Martin 1998; Jackson et al. 2005).

The concept of a *key scenario* is powerful because it describes actions of actors in the context of their cultures (Ortner 1973). Acquiring higher education is part of the key scenario in the transition to adulthood in most industrial countries, including Israel. The three narratives of care leavers who *made it* into higher education can teach us about the majority of care leavers that *do not* succeed to conform to the scenario of higher education. Given the various needs of many adolescents in care, professionals often give more attention to keeping them *on track* in terms of their emotional and social behaviour rather than promoting their education (Jackson and Cameron 2014). The background of children in care implies that many of them come from families that do not include higher education in their key scenario of transition to adulthood. When such young people stay in care facilities that do not promote education, they age out of the care system with significant educational gaps, which, in turn, work against their integration into higher education.

Keeping in mind the unique features of the Israeli educational residential system, the study findings show that care facilities have an ability to help young people realize their key scenario or revise it in order to support their integration into higher education. Care facilities should make greater efforts to impart the value of education. This could be done by providing active supervision and general empowerment of the young people during the stay at the facility (e.g. by tutoring, talking about the importance of higher education, supervising the educational achievements and being role models).

While the message from this study is clear, we would like to add a note for the future. The results of this study offer a theoretical corroboration to existing knowledge on factors supporting care leavers' positive educational outcomes and, in particular, their integration into higher education. These findings should be further explored using other research methods and larger representative samples. Finally, the results of this study could be an important step in efforts to improve programmes and services in care facilities in order to assist care leavers to reach positive outcomes and enable them to successfully integrate into society.

References

Arnett, J. J. (2000). Emerging adulthood: A theory of development from the late teens through the twenties. *American Psychologist, 55*, 469–480.

Casas, F., & Montserrat, C. B. (2010). Young people from a public care background: Establishing a baseline of attainment and progression beyond compulsory schooling in five EU countries. In S. Jackson & C. Cameron (Eds.), *Young people in public care—Pathways to education in Europe*. London: University of London.

Courtney, M. E., & Dworsky, A. (2006). Early outcomes for young adults transitioning from out-of-home care in the USA. *Child and Family Social Work, 11*, 191–198.

Department for Education. (2014). Outcomes for children looked after by local authorities in England as at 31 March 2014, https://www.gov.uk/government/uploads/system/uploads/attachment_data/file/384781/Outcomes_SFR49_2014_Text.pdf. Accessed 16 Oct 2015.

Hines, A. M., Merdinger, J., & Wyatt, P. (2005). Former foster youth attending college: Resilience and the transition to young adulthood. *American Journal of Orthopsychiatry, 75*, 381–394.

Jackson, S., & Cameron, C. (2011). *Young people from a public care background: Pathways to further and higher education in five European countries—Final report of the YiPPEE project.* London: University of London.

Jackson, S., & Cameron, C. (2014). *Improving access to further and higher education for young people in public care: European policy and practice.* London: Jessica Kingsley Publishers.

Jackson, S., & Martin, P. Y. (1998). Surviving the care system: Education and resilience. *Journal of Adolescence, 21*, 569–583.

Jackson, S., Ajayi, S., & Quigley, M. (2005). *Going to university from care.* London: University of London.

Kashti, Y., Shlasky, S., & Arieli, M. (2000). *Communities of youth: Studies on Israeli boarding schools.* Tel Aviv: Ramot (Hebrew).

Kvale, S. (1996). *Interviews: An introduction to qualitative research interviewing.* Thousand Oaks: Sage.

Maoz, D. (2004). *Aspects of life cycle in the journey of Israelis to India.* Unpublished Doctoral Dissertation, Hebrew University, Israel (Hebrew).

Martin, P. Y., & Jackson, S. (2002). Educational success for children in public care: Advice from group of high achievers. *Child and Family Social Work, 7*, 120–130.

Mayseless, O. (2002). Young Israeli men in the transition from adolescence to adulthood: The role of military service. *Studies in Education, 5*, 159–190 (Hebrew).

Mendes, P., & Moslehuddin, B. (2004). Graduating from the child welfare system: A comparison of the UK and Australian leaving care debates. *International Journal of Social Welfare, 13*(4), 332–339.

Mendes, P., & Moslehuddin, B. (2006). From dependence to interdependence: Towards better outcomes for young people leaving state care. *Child Abuse Review, 15*(2), 110–126.

Merdinger, J. M., Hines, A. M., Osterling, K. L., & Wyatt, P. (2005). Pathways to college for former foster youth: Understanding factors that contribute to educational success. *Child Welfare, 84*, 867–896.

National Council for the Child. (2014). *Children in Israel: Statistical abstract.* Jerusalem: Author (Hebrew).

Ortner, S. (1973). On key symbols. *American Anthropologist, 75*, 1338–1346.

Pecora, P. J., Kessler, R. C., O'Brien, K., White, C. R., Williams, J., Hiripi, E., et al. (2006). Educational and employment outcomes of adults formerly placed in foster care: Results from the Northwest Foster Care Alumni Study. *Children and Youth Services Review, 28*(12), 1459–1481.

Rosenthal, G. (1993). Reconsideration of life stories: Principles of selection in generating stories for narrative bibliographical interviews. In R. Josselson & A. Lieblich (Eds.), *The narrative study of lives* (pp. 59–91). Newbury Park: Sage.

Strauss, A., & Corbin, J. (1990). *Basics of qualitative research: Techniques and procedures for developing grounded theory* (2nd ed.). Newbury Park: Sage.

Zeira, A., & Benbenishty, R. (2008). The status of alumni of educational residential care settings in Israel. *Mifgash: Journal of Social-Educational Work, 28*, 95–134 (Hebrew).

Zeira, A., Arzev, S., Benbenishty, R., & Portnoy, H. (2014). Children in educational residential care: A cohort study of Israeli youth. *Australian Social Work, 67*(1), 55–70.

9

The Drawback of Getting By—Implicit Imbalances in the Educational Support of Young People in and Leaving Care in Germany

Stefan Köngeter, Wolfgang Schröer, and Maren Zeller

Introduction

Young people who grow up in institutions with public-sector responsibility (e.g. residential homes, foster families) are disproportionately affected in nearly all countries by social disadvantage and exclusion. Throughout their educational careers and on their way to adulthood, they are often unable to fall back on family support and are, in this respect, dependent on public infrastructure and extra-familial forms of informal support. As a result, the path to adulthood for these young people, as shown by nearly all international studies, is marked by many barriers to transition. Extensive research indicates that care leavers are one of the most vulnerable and excluded groups of young people (Knorth et al. 2008; Stein 2006, 2012).

S. Köngeter (✉) • M. Zeller
Department of Education, Trier University, Trier, Germany

W. Schröer
Department of Social Pedagogy and Organizational Studies,
University of Hildesheim, Magdeburg, Germany

As good school results are more than ever stressed as the key to a good life, low educational attainment puts looked-after children at risk of social exclusion during their transition to adulthood (Jackson and Cameron 2012). Although educational policy has been at the centre of European politics for several years, young people growing up under public-sector responsibility have scarcely been considered. Very few countries have developed government policies that explicitly support care leavers to pursue education beyond compulsory school age and to enter higher education (Jackson et al. 2005; Hyde-Dryden 2014). To date, German social and educational policies have concentrated on the integration of socially disadvantaged young people into the labour market. Consequently, the educational aspirations and capabilities of young people leaving care have been systematically neglected. One can find this lack of awareness of post-secondary education for care leavers in higher education institutions (HEI), in social policy and in care facilities.

The findings that we present in this chapter are based on the research study 'Higher Education without Family Support' (www.hei4cal.de), financed by the Jacobs Foundation.[1] This research endeavour was a collaborative project of the Stiftung University of Hildesheim in Germany, the Hebrew University of Jerusalem and the Bar-Ilan University in Ramat Gan, Israel. The study used a mixed-methods approach focusing on young people in care and after care. As one part of this study, in-depth, qualitative interviews were conducted. These interviews provide evidence that education is an important protective factor in their lives, as it enhances their self-efficacy, allows them to experience permanence and security, provides them with recognition from adults and helps care leavers to set themselves apart from peers and family members with low school achievements and difficult occupational careers (Refaeli and Strahl 2014; Köngeter et al. 2016; Melkman et al. 2015; Refaeli et al. 2016). A cross-sectional survey was used to examine the educational climate among older adolescents (16 years or older) in out-of-home care (OHC). This survey of 237 students is the first in Germany to provide insights into this topic.

---

[1] This research was supported by the Jacobs Foundation. We thank Carolin Jänisch for assistance in developing and analysing the survey, and our colleagues Katharina Mangold and Benjamin Strahl who greatly contributed to this study.

Review of Key Literature

International literature suggests that young people growing up in residential or foster care are frequently less successful in their educational and academic careers compared to their peers in the general population (Benbenishty and Shimoni 2012; Berridge 2008; Jackson 2013; Schaffner and Rein 2013; Trout et al. 2008; Zeller and Köngeter 2012). Research has shown that school performance and educational attainment of young people in residential care are generally poor when compared to their peers who have not been in care (Trout et al. 2008). The difficulties experienced by young care leavers are indicated by the high likelihood of them leaving the school system without obtaining a formal qualification (Berridge 2012; Brodie 2009; Stein and Munro 2008). This fact was highlighted in a study conducted in five European countries (Jackson and Cameron 2010). Overall, it is evident that young people in care not only take longer to obtain a qualification, but also achieve lower levels than their peers (Courtney et al. 2010; Jackson and Cameron 2011).

Research on the educational experiences of young people in OHC, which includes young people in residential and foster care, provides several explanations for poor school performance (Berridge 2008; Jackson and Cameron 2012). In many studies, it has been shown that pre-care experiences, such as maltreatment and neglect, a low priority on education in their families of origin and family disruptions, lead to young people performing more poorly when they enter care (O'Higgins et al. 2015). This is in line with findings on socially disadvantaged young people who have lower educational achievements than their same-aged peers. In contrast, more recent findings show how these results are related to failures in the care system:

> Even though less successful school performance may be explained by difficulties connected to children's and young people's situation pre care, it is still a fact that a placement in care has not compensated young people for previous difficulties and shortcomings at school. (Höjer and Johansson 2013, p. 26)

At the same time, residential care institutions are often not focused on educational performance but on behavioural issues (Gharabaghi 2012).

School-related factors, such as a failure to monitor attendance, learning problems faced by young people, a lack of services for learning disabilities and unsympathetic responses to behavioural difficulties, are also mentioned as obstacles to good school performance (Jackson and Cameron 2012).

The most recent studies on residential care throughout Germany are already several years old and do not closely examine academic factors (Bürger 1990; Baur et al. 1998; Schmidt et al. 2002). However, current statistical data can give some indication of the school attendance of young people in, and after, care. These data suggest that nearly a third of young adults provided with residential care are, at the time their care ends, neither attending school nor receiving vocational training or career-related support (Köngeter et al. 2008). These high figures, particularly among the 15–18-year-olds, suggest that the number of early school leavers and school refusers is comparatively high among young people in care.

Statistical data also indicate that residential and foster care provides support for families in precarious life situations. A disproportionally large number of parents, whose children are placed in residential or foster care, are single parents and/or recipients of social welfare (Fendrich et al. 2012). Since there is a strong association between a precarious life situation and low educational outcomes in general, the low educational achievements of children in care are, to some extent, not surprising (Müller 2009), though not fully accounted for. Furthermore, psychosocial crises can prolong the time spent in education and/or training (Hansbauer and Kress 2012). There are two more recent studies related to the academic performance of children in care. First, Esser (2011) conducted a survey in six residential care homes and analysed almost 350 questionnaires (a 25 per cent return rate). In all, 10 per cent of the sample graduated from high school, and 5 per cent went on to study either at college or at university. Secondly, a study involving 378 participants in different fields of institutional care analysed the importance of schooling for the developmental process of children in care. This study demonstrated that better grades at school are closely associated with the well-being of children in care, and that this higher school attainment is connected with a trusting relationship between the young person and adults in care facilities and young people's perception of their ability and possibilities to participate in the care planning process (Albus et al. 2010).

Despite the challenge presented by the lack of research on this topic, it is notable that, in practice, schooling and residential or foster care overlap at some point. In approximately 50 per cent of all cases where child and youth services are offered, the initial assessment indicates 'difficulties with school and learning' as an important reason (but not the only one) why a young person is placed in residential or foster care (Fendrich et al. 2009). This highlights the importance of exploring ways in which schools and residential care facilities can cooperate in the child's best interests. Interestingly, Pothmann (2007) also analysed the connection between placements in residential care and educational mobility within the school system, which, in Germany, is a highly selective one.[2] He concluded that placements in residential care result in a stabilization of school attainment. He showed that compared to their same-aged peers, young people in residential care have to change to a lower school type (such as Hauptschule/lower secondary school or a school for children with special needs) less often. As a reason for these slightly positive results, Pothmann refers to other German studies that show how residential care has an impact on stabilizing the children's social environment in general (e.g. Baur et al. 1998). Interestingly, these results are, to some extent, in line with the meta-analyses recently conducted by O'Higgins et al. (2015). By analysing 28 studies from the UK, USA, Canada and Australia, they found that there is '…a correlation between being in care and educational outcomes, but this relationship is mediated by a number of individual, family and environmental risk factors…. There was little support for the claim that being in care *per se* is detrimental to educational outcomes of children in care' (O'Higgins et al. 2015, p. 5).

---

[2] After four years of elementary/primary school in Germany, children choose to attend either Gymnasium/upper secondary school (which leads to a degree that allows to study at colleges or universities), or Realschule/intermediary secondary school or Hauptschule/lower secondary school (both lead to a degree that allows to take on an apprenticeship), or a school for children with so-called special needs.

Educational Support in Germany

In 2013, in Germany, 189,414 adolescents (121 per 10,000 of under 21-year-olds) lived in a residential care facility or with a foster family. Evidence shows that these young people are systematically disadvantaged with respect to their academic and vocational career (Köngeter et al. 2008).

The basic federal legal framework in Germany for care of children and youth with problems is the Social Code, *Sozialgesetzbuch* (SGB) VIII. The central platform of this framework, pertaining to all young people aged up to 21 years (and in exceptional cases until the age of 27), is the child's right to assistance in their upbringing and education. The implementation of the state's policy is carried out by the statutory local services for child and youth care and education, and the communal Child and Youth Welfare Office usually implement these. However, SGB VIII explicitly draws attention to the variety of 'organizational bodies' that may provide services, and to the option of services also being provided by private bodies, meaning that the majority of child-raising support is performed by such institutions. Nevertheless, the Child and Youth Welfare Office has a major role, as it is responsible for the overall care management process.

Older youth and young adults have, in principle, access to the same spectrum of residential and non-residential care services as that which exists for younger children and adolescents. In addition, special provisions have been developed either in the form of (single or group) accommodation with social worker support (assisted living) or with non-residential assistance (e.g. counseling) (SGB VIII, Section 41). In particular, accommodation is provided for via assisted living (SGB VIII, Section 13) for young adults with a socially disadvantaged background who are enrolled in a scholastic or vocational education programme.

As part of becoming independent in the transition to adulthood, the entry into vocational training and employment is considered to be of vital importance. In this regard, for socially disadvantaged young people, who can be found in disproportionately high numbers in care, SGB II (basic job-seekers' benefits) and SGB III (employment promotion) become relevant. In particular, a number of new divisions have emerged in practice between SGB II and SGB VIII since the implementation of

SGB II, in early 2005. As part of these statutory guidelines, employable young people receive basic social services and partly pedagogically orientated assistance. Although SGB VIII has a clear legal priority of guaranteeing the best interests of the child, in practice it can be observed that town councils administer the provision of services for young people aged between 16 and 18 years considerably more strictly. Thus, more and more young people are being released early from care, and the legal scope of SGB II is being applied to them, which may lead to an increase in the implementation of tough sanctions for young adults under the age of 25.

The public discourse on young people at risk in Germany is dominated by the idea that socially disadvantaged young people have difficulties entering training and finding employment in the so-called primary labour market. Therefore, the vast majority of programmes for youth at risk focus on their integration into the 'lower' segments of the labour market.[3]

Programmes that address the challenges of entering HIE are mostly focused on the lack of financial support available to socially disadvantaged students. The largest of these programmes provides only financial benefits, yet the federal training assistance act (Bundesausbildungsförderungsgesetz, BaFöG) fails to take into account that socially disadvantaged young people need more than mere financial support.

A programme at the University of Applied Sciences in Frankfurt am Main focuses on students from non-academic families. Their collaboration with schools to promote HEI and to encourage socially disadvantaged young people to engage in higher education is particularly relevant to care leavers. This programme acknowledges that many young students without an academic background need ongoing social and technical support to continue their studies once they enter higher education.[4]

A recently published report by the Centre for Higher Education Development (CHE) in Gütersloh (Germany) outlines the different pathways for entering post-secondary education in Germany without having an *Abitur* (higher secondary degree). These options vary from county to county; however, the study options offered are largely directed

---

[3] http://www.bildungsserver.de
[4] http://www.fh-frankfurt.de/de/studienangebot/schuelerinnen_lehrerinnen/chancen_bilden.html

at qualified persons who are already successful in their career. In contrast to many other European countries, Germany's tertiary system still insufficiently attracts people from non-academic backgrounds or non-standard educational pathways (Nickel and Duong 2012).

This study is part of a transnational research project in Israel and Germany that examined the integration of care leavers who aspire to or have already entered post-secondary (higher) education. The aim of this study was to explore the educational aspirations of older adolescents in OHC in Germany, the social support they receive to pursue their educational goals and the factors that promote or block care leavers' successful transition to, and integration into, higher education.

Methods

We employed a mixed-methods design starting with qualitative, in-depth interviews with care leavers who had already entered HEI in Germany. The care leavers' personal narratives, which we collected in our study, informed the subsequent development of a survey among young people who were about to leave care. In this chapter, we focus on the results of the cross-sectional survey instrument to explore the perceived educational climate experienced by older adolescents in OHC. By the means of a questionnaire, youth aged 16 or older and currently living in OHC facilities were asked about several aspects regarding their educational status and further aspirations.

The survey included items on several life domains: general data about the young person and his/her family background (year of birth, gender, immigration and parents' education), their OHC, and their educational characteristics (e.g. type of school, grades, diagnosis of learning disability). A second part focused on the current educational support in school and care facilities. This included first a scale measuring the sense of belongingness to school. The scale comprised 16 items (four-point Likert scale), with four subscales (belonging, teacher support, peer support, and study support). Second, youths' perceptions regarding educational involvement and support of staff in residential care facilities were examined with a scale consisting of eight items (e.g. educational assistance and encouragement by staff). Third, a scale of four items measured the learning conditions in the facility (e.g. peer support). Finally, a third part focused on (educational) plans after leaving care and whether participants felt able to cope with future challenges in their education career.

The study sample comprised 237 youth in care from 37 different institutions. The questionnaire was distributed mainly in the Bundesland, Lower Saxony, but also in Baden-Württemberg, Bavaria, Berlin, Hessen and North Rhine-Westphalia. To collect information about children placed in care, the care facilities were contacted with a request to participate in the survey. If they agreed to take part, a package of blank questionnaires was sent to the institutions. It included instructions for the institution on how to distribute and collect the questionnaires. The study was approved by the University of Hildesheim ethics committee.

We studied a convenience sample, without structured or regional consultancy with specific institutions, and were dependent on the support of the staff in charge in sharing the questionnaires and returning them to the researchers. Institutions were individually responsible for the distribution and return of the surveys, and some variation in response patterns occurred. Most institutions distributed the questionnaires to the young people aged 16 and older, and requested their independent completion and return. Other institutions told them about the survey, and interested youth were asked to complete and return the questionnaires. Youths responded anonymously, but did so in a group context. The response rate was 94.9 per cent.

Findings

The study sample comprised 237 youth in care from 37 different care facilities. It included 33 from a foster family (14.7 per cent), 64 from residential care group on premise (28.4 per cent), 58 in residential care group in community (25.8 per cent), 57 in assisted accommodation (25.3 per cent), 13 in other types of settings (5.8 per cent) and for 12 youth data are missing. A small majority of the respondents were girls (127, i.e. 54.5 per cent). The age of the youths ranged between 16 and 26 years, but most of the participants were 16 (17.3 per cent), 17 (33.3 per cent) and 18 (22.1 per cent) years old, with the median age being 17 years.

Educational Situation

Educational Characteristics of the Youth

The majority of youth in our sample had already left school and moved to vocational school (32.9 per cent). A relatively low percentage of the sample attended the higher secondary school (Gymnasium), achieving an enabling degree for university entrance. The respondents who were attending a regular school (n = 128) were generally in the ninth or tenth grade. A history of attendance of special education (in special education schools or special education classes inside regular schools) was the case for 25.5 per cent of respondents. This proportion is significantly higher than that of the general population rate of around 4.1 per cent (see www.destatis.de, own calculations).

School Climate

Overall, the youth assessed the school climate as positive, and expressed a strong sense of belonging to the school (73.1 per cent agreed on this) and a high rate of satisfaction (72.3 per cent). In the context of teacher support, the overall assessment was positive, and agreement related to respect from the teachers was highest (84.2 per cent). A positive personal connection between students and teachers was perceived by 71.6 per cent of respondents. However, a relatively high percentage (18 per cent) indicated that others were making fun of them in school.

Educational Staff Support and Involvement

Overall, respondents assessed staff support and involvement in their studies as very high. This is evident in their perceptions that staff were interested in their educational performance (95.2 per cent agreement), and provided help for an improvement of educational achievement as well as assisting them in coping with educational difficulties (91.2 per cent and 89.3 per cent respectively agreed). The perceived assessment of the extent of the staff's involvement in encouraging youth to think about future post-secondary studies was, however, relatively low (65.8 per cent agree).

Study Conditions in the Facility

In addition to the above-mentioned support from staff, a large proportion of youth reported that they had conditions beneficial for learning. In particular, respondents indicated that they could access help for their studies (92 per cent agree). However, a much lower proportion felt that they were able to find friends to study with (59.7 per cent) or that their peers were interested in school (67.2 per cent).

Thoughts About the Future and Importance of Education

The vast majority of participants did not expect to complete their higher secondary degree (Abitur, the higher education entrance qualification) when leaving care, or were not intending to complete it (59.5 per cent). Rather, they planned to complete vocational training (51.3 per cent), or to commence work (28.4 per cent). A minority had educational aims such as school (16.5 per cent) or secondary school completion (14.4 per cent), but a group of 17.7 per cent planned to study in the future. A small, but significant, group planned to enlist in military or national service (13.3 per cent). A large proportion of the youth perceived future education, in general, as very important (59.8 per cent). Higher education was a goal for 34.6 per cent of the sample, but in contrast to these findings, the importance of higher education for their (future) children was very high (71.4 per cent). A third of the sample actively sought information about educational programmes for their future career (34.8 per cent) and invested efforts in planning their education (30.2 per cent).

Support of Educational Aspirations

To identify young people who were interested in continuing their educational career after finishing secondary education, we conducted a cluster analysis (Garson 2014). Cluster analysis is used to identify homogenous groups in a sample, by minimizing within-group variance and maximizing between-group variance (Wiedenbeck and Züll 2001). Our cluster analysis aimed at identifying the educational aspirations of young people who were on the verge of leaving care, and included three variables:

- School type (lower secondary, intermediary secondary school, upper secondary school, vocational school/training, special school)
- Expected degree at the time of leaving the care system
- Educational and vocational plans for the future (after having left care).

We conducted a hierarchical cluster analysis using the Statistical Package for the Social Sciences (SPSS) 22.0.[5] We excluded 33 cases because of missing values. On the basis of the dendrogram, we decided to choose a four-cluster solution, and validated this by a K-Means analysis. Cluster centres for the K-Means algorithm were chosen from the hierarchical cluster analysis. The clusters proved to be stable, and we proceeded with the K-Means cluster. We identified four clusters that represent different educational aspirations of the young participants in the sample:

- Cluster I: 'The pragmatic group' – 46 cases
- Cluster II: 'The interested group' – 45 cases
- Cluster III: 'The motivated group' – 55 cases
- Cluster IV: 'The weary group' – 58 cases.

---

[5] We chose the squared Euclidean distance as default settings for this procedure and presumed the dichotomized variables as metric. The single-linkage algorithm did not show any outlier. Variables were not standardized on the basis of z scores.

Cluster I (46): The Pragmatic Group

The first cluster is mainly made up of young people attending a *Hauptschule* (the lowest secondary level; 28.3 per cent) or vocational school (37.0 per cent). Despite the low number of people (three), 25 per cent of all special needs schoolchildren were in Cluster 1 ($SR = 0.2$). This cluster mostly contained young people (73.9 per cent) who expected to gain a qualification from the lowest secondary level. By contrast, only 6.5 per cent of those asked expected to take the *Abitur* higher education entrance qualification, and none thought they would leave the youth welfare services with a qualification leading to the upper secondary level. Most of the young people in Cluster I (91.3 per cent) were planning to enter vocational training after leaving the youth welfare services. None of the young people in the first cluster were planning to gain school qualifications or start work. Only a small number (8.7 per cent) saw further or higher education as relevant for their future.

Cluster II (45): The Interested Group

Cluster II particularly contained cases of young people attending *Realschule* (intermediary secondary level, 31.1 per cent) and vocational schools (35.6 per cent). A smaller number of the young people in this cluster (13.3 per cent) were at a lower secondary school or were not attending any school (17.3 per cent). This cluster mainly contained young people who expected to gain an intermediary secondary school qualification after leaving the youth welfare services (97.8 per cent) and then to complete vocational training.

Cluster III (32): The Motivated Group

In the third cluster, almost a third were schoolchildren attending a *Gymnasium* (upper secondary school, 29.1 per cent). Another 29.1 per cent of young people in this cluster were at intermediary secondary level.

Young people at vocational school (20.0 per cent) were also in this cluster. An even lower number were children attending other school types (10.9 per cent) or not attending school (7.3 per cent). Cluster III is also characterized by a very high percentage (52.7 per cent) of schoolchildren, indicating that they expect to gain the *Abitur* as their future qualification. All respondents in Cluster III aimed to attend further or higher education.

Cluster IV (52): The Weary Group

Cluster IV contained 28 young people at vocational school (48.3 per cent). Another 11 young people are at lower secondary schools, seven at special educational needs (SEN) schools and 11 more had left the school system or were in school elsewhere. Furthermore, 29 young people (50.0 per cent) expected to achieve a lower secondary qualification and 16 (27.6 per cent) an intermediary qualification. All the respondents in Cluster IV aimed to start work or gain a school qualification in future.In the following section, we consider how much support the young people in residential care experienced during their attempts to gain qualifications.

Educational Aspirations and Expectations

The state of the research on formal educational success among young people in residential care shows clearly that their expectations for the future are one of the most important factors influencing young people's scholastic situation (see Berridge 2008; Jackson and Cameron 2014). Our study mainly gathered data on the importance of future courses of higher education,[6] distinguishing between how important this kind of course is for the young people themselves and how important it is for their parents or the adults looking after them in residential care (see Table 9.1). What is of particular interest here is the expectations which other people placed on the young people and the extent to which these differed from the young people's own expectations. These expectations are important

---

[6] Ticked the option 'applies fully'.

Table 9.1 Importance of higher education

	How important is it for you that you have higher education		How important is it for your parents that you have higher education		How important is it for your staff that you have higher education	
	M	SD	M	SD	M	SD
I	1.82	0.89	2.05	0.99	1.98	0.83
II	2.04	0.74	2.02	0.84	2.05	0.69
III	3.15	1.05	2.63	0.89	2.47	0.77
IV	1.84	0.86	2.06	0.97	1.94	0.88
Average	2.24	1.05	2.20	0.95	2.12	0.82

not only because they reveal different interests, but also because they can affect young people's actual performance at school.

What stands out here is the fact that the expectations of staff at the youth welfare services were considerably lower than those of the young people themselves, or those of their parents. It is particularly interesting that others' expectations of young people who were motivated to gain qualifications were comparably low (M = 2.47; SD = 0.77). A similar discrepancy can be seen in the group of young people interested in gaining qualifications, who had higher expectations than their parents or the adults looking after them in residential homes ($M_{\text{own expectation}}$ = 2.04; $M_{\text{parents' expectations}}$ = 2.02; $M_{\text{youth welfare staff's expectation}}$ = 2.05) (see Table 9.1). In contrast, young people who are pragmatic about gaining qualifications tended to have slightly lower expectations than the people responsible for them. In other words, the adults around those who were motivated to gain qualifications have lower expectations while they are expecting more of those who are pragmatic about gaining qualifications.

Educational Support in School

In the case of difficulties with coursework, those who were pragmatic and weary about qualifications assigned a higher rating to the support they received (M_I = 3.51; SD = 0.63; M_{IV} = 3.31; SD_{IV} = 0.66), while participants in Clusters II and III perceived less support (M_{II} = 3.14; SD_{II} = 0.61; M_{III} = 3.13; SD_{III} = 0.60). Table 9.2 shows that support in school is significantly dependent on the school type young people attend.

Table 9.2 Support in school

"If I have difficulty in school I get help" (in school)		
School Type	M	SD
Upper secondary school	3.11	0.47
Intermediary secondary school	2.81	0.79
Lower secondary school	3.27	0.67
Vocational school	3.05	0.73
Special needs school	3.50	0.52
Other	3.12	0.49
Average	3.07	0.72

These data suggest that more support is generally provided in schools with less well-performing pupils. In SEN schools, especially, there is a strong pedagogical and social emphasis. Here, too, it can thus be seen that lower secondary and SEN schools, especially, appear to respond to pupils' difficulties with learning content by providing increased support.

Educational Support and School Climate

Significant differences between the young people looking to achieve different qualifications can be seen when it comes to the question of how well they get on with the teachers at their school. A large number of those who were motivated to gain qualifications had positive relationships with teaching staff (M = 3.18; SD = 0.59), whereas numbers were lower in the other clusters (M_I = 2.86; SD_I = 0.81; M_{II} = 2.67; SD_{II} = 0.82; M_{IV} = 2.82; SD_{IV} = 0.83).

There were also notable differences between the clusters with regard to social ties to their fellow schoolchildren. While those who were motivated to gain qualifications frequently felt that people were laughing at them, far fewer felt this way among those in the pragmatic group. Taking into account findings on pupils' relationships with their teacher, it can be posited here that young people who were motivated to gain qualifications tended to develop positive relationships with the teachers rather than with their fellow pupils.

Calmbach et al. (2012) showed that almost all young people, whatever their life experiences may be, see the relationship between teachers and pupils, or the teacher's personality, as important. Young people expect teaching staff to encourage their strengths and provide individual support for their weaknesses. This relationship may be of increased importance to young people in residential care, as they more rarely come across peers at upper secondary school with whom they have much in common. Teachers appear to have a mediating function, especially when it comes to the relationship between young people in residential care and their peers. For example, fellow pupils make fun of young people in residential care less often if they feel they are respected by their teachers (Kendall Tau-b = −0.173**; sig. (2-sided)). This correlation may indicate the importance of the teacher as a figure whose support may be able to minimize exclusion.

Support Through the Youth Care System

The following findings concern how well the youth welfare services were seen to react to young people's different attitudes towards qualifications. In general, it can first be said that young people in forms of residential care felt that they received support with school matters from the youth welfare services. Looking at the four attitudes towards qualifications and comparing the mean values of the aspects of support among the clusters, it can be seen that in six of seven aspects of support studied, those who were interested in qualifications felt the least supported. This difference stands out particularly in one aspect: while Cluster I (pragmatic about qualifications) and Cluster IV (weary) themselves judged that they received a high degree of support from staff in the children's social care services when they had difficulties with learning content (M_I = 3.51; SD_I = 0.63 and M_{IV} = 3.31; SD_{IV} = 0.66), the results are different for Cluster II (those interested in qualifications) and Cluster III (those motivated to gain qualifications) (M_{II} = 3.14; SD_{II} = 0.60 and M_{III} = 3.13; SD_{III} = 0.60).

Discussion

Our findings show that young people in care display a great diversity of educational aspirations. The stereotyped, one-dimensional image of young people in care who are not interested in their educational career must be challenged (see also Jackson 2013). In both, the in-depth interviews

(Melkman et al. 2015; Refaeli et al. 2016) and in the quantitative survey data, we found a broad range of different life courses, attitudes and aspirations regarding education and vocational training, and access to support from social work and other professionals.

Furthermore, it is important to highlight the high number of those young people who are interested or even highly motivated to continue their education after their secondary schooling. On the basis of our survey, we could distinguish four different types of educational aspirations: the pragmatic group was interested in basic educational attainments and planning to enter vocational training; the interested group aimed to obtain an intermediary secondary school qualification and planned further education or vocational training; the motivated group expected to receive a general qualification for university entrance and aimed for higher education; and, finally, the weary group was not interested in school and educational qualifications, but wanted to get a job as soon as possible. Almost half of the young participants in our survey were either interested in their educational career or motivated to continue with their education. The pragmatic group was still interested in completing a vocational training, whereas a subgroup of 58 young people seemed weary with education.

The high diversity of educational aspirations, however, is not recognized within the transition system, and particularly the need for ongoing educational support, especially for the care leavers with higher educational aspirations. Altogether, it is a major challenge in the transition to adulthood for care leavers to realize their educational goals. This is partly due to the system of social services in Germany, which clearly focuses on the transition to work, but not so much on the transition to higher education. After young people in care leave the residential care system, they will be supported by organizations and interventions of the so-called transition system (*Übergangssystem*) in Germany. This system—very often called a 'transition jungle'—is focused on young adults with low educational achievements. It covers all the educational and job creation schemes, which provide support in the transition to adulthood, but not the HEI. After finishing school in 2008, a total of 34 per cent of all young people who did not start university ended up on one of these schemes (Bundesministerium für Bildung und Forschung 2010).

Furthermore, our survey revealed that these institutional conditions discourage young people with a care background from continuing with their education. Our data support previous findings (e.g. Pfeffer 2008) that the family of origin and the social context in which these young people grow up are strong influence on their future education trajectory. Two clusters of young people (the interested and the motivated group) have more role models with respect to their educational careers and aspirations. However, they feel significantly more often alienated from their peers in school, which is indicated by a lack of friends in school, and the fact that that they perceive that they are made fun of by peers.

Even more surprising and significant was the comparably lower support those interested and motivated young people received from professionals in school and in the care system. One of the most important findings was the prevalence of low expectations among staff in the care system when considering the educational potential of highly motivated young people in care. Also, their parents seem to have lower expectations compared with the young people in care themselves. These low expectations correspond with significantly lower levels of support provided by teachers in school and by staff in the residential care system. The lower amount of support may be explained by the fact that their school performance is judged to be more successful. This finding would accord with previous research evidence that less is also expected of young people in residential care with regard to educational achievement. However, if others gave them more time and support, believed in them and expected more of them, their aspirations and achievements regarding formal education could be raised (see Stein 2012).

These results have to be interpreted against the background of limitations of our study. First of all, this is not a representative study, as we employed a convenience sampling strategy. For this reason, our sample may be biased, overestimating the proportion of young people in care who are motivated towards, or interested in, formal education. As our project emphasized higher education in the study title, care facilities with a focus on education may have responded more often than others. However, it is even more surprising that the groups of young people with educational aspirations do receive less support in such care facilities.

In summary, young people in care, who show at least some educational aspirations, face a range of amplifying challenges. We have identified obstacles on all levels. They experience themselves as outsiders in the educational system and receive less support to realize their educational aspirations. The expectations regarding their educational careers are focused on the goal of early independence, which works against participation in post-secondary education. This is reinforced by a care system, which reduces care provisions for young adults (Sievers et al. 2015) and emphasizes support for those who are in danger of failing to become independent. Finally, these young peoples' circumstances are perpetuated by a social service system, which is focused on employment and not on (higher) education.

These results have implications for both policy and practice. The transition to adulthood and the support systems relevant to this transition emphasize (as established in the German social code books) early independence and transition to work, as has been shown in the European young people from a public care background pathways to education in Europe (YiPPEE) project for several other countries in the EU (Jackson and Cameron 2011). Educational aspirations of young people leaving care need to be recognized and supported by social work practice. However, job centres and employment agencies must also provide support not only in the transition to work, but in HEI. As we know from previous studies (Montserrat et al. 2012), educational pathways of young people leaving care may be longer than those of non–care leavers, and this needs to be acknowledged. This delay in their educational careers is caused first of all by crises during their youth, but care leavers in their 20s need emotional support to cope with recurring crises. Another reason for delays in their educational careers is financial challenges. Only with adequate financial support can they take the risk to invest their time in higher education. Finally, social support through peers seems an important protective factor, as our qualitative data and other research suggests (see e.g. Hiles et al. 2013). In sum, a better understanding of the social, emotional and financial interdependencies of emerging adults (Mendes 2010) would contribute to improved and more sustainable outcomes of transitions to adulthood.

References

Albus, S., Greschke, H., Klingler, B., Messmer, H., Micheel, H.-G., Otto, H.-U., et al. (2010). *Wirkungsorientierte Jugendhilfe*. Münster: Waxmann.

Baur, D., Finkel, M., Hamberger, M., Kühn, A., & Thiersch, H. (1998). *Leistungen und Grenzen von Heimerziehung. (JULE-Studie)*. Stuttgart: W. Kohlhammer.

Benbenishty, R., & Shimoni, E. (2012). Educational achivements of children and youth in out of home placements and in community child welfare treatment. *Mifgash: Journal of Social-Educational Work, 36*(December), 185–204 (Hebrew).

Berridge, D. (2008). *Educating difficult adolescents: Effective education for children in public care or with emotional and behavioural difficulties*. London: Jessica Kingsley Publishers.

Berridge, D. (2012). Educating young people in care: What have we learned? *Children and Youth Services Review, 34*(6), 1171–1175.

Brodie, I. (2009). *Improving educational outcomes for looked-after children and young people*. London: Centre for Excellence and Outcomes in Children and Young People's Services.

Bundesministerium für Bildung und Forschung. (2010). *Berufsbildungsbericht [National report on education]*. Bonn: Bundesministerium für Bildung und Forschung.

Bürger, U. (1990). *Heimerziehung und soziale Teilnahmechancen. Eine empirische Untersuchung zum Erfolg öffentlicher Erziehung*. Pfaffenweiler: Centaurus.

Calmbach, M., Thomas, P. M., Borchard, I., & Flaig, B. (2012). *Wie ticken Jugendliche 2012? Lebenswelten von Jugendlichen im Alter von 14 bis 17 Jahren in Deutschland*. Düsseldorf: Verlag Haus Altenberg.

Courtney, M. E., Dworsky, A., Lee, J., & Raap, M. (2010). *Midwest evaluation of the adult functioning of former foster youth: Outcomes at age 23 and 24*. Chicago: Chapin Hall at the University of Chicago.

Esser, K. (2011). *Zwischen Albtraum und Dankbarkeit. Ehemalige Heimkinder kommen zu Wort*. Freiburg im Breisgau: Lambertus-Verlag.

Fendrich, S., Pothmann, J., & Wilk, A. (2009). Welche Probleme führen zu einer Hilfe zur Erziehung. *KOM Dat, 12*(3), 5–6.

Fendrich, S., Pothmann, J., & Tabel, A. (2012). *Monitor Hilfen zur Erziehung 2012*. Dortmund: Eigenverlag Forschungsverbund DJI/TU Dortmund.

Garson, G. D. (2014). *Cluster analysis*. Asheboro: Statistical Associates Publishers.

Gharabaghi, K. (2012). Translating evidence into practice: Supporting the school performance of young people living in residential group care in Ontario. *Children and Youth Services Review, 34*, 1130–1134.

Hansbauer, P., & Kress, L. (2012). *Übergänge in die Zeit nach dem Heim. Ergebnisse aus einem Projekt mit ehemaligen Jugendlichen aus den Erziehungshilfen*. Münster: Broschüre herausgegeben von der Diakonie Rheinland-Westfalen-Lippe e.V.

Hiles, D., Moss, D., Wright, J. & Dallos, R. (2013). Young people's experience of social support during the process of leaving care: A review of the literature. *Children and Youth Services Review, 35*, 2059–2071. doi:http://dx.doi.org/10.1016/j.childyouth.2013.10.008.

Höjer, I., & Johansson, H. (2013). School as an opportunity and resilience factor of young people placed in care. *European Journal of Social Work, 16*(1), 22–36.

Hyde-Dryden, G. (2014). Overcoming self-reliance and lack of expectation among care leavers in higher education in England: The role of inter-agency working. *Schweizerische Zeitschrift für Soziale Arbeit, 9*(1), 75–93.

Jackson, S. (2013). *Pathways through education for young people in care: Ideas from research and practice*. London: British Association for Adoption and Fostering.

Jackson, S., & Cameron, C. (2010). *Young people from a public care background: Establishing a baseline of attainment and progression beyond compulsory schooling in five EU countries*. London: Thomas Coram Research Unit.

Jackson, S., & Cameron, C. (2011). *Young people from a public care background: Pathways to further and higher education in five European countries*. London: Thomas Coram Research Unit.

Jackson, S., & Cameron, C. (2012). Leaving care: Looking ahead and aiming higher. *Children and Youth Services Review, 34*(6), 1107–1114.

Jackson, S., & Cameron, C. (2014). *Improving access to further and higher education for young people in public care*. London: Jessica Kingsley Publishers.

Jackson, S., Ajayi, S., & Quigley, M. (2005). *Going to university from care*. London: Institute of Education.

Knorth, E., Harder, A., Zandberg, T., & Kendrick, A. (2008). Under one roof. A review and selective meta-analysis on the outcomes of residential child and youth care. *Children and Youth Services Review, 30*(2), 123–140.

Köngeter, S., Schröer, W., & Zeller, M. (2008). Germany. In M. Stein & E. Munro (Eds.), *Young people's transitions from care to adulthood. International research and practice* (pp. 64–78). London/Philadelphia: Jessica Kingsley Publishers.

Köngeter, S., Mangold, K., & Strahl, B. (2016). *Bildung zwischen Heimerziehung und Schule. Ein vergessener Zusammenhang.* Weinheim: Juventa.

Melkman, E., Mor-Salwo, Y., Mangold, K., Zeller, M., & Benbenishty, R. (2015). Care leavers as helpers: Motivations for and benefits of helping others. *Children and Youth Services Review, 54*, 41–48.

Mendes, P. (2010). Moving from dependence to independence. A study of the experiences of 18 care leavers in a leaving care and after care support service in Victoria. *Children Australia, 35*(1), 14–21.

Montserrat, C., Casas, F., & Malo, S. (2012). Delayed educational pathways and risk of social exclusion: The case of young people from public care in Spain. *European Journal of Social Work, 16*(1), 6–21.

Müller, H. (2009). Heimerziehung und Bildungsgerechtigkeit: Rahmenbedingungen und Anforderungen für die Kooperation mit Schule. In J. Hast, D. Nüsken, G. Rieken, H. Schlippert, X. Spernau, & M. Zipperle (Eds.), *Heimerziehung und Bildung* (pp. 149–167). Frankfurt am: IGFH-Eigenverlag.

Nickel, S., & Duong, S. (2012). *Studieren ohne Abitur: Monitoring der Entwicklungen in Bund, Ländern und Hochschulen.* Gütersloh: CHE Gemeinnütziges Centrum für Hochschulentwicklung.

O'Higgins, A., Sebba, J., & Luke, N. (2015). *What is the relationship between being in care and the educational outcomes of children?* Oxford: Rees Centre for Research in fostering and education, University of Oxford.

Pfeffer, F. T. (2008). Persistent inequality in educational attainment and its institutional context. *European Sociological Review, 24*(5), 543–565.

Pothmann, J. (2007). 'Bildungsverlierer' – eine Herausforderung für die Heimerziehung. Schulbesuch von 12- bis 17-Jährigen in Heimen und betreuten Wohnformen. *Forum Erziehungshilfen, 13*(3), 179–188.

Refaeli, T., & Strahl, B. (2014). Turning point processes to higher education among care leavers. *Social Work & Society, 12*(1). http://www.socwork.net/sws/article/view/388/736.

Refaeli, T., Mangold, K., Köngeter, S., & Zeira, A. (2016). Continuity and discontinuity in the transition from care to adulthood – Challenges for social work research and practice. *British Journal of Social Work.* doi:10.1093/bjsw/bcw016.

Schaffner, D., & Rein, A. (2013). Jugendliche aus einem Sonderschulheim auf dem Weg in die Selbstständigkeit – Übergänge und Verläufe. Anregungen für die Heimpraxis aus der Perspektive von Adressat/innen. In E. M. Piller & S. Schnurr (Eds.), *Kinder- und Jugendhilfe in der Schweiz* (pp. 53–78). Wiesbaden: VS Verlag.

Schmidt, M., Schneider, K., Hohm, E., Pickartz, A., Mascnaere, M., Petermann, F., et al. (2002). *Effekte erzieherischer Hilfen und ihre Hintergründe*. Stuttgart: Kohlhammer.

Sievers, B., Thomas, S., & Zeller, M. (2015). *Jugendhilfe – und dann? Zur Gestaltung der Übergänge junger Erwachsener aus stationären Erziehungshilfen - Ein Arbeitsbuch*. Frankfurt am Main: Internationale Ges. f. erzieherische Hilfen.

Stein, M. (2006). Research review: Young people leaving care. *Child and Family Social Work, 11*(3), 273–279.

Stein, M. (2012). *Young people leaving care. Supporting pathways to adulthood*. London: Jessica Kingsley Publishers.

Stein, M., & Munro, E. (Eds.) (2008). *Young people's transitions from care to adulthood. International research and practice*. London: Jessica Kingsley Publishers.

Trout, A. L., Hagaman, J., Casey, K., Reid, R., & Epstein, M. H. (2008). The academic status of children and youth in out-of-home care: A review of the literature. *Children and Youth Services Review, 30*(9), 979–994.

Wiedenbeck, M., & Züll, C. (2001). Klassifikation mit Clusteranalyse: Grundlegende Techniken hierarchischer und K-Means-Verfahren. *ZUMA-How-to-Reihe*. http://www.gesis.org/fileadmin/upload/forschung/publikationen/gesis_reihen/howto/how-to10mwcz.pdf

Zeller, M., & Köngeter, S. (2012). Education in residential care and in school. A social-pedagogical perspective on the educational attainment of young women leaving care. *Children and Youth Services Review, 34*(6), 1190–1196.

Part III

Comparative Policy and Practice in Different Jurisdictions

10

Leaving Care in the UK and Scandinavia: Is It All That Different in Contrasting Welfare Regimes?

Emily R. Munro, Anne-Kirstine Mølholt, and Katie Hollingworth

Introduction

In the past decade, international research on young people leaving out-of-home care (OHC) has sought to analyse causes of, and responses to, a consistent profile of disadvantage and poor outcomes (Gabriel and Keller 2014; Mendes et al. 2014; Stein and Munro 2008; Stein et al. 2011). Initial mapping exercises, outlining legal and policy frameworks and presenting research and data on young people leaving care (Stein 2014; Stein and Munro 2008; Stein and Verweijen-Slamnescu 2012), have laid the foundations for more comparative work to assist countries as they seek to

---

E.R. Munro (✉)
Institute of Applied Social Research, University of Bedfordshire, Luton, UK

A.-K. Mølholt
Department of Sociology and Social Work, Aalborg University – CPH, Copenhagen, Denmark

K. Hollingworth
UCL Institute of Education, University College London, London, UK

respond to the opportunities and/or risks associated with globalization. This chapter contributes to this emerging literature and explores the transitions of young people leaving care in the UK and Scandinavia: clusters that are typified as operating contrasting welfare regimes.

The UK has been categorized as a liberal welfare regime by Esping-Andersen (1990). Classical features of this type of regime include private rather than collective or government responsibility for individual and family well-being; and strict entitlement rules governing access to modest public benefits. In contrast, the Scandinavian countries of Denmark, Norway, and Sweden have been classified as social democratic regimes, built on the principles of universalism and de-commodification of social rights (Esping-Andersen 1990). Esping-Andersen (1997) cautioned that the generalizations inherent in the models '…contribute to seeing the forest – rather than the myriad of trees' (p. 179), but, from the descriptions, it could be predicted that:

> Liberal regimes will pay particular attention to preparation for independent living…and social democratic regimes will be prepared to provide extensive after care support. (Pinkerton 2008, p. 252)

Although it is important not to overstate the homogeneity of nations in specific welfare regime clusters, one might hypothesize that young people making the transition from care to adulthood in Scandinavia would benefit from higher levels of public service than their counterparts in the UK. In practice, research shows that in the child welfare and leaving care field, the picture is much more complex (Backe-Hansen et al. 2013b; Bengtsson and Böcker Jakobsen 2009; Mendes 2009; Munro and Manful 2012; Stein and Munro 2008).

In this chapter, we draw on Pinkerton's (2008) model for international comparison to investigate the dynamics of leaving care policy, and implications for young people leaving OHC in contrasting welfare regimes (Liberal/UK and Social Democratic/Scandinavia). The model illustrates three domains, namely, the macro, the mezzo, and the micro. The macro domain refers to international social processes affecting states and indirectly affecting local practices (Houston and Campbell 2001). The mezzo domain consists of relations between the nation-state, welfare regimes and social professions. The micro domain contains the practices of everyday life. Dimensions of culture, politics and economics are included within each of the domains (Pinkerton 2008, p. 249). The figure below represents two countries within a global setting, with the young people leaving care placed in the centre (Fig. 10.1).

In this chapter, we first provide a brief overview of the global processes that have shaped, and will continue to shape, youth transitions. Second, we explore subsequent policy responses for young people leaving OHC and examine the degree to which leaving care policies in liberal welfare regimes (UK) and social democratic regimes (Scandinavia) conform to, or deviate from, archetypal regime types. Finally, we examine how mezzo responses influence the everyday lives of young people making the transition from care to adulthood.

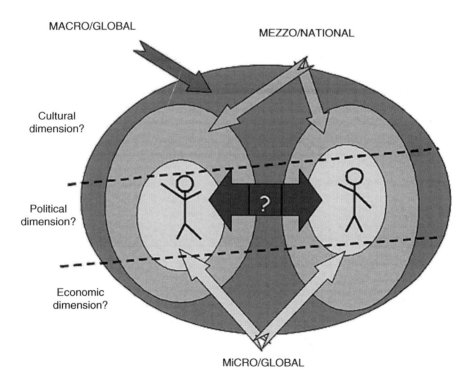

Fig. 10.1 Pinkerton's three-domain model for international comparison (Pinkerton 2008, p. 249)

Global Processes and Their Impact on Youth Transitions

Life course transitions need to be understood in the context of particular times and places. During times of rapid global change, cohorts of people at different stages in the life course may experience and negotiate these changes in very different ways (Elder and Rockwell 1979). Economic conditions, the state of the labour market and general levels of education play an important role in shaping the opportunities available to a given generation and the risks they are exposed to (Settersten et al. 2008; Walther 2009). Across Europe, recent global changes and economic conditions have served to disrupt many young people's life course transitions. However, it is important to recognize that trajectories and (poor) outcomes are not inevitable or 'impervious to political intervention' (Nilsen and Brannen 2014, p. 9). That said, since the global economic crisis in 2008, the number of young people not in employment, education or training (NEET) has risen among the member states of the European Union (EU), and is now at one of the highest levels ever recorded. In 2013, 23 per cent of young people, on average, were NEET, which is 8 per cent higher than in 2007 (Eurofound 2014). Although Norway is not part of the EU, the rise in the proportion of young people who are NEET also applies, but the rate of unemployment there remains slightly lower than in Sweden and Denmark (Backe-Hansen et al. 2013a, b; Bø and Vigran 2014).

The challenges and unpredictability of the labour market have not only prolonged school-to-work transitions, but have also influenced the timing and sequencing of other transitions. For example, young people tend to remain living with their parents for longer than earlier generations (Mølholt 2014; Yen et al. 2009). In the UK, 50 per cent of young people have left the parental home at the age of 25, compared with age 20 in Denmark (Eurofound 2014). Moreover, returning to the family home has become more common in '…cases of unemployment, partnership break up, or because other options appear more attractive' (Walther 2009, p. 123).

The option of postponing departure from foster care or residential care has not been routinely available to young people approaching legal adulthood. Thus, compared to their peers in the general population, young people leaving care have tended to experience *accelerated* and *compressed* pathways to adulthood and have had to:

Cope with challenges and responsibilities of major changes in their lives – leaving care and setting up home, leaving school and entering the world of work, (or more likely being unemployed and surviving on benefits) and being parents – at a far younger age than other young people. (Stein 2002, p. 68)

The timing and quick succession of these major events deny young people the psychological space to negotiate changes of circumstance sequentially, which is how most young people cope during periods of transition (Coleman and Hendry 1999; Stein 2002, 2012).

The risks inherent for care leavers during late adolescence and early adulthood are also elevated in a number of ways: they have to overcome pre-care adversities and disadvantages; they face additional obstacles to educational achievement; and they cannot necessarily rely on their birth family, or on former carers for ongoing emotional or financial support (Antle et al. 2009; Bakketeig and Backe-Hansen 2008; Jackson and Höjer 2013; Mendes 2005; Storø 2005). Transitions to stable and secure employment are particularly challenging, as the educational attainment of young people in care is lower than that of their peers in the general population (Bryderup and Trentel 2013; Cameron et al. 2011; Department for Education 2014; Höjer et al. 2008; Vinnerljung et al. 2005).

Arguably, given the risks inherent for young people leaving care, governments have a moral and legal responsibility to intervene to improve outcomes for this group, especially since the state was, in part, responsible for separating them from their biological families (Courtney et al. 2007; Mendes et al. 2014). In practice, states acting as corporate parents have responded differently to calls to improve preparation and support for young people negotiating the transition from care to adulthood (Munro et al. 2011c).

Children in and Leaving OHC at the Mezzo Domain

In both the UK and Scandinavia, many young people's life course transitions are being influenced by globalization and austerity measures. The impact of these changes on the circumstances of young people will be influenced by a complex interplay of social, political, and economic factors and mediated through state provisions and social welfare institutions at the mezzo level. There are ideological differences governing perceptions of the role and purpose of care, which serve to influence who enters the care system, how long they stay and the support provided when they leave (Bengtsson and Böcker Jakobsen 2009; Fernandez and Barth 2010; Munro and Manful 2012; Stein and Munro 2008; Thoburn 2007).

In the UK, the rate of young people in state care per 1,000 of the child population ranges from 5.9 in England to 10.7 in Scotland (Department for Education 2014; Scottish Government 2014). One reason for the apparently larger care population in Scotland is that children and young people living with their biological parents under supervision arrangements are included in the statistics.[1] Traditionally, Denmark has had the highest rate of children in care in Scandinavia, standing at 9.8 per 1,000 child population aged 0–17 in 2013, compared to 8.5 and 9.6 in Sweden and Norway, respectively (National Board of Health and Welfare 2014; Statistics Denmark 2013; Statistics Norway 2013). However, the rate in Denmark has remained stable over recent years, whereas in Sweden and Norway rates have been on the rise (Backe-Hansen et al. 2013a, b; Mølholt et al. 2012; National Board of Health and Welfare 2014). Reflecting the international trend towards reduced use of residential care, in both the UK and Scandinavia, the majority of children in care live with foster carers (ranging from 54 per cent in Denmark to 82 per cent in Norway) (National Board of Health and Welfare 2014; Statistics Denmark 2013; Statistics Norway 2013). Those placed in residential settings tend to be adolescents with complex needs and/or emotional and behavioural difficulties that can be difficult to manage in family settings (Bengtsson and Böcker Jakobsen 2009; Berridge et al. 2012; Hart et al. 2015). In Scandinavia, questions have been raised about the drive to increase the use of foster family care, and Norwegian academics have reflected that:

---

[1] It is possible to be placed with parents under a legal order in England, Wales, and Northern Ireland, but this measure is not used as often. See Munro et al. (2011a) for an overview of the availability and comparability of UK safeguarding statistics.

An additional reduction of residential care can easily induce that groups traditionally not seen in family foster care will increase the probability of placement breakdowns...A discussion of the role of foster families is necessary and who each type of placement benefits. (Backe-Hansen et al. 2013a, b, p. 232) (authors' translation of the original text)

In England, residential care tends to be seen as a measure of last resort, and concerns have been raised about skills and qualifications of the workforce, and its capacity to meet the complex needs of those placed (House of Commons Education Committee 2014a; National Audit Office 2014). The high cost of residential placements, compared to foster placements, particularly in the context of the poor outcomes achieved, has also featured in the debate. Perceptions concerning appropriate placements are shaped to varying degrees by culture and politics, as well as the economic conditions in each country. These three dimensions (culture, politics and economics) have, to varying degrees, influenced policy development and the opportunities open to young people negotiating the transition from care to adulthood.

In the UK and Scandinavia, the majority of young people leave care before, or at the age of, 18 years, although in some circumstances it is possible for them to remain with their carers until their early 20s (Backe-Hansen et al. 2013a, b; Children and Families Act 2014; Children and Young People (Scotland) Act 2014; Social Services and Well-being (Wales) Act 2014). In Northern Ireland, recent data show that 10 per cent of young adults on the *Going the Extra Mile Scheme* remain with their foster carers beyond the age of 21 (Coyle 2015).

Across the UK, local authorities' responsibilities towards young people leaving care have grown considerably in the past 20 years. Top-down legislation and regulation has been a vehicle to support implementation of targeted services and support of young people leaving care. While preparation for leaving care is a central plank of the policy framework, so too is aftercare support from leaving care personal advisers. Broadly speaking, these changes have sought to move beyond *accelerated* and *compressed* transitions to *extended* and *graduated* transitions. That is, legal and policy developments have sought to ensure that young people leaving OHC are prepared and equipped with the skills to live independently, and have extended entitlement to accommodation and/or social work support into early adulthood.[2] This more direct and generous state intervention does not conform to the traditions of liberal welfare regime types, which classically feature individual responsibility. However, it is noteworthy that extended support may be conditional upon fulfilment of certain conditions (e.g. engagement or re-engagement with EET), which is more in keeping with conditional entitlement to modest benefits.

Arguably, across the UK, a cluster of political and economic factors has served as a catalyst for policy development. First, administrative data and research have heightened awareness of the poor outcomes experienced by young people leaving care (Biehal et al. 1995; Broad 1998; Department for Education 2014; Dixon and Stein 2005; Jackson and Cameron 2012). Second, there has been a political orientation towards investing in children and young people, and particularly those at high risk of social exclusion or low educational achievement, to reduce the likelihood of long-term and costly reliance on the welfare state in adulthood (Fawcett et al. 2003; Williams 2004).

In England, for example, political debates preceding implementation of the Children (Leaving Care) Act 2000 signalled an acceptance that the state has *assumed* and has *reparatory* responsibilities towards young people in and leaving care (Hollingsworth 2012). The former is grounded in a belief that having voluntarily accommodated or compulsorily removed children from their birth families, the state has a duty to fulfil the parenting role to the best of its ability, and, in doing so, there is a need to recognize that this role extends beyond young people's eighteenth birthdays. The latter principle demonstrates an acknowledgement that as a matter of social justice, children in OHC are owed support to *redress harm* caused prior to entry and/or as a result of weaknesses in quality of care provided by the corporate parent. Charities and members of parliament have also lobbied the government when they have perceived that there are inequities or gaps in provision to meet the needs of young people leaving care

---

[2] This top-down prescription will encounter a practice 'reality' (Preston-Shoot 2001 p.13), and local authorities may struggle to implement changes on the front-line, particularly given that extended duties have come during a period of extensive budget cuts.

(House of Commons Education Select Committee 2014b; Voices from Care Wales 2012).

The targeted legislation that has been introduced across the UK has imposed new duties on local authorities, and compelled them to provide specific services and support. Legislative changes have also supported the development of specialist services and contributed to the establishment of multi-agency teams in some areas, with housing, employment and health specialists working alongside leaving care personal advisers (Stein 2012).

Going the Extra Mile (GEM), the first scheme permitting young people to stay in their *foster care placements* beyond the age of 18, was introduced in Northern Ireland in 2006 (McCrea 2008). Twenty-eight per cent of former relevant children stay with their foster carers beyond the age of 18, a higher percentage than in other parts of the UK (Coyle 2015; Department for Education 2014). More recently, England, Scotland, and Wales have piloted and subsequently implemented similar schemes, and placed these on a statutory footing (Children & Families, Act 2014 section 98; Children &Young People [Scotland] Act 2014 part 10; Munro et al. 2012; Social Services and Well-being (Wales) Act 2014 section 108; Children &Young People [Scotland] Act 2014 part 10). So far, Scotland is the only jurisdiction in which young people can remain in *residential care* up to the age of 21, even though young people in these placements tend to have the most complex needs (Hart et al. 2015).

In Denmark, Norway and Sweden, there are no specific Acts governing the provision of services to prepare and support young people leaving care, but they are referred to in the general child welfare legislation. It has been argued that 'care leavers may "disappear" in a welfare system based on universalistic distribution of services' (Backe-Hansen et al. 2013a, b, pp. 200–201). Decisions on the arrangements of aftercare support for care leavers are less prescribed than in the UK. Case-by-case decision-making by frontline workers is influential in shaping the support young people receive, but this can be affected by differences in local resources (Ejrnæs et al. 2010; Mølholt et al. 2012; Oterholm 2008, 2015).

The Danish Act is the most specific of the three Scandinavian child welfare acts, and the Swedish the least so. In Denmark, specific reference is made to the time at which the municipality must decide whether a young person leaving care has a need for aftercare support, and four types of aftercare support are outlined (Socialministeriet 2011). In contrast, in Sweden, there is no mandatory legislation governing aftercare. Aftercare decisions are decentralized to municipal social services, and thus the support young people receive varies significantly in different localities, depending upon local resources and the attitudes of individual social workers (Backe-Hansen et al. 2013a, b; Höjer and Sjöblom 2014). This affords flexibility, but does not guarantee entitlement to the substantial aftercare support one would anticipate provision of in social democratic welfare regimes.

Young People's Voices: Everyday Experiences in the Micro Domain

Despite considerable differences in legal and policy frameworks affecting youth transitions in general, and those of young people leaving care more specifically, research in Western Europe, Australia, Canada and the USA highlights that the experiences of young people leaving care in the micro domain are remarkably consistent (Stein and Munro 2008). This section highlights a number of recurring themes in the narratives of young people leaving care in Scandinavia and the UK.

From a life course perspective, it is important that people experience a 'goodness of fit' between their plans for the life course and the timing and pacing of key events and transitions (Elder 1995, p. 115). Although the *UN Guidelines for the Alternative Care of Children* (General Assembly of the United Nations 2010) specify that states should take into consideration children's age, gender, maturity, and particular circumstances in the process of transition from care to aftercare, and legal and policy frameworks acknowledge the importance of young people's active participation in decisions affecting their lives, in practice, many young people continue to experience age-related transitions to semi-independent or independent living due to administrative rules and regulations (Höjer and Sjöblom 2014; Mølholt et al. 2012; Munro et al. 2011b, 2012). In both the UK and Scandinavia, young people may feel that they have little or no choice about the timing of their transition, as one young woman in England reflected[3]:

> I didn't want to go. I still had to go anyway. I didn't have a choice...I was moving out at eighteen, end of discussion, and the bit that really pissed me [off] is [that] they chucked me out on my eighteenth birthday. (Young woman, England in Munro et al. 2011b, p. 21)

Similar messages feature in Danish and Swedish research, as the quotes below illustrate:

> I left care at age 17 1/2. But I couldn't move back to my mom, 'cause that's where it all went wrong… A contact person supported me until I turned 18, then I was on my own. But I couldn't take care of myself…I felt lost. It was a nightmare. (Young woman, Denmark in Mølholt 2017)

A young man in a Swedish study reflected that:

> The care stopped because I turned 18 years old and it was time to move on. The social services did not want to pay for me any longer…But really I would like to have stayed in that foster home… I would have preferred to stay there until I had finished my education at college…I didn't feel ready to move out on my own. (Gunnar, Sweden in Höjer and Sjöblom 2014, p. 35)

These experiences also highlight that although the principle that young people should be active participants in social work decision-making processes is embedded in child welfare legislation in the UK and Scandinavia, frontline practice is highly varied.

Qualitative research findings show that professionals and young people often have different views on whether the young people have been active participants in decision-making processes (Mølholt et al. 2012; Munro et al. 2011b; Oterholm 2008). While child welfare services emphasize that they have engaged and involved the young people per the require-

---

[3] In England, the option of remaining in placement beyond 18 years is not available to young people leaving residential care, and the option of staying put with foster carers is conditional upon the carer being willing and able to extend the placement.

ments of the law, young people do not necessarily experience participation or consider that they are able to influence decisions concerning their care or aftercare (Binde 2008; Bratterud et al. 2006; Egelund et al. 2005; Höjer and Sjöblom 2014; Jackson et al. 2005). Furthermore, the decisions or options on offer do not always seem relevant to young people in the here and now (Böcker Jakobsen et al. 2010; Oterholm 2008).

Lack of provision of the help and support that are wanted and needed can be a source of frustration to young people. The following account from a young Danish woman emphasizes how she experiences that she cannot get the help that she needs, since it is not part of the aftercare services provided by the state:

> It's probably the family-relation thing that we often need, and the law and society isn't always built for that. We [young people leaving care] often behave inappropriately because we become frustrated. I mean, I can only talk from my own experiences, but it's definitely a huge problem in my world, that it is often a contact person and practical help that I'm offered… So the help that I seek, or what I need…they can't give me. (Young woman who has left care, Denmark in Mølholt 2017)

This reflection also highlights a mismatch between children's services orientation towards providing financial or practical help and the importance young people place on relationships and emotional support.

Discontinuities and difficult transitions in life are easier to deal with if young people have resources, attributes,[4] and what has been termed by Simmons et al. (1987) as, 'arenas of comfort' in which they can find sanctuary. Supportive relationships are recurrent features within positive leaving care discourses (Cameron et al. 2011; Egelund Nielsen et al. 2005; Höjer and Sjöblom 2014; Jackson et al. 2005; Munro et al. 2012). Research findings from the UK and Scandinavian countries show that some young people in foster care experience a secure stable base and benefit from feeling that they are accepted and are part of the family (Höjer and Sjöblom 2014; Munro et al. 2012). These young people acknowledge that their foster families provide an important source of ongoing

---

[4] For example, self-worth, self-perceived social acceptance, and social support (Grills-Taquechel et al. 2011; Simmons et al. 1987).

support as they negotiate the transition to adulthood and independence. For example, an interviewee in Höjer and Sjöblom's study of leaving care in Sweden explained:

> I was like a son in the house so I knew I could come back home if I wanted to, so I had a permanent place in that family. (Höjer and Sjöblom 2014, p. 41)

Research examining the educational pathways of young people leaving care in England, Sweden, and Denmark also highlights the importance of supportive, long-term, and stable care in facilitating successful transitions to independence and educational success (Bryderup and Trentel 2013; Cameron et al. 2011; Jackson and Cameron 2012; Jackson et al. 2005). Jackson et al. (2005) found that care leavers with the fewest problems, and who made the most successful transitions, were those who had a successful final foster placement, which provided an ongoing secure base after moving to university or independent living. Continuing support (emotional, practical, and, in some cases, financial) from foster carers during and after this transition was a key protective factor helping to ameliorate the young person's feelings of stress and loneliness. Knowing they had this ongoing support and 'arena of comfort' to fall back on, similar to the parental support afforded to their non-care peers, made the process far more manageable. However, it is also important to recognize that supportive bonds with non-parental figures, such as mentors, can also have a profound significance in the lives of young people leaving care (Egelund Nielsen et al. 2005; Mølholt et al. 2012; Storø 2005).

Conclusion

In recent years, globalization and socio-economic changes have influenced and shaped youth transitions. A complex interplay of factors impact the opportunities and risks to which young people leaving care are exposed to. What is clear from international research is that young people negotiating the transition from care to adulthood have to face additional hurdles and challenges compared to their peers in the general population. In both the UK and Scandinavia, young people leaving care have traditionally experienced *accelerated* and *compressed* transition pathways, without access to the levels of practical, financial, and emotional support that are typically available to their peers in the general population. Heightened awareness that young people leaving care are vulnerable to poor outcomes has led academics and (to varying degrees) the charitable sector and politicians to consider (and, in some cases, implement) changes designed to meet their needs, or promote their rights.

The hypothesis that social democratic regimes in Scandinavia would provide extensive aftercare support and the liberal welfare regimes in the UK would be orientated towards preparation for independence, rather than longer-term care, is an oversimplification. In both the UK and Scandinavia, the frameworks that are in place do not preclude moving beyond *accelerated* and *compressed* transitions, towards *extended and graduated* transitions that are more akin to those experienced by the general population. What differs, at the mezzo domain, is the level of discretion afforded to localities and frontline social workers to make decisions about what preparation and support are provided, by whom, and for how long.

In Denmark and Norway, young people may receive aftercare support until the age of 23, but the nature and the extent of support provided are largely determined at municipality level and by frontline social workers, who make decisions on a case-by-case basis. In part, the lack of central prescription reflects a societal expectation that high-quality universal support and services should be sufficient to meet the needs of the population.

In contrast, in the UK, the politics of the social investment state and moral arguments have been used to advocate for specialist support and services for young people leaving OHC. Charities, cross-party select committees and service users have also lobbied to increase entitlements and extend provision, particularly for those with the most complex needs. Targeted legislation and regulations have been introduced to impose specific duties upon local authorities. Formal schemes have also been implemented to permit young people in foster care to remain living with their carers up to the age of 21. Aftercare support from leaving care personal advisers is also provided until young people reach the age of 21 (or 25 in some circumstances).

Although models of delivery in Scandinavia and the UK are different, at the micro domain, the experiences of young people leaving care

are rather similar. The option to remain in OHC placements beyond the age of 18 is not open to all; a high proportion of young people continue to experience age-related transitions. Many report a lack of choice and that they have not been active participants in decision-making processes. This does not necessarily mean that the child welfare system has not tried to engage them, but the options available are limited or do not seem relevant to the young people concerned. There may also be a mismatch between the services and support on offer (often financial or practical provision), and what young people desire (consistent emotional support).

So, is it all that different? Research in both the UK and Scandinavian contexts reveals that still more needs to be done to ensure that services' responses are rights based, rather than being determined by young people's age or placement type (Munro et al. 2011b, 2012). While enhanced legal entitlements and policy developments are to be welcomed to establish minimum expectations, it is clear that regulation alone is insufficient to deliver improved outcomes (House of Commons Committee of Public Accounts 2015; Munro and Gilligan 2013). First, where duties are imposed, these need to be accompanied with sufficient resources to support effective delivery. Second, as messages from young people consistently show, secure, stable, and enduring relationships with carers, professionals, peers and members of the wider community, both in and after care, are an important underpinning and springboard for positive outcomes into adulthood.

References

Antle, B. F., Johnson, L., Barbee, A., & Sullivan, D. (2009). Fostering interdependent versus independent living in youth aging out of care through healthy relationships. *Families in Society-the Journal of Contemporary Social Services, XC*(3), 309–315.

Backe-Hansen, E., Havik, T., & Grønningsæter, A. B. (2013a). På vei mot et fosterhjemsløft. In E. Backe-Hansen, T. Havik, & A. B. Grønningsæter (Eds.), *Fosterhjem for barns behov. Rapport fra et fireårig forskningsprogram* (pp. 223–234). Oslo: Norsk institutt for forskning om oppvekst, velferd og aldring.

Backe-Hansen, E., Højer, I., Sjöblom, Y., & Storø, J. (2013b). Out of home care in Norway and Sweden – Similar and different. *Psychosocial Intervention, XXII*(3), 193–202.

Bakketeig, E., & Backe-Hansen, E. (2008). *Forskningskunnskap om ettervern*. Oslo: Norsk institutt for forskning om opvekst, velferd og aldring.

Bengtsson, T. T., & Böcker Jakobsen, T. (2009). *Institutionsanbringelse af unge i Norden: en komparativ undersøgelse af lovgrundlag, institutionsformer, og udviklingstendenser*. København: SFI - Det Nationale Forskningscenter for Velfærd, København.

Berridge, D., Biehal, N., & Henry, L. (2012). *Living in children's residential homes*. London: Department for Education.

Biehal, N., Clayden, J., Stein, M., & Wade, J. (1995). *Moving on: Young people and leaving care schemes*. London: Her Majesty's Stationery Office.

Binde, R. (2008). Oppføling av ungdom i barnevernet. In B. Storhaug & S. Storhaug (Eds.), *Overgangen fra barnevern til voksenliv i Trondheim. Slutrapport fra OBVIT-prosjektet*. Trondheim: NTNU Samfunnsforskning.

Bø, T. P., & Vigran, Å. (2014). *Ungdom som verken er i arbeid eller utdanning*. Oslo: Statistics Norway.

Böcker Jakobsen, T., Hammen, I., & Steen, L. (2010). *Efterværn – støtte til tidligere anbragte unge: midtvejsevaluering af forsøg med efterværn under handlingsprogrammet "Lige muligheder"*. København: SFI – Det Nationale Forskningscenter for Velfærd.

Bratterud, Å., Binde, R,. Horneman, K., Husby, I., Dahlø, S., Iversen, O., Munkeby, L., & Sårstad, A. (2006). Ungdom med barneverntiltak – på vei mot voksenlivet. Delrapport 1. Trondheim: NTNU, Barnevernets utviklingssenter.

Broad, B. (1998). *Young people leaving care: Life since the Children Act 1989*. London: Jessica Kingsley Publishers.

Bryderup, I. M., & Trentel, M. Q. (2013). The importance of social relationships for young people from a public care background. *European Social Work, XVI*(1), 37–54.

Cameron, C., Jackson, S., Hauari, H., & Hollingworth, K. (2011). *Young people from a public care background: Pathways to further and higher education in England. A case study*. London: Institute of Education.

Children (Leaving Care) Act (2000). London: The Stationery Office.

Children and Families Act (2014). London: The Stationery Office.

Children and Young People (Scotland) *Act* (2014). Edinburgh: The Scottish Government.

Coleman, J., & Hendry, L. B. (1999). *The nature of adolescence*. London: Routledge.

Courtney, M. E., Dworsky, A., & Pollack, H. (2007). When should the state cease parenting? Evidence from the Midwest study. In *Issue Brief* (Vol. 115). Chicago: Chaplin Hall.

Coyle, D. (2015). *G.E.M. Scheme: Regional overview. Northern Ireland benchmarking presentation 26 June 2015.*

Department for Education. (2014). *Outcomes for children looked after by local authorities in England as at 31 March 2014.* London: Department for Education.

Dixon, J., & Stein, M. (2005). *Leaving care: Throughcare and aftercare in Scotland.* London: Jessica Kingsley.

Egelund Nielsen, H., Andersen, D., Ankerbo, A., Ericson, N., Jul Gunnersen, S., Jensen, C., et al. (2005). *TABUKA: tidligere anbragtes bud på kvalitet i anbringelsen af børn og unge.* København: Børn & Unge.

Ejrnæs, M., Ejrnæs, M., & Frederiksen, S. (2010). Socialt udsatte børn og unge – Forebyggelse og anbringelse i kommunerne. In S. H. Andersen (Ed.), *Når man anbringer et barn. Baggrund, stabilitet i anbringelsen og det videre liv.* København: Rockwool Fonden.

Elder, G. H. (1995). The life course paradigm: Social change and individual development. In P. Moen, G. H. Elder, & K. Lüscher (Eds.), *Examining lives in context. perspectives on the ecology of human development* (pp. 101–139). Washington, DC: American Psychological Association.

Elder, G. H., & Rockwell, R. C. (1979). The life-course and human development: An ecological perspective. *International Journal of Behavioral Development, II*(1), 1–21.

Esping-Andersen, G. (1990). *The three worlds of welfare capitalism.* Princeton: Princeton University Press.

Esping-Andersen, G. (1997). Hybrid or unique?: The Japanese welfare state between Europe and America. *Journal of European Social Policy, VII*(3), 179–189.

Eurofound. (2014). *Mapping youth transitions in Europe.* Luxembourg: Publications Office of the European Union.

Fawcett, B., Featherstone, B., & Goddard, J. (2003, July 15). *From the womb to the workplace: Child welfare under new labour.* Paper presented to the Annual Conference of the Social Policy Association, University of Teesside, Middlesbrough.

Fernandez, E., & Barth, R. P. (2010). *How does foster care work?: International evidence on outcomes.* London: Jessica Kingsley Publishers.

Gabriel, T., & Keller, S. (2014). Les care leavers: quelles transition après les mesures de protection de la jeunesse? *Revue Suisse de travail social, XVI*(4), 6–8.

General Assembly of the United Nations. (2010). *Guidelines for the alternative care of children*. New York: United Nations.

Grills-Taquechel, A. E., Norton, P., & Ollendick, T. H. (2011). A longitudinal examination of factors predicting anxiety during the transition to middle school. *Anxiety, Stress, Coping, XXIII*(5), 493–513.

Hart, D., La Valle, I., & Holmes, L. (2015). *The place of residential care in the English child welfare system*. London: Department for Education.

Höjer, I., & Sjöblom, Y. (2014). *Young people's experience of participation when exiting out of care* (pp. 27–45). XVI: Schweizerische Zeitschrift für Soziale Arbeit.

Höjer, I., Johansson, H., Hill, M., Cameron, C., & Jackson, S. (2008). *State of the art consolidated literature review. The educational pathways of young people from a public care background in five EU countries*. London: Thomas Coram Research Unit.

Hollingsworth, K. (2012). Securing responsibility, achieving parity? The legal support for children leaving custody. *Legal Studies, XXXIII*(1), 22–45.

House of Commons Committee of Public Accounts. (2015). *Care leavers transition to adulthood. Fifth report of session 2015–2016*. London: The Stationery Office.

House of Commons Education Committee. (2014a) *Residential children's homes*, Sixth report. London: The Stationery Office.

House of Commons Education Committee. (2014b). *Into independence, not out of care: 16 plus care options. Government response to the committee's second report of session 2014–15*. London: The Stationery Office.

Houston, S., & Campbell, J. (2001). Using critical social theory to develop a conceptual framework for comparative social work. *International Journal of Social Welfare, X*(1), 66–73.

Jackson, S., & Cameron, C. (2012). *Final report of the YIPEE project. Young people from a public care background: Pathways to further and higher education in five European countries*. London: Thomas Coram Research Unit.

Jackson, S., Ajayi, S., & Quigley, M. (2005). *Going to university from care*. London: Institute of Education.

McCrea, R. (2008) Evaluation of the former foster care scheme. *Leaving Care Implementation Project*. Belfast: The Fostering Network

Mendes, P. (2005). From state care to independence: A comparison of the Australian and American leaving care debates. *The Social Policy Journal, IV*(1), 51–63.

Mendes, P. (2009). Globalization, the welfare state and young people leaving state out-of-home care. *Asian Social Work and Policy Review, 3*, 85–94.

Mendes, P., Pinkerton, J., & Munro, E. (2014). Young people transitioning from out-of-home care: An issue of social justice. *Australian Social Work, LXVII*(1), 1–4.

Mølholt, A. K. (2014). Opvækstvilkår. In B. Greve, A. Jørgensen, & J. E. Larsen (Eds.), *Det danske samfund* (pp. 263–286). København: Hans Reitzels Forlag.

Mølholt, A. K. (forthcoming, 2017) *Young people who have been in care. Narratives of the past, the present, and expectations for the future* (Preliminary title). Aalborg: Aalborg University.

Mølholt, A. K., Stage, S., Pejtersen, J. H., & Thomsen, P. (2012). *Efterværn for tidligere anbragte unge: En videns- og erfaringsopsamling*. København: SFI – Det Nationale Forskningscenter for Velfærd.

Munro, E. R., & Gilligan, R. (2013). The 'dance' of kinship care in England and Ireland: Navigating a course between regulation and relationships. *Psychosocial Intervention, 22*, 185–192.

Munro, E. R., & Manful, E. (2012). *Safeguarding children: A comparison of England's data with that of Australia, Norway and the United States*. London: Department for Education.

Munro, E. R., Brown, R., & Manful, E. (2011a). *Safeguarding children statistics: The availability and comparability of data in the UK. Research brief. DFE-RB153*. London: Department for Education.

Munro, E. R., Lushey, C., Ward, H., & National Care Advisory Service. (2011b). *Right2BCared4: Final report. Research Report DFE-RR106*. London: Department for Education.

Munro, E. R., Pinkerton, J., Mendes, P., Hyde-Dryden, G., Herczog, M., & Benbenishty, R. (2011c). The contribution of the United Nations convention on the rights of the child to understanding and promoting the interests of young people making the transition from care to adulthood. *Children and Youth Services Review, XXXIII*(12), 2417–2423.

Munro, E. R., Lushey, C., National Care Advisory Service, Maskell-Graham, D., Ward, H. with Holmes, L. (2012). *Evaluation of the staying put: 18+ family placement programme pilot: Final report. Research report DFE-RR191* (London: Department for Education).

National Audit Office. (2014). *Children in care*. London: National Audit Office.

National Board of Health and Welfare. (2014). *Children and young person's subjected to measures 2013. Measures under the Social Services Act (SOL) and the Care of Young persons Act (LVU)*. Stockholm: Socialstyrelsen.

Nilsen, A., & Brannen, J. (2014). An intergenerational approach to transitions to adulthood: The importance of history and biography. *Sociological Research Online, XIX*, 2.

Oterholm, I. (2008). Barneverntjenestens arbeid med ettervern. In E. Bakketeig & E. Backe-Hansen (Eds.), *Forskningskunnskap om ettervern* (pp. 161–206). Oslo: Norsk institutt for forskning om oppvekst, velferd og aldring.

Oterholm, I. (2015). *Organisasjonens betydning for sosialarbeideres vurderinger.* Oslo: Høgskolen i Oslo og Akershus.

Pinkerton, J. (2008). States of care leaving. Towards international exchange as a global resource. In M. Stein & E. Munro (Eds.), *Young people's transitions from care to adulthood: International comparisons and perspectives* (pp. 241–257). London: Jessica Kingsley Publishers.

Preston-Shoot, M. (2001). Regulating the road of good intentions: Observations on the relationships between policy, regulations and practice in social work. *Social Work in Action, XIII*(4), 5–20.

Scottish Government. (2014). *Children's social work statistics 2013/2014.*

Settersten Jr., R. A., Furstenberg, F. F., & Rumbaut, R. G. (2008). *On the frontier of adulthood: Theory, research, and public policy.* Chicago: University of Chicago Press.

Simmons, R. G., Burgeson, R., Carlton-Ford, S., & Blyth, D. A. (1987). The impact of cumulative change in early adolescence. *Child Development, LVIII*(5), 1220–1234.

Social Services & Well-being (Wales) Act (2014). Cardiff: Welsh Government.

Socialministeriet. (2011) *Bekendtgørelse af lov om social service.*

Statistics Denmark. (2013). www.danmarksstatistik.dk. Accessed August 2015.

Statistics Norway. (2013). www.ssb.no. Accessed August 2015.

Stein, M. (2002). Leaving care. In D. McNeish, T. Newman, & H. Roberts (Eds.), *What works for children?* (pp. 59–82). Milton Keynes: Open University Press.

Stein, M. (2012). *Young people leaving care: Supporting pathways to adulthood.* London: Jessica Kingsley.

Stein, M. (2014). Young people's transition from care to adulthood in European and Postcommunist Eastern European and Central Asian societies. *Australian Social Work, LXVII*(1), 24–38.

Stein, M., & Munro, E. R. (2008). *Young people's transitions from care to adulthood: International comparisons and perspectives.* London: Jessica Kingsley Publishers.

Stein, M., & Verweijen-Slamnescu, R. (2012). *When care ends, lessons from peer research, insights from young people on leaving care in Albania, the Czech Republic, Finland and Poland.* Innsbruck: SOS Children's Villages International.

Stein, M., Ward, H., & Courtney, M. (2011). Editorial: International perspective on young people's transitions from care to adulthood. *Children and Youth Services Review, XXXII*(12), 2409–2411.

Storø, J. (2005). *Å gå over brennende bruer*. Oslo: Høgskolen i Olso.

Thoburn, J. (2007). *Globalisation & child welfare: Some lessons from a cross-national study of children in out-of-home care*. Norwich: School of Social Work & Psychosocial Studies, University of East Anglia.

Vinnerljung, B., Oman, M., & Gunnarson, T. (2005). Educational attainments of former child welfare clients – A Swedish national cohort study. *International Journal of Social Welfare, XIV*(4), 265–276.

Voices from Care Wales. (2012). *Social service Wales Bill: Organisational response*. Cardiff: Voices From Care.

Walther, A. (2009). "It was not my choice, you know?": Young people's subjective views and decision-making processes in biographical transitions. In I. Schoon & R. K. Silbereisen (Eds.), *Transitions from school to work: Globalization, individualization, and patterns of diversity* (pp. 121–144). Cambridge: Cambridge University Press.

Williams, F. (2004). What matters is who works: Why every child matters to new labour. Commentary on the DfES green paper every child matters. *Critical Social Policy, XXIV*(3), 406–427.

Yen, I. H., Powell Hammond, W., & Kushel, M. B. (2009). From homeless to hopeless and healthless?: The health impacts of housing challenges among former foster care youth transitioning to adulthood in California. *Issues in comprehensive pediatric nursing, XXXII*(2), 77–93.

11

Peer Research with Young People Leaving Care: Reflections from Research in England, Northern Ireland and Argentina

Berni Kelly, Jo Dixon, and Mariana Incarnato

Introduction

In recent decades, there has been a developing body of youth research utilizing peer research (PR) methods. Whilst the general benefits of participatory research have been highlighted, less is known about the real contributions and challenges of involving young people as peer researchers, particularly care leavers. In this chapter, we draw on the PR approaches used in three care leaver studies based in England, Northern

---

B. Kelly (✉)
School of Social Sciences, Education and Social Work, Queen's University Belfast, Belfast, UK

J. Dixon
Department of Social Policy and Social Work, Research & Teaching Unit, University of York, York, UK

M. Incarnato
Executive Director DONCEL Civil Association, Buenos Aires, Argentina

© The Author(s) 2016
P. Mendes, P. Snow (eds.), *Young People Transitioning from Out-of-Home Care*, DOI 10.1057/978-1-137-55639-4_11

Ireland (NI) and Argentina. We explore the processes of implementing PR approaches, the benefits of the methodology and the limitations of using this method in our research with care leavers. In doing so, we suggest learning points for using PR in future studies with care-experienced youth.

Background

PR is embedded within the tradition of empowerment and service- user involvement. Although there is no strict definition of what PR should involve, Bourke (2009, p. 458) provides a working definition as '…a research process which involves those being researched in the… project planning, research design, data collection and analysis, and/or the distribution and application of the research findings'. In this sense, peer researchers should be involved from the beginning of the study and throughout all elements of the research process.

Participatory approaches have found particular traction in research on marginalized groups, the 'difficult to reach' and those who have historically 'lacked a voice', including young people (Nind 2011; SOVA 2005). The impetus for the increased use of participatory approaches in research with young people can, indeed, be located within the children's rights agenda. The United Nations Convention on the Rights of the Child, ratified by Argentina in 1990 and the UK (including NI) in 1991, calls for greater provision for children to have a say in decisions and issues that affect them, including research that directly engages with children. PR has also evolved alongside sociological paradigm shifts that have led to the re-conceptualization of childhood, where children are seen as competent social actors (Greene and Hill 2005; Nind 2011).

Involving peer researchers seeks to redress hierarchical relationships within research by minimizing the potential for power imbalances between professional adult researchers and young people. This assumes that peer researchers can facilitate a less threatening environment where greater rapport and openness can be fostered, based on empathy and shared understanding. Furthermore, peer researchers may well be regarded as experts by experience, and positive role models (SOVA

2005). Importantly, employing care leavers as peer researchers also provides them with actual work experience, which brings with it opportunities to gain valuable training and wider life and employment skills that can increase future employability (Dixon et al. 2015; JRF 2000; Curtis et al. 2004; Kilpatrick et al. 2007).

Such benefits, however, are not assured, and commentators have drawn attention to reservations about the actual added value of the approach and concerns about the potential for bias and poorer quality data (Nind 2011). Holland et al. (2010) also questioned the analytic competence of non-professional researchers. In this chapter, we address some of these concerns, drawing on the experiences of three PR studies with care-experienced young people in England, NI and Argentina. Although each study had unique aims and objectives and different stages of data collection, they all had a common commitment to adopting a PR approach to interviews with care leavers. Before commencement, all three studies secured ethical approval from their respective agencies and relevant local authorities. We begin with an overview of the methods and processes adopted in each study, including stages of recruitment, training and support for peer researchers. We also explore our varying experiences of implementing PR approaches, highlighting not only the benefits, but also the challenges and lessons for future research.

The English Corporate Parenting Study

The English Corporate Parenting (CP) study is one of the largest to use a PR approach with care-experienced youth. The study explored young people's experiences of care, their engagement in education and employment, perceptions of home, general well-being and their views on the local authority's role as 'corporate parent'. The study provided training and support to enable 36 care leavers to become peer researchers, using the National Care Advisory Service (NCAS) model, which promotes care leavers' involvement in all aspects of the research process. Peer researchers were, therefore, involved in developing interview guides to ensure that questions were relevant and meaningful to young people; carrying out interviews with 579 young people in and from care; contributing to qualitative analysis; and presenting findings to practitioner and academic audiences.

The PR approach began with the design of recruitment information including comprehensive job specifications, in collaboration with a Young People's Advisory Group. The opportunity was offered to as broad a group of care leavers as possible. However, the importance of having realistic expectations around basic literacy skills and commitment meant that, in reality, those with highly complex needs were not included in the PR team, the overriding aim being to ensure the interviews were successful and positive for all concerned. The role involved contact with vulnerable young people, so criminal clearance checks were required. Peer researchers were paid per interview, mostly arranged through the local authority. Local authorities also took responsibility for recruiting peer researchers, with some holding recruitment interviews and others selecting young people they considered suitable; however, at least one sent young people to training without fully explaining the study.

Two care-experienced young people aged 18 and over were recruited from each of the 12 local authorities (n = 24). There was a high level of engagement, with most remaining with the study for two years, and nine remaining throughout the three years. Six young people left in years two and three left due to other commitments, including work, studies and parenthood. These young people were replaced, resulting in a total of 36 peer researchers working with the study. Peer researchers ranged from 19 to 22 years of age, with slightly more young women taking on the role. Most of the peer researchers were in education or part-time work, though around six were out of work and education, and two were young parents.

The peer researchers were supported by an academic researcher, a student intern, a participation worker and a research administrator. They also received training and support from the NCAS participation workers. Two training events were held each year for peer researchers, which involved a two-day residential workshop and refresher courses in the second and third years. The training was comprehensive, covering data collection approaches, ethics and data protection, interview techniques, effective communication skills, fieldwork safety procedures, thematic analysis and presentation skills. The workshops also provided opportunities for the peer researchers to meet and share experiences, offering both peer support and further learning to address issues that had arisen. The training workshops were evaluated and peer researchers' comments were taken on board in the planning of subsequent workshops, for example, more ice breakers and interactive activities were introduced to reflect PR feedback on the intensity of the initial training sessions. The PR and professional team indicated that young people benefited from the training in terms of increased skills in communication, listening and team work. Three young people felt unable or unwilling to continue with the role after the training due to the level of commitment required or concerns about the interview subject matter, demonstrating the need for careful recruitment and selection for the role.

The peer researchers used structured interviews in year one to promote consistency of data across the large and inexperienced interview team. In years two and three, interviews became more semi-structured, which provided greater scope for peer researchers to direct the interviews and explore topics in more detail. Though mostly successful, some peer researchers were clearly less comfortable and competent with the semi-structured approach.

Fieldwork for the CP study took place during three summers, with individual interviews held for two to three days within a local authority venue. Concerns around the ethical implications of carrying out interviews in their own local areas meant that the peer researchers were required to travel to another fieldwork area to interview, which worked relatively well. Participating local authorities appointed a member of staff to liaise directly with the research team and peer researchers. These Area Research Coordinators (ARCS) were crucial, helping to set up interview days and recruit interviewees. This proved time-consuming and required considerable commitment from ARCS to ensure that the interview days were successful.

Participation workers and ARCs also provided emotional and practical support and managed the PR team on a daily basis during fieldwork. This involved maintaining regular contact to ensure that individual needs were addressed and accompanying peer researchers who were travelling to interviews outside their local area. Arranging travel and hotel accommodation for 36 peer researchers and maintaining contact during the fieldwork visits were also highly time-consuming tasks for the research team, and significantly altered the overall role of the academic researchers from undertaking fieldwork to, instead, the administration of fieldwork. The participation workers were also responsible for conducting debriefing sessions after fieldwork. Very occasionally, this resulted in supporting peer researchers to address difficult issues that had arisen during interviews. All peer researchers received a certificate of participation and achievement at the end of the project. They were also offered support with thier CVs and the opportnity to obtain a reference from the research and participation managers.

The Northern Irish YOLO Study

The YOLO (You Only Leave Once?) study of transitions and outcomes for care leavers with mental health and/or intellectual disabilities in NI also adopted a PR approach to the qualitative phase of data collection. A total of 31 care leavers were interviewed across NI up to three times over the course of a year to track their experience of transition from care and explore their views on their support needs and access to services. Peer researchers were involved in the production of a recruitment DVD, development of interview questions and tools, interviews with care leavers and analysis and presentation of the findings.

To recruit peer researchers, the study's Care Leaver Advisory Group helped to design a one-page job specification and a one-page application form to ensure accessibility of information and application process. Advertisements for the post were circulated via universities, non-governmental organizations (NGOs) and statutory leaving care services. Following screening of applications received, applicants were invited for interview. This stage of the recruitment process offered an opportunity for applicants to experience a formal interview, as, for some young people, this was their first experience of applying for a job. Some candidates did not attend the interview, and several candidates were unsuccessful. These young people were given the opportunity for verbal and written feedback from the interview panel to ensure they were informed of areas for improvement for future job opportunities. Criminal clearance checks were also required for the post.

A total of ten young people were recruited to participate in training; however, due to new jobs and parenting roles, two withdrew before training began. From the outset, peer researchers were informed that it was mandatory to complete five full days of training. As three young people failed to attend some training sessions, they also exited the study. The training programme addressed the study aims; mental health and disability issues; interviewing skills; and ethical issues. A range of participatory training approaches was employed including role plays, practical exercises and contributions from previous peer researchers. At the end of the training programme, the remaining five peer researchers participated in an individual appraisal with the training team, reflecting on their strengths, weaknesses and support needs; and were informally assessed by the training team using a role-play scenario. All five young people received a certificate of completion, but one young person was unable to undertake the PR role due to the commencement of a new college course. Feedback from peer researchers on the training programme indicated that they felt they had benefitted from the training offered, gaining more insight into issues for disabled care leavers and acquiring new interviewing skills.

The four peer researchers recruited (two males and two females) had a range of previous care experiences and were aged between 20 and 24 years. Two of these young people were studying for university degrees, third was working part-time having previously completed a university degree and the fourth was in part-time employment, having left school early with few qualifications. At a later stage of the study, the fourth young person withdrew from the study for personal reasons, and was replaced by a new peer researcher with a similar background, who undertook a bespoke training programme. All peer researchers were paid at a daily rate via the Voice of Young People in care (VOYPIC). Interestingly, those young people who exited the study post-interview tended to have lower levels of engagement in education or training, which has implications for supporting a peer research team with varying care and educational experiences.

Although the original intention was to have peer researchers conducting interviews in pairs, they chose to be paired with the professional researcher for the first interview. These interviews were usually conducted in the young person's own home, and the professional researcher played a supporting role by arranging the interview, transporting the peer researcher and prompting when required during the interview. The interview schedule was semi-structured and used visual aids to map the leaving care journey and social networks. Interviews ended with administration of the 12-item version of the General Health Questionnaire (GHQ) to rate their general level of health and mental well-being across the data collection period (Goldberg 1978).

It became apparent during the course of the first interviews that some peer researchers were uncomfortable with some aspects of the interview, including questions about mental illness and administering the structured GHQ tool. During the first round of interviews, the professional researcher assisted with some of these more challenging aspects of the interview, and these issues were then addressed in refresher training for peer researchers to increase their skills and confidence in these areas.

The second stage entailed follow-up telephone interviews usually conducted by the same peer researcher on their own. Peer researchers analysed transcripts of the first interviews to establish questions for this second interview, and conducted these follow-up interviews with confidence. For some participants, the second interview was held in person due to the participant's level of impairment. In such cases, the professional researcher was present as before, although the peer researcher took a stronger lead in all aspects of the interview. For the final phase of in-person interviews, peer researchers conducted more interviews alone, although the professional researcher still provided support for some interviews due to the needs of the participant or concern about the unpredictability of the research context (e.g., challenging behaviours).

The peer researchers were supported by a team comprising two professional researchers and a team member from VOYPIC. The professional researchers played important, often time-consuming roles in relation to the logistics of setting up interviews and ensuring peer researchers were practically able to travel to and from interviews. Each peer researcher also had a named support person from VOYPIC who could offer independent support and advice; however, only one young person took up this support. Other peer researchers felt adequately supported already by the research team. Regular individual and group meetings were held with the peer researchers throughout the study, and each peer researcher had briefings before and after interviews to ensure adequate preparation and reflection on experiential learning. As a result, close working relationships were developed, and peer researchers often shared personal reflections on the emotional impact of the interviews and ongoing personal issues impacting their lives (e.g., family, education or employment-related issues). This level of engagement provided an opportunity for the professional researchers to provide emotional and practical support beyond initial expectations, reflecting the importance of acknowledging the issues at play for peer researchers who faced their own challenges related to leaving care.

Three further formal training programmes were provided for the peer researchers. Following completion of the first round of interviews, peer researchers joined the professional researchers for a collaborative training day on qualitative data analysis. The third training day focused on comparative analysis of a sample of transcripts to provide an interpretive validity check and develop a shared coding framework. The final training day was held prior to the last round of interviews, and focused on learning from the first two phases of data collection and preparing for the final interviews.

The Argentinian Building Independence (CA) Study

The Argentinian CA (Construyendo Autonomía, or Building Independence) study aimed to examine the process of transition for young people in and leaving care in four provinces (Buenos Aires, Tucuman, Chaco and Santiago del Estero); and develop tools to improve approaches to transition. The project, a joint venture between the Faculty of Social Sciences in Argentina (FLACSO) and the DONCEL NGO, was aimed at addressing the needs of a large number of young people aged over 18 who were transitioning from care to independent living. It is the first study to use PR approaches to investigate leaving care processes in Latin America. Seven young care leavers were trained to conduct structured interviews and focus groups with youths in and leaving out-of-home care (OHC). However, two of these young people did not progress to the fieldwork role due to other employment demands.

At the beginning of the project, two training and exchange sessions were organized for the project's professional research team, with input from an independent specialist trainer. In these sessions, the workings of PR methodology and plans for training peer researchers were discussed in detail. Following these sessions, a team of seven young people (two females and five males) aged over 21 years who had left the care system was established to take on the role of peer researchers. These young people were required to have a range of prior experience and characteristics: previous participation in DONCEL's Exit Guide project (www.guiaegreso.com.ar), secondary education to at least third year, interest in mentoring other young people, time and availability to travel and organizational and collaborative skills. All peer researchers had previous experience of facilitating workshops on care and protection issues in residential homes. Given their previous roles, they were already aware of the project and had developed a climate of trust with the young people and the research team. Training was delivered over the course of three days at FLACSO's office, in order to prepare them for their participation in the design and implementation of the research tools, the processing of data collected and the interpretation of findings.

A booklet written to aid the training process proved valuable to the team throughout the duration of the project, as it included administrative information (including contracts, travel expenses, office hours and contact telephone numbers); project information (including the conceptual framework, objectives, and roles of the research team and peer researchers); and methodology (including principal elements of the data collection process and research instruments).

The study used two structured interview schedules, one for in-care adolescents and another for care leavers. The interview questions were developed jointly by the professional and PR team. The questions were based on the criteria detailed in the 'Pathway Plan', as this provides an organizational framework to prepare the young person for after-care life, both on material and subjective levels. The same criteria used in the structured interviews were applied in the preparation of guidelines for the focus groups.

Peer researchers conducted a total of 69 structured interviews in the four provinces involved in the project, 49 in in-care, with adolescents residing in care institutions, and 20 with young care leavers. In three provinces (Chaco, Tucuman and Santiago del Estero), intensive workshops were also held, based on two main objectives: to investigate the perceptions of young people and their institutional referents regarding the transition from in-care to after-care, and to provide a meeting space for young people and adults working in the institutions to exchange experiences and tools to facilitate practice development. In this context, the peer researchers undertook individual interviews and focus groups with adolescents, and contributed to group interviews and workshops with professionals, which were led by the project team.

A database for processing the information gathered in the interviews was created, which included the transcription of open-ended questions. All audio material recorded in the focus groups and individual interviews was transcribed in order to process and analyse the information. While the professional team was responsible for the preliminary processing and analysis of quantitative and qualitative data, the peer researchers also participated actively in this part of the process through two workshops focused on analysis of the findings.

Overall, the peer researchers made an extremely valuable contribution to the CA study. However, their lack of experience posed serious challenges, and peer researchers often found themselves in critical personal situations that prevented them from seriously committing to the study. Interviews also had an emotional impact on the peer researchers, requiring professional researchers to play a dual role of meeting the personal, emotional needs of peer researchers and supporting them to fulfil their PR role.

Unlike their previous work on the Exit Guide, this project required the young people to put aside their own personal experiences and take on a new role. Skills for undertaking this PR role must be built over time; however, further training is also required, not so much in terms of using data collection tools or interviewing, but with respect to subjective tools to enable care leavers to adopt a new role as a peer researcher, and not only as a care leaver. However, over the course of the study, there was a visible change in the way the peer researchers viewed the care system, its weaknesses, shortcomings and strengths. It was evident that there had been a change in discourse, in how they described their experiences and in how they talked about what had happened to them. In testimony to their PR experience, the CA study interviewed each peer researcher to develop a video based on their work on the project (DONCEL & FLACSO 2015).

Benefits and Challenges of PR

Whilst it was hoped that PR would enhance the interview experience for participants across all three studies, there had been little robust evidence that PR actually achieves this. Some researchers have claimed that young people's participation can produce 'better or at least different data' (Holland et al. 2010), but this had not been systematically established to date (Smith et al. 2002). Although the PR model in the CP study had been successfully used in earlier NCAS research on care leavers (WMTD & Catch22 2007; Lushey and Munro 2014), these previous studies had not routinely assessed the method. Both the CP and YOLO studies, therefore, commissioned an independent evaluation of the PR methodology, exploring the perspectives of peer researchers, interviewees and staff supporting peer researchers. The CA study also sought feedback from the peer and professional researchers. Overall, across the studies, there were benefits and challenges of the PR approach for the research process, the participants and the peer researchers themselves. Three core themes emerged and are discussed below: the personal and professional development of peer researchers, the benefits for research participants and the impact on the research process.

Personal and Professional Development of Peer Researchers

Involving care leavers as peer researchers must be meaningful and provide both them and the young people they interview with a positive experience. Feedback from peer researchers across all three studies demonstrates that they were successful in this sense as many peer researchers considered the training to have been comprehensive and valuable, providing them with wider skills. Undertaking interviews also proved a valuable learning

11 Peer Research with Young People Leaving Care: Reflections...

and development experience. The CP and CA studies provided young people who had previously only experienced their local areas, with their first opportunity to travel further afield. Moreover, peer researchers felt that the role had improved their interpersonal, social and practical skills, including timekeeping, professional responsibility and confidence to talk to new people. In this way, the young people felt they had developed skills and experiences that could help them secure future training and employment opportunities:

> I gained more self-esteem and confidence as a result of doing the peer research. I was able to relate to young people better and it also led to me doing different pieces of work with young people within the local authority. (CP peer researcher).

Professional researchers and support staff commented on how much the peer researchers had enjoyed and benefited from the experience in terms of knowledge, awareness, confidence and communication skills. Peer researchers also gained new insights into issues of which they had limited prior experience, including understanding mental health and disability issues, and the importance of social inclusion:

> If I saw someone in a wheelchair… I want them to feel better and be not left out. I have learnt to include people more that I might have ignored before. (YOLO peer researcher).

As with most research in this area, there is the potential for peer researchers to hear sensitive and distressing information. One peer researcher noted: 'it was emotional and physically draining…but valuable life experience', highlighting the importance of training and support to cope with such information. Gaining insight into other care leavers' experiences also prompted peer researchers to reflect and gain new insight into their own care identities:

> It is helping me shape my own journey – where I came from and where I am at now, things seem to be meant to be, just falling into place. (YOLO peer researcher).

Finally, peer researchers benefited from the establishment of new friendships and support networks with their fellow peer researchers and other members of the research team. They described feeling inspired by the opportunity to have a say and contribute to a project that will make an impact on policy or practice, for example: 'I feel I have done something meaningful for my life… I feel hope that what we are doing will help in the future…' (CA peer researcher).

Impact on Research Participants

The evaluation of both the YOLO and CP studies sought the views of research participants on their experience of being interviewed by a peer researcher. In the CP study, a survey of 120 participants confirmed the value of the PR approach, with two-thirds agreeing that young people should always be involved in research that is about them, whilst 57 per cent felt it important to be interviewed by someone with a similar experience to them (32 per cent felt that shared experience was not important).

In the YOLO study, participants rated the PR experience very positively and recommended participatory approaches for other care leaver studies. Interestingly, one young person added that it was the first time they had met another care leaver. Some young people also viewed peer researchers as role models, as they were successfully working on the project, had skills and confidence for meeting new people and interviewing and had secured places at University or in employment. Indeed, peer researchers could sometimes direct participants to sources of practical support (e.g., a funding stream to help with education), although they handled such situations with objective professionalism.

Impact on Research Process

Given the time, resources and effort required to facilitate PR, it is important that there are benefits for the study in terms of the quality of data and added value during planning, data analysis and dissemination phases. All three studies have found that the quality of interview data was enhanced by the involvement of peer researchers who could share a mutual understanding of the research topic with participants and a common language that helped build rapport and support communication. Young people who might usually avoid research participation may also feel more inclined to engage in the process, facilitating participation of traditionally 'hard to reach' voices and minimizing attrition. There was certainly evidence of high participation rates in the three studies, and, in the majority of cases, the quality of data suggested that interviews had gone well and that participants had been willing to share their views and experiences openly. While some peer researchers were natural interviewers from the start, many improved as they gained experience (e.g., screening out irrelevant questions or using appropriate prompts). However, such variations in approach are to be expected in any study with multiple newly recruited researchers who need to develop their familiarity with the interview schedule and process.

Peer researchers often required support from the professional researcher when unexpected issues arose during fieldwork (e.g., unexpectedly having a young child present during the interview), or when they needed to debrief in order to process the emotional impact of the care leaver's story, or witnessing the adverse living circumstances of some young people (which may, or may not, contrast with their own experiences). In the YOLO study, the presence of the professional researcher gave them an opportunity to observe how to respond to unexpected challenges, highlighting the value of co-producing interviews. In the other studies, where peer researchers interviewed independently, high levels of support were offered by the professional staff when required.

Close attention to research ethics and fieldwork safety procedures was also necessary, for example, carrying out risk assessments for peer researchers and developing protocols for safe exit strategies should an interviewee or peer researcher become uncomfortable or upset. Of course, this is good practice with any research, but there was a heightened sense of responsibility to ensure that peer researchers had a safe and positive fieldwork experience.

Managing the logistics of supporting peer researchers to travel to unfamiliar areas proved to be time-consuming and required almost military precision planning. However, such careful planning was important to ensure safety and to minimize the likelihood that peer researchers would arrive to interview someone they knew. As some research participants led chaotic lives, appointments were often cancelled or forgotten. The need for repeated visits and re-arranged interviews discouraged peer researchers and added to the volume of work. In addition, there were more costs for the study, as peer researchers still needed to be paid for their time and travel.

Across all three studies, the professional research team benefited from the involvement of young people who understood the research project but also had direct experience of living in, and leaving, care. Peer researchers' personal knowledge and experience helped to create more appropriate interview questions, and enabled an empathic and supportive questioning style. During analysis processes, the mutual exchange of ideas and critical questioning of assumptions led to a more sensitive and critical analytical approach. Peer researchers used their insider knowledge of service systems and each care leaver's story to inform the interpretation of the data without losing the context of the original meaning from the young person's perspective. In this way, the peer researchers helped to inductively identify common or divergent themes in the interview data.

Finally, across the three studies, the peer researchers were a highly talented group of young people for whom presentation skills were quickly acquired and refined during training. The experience of peer researchers presenting findings to practitioner and academic audiences has been extremely positive to date. Their authentic presentational style as a care-experienced young person has a powerful impact, evidenced by the direct feedback from audiences.

Lessons for Future Research

Whilst researchers in the field of leaving care can have a strong commitment to the rights of care leavers, consideration of a PR methodology is often based on the balance between the extra effort or cost required and the added value peer researchers can bring to a study. Across all three studies, we found that PR improves recruitment, reduces attrition, enhances rapport and empathy with participants and encourages an open and ethical research approach. Whilst previous commentators have also noted such benefits of PR for the research process (Lushey and Munro 2014; Verweijen-Slamnescu and Bowley 2014), our studies further extend our knowledge of the benefits for peer researchers themselves who benefit from building their professional skills and experience, feeling a sense of 'giving something back' and reflecting on their own care leaver experience and identity. However, PR is not without its challenges in terms of practicalities, resources and added ethical considerations. On the basis of our experiences of PR, core lessons for future PR studies have been identified:

- An intensive and tailored training programme covering the skills and ethics of interviewing is very important, including an opportunity to role-play interviews and practise responding to challenging situations. Training programmes should also provide an opportunity to share their experiences and bond as a group for peer support. Interactive activities, social events and residential programmes are helpful ways to develop peer and professional relationships as part of the training process. An assessment point at the end of the training programme is also helpful.
- Clear pathways to personal support for peer researchers during the research process are crucial. Hearing the narratives of other care leavers and witnessing first hand their difficult living circumstances can be emotionally challenging for peer researchers, bringing reminders of their own care story or leading to a re-analysis of their own experiences. In care leaver studies, peer researchers are also likely to have ongoing challenges in their own lives that require a flexible approach to the timing of data collection and the need for extra support. Emotional support during this time of reflection and personal learning is important; this could be provided by professionals engaged with the study or by an external counsellor or participation worker.
- The logistics of organizing peer research activities produces much additional resources and administrative work for the research team; this should be costed into the research budget, including a dedicated project worker to undertake this role. It is essential that sufficient resources, support and procedures are in place to ensure PR is carried out safely, effectively and successfully.
- For projects involving multiple data collection points over time, it is important to also provide refresher training days and fast track training

- programmes for peer researchers who join the PR team at a later stage, given the high risk of peer researchers exiting the project due to demands of further education, jobs or parenting.
- Adopting a PR approach does not necessarily mean that young people should be expected to conduct interviews alone or with their peers. Co-production of research, with peer researchers and professional researchers working together, provides unique opportunities to support and learn from each other, share different areas of expertise and ensure academic rigour throughout the research process.
- Peer researchers should continue with their involvement in studies beyond the point of data collection to analysis and dissemination of findings. Conducting interpretive validation activities, such as comparisons of independent analysis of transcripts, can assist with a shared approach to thematic analysis and interpretation. In addition, peer researchers often undertook the PR role for altruistic reasons based on an innate desire to help other young people leaving care and effect change in care leaver policy and practice. It is important, therefore, to facilitate their engagement with policy makers, service providers and other research users as part of the dissemination of the research findings to acknowledge and build respect for the PR role.

These messages both echo and strengthen those from existing literature on participatory research, particularly PR with care-experienced youth (Lushey and Munro 2014; Verweijen-Slamnescu and Bowley 2014). The recognition that PR can take longer and require greater resources than more traditional approaches is a common theme running through our own studies and earlier research, as is the need for comprehensive and ongoing training and support (Bourke 2009; Lushey and Munro 2014). Our studies add to this existing knowledge base by highlighting the particular benefits and challenges for the peer researcher. The PR approach across the three studies varied over time in response to the practical, technical and emotional needs of peer researchers. Such flexibility is essential with care-experienced peer researchers in the context of ongoing personal challenges as they navigate their own pathways from care, and encounter the stories of other care leavers participating in the research.

Conclusion

Drawing on the experiences of these three studies, this chapter has considered the wider impact and experience of PR. The findings demonstrate that despite core challenges, young people's participation as peer researchers does have benefits for the research participants, type and quality of data and peer researchers themselves. However, these benefits of involving peer researchers in qualitative research with care leavers are by no means automatic. Whilst it is important that research is inclusive, and that those involved in research are empowered, it is equally important that the research maintains academic rigour and is ethically sound. Careful planning and training, additional resources, clear pathways to support peer researchers and co-production of data collection, analysis and dissemination are critical. Given our experiences of PR across our studies, we strongly encourage other researchers to consider a PR approach, if it is suitable to the aims and objectives of their future studies, and to use our reflections on the benefits and challenges of implementing PR in care leaver studies to help navigate their way towards a successful peer research model.

References

Bourke, L. (2009). Reflections on doing participatory research in health: Participation, method and power. *International Journal of Social Research Methodology, 12*(5), 457–474.

Curtis, K., Roberts, H., Copperman, J., Downies, A., & Liabo, K. (2004). How come I don't get asked no *questions? Researching 'hard to reach' children and teenagers. Child and Family Social Work, 9*, 167–175.

Dixon, J., Lee, J., Stein, M., Guhirwa, H., Bowley, S., & Catch 22 Peer Researchers (2015). *Corporate parenting for young people in care: Making the difference?* London: Catch22.

DONCEL and Faculty of Social Sciences in Argentina. (2015). Building independence, a peer research video project. Buenos Aries: DONCEL & FLACSO. https://www.youtube.com/watch?v=3NvxJOOS3A4

Goldberg, D. (1978). *Manual of the general health questionnaire*. Windsor: NFER-Nelson.

Greene, S., & Hill, M. (2005). Researching children's experiences: Methods and methodological issues. In S. Greene & D. Hogan (Eds.), *Researching children's experiences: Approaches and methods* (pp. 1–21). London: Sage.

Holland, S., Ronold, E., Ross, N. J., & Hillman, A. (2010). Power, agency and participatory agendas: A critical exploration of young people's engagement in participative qualitative research. *Childhood, 17*, 360.

Joseph Rowntree Foundation (2000). *Involving young people in research projects, Findings.* York: JRF.

Kilpatrick, R., McCartan, C., McAllister, S., & McKeown, P. (2007). If I am brutally honest, research has never appealed to me…The problems and successes of a peer research project. *Education Action Research, 15*, 351–369.

Lushey, C., & Munro, E. (2014). Peer research methodology: An effective method for obtaining young people's perspectives on transitions from care to adulthood? *Qualitative Social Work, 14*(4), 522–537.

Nind, M. (2011). Participatory data analysis: A step too far? *Qualitative Research, 11*, 349.

Smith, R., Monaghan, M., & Broad, B. (2002). Involving young people as co-researchers: Facing up to methodological issues. *Qualitative Social Work, 1*, 191–207.

SOVA. (2005). *Women into work pilot project evaluation report. Peer mentoring support and resettlement pilot.* Sheffield: Sheffield Hallam University. https://www.shu.ac.uk/_assets/pdf/hccj-sovareport.pdf. https://www.shu.ac.uk/_assets/pdf/hccj-ResearchMethodology.pdf. Accessed 10 Sept 15.

Verweijen-Slamnescu, R., & Bowley, S. (2014). Empowering young care leavers through peer research. In T. Stern (Ed.), *Action research, innovation and change: International perspectives across disciplines* (pp. 89–100). Oxon: Routledge.

WMTD Catch22 & National Children's Bureau (2007). *What makes the difference?* London: WMTD/Catch22 & NCB.

12

Researching Care Leavers in an Ethical Manner in Switzerland, Germany, Israel and China

Samuel Keller, Benjamin Strahl, Tehila Refaeli, and Claire (Ting) Zhao

Introduction

Ethical issues are pivotal elements of the practice and profession of social work and child and youth services (henceforth described in this chapter as 'social work') regarding social workers' power, role and reciprocity, norms and decision-making processes (e.g. IASSW and IFSW 2004). But

---

S. Keller (✉)
School of Social Work, ZHAW Zürich Universitiy of Applied Sciences, Zürich, Switzerland

B. Strahl
Department for Social Pedagogics and Organisation Studies,
University of Hilfesheim, Hildesheim, Lower Saxony, Germany

T. Refaeli
Department of Social Work, Ben-Gurion University, Beer-Sheva, Israel

C. Zhao
School of Social Sciences, Education and Social Work, Queen's University Belfast, Belfast, UK

© The Author(s) 2016
P. Mendes, P. Snow (eds.), *Young People Transitioning from Out-of-Home Care*, DOI 10.1057/978-1-137-55639-4_12

when looking for ethical guidelines in research, only a limited number of comprehensive discussions can be found. An exception is Mendes et al. (2014) who proposed an ethical framework for the specific research field of leaving care. It is important to note that research ethics cannot be borrowed directly from practice ethics (Shaw 2003). To reflect on ethical questions in research means recognizing the expectations, roles and dignity of participants concerning research questions and research methods. Most importantly, those reflections should be implemented within the context of interaction, methods, data and results (Josselson 2007).

The transition to adulthood creates a number of challenges for this group, including family conflicts, obstacles to gaining stable employment and pursuing higher education (Arnett 2007; Stein 2006). The experience of being placed in out-of-home care can present a barrier for researchers seeking to contact those individuals who have left care, since in their everyday adult life, care leavers often try to hide this aspect of their upbringing. This challenge highlights the need for researchers to proceed ethically in the process of trying to find adult individuals from this vulnerable group, and encourage them to participate in research. It also needs to be recognized that such research involves a vulnerable group with histories of trauma and abuse. This context demands extra care to avoid the creation of harm associated with participation in research. In addition, research on care leavers is done with children, young people or young adults who are usually not sufficiently supported and advised by family members or other mentors. Therefore, adequate support should be offered after the interview, in the form of professional help and intervention, if needed. This can lead to questions of what role the researchers play in the lives of care leavers, and what assistance care leavers can expect from researchers. Keeping in mind that care leavers are different from each other and come from a variety of cultures and ethnicities, it is impossible to find general, all-encompassing answers to ethical questions. However, regardless of the differences in context, this chapter argues that certain commonalities exist in the ethical conduct of leaving care research, and these are described across four different national studies.

The aim of this chapter is to explore what constitutes an ethical approach when researching youth leaving care, by identifying certain core ethical principles and examining the challenges of maintaining an ethical approach to fieldwork. The ethical challenges will be divided into four chronological dimensions based on the field experience: entering the field, completing the interview, leaving the field and reflections on cultural factors in ethical decision-making. This chapter draws attention to the importance of applying ethical standards within each research component through developing professional relationships, assessing and managing risks and respecting looked-after youth.

Four Qualitative Studies with Care Leavers in Four Countries

The authors conducted leaving care research in China, Israel, Germany and Switzerland. In all four countries, there is a notable lack of research and theory that directly investigates the process of leaving care. The four authors' shared experiences on ethical considerations were based on the below-mentioned four qualitative research projects on care leavers:

Israel

The aim of the study was to examine care leavers' experiences in transitions, specifically the transition from military service to civilian life, and the sources of resilience in periods of transition. The research project included a qualitative component where 16 life story interviews were conducted with young people who had aged out of residential facilities four years earlier.

Germany

The aim of the study was to investigate the transition of care leavers into higher educational institutions. Seventeen open-ended biographical interviews were conducted in order to (re)construct the care leaver's life from the care leaver's perspective, and to investigate the transition process in the context of biographical matters (especially family, care history and school career). In response to the interviews with care leavers in higher education, a self-organized network of students without family support was subsequently initiated.

Switzerland

The goal of the study was to define and raise the quality of mother–child-care and transitions by taking into consideration social workers' and users' perspective as well as individual development over time. Mother–child-care is a setting for young mothers and their babies to whom child-care-authorities provide support to promote successful mothering. Thirty young mothers living in seven different institutions were interviewed (semi-structured narrative interviews) both after having entered and after having left care.

China

The research aimed to provide insights into youth in residential care in China to illustrate the challenges they face when transitioning to adulthood. This was designed as a qualitative case study and included twelve young people and four care workers as participants. Semi-structured interviews, observations and document analysis were employed to provide a triangulated understanding of the leaving care process.

By bringing these four studies together, it has become apparent that approaching research with care leavers in an ethical manner is full of complexities. The challenges are discussed through a comparative analysis of these four studies by following the chronology of research field work (entering the field, interview situation, ending the interview and reflecting on the cultural context), as summarized in Fig. 12.1.

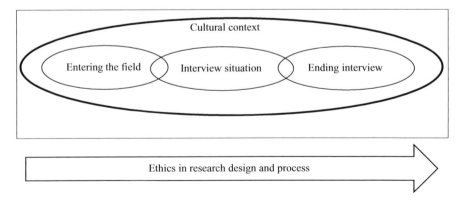

Fig. 12.1 Ethically relevant dimensions in research design and process

Entering the Field

Elementary Considerations: Addressing Care Leavers as Interviewees

The way to address care leavers as potential interview partners must be considered before entering the field. First, the terms that are used to address interviewees must fit within their self-perception without being stigmatizing. In most countries, the term 'care leaver' is not known by the youths themselves. Translations or synonyms do not always exist, and for those who have left care, such specific designations referring to their out-of-home care experience might appear to be stigmatizing. Some young people have problems understanding why they were asked to be interviewed and may believe that it is because they are viewed as 'special', which could have negative connotations. This automatic basis of mistrust can lead to refusals and cancelations of meetings even if they have agreed to be interviewed, which can be understood as the strategy of a stigmatized person to deal with the expectations of others (Goffman 1963).

How can researchers deal with this difficulty of addressing care leavers as interviewees? Considering the research studies reviewed here, we suggest addressing care leavers in a resource-oriented way, by addressing them as experts in their life situation. For example, the German study on care leavers in higher education highlighted their educational achievements (as students) and their ability to overcome their difficult preconditions. The positive impact of this was finding more interviewees than needed, who were willing to tell their story.

Access to the Field/How to Find Interviewees

The research experiences of all considered studies demonstrated the difficulty of tracing care leavers after they had left care (e.g. due to change of mobile phone numbers and unstable accommodation). The ethical challenge arising out of this problem is how to find a voluntary, but also adequate, sample, without neglecting the importance of confidentiality (Mendes et al. 2014). In countries where no association or (self-)

organization of care leavers exists, care institutions or care workers are the only reliable formal connection to former institutionalized or foster children. This approach is delicate for ethical reasons; using (former) caregivers as facilitators of research participation may create questions of true voluntariness, as interviewees might feel obliged to participate when asked to do so by their former carers (Narimani 2014). It is possible that former care workers may forward contact details of care leavers without permission of the interviewees, which could be seen as a breach of the approved ethics explanatory statement. While this may be more convenient for recruitment purposes, researchers should reflect on the potential influence of caregivers, and be aware that they may not know how consent for participation in the interview has been obtained. For these reasons, alternative ways of reaching care leavers need to be pursued first. Depending on the research question and the target group, contact could be made using mailing lists of universities, social networks (like Facebook, among others), contacting correctional facilities or homeless shelters, placing posters and flyers in selected places, placing advertisements in newspapers and using snowball sampling. Also, authorities and youth welfare offices may be an option to contact care leavers. Distributing information about a research project must be done without breaching client confidentiality.

Not all methods of reaching care leavers are equally effective. Further, as making contact with care leavers can be difficult, employing different recruitment strategies can ensure access to a sample that is as varied as possible. This is important to gain a sample that includes a range of experiences (Mendes et al. 2014); therefore, researchers should not to be solely dependent on directly mediated contacts through former service providers.

Place of Interview/Choice of Interview Partner

A fundamental consideration of doing ethical research is to observe the principle of 'first do no harm', derived from the field of medical practice and research (Jonsen 1977). This is done by identifying and managing risks associated with the care leaver's participation in the project (Mendes et al. 2014; Unger et al. 2014). As care leavers are asked to narrate their personal experiences, including trauma, maltreatment and relationship breakdowns, in the interview situation, the environment should be comfortable, safe and inspire confidence. As the care leavers know best, in terms of what suits their emotional/psychological condition, they must be carefully involved in the organization of the interview arrangement. This concerns aspects of the location and the involved persons in the interview situation. Locations may range from the researcher's office to the home of the interviewee. The latter option may best meet the wishes of the interviewee, but could be problematic for safety reasons for the interviewer (Mendes et al. 2014).

Alternatively, neutral, semi-public places like coffee shops or parks may be appropriate, though settings such as these can be problematic for audio-recording if there is background noise. The gender of the interviewer was important in the German research project in cases of care leavers with traumatic experiences (e.g. childhood sexual abuse). If the interviewee still feels uncomfortable, an option could be to allow a friend to be brought along or to change the location. To conclude, interviewees should be able to participate in all matters relating to the planning of the interview setting, as they are the most important, but also vulnerable persons in this process, and their convenience and well-being should have the highest priority, notwithstanding the importance of researcher safety.

Interview Situation and Role of Interviewers

The next step in the interview process is the actual meeting with the interviewee and the interview process which arise other ethical issues.

Formal Consents Versus Informal Expectations

The first ethical issue concerns what the interviewees understand before they agree to participate in the interview concerning the possible emotional harm they might experience as a result of participating. The use of an 'informed consent' form in any study is typically obligatory today in social science studies (Israel and Hay 2006). At the outset, researchers describe the aim of the interview before presenting the consent form. According to Meade and Slesnick (2002), in order to obtain valid and completely voluntary consent, the researcher must provide the maximum information that will help the participants decide whether they are ready to participate after they consider any possible risk and benefit (Israel and Hay 2006; Halse and Honey 2005). Mendes et al. (2014) highlight, and indeed our experiences in the studies underline, the need to read the consent form aloud for participants, because some of them may have difficulties in reading and understanding. Reading aloud the form, which should be written in a clear language, can assist the young person to fully understand what they are signing. In addition, one section in the (Israeli) form claims that the interviewer explained to the interviewee the kinds of inconveniences that he/she might experience during the interview. We know we can arouse some unwanted memories (from the perspective of the interviewee), which the interviewee may or may not disclose. Since the informed consent form does not include detailed data on this kind of risk, one solution is to fully describe the emotional consequences that may accour (as is done in the Chinese research). Nevertheless, it is not possible for the researcher to know what the full range of emotional consequences is for each individual, and going in too hard on this may deter participation.

Presenting the Researcher

The researchers in our studies were all qualified social workers who have the professional ability to deliver emotional support to participants, as suggested by Mendes et al. (2014). However, this highlighted the ethical question of how to present the researcher. First, the participants in the Chinese study demonstrated limited understanding of the researcher's role. Owing to the limited role of social workers and research studies in China, most of them interpreted the researcher as a public servant or journalist. That mistaken understanding of the duty of the researcher might affect the way in which participants respond to interview questions, or may negatively impact their 'free will' to participate and/or stop when they choose to do so (Israel and Hay 2006). In this situation, interviewers need to outline what the researcher's duty is, what the interviewees can expect and what benefits (if any) they may receive from participating, in order to comply with ethical requirements.

In Israel, presenting the researcher as coming from the social work field led to the question of how to make it clear that we do not have the resources to provide ongoing help as social workers typically do. In the interviews in Israel, some references to social workers arose in the life stories. While analysing the data, we understood that these references could be interpreted as a request for help, and even be viewed as an expectation of help from the researcher. In one example, an interviewee was describing economic distress and claimed that social services were not helping. This could be interpreted as a request to the interviewer to intervene and help him/her directly, or through his/her connections with social services. We saw that as an unwanted effect on the content of the interview, since the life story may have been affected by the interviewee's wish to attain secondary assistance from the interviewer. However, the ethical duty to share the data about the aim and the context of the research is obligatory. Therefore, the decision was made to emphasize that we are social work *researchers*, carefully taking into account the meaning of any reference concerning experiences with social workers during the interviews. We also suggested a list of social services to the interviewees at the end of the interview, which would possibly be able to help them.

Enhance Confidence at the Beginning of the Interviews

At the beginning of the interview, we sometimes felt we needed a longer process to create a feeling of confidence and trust. This was the main issue in the study in China. Culturally, the process of strangers getting to know each other required several meetings, preferably informal ones, which posed a challenge for this type of research. The research process demands that in order to maintain objectivity, some distance has to be maintained. The dilemma is to either keep the process of the research 'clean' while paying the price of potentially eliciting poor-quality information from the interviewees, or to establish a longer relationship with the interviewees before the interviews in order to attain richer data, but then the process of collecting the data is potentially compromised. In Israel, conducting 'small talk' before the interview actually led, in some cases, to important data being discussed at this point and it therefore was not technically part of the interviews. Consequently, we try to turn on the recorder right after the signing of the formal consent form, and treat the 'small talk' as part of the interview. Josselson's concept (2007) of repetitive explanation about the contribution the interview can make in the relevant field (e.g. promoting services for care leavers) can be another way to encourage rapport at the beginning and throughout the interview.

Uncovering Biographical, Traumatic Memories Without Giving Therapy

The ethical issue here concerns who has the responsibility to protect the adult interviewee. As mentioned earlier, the interview situation, especially when seeking narrative or biographical information from care leavers, can provoke traumatic memories. While discussing the care leavers' life, the interview situation is often highly sensitive. However, as researchers, we cannot offer to provide therapy afterwards (Halse and Honey 2005).

In most of our cases, interviewees seemed to know how to protect themselves during the interview. Most of them maintained a calm manner while speaking about their trauma and losses. Occasionally, participants decided not to keep talking if they felt they would not be able to control their emotions, as a way of protecting themselves against distress. However, some interviewees became upset during the interview, and expressed their feelings by crying or raising their voices.

The ethical question is whether to stop the interview and suggest continuing it in another meeting given that we are aware that the process of contacting care leavers is not easy, and that if we stop the interview, it may be the end of the contact with this person. In our interviews, the interviewer provided the option to stop or take a few minutes' break. In all the cases, the interviewees preferred not to stop completely and sometimes just to stop for few minutes. However, the ethical question remains: do we need to be active in stopping the interview when we can see that it is upsetting for the interviewee? According to Josselson (2007), participants know how to protect themselves, and choose what to share and what to keep to themselves.

We are also left with the question as to how participants cope after the interview with issues they talked about during the interview. Who is responsible to make sure that they can manage the trauma or any negative feelings they are left with? In line with recommendations made by Mendes et al. (2014), interviews in the four projects were coducted by qualified social workers who have clinical experience as well as previous experience interviewing young people in distress. In addition, there are agreements that relationships with the interviewees are for the research only and not therapeutic ones and therefore they will end at the end of the interviews. The question that remains open is whether it is ethical to call the interviewee to check on how he/she is feeling a few days after the interview. The unwritten contract in most of our interviews is that there are professional boundaries, according to which no ongoing contact will be pursued by either party after the interview. However, these boundaries leave certain ethical unanswered questions about participant welfare and open for further inquiry.

Ending the Interview

Preceding sections showed that each interview situation must be seen as a unique and communally constructed social interaction—even more so when open questions allow participants to define topics and extensions of their narratives (Rosenthal 2003). As narratives can describe private and emotional experiences and feelings, the time just after having officially finished the interview is an important and sensitive period, as will be explored further below.

How to End on a Positive Note?

Turning off the recorder can relieve the tension of what is sometimes seen as an official or formal experience. Interviewees might now start to realize whether their initial expectations were met (or not), and/or if they feel confident or suspicious, empowered or dependent. This leads to the following ethical dilemma: on the one hand, the more you were able to create an atmosphere of privacy and confidence before and during the interview, the more the likelihood of better quality of the data. On the other hand, the annoyance, frustration and vulnerability of participants could increase afterwards if they feel they were emotionally exploited. For this reason, it is important to 'end on a positive note' (Josselson 2007, p. 544), and to have enough time for mutual reflection after turning off the recorder in order to find a balance between closeness and distance.

Based on this sensitive ending, it is also easier for all participants to find a transparent and open-minded way to clarify if and how to stay in contact (as far as roles and expectations are concerned). To clarify, further contact on a positive note is relevant for different reasons: researchers must be contactable after the interview to answer questions coming up a few days later, and, in specific cases, to refer to further professionals such as counsellors or therapists. Later, they should be able to contact care leavers to manage expectations, and to check that privacy is preserved when results are published.

Buying Information or Esteeming Participation?

Care leavers are a hard-to-reach population. The possible reasons for this include the fact that they are young people in changing and unstable circumstances, and also, based on their experiences in care, they tend to have mixed feelings towards official conversations with adult 'professionals'. Thus, it is folly to assume that participants will make a substantial effort to allocate time to share personal and maybe unpleasant experiences with a stranger. A small gift at the end (besides paying for travel expenses and paying for drinks) might help provide motivation and acknowledge effort. This, however, leads to another ethical dilemma: what sort of gift is appropriate without becoming an inappropriate incentive? Is it not the case that motivation should be intrinsic?

Although it can be seen as an (ethical) practice in research in many countries to pay for the effort associated with long interviews, there is a difference between money and a non-paternalist stance on payment

(Shaw 2003), which addresses individual motivation instead of monetary incentives. It also depends on the cultural and subcultural context as to how care leavers and their social networks react to gifts or payment. In our projects, all care leavers received about €20 as a form of appreciation for their willingness and time, and some of them received a gift card or movie tickets to the value of €20. The balance between purchase of information and lack of recognition should be carefully negotiated with different parties.

Triggering Emotions, Answering Emotions, Helping?

The opportunity to talk is also a motivation for youth participants to engage in research, regardless of the material reward. After having ended the interview, care leavers might see the interviewer as a confidant who has been interested, and has listened and understood without judging them. Or, alternatively, they could see him/her as another professionally motivated 'pretender' who was 'faking friendship' (Duncombe and Jessop 2002) to pursue his/her own goals. Confidence, as well as mistrust, can lead to a misunderstanding of the relationship with the researcher.

In some of our studies, participants sent personal text messages and pictures to the interviewer's business mobile phone or chat after the interview. Though mobile phones and chats are important means to enter the field and to stay in contact with young people leaving care, researchers must see new media as unchartered ways to communicate that come with many possible misunderstandings. In those cases, the interviewers answered immediately, asked if there were further questions, and gave thanks in a polite, but formal, way. Thus, care leavers felt neither rejected (again) nor that the interviewer was a close friend.

Researchers are responsible for care leavers' well-being after the interview, and for providing access to possible further support (Birch and Miller 2000). Although the close rapport achieved for the interview could be viewed as a quasi-therapeutic interaction, this should be avoided during the research process (Brinkman and Kvale 2008). To be prepared for this particular possibility, interviewers need to prepare at least a leaflet, with important and easily reachable addresses concerning suitable agencies, including counseling or therapy, and provide contact details. In Israel, we gave the participant a list of social services that can provide emotional and practical support.

Impact of Culture/Understanding Differences

Ethical values are not universal. Moreover, regardless of national and cultural differences, a researcher encounters additional challenges when working with various subcultural groups. This section illustrates the fact that culture is an overlooked factor in research; however, this needs to be acknowledged, while the transition from out-of-home-care research continues to expand internationally.

It has been mentioned that the modern concept of research ethics was developed within the Western context, which is a particular ideological and cultural framework that is not shared universally. Within this Western social context, such as Germany, Switzerland and Israel, a participant is, perhaps, able to understand the meaning of the ethical approach more thoroughly and use it more naturally, since the ethical values are not far removed from their native cultural traditions. Yet, in the case study of China, it is clear that the concept of research ethics, as discussed here from within an admittedly Western perspective, may not be fully understood and acted upon.

The participants and gatekeepers in China are not familiar with the ethical tradition whereby the researcher approaches the gatekeepers, including the institution manager, administrative team and care workers. The majority of them do not have any knowledge regarding research ethics, and they care solely about whether the senior leadership of the institution has agreed to the initiative.

Accordingly, the Chinese young people questioned the necessity of the consent form and were reluctant to protect themselves by using the rights they were informed of by the researcher. One of the participants said that as long as the gatekeepers agreed, he would not have a problem with participating. He did not bother to even glance at the consent form before signing. So, the researcher felt obliged to remind him of the relevant information about the research and the participants' rights before the interview commenced.

Another case refers to a Chinese young person's lack of willingness to protect his own rights. In one interview, when it touched upon a young person's painful past, he was observed to break down emotionally and was unable to continue the conversation. The researcher offered him the right to refuse to answer or to modify the continuation of the interview as he wished; however, he chose to surrender these rights and kept going. Eventually, the researcher stopped interviewing because of the observed harm to the young person.

The young person described above revealed his reasons for continuing, which were all related to traditional Chinese culture. Firstly, he felt uncomfortable to refuse requests, because this could be seen to raise tension and disagreement during a face-to-face interaction, which is not tolerable in Chinese culture. Secondly, if he failed to complete the interview as promised, he would judge himself as a dishonourable human being. It is related to Chinese culture evaluates a person's credibility by his/her ability to match his/her words with behaviours. In addition to that, it is seen as shameful to stand up for individual rights, which is in contradiction with the collective cultural environment in China. These issues have also arisen while interviewing care leavers in Israel who had emigrated from Ethiopia.

However, it was encouraging that the case study in China found that there is an emerging awareness of the need for ethical approaches, particularly when these aligned with participants' other motivations. For example, there were two care workers who questioned the aims of the research before allowing their children to meet with the researcher. Their questions were about the purpose of protecting children, which aligned with the ethical values of the research. Also, several young people accepted the option of not answering certain questions, when they expected the questions might raise undesirable emotional reactions.

In addition, it should also be noted that the research question about 'transitioning from out-of-home care' comes with a certain cultural assumption linked to modern Western middle-class values. However, children in care are various subgroups who hold different opinions about mainstream values. Ethical questions arise when interpreting independence as an agreed aim for the care leavers. The existing research has indicated that returning to one's original family has become a very common response to the notion that one would wish to seek independence (Courtney and Dworsky 2006; Dixon et al. 2006), and is in alignment with Chinese culture and society (Zhao 2015). It raises the notion that care leavers may appreciate dependence over independence, which is in direct contradiction to goals set by policy makers and social work practitioners, and might be unjustifiably interpreted by researchers as a 'deficit'.

Conclusion and Further Thoughts

This chapter aimed to connect theories and practices on ethical issues in interviewing care leavers. Our main goal was to highlight the complexity of this issue by presenting some examples of the ethical concerns we uncovered during our interviews in four different countries with individuals from different cultural backgrounds. We are well aware that these concerns are not all-encompassing when it comes to the ethical issues of researching these and other vulnerable groups. However, to support researchers' critical reflexivity concerning their methods, ideals, roles, impact and empathy as one of the major tasks and methodical requirements (Unger et al. 2014), certain common important factors have been articulated:

Enter the Field Considerately and with an Intent to Respect Young People

Care leavers will likely internalize the stigma of their group identity (Goffman 1963). Therefore, it seems important to not only address them not just as vulnerable youths, but also to highlight their achievements. As care leavers are first-hand experts about their situation and experiences, they must be viewed as serious interview partners, and respected as being able to be involved in all aspects of the interview process as means of preventing any harm.

Give a Real Choice About Participating

Respecting care leavers as serious interview partners, as autonomous human beings and not just as (potential) participants and objects of research, also means to give them a real choice whether or not to participate. We define having a real choice as including the decision whether or not to use a researcher or adult's power when approaching them, an independent and private process regarding their decision whether or not to participate, and the option of changing one's mind, depending on any time limits or other conditions included in the consent form, for as long as data analysis or the study runs. Even better, of course, would be if care leavers were able to participate when research projects are first designed.

Avoid Misunderstood Meanings of a Quasi-Intimate Relationship

The direction and potential revelations of an interview simply cannot be anticipated in advance. From a researcher's perspective, the time when participants were able to influence the quality of data might technically be over when the recorder is turned off. Nevertheless, from an ethical perspective, the interviewees' views and possible sensitivity after having ended the interview must still be taken very seriously. This is often a time of vulnerability for interviewees who have just exposed important aspects of their lives. They may feel intimately connected to the interviewer, who they now realize they will likely never see again (Josselson 2007). Thus, it is not enough to merely clarify the role of the relationship before the interview; time must also be taken to answer any questions at the end.

Clarify Expectations and Roles: Before and After the Interview

Interviewers might underestimate how much care leavers are used to be 'interviewed' with concrete, sometimes hidden, consequences, when professionals want to decide about next steps of intervention. They might define an interviewer's role as a professional, as a politically motivated activist, as a friend, as an adversary representing bad experiences in child and youth care or as an objective, impersonal researcher. As much as possible, researchers must be aware of care leavers' feelings during the interview and offer time-outs if they think it is needed. It is also important to lead the interviewed young person back into their everyday life by integrating some informal 'chatting' after the interview.

Avoid Spoiling the Field

If we understand the research field as an eco-system, the researcher's activity could cause potential 'pollution' to the participants, their social networks and in the research field itself, which would harm further research. As members of the academic community, researchers should be careful to avoid any unethical behaviour towards participants.

Offer Supervision to Social Work Researchers

Offering supervision must be seen as extremely important for developing a coherent research context. In research processes, there is often little time to reflect on roles, situations or impacts, as presented in this chapter. Supervision offers a regular and professional structured opportunity to reflect, to learn and to avoid causing harm or misunderstandings, and also to ensure that qualitative research is of high methodological quality and conducted only by appropriately skilled interviewers (Mendes et al. 2014).

Share Knowledge

Examining ethical issues from different (international) perspectives can lead to an expansion of our options as to how to deal with different dilemmas. Being exposed to other opinions can sometimes undermine researchers' feelings on to how to conduct research appropriately, but also gives them a second chance to confirm that their process of conducting research would avoid causing harm.

One of the common findings from the experience of presenting the four sets of studies in this chapter is that a so-called ethical approach is not limited to the ethical approval procedures, and yet there is little guidance on matters outside of this process. In this sense, it is important to address the question as to what is to be done when the researcher meets an ethically challenging situation, which falls out of the realm of their ethical approval. From supervision by other researchers, interviewers can develop skills that balance these various, largely undefined, practical and emotional difficulties.

Notice Culture as an Overlooked Factor

The transition from out-of-home care research aims to decrease the social exclusion of marginalized groups, and in this sense, culture is a key indicator of understanding the experiences of minority ethnic groups or other under-researched groups. However, the cultural definition of 'transition from out-of-home care' research should also be explored further. In particular, the current research has a preset tone, which generally carries the mainstream ideology of the West; therefore, the baseline perspective may be in direct contradiction with the researched subculture and non-Western cultural values.

Conclusion

To summarize, this chapter examines the process of exploring ethical issues in research among care leavers from an international point of view. This process leads to an observation of the different stages in which ethical issues can arise, and their complexity in different cultural groups, as well as offering some methodological orientation that can address these issues. Our main recommendations for other researchers are to examine at each step of their research the possibility for ethical issues; to create a researchers' community to discuss and consult whenever dilemmas arise; and to create an open dialogue about these ethical issues with care leavers as well as other vulnerable groups in order to respect their opinions about what processes will best serve their interests. We highlight that whilst researchers involved in these studies may intend to promote the welfare of vulnerable groups, they should invest extra efforts to avoid any harm to individuals in these groups. They can arguably achieve this aim by critically reflecting on their role and on unintended impacts and cultural ideals behind goals and methods during the whole research process.

References

Arnett, J. (2007). *Adolescence and emerging adulthood: A cultural approach* (3 ed.). Upper Saddle River: Prentice Hall.

Birch, M., & Miller, T. A. (2000). Inviting intimacy: The interview as, therapeutic opportunity. *International Journal of Social Research Methodology, 3*(3), 189–202.

Brinkmann, S., & Kvale, S. (2008). Ethics in qualitative psychological research. In C. Willig & W. Stainton-Rogers (Eds.), *The SAGE handbook of qualitative research in psychology* (pp. 262–280). London: Sage.

Courtney, M., & Dworsky, A. (2006). Early outcomes for young adults transitioning from out-of- home care in the USA correspondence. *Child and Family Social Work, 11*(3), 209–219.

Dixon, J., Wade, J., Byford, S., Weatherly, H., & Lee, J. (2006). *Young people leaving care: A study of costs and outcomes: Final report to the department for education and skills*. York: Social Work Research and Development Unit, University of York.

Duncombe, J., & Jessop, J. (2002). Doing rapport and the ethics of faking friendship. In M. Mauthner, M. Birch, J. Jessop, & T. Miller (Eds.), *Ethics in qualitative research* (pp. 108–121). London: Sage.

Goffmann, E. (1963). *Stigma. Notes on the management of spoiled identity*. Englewood Cliffs: Prentice-Hall.

Halse, C., & Honey, A. (2005). Unraveling ethics: Illuminating the moral dilemmas of research ethics. *Journal of Women in Culture and Society, 30*(4), 2141–2162.

International Association of Schools of Social Work (IASSW) and International Federation of Social Workers (IFSW). (2004). http://ifsw.org/policies/statement-of-ethical-principles/. Accessed 18 Aug 2015.

Israel, M., & Hay, I. (2006). Informed consent. In M. Israel & I. Hay (Eds.), *Research ethics for social scientists* (pp. 60–77). London: Sage.

Jonsen, A. R. (1977). Do no harm: Axiom of medical ethics. In S. Spicker & H. T. Engelhardt (Eds.), *Philosophical medical ethics: Its nature and significance* (pp. 27–41). Dordrecht: Kluwer.

Josselson, R. (2007). The ethical attitude in narrative research: Principles and practicalities. In D. J. Clandinin (Ed.), *Handbook of narrative inquiry: Mapping a methodology* (pp. 537–566). Thousand Oaks: Sage.

Meade, M., & Slesnick, N. (2002). Ethical considerations for research and treatment with runaway and homeless adolescents. *Journal of Psychology, 136*(4), 449–463.

Mendes, P., Snow, P., & Baidawi, S. (2014). Some ethical considerations associated with researching young people transitioning from out-of-home care. *Community, Children and Families Australia, 8*(2), 81–92.

Narimani, P. (2014). Zustimmung als Prozess: Informiertes Einverständnis in der Praxisforschung mit von Ausweisung bedrohten Drogenabhängigen. In H. V. Unger, P. Narimani, & R. M'Bayo (Eds.), *Forschungsethik in der qualitativen Forschung Reflexivität, Perspektiven, Positionen* (pp. 41–58). Wiesbaden: Springer Fachmedien.

Rosenthal, G. (2003). The healing effects of storytelling: On the conditions of curative storytelling in the context of research and counseling. *Qualitative Inquiry, 9*(6), 915–933.

Shaw, F. (2003). Ethics in qualitative research and evaluation. *Journal of Social Work, 3*(1), 9–29.

Stein, M. (2006). Research review: Young people leaving care. *Child and Family Social Work, 11*(3), 273–279.

Unger, H. V., Narimani, P., & M'Bayo, R. (2014). *Forschungsethik in der qualitativen Forschung Reflexivität, Perspektiven, Positionen*. Wiesbaden: Springer Fachmedien.

Zhao, T. (2015) *A qualitative case study of youth transition from out-of-home care (Residential care) in China: Variation on an international theme?* Unpublished PhD thesis. Queen's University Belfast.

Part IV

An Analysis of Policy and Practice in Specific Jurisdictions

13

Young People Transitioning from Care in Australia: A Critical But Neglected Area of Policy Development

Toni Beauchamp

This chapter examines policy frameworks for young people transitioning from out-of-home care (OHC) in Australia and draws comparisons with the UK and the USA. In Australia, a raft of reviews and inquiries at state and national levels has highlighted the need to strengthen provisions for transition planning and aftercare support. While there are some examples of innovative policy responses, overall, the pace of reform in Australia has been slow. In most states and territories, legal provisions are discretionary, and access to aftercare support is not viewed as an automatic entitlement. The challenges that young people face in accessing appropriate support are often exacerbated by fragmented responsibilities and lack of coordination across government departments. There is also little monitoring of compliance with legal requirements for transition planning or outcomes of care leavers.

T. Beauchamp (✉)
Abbotsford, NSW, Australia

About Children and Young People in Care and Transitioning from Care

In Australia, policy debates on this issue have been fragmented due to a federal system of government and policy and practice differences between states and territories (Mendes et al. 2011a). State and territory governments are responsible for the administration of statutory child protection, including OHC. The Commonwealth Government has a minor role in child protection, including funding services that focus on prevention and early intervention (Senate Community Affairs Reference Committee 2015).

According to data from the Australian Institute of Health and Welfare (AIHW 2015a), on 30 June 2014, there were 43,009 children and young people in statutory OHC, including those in foster care, kinship care and residential care. Over the past 15 years, the number of children and young people in OHC nationally has more than doubled (Australian Institute of Family Studies [AIFS], cited in Senate Community Affairs Reference Committee 2015). Aboriginal and Torres Strait Islander children are significantly over-represented in the OHC system and are over nine times more likely to be in OHC than non-Indigenous children (AIHW 2015a). In addition to children and young people in statutory OHC, a large number of children and young people are in informal arrangements with relatives and kin.[1] The AIHW (2015a) indicates that 3124 young people aged 15–17 were discharged from OHC in 2013–14.[2]

International research consistently shows that young people transitioning from care are at high risk of social exclusion, poverty and poor outcomes in later life (Stein and Munro 2008; Höjer and Sjöblom 2014). Findings from Australian research are consistent with the international evidence. For example, a survey of 471 young care leavers, conducted for the CREATE Foundation, found that nationally 35 per cent of the young people were homeless in the first year of leaving care, 46 per cent

---

[1] It has been estimated that the Australian ratio of informal to formal kinship care arrangements is three to one (Smyth and Eardley 2008).
[2] This figure includes some young people returning to families or other placements and does not clearly distinguish young people transitioning to independence.

of young men and 22 per cent of young women had been involved in the youth justice system, 65 per cent of young people did not complete Year 12 and 29 per cent were unemployed compared to the national average of 9.75 per cent (McDowall 2009). Notably, 28 per cent were already parents themselves. A recent national study found that 63 per cent of young people in the study group who were receiving support from homelessness services had come out of state care, although no data were provided regarding how long, on average, the OHC cohort had been in care, or the average age at which they left care (Flatau et al. 2015). Another recent study found that care leavers rarely transition to higher education (Harvey et al. 2015).

As Wade and Munro (2008) argue, how young people fare in the transition process is not completely pre-determined by their past experiences, and there is considerable scope to provide them with turning points and opportunities for change. Research consistently indicates three key factors that are critical to achieving better outcomes: improving the quality of care, a more gradual and flexible transition process and more specialized aftercare supports, including access to stable accommodation arrangements (Stein 2008).

The National Policy Context

In 2009, the Commonwealth, state and territory governments and a coalition of non-government organizations agreed to a *National Framework for Protecting Australia's Children 2009–2020*. The National Framework is underpinned by a public health model, which, if realized, would shift the child protection system to place greater emphasis on preventing child abuse and neglect and early intervention. The National Framework includes a commitment to improving support for young people who are transitioning from care.

In 2010, the Commonwealth Government also introduced *National Standards for Out-of-Home Care* to drive improvements in the quality of care. The standards include a requirement that all young people have a transition from care plan commencing at age 15 (Department of Families, Housing, Community Services and Indigenous Affairs 2011). However, there is still poor compliance with this standard across most states and territories, and no concrete supports are prescribed for young people who have left state care. The key problem with both the National Standards and the National Framework is the lack of accountability and enforceable measures. A related issue is the lack of funding associated with the National Framework to support implementation or provide incentives for investment by state and territory governments.

Currently, there is some optimism that the National Framework will be reinvigorated through the Third Action Plan, which includes some measures to strengthen implementation, governance and accountability. The need to improve support for young people transitioning from care is recognized as a key priority in the plan (Department of Social Services 2015).

Giving Young People the Option to Stay in Care Longer

There is an international consensus among researchers and practitioners that the transition process from care needs to be much more gradual and flexible, based on the levels of maturity and the needs of the young person rather than simply chronological age (Mendes et al. 2011b).

Allowing young people to remain in care longer is also consistent with research on brain development, which shows that critical areas of the brain required for effective decision-making are not fully developed until the mid-20s (Bava and Tapert 2010). The pre-frontal cortex, which is involved with social interaction and self-awareness and regulates risk-taking behaviour, is the region of the brain that changes most during adolescence. Research also tells us that brain development of children who have suffered trauma is delayed, if not disordered (Child Welfare Information Gateway 2015), supporting the argument that care should be extended beyond the age of 18.

It is now increasingly common for young people in the general population to live at home with their parents, or remain financially dependent on them, beyond the school years, and often up to the mid-20s. They also have the security of knowing they have a safety net to rely on if they encounter difficulties. It is notable that the Commonwealth Government's recent report on welfare reform proposes that the age of independence for welfare support should be 22 years (Reference Group on Welfare Reform 2015). In setting the age of independence, the Reference Group notes that the age at which young people leave home in Australia has been rising over time. Data from the Household, Income and Labour Dynamics survey show that in 2012, a total of 81.7 per cent of young men and 72.5 per cent of young women aged 18–21 were living at home with parents or guardians (Wilkins 2015). Just over half (52.1 per cent) of young men and 41.9 per cent of young women aged 22–25 were still living at home with their parents.

Young people growing up in care are more vulnerable and have less support and fewer resources than other young people. Yet, generally, government policies across all Australian states and territories are framed around the expectation that young people leave care at the age of 18, regardless of their individual readiness to do so.

The Australian Capital Territory (ACT) Government has recently released a new five-year strategy to reform OHC. Under the strategy, the subsidy paid to foster and kinship carers will be extended to age 21 in 'select cases where it can be demonstrated that the young person's well-being would otherwise be jeopardized by the cessation of subsidy at 18' (ACT Government 2014). The New South Wales (NSW) Government has recently announced a new 'post care education financial support' payment aimed at helping young people aged 18–25 to complete their Higher School Certificate (Year 12) or equivalent studies (Family and Community Services 2015). The payment provides financial support to carers to maintain current support arrangements while the young person is completing their secondary studies. However, this does not extend to supporting young people to participate in higher education, and there is no provision for continued casework support.

In the UK and the USA, recent legislative reforms, which give young people the option to stay in care until the age of 21, were driven by evidence that young people who remain in care longer generally have better outcomes. Young people who leave care at an early age display higher rates of substance abuse, homelessness, unemployment and poor educational outcomes (Wade and Dixon 2006). Conversely, young people who stay in care longer, particularly beyond the age of 18, experience smoother transitions and are more likely to continue their education and have stable housing (Peters et al. 2009; Raman et al. 2005).

The evaluation of the 'Staying Put' pilot programme, which was trialled in 11 local authorities in England, found that young people who stayed on with carers were twice as likely to be in full-time education at the age of 19 compared with those who did not (Munro et al. 2012). Those who did not stay put were also more likely to experience housing instability after they left care. This provided the impetus for legislative reform, which gave young people the right to remain with their carers until age 21, with financial support. In England, the right to stay in care is currently limited to young people in foster care. However, a campaign group, Every Child Leaving Care Matters, is continuing to advocate for an equivalent level of support to be available to young people in residential care (Rogers 2015). Similar legislation has recently come into effect in Scotland and Wales. Notably, Scotland has gone further than England and extended the right to stay in care to young people in residential care (The Scottish Government 2014). Young people can also re-enter care until the age of 21 if they encounter difficulties. Policy explicitly recognizes the concept of 'interdependence' and emphasizes that accelerated or abrupt transitions should be avoided wherever possible (The Scottish Government 2013).

In the USA, policy and legislative reform has also focused on extending foster care services beyond the age of 18. The MidWest evaluation of the Adult Functioning of Former Foster Youth, a longitudinal study of young people in Illinois, Iowa and Wisconsin, compared the outcomes of young people who were still in care at the age of 19 with those who had already left care. Young people who remained in care for an additional year were more than twice as likely to be continuing their education (Peters et al. 2009). They were also more likely to delay pregnancy (Dworsky and Courtney 2010) and less likely to be involved in the criminal justice system (Courtney et al. 2005).

These findings from the MidWest evaluation provided the impetus for legislative change. The *Fostering Connections to Success and Increasing Adoptions* Act 2008 gives states the option of allowing eligible young people to remain in care until they are 21 years old. States are able to claim federal reimbursement for the costs of extended care. However, young people are only eligible if they are engaged in education or employment, or have a medical condition that prevents such activity. They can be living in a foster home, residential setting or living semi-independently. So far, at least 22 states have extended foster care services to young people beyond the age of 18 (Putnam-Hornstein et al. 2015).

Planning for the Transition

Research has consistently shown that there is a strong association between good preparation and planning and positive post-care experiences (Mendes et al. 2011b). Effective transition planning includes the development of an individual plan, which actively involves the young person in decision-making and includes a comprehensive assessment of individual needs (McDowall 2009). Progress in meeting goals should be regularly reviewed. Preparation needs to be holistic and place equal importance on building practical, emotional and interpersonal skills (Stein 2012).

All Australian jurisdictions have recognized the importance of planning for the transition in legislation or policy. On 30 June 2014, a total of 59.5 per cent of young people aged 15 and over had a current and approved leaving care plan (AIHW 2015b). However, this estimate was based on data available from only four states, namely, Victoria, Queensland, NSW and Western Australia, as the other four jurisdictions were unable to provide data for this measure.

The issue of poor transition planning has been raised in a number of independent reviews and inquiries. A review by the NSW Ombudsman (2013) of young people leaving care found that a large majority of the review group (78 per cent) left care without an approved transition plan. Without this approval (by the NSW Department of Family and Community Services), a young person is not able to access financial support to assist him/her in the transition process. Where transition plans did exist, nearly half were inadequate, or only developed in the two months before the young person turned 18 years. The Ombudsman also raised concern about the failure to address the specific circumstances and needs of high-risk young people, particularly young mothers, Aboriginal young people and young people in juvenile detention prior to leaving care.

The Commissioner for Children in Tasmania (2012) has raised concern about the uncertain road many young people face when they leave state care. As on 30 June 2012, just 20 per cent of 15–18-year-old care leavers in Tasmania had a transition plan. The Queensland Commission of Inquiry into Child Protection (2013) also highlighted significant concerns about poor transition planning. These issues are echoed in a series of three national report cards by the CREATE Foundation. The surveys conducted in 2009, 2011 and 2013 found little improvement in the number of young people aged 15–17 who were aware of having a transition plan (McDowall 2009, 2011, 2013). Hence the challenge is not simply ensuring that such plans are drawn up; they need to be developed in consultation with the young person, who needs to understand their role and purpose.

Support After Leaving Care

Not all young people want to remain in care longer, irrespective of what professionals believe to be in their best interests. An appropriate suite of supports should be available to meet the needs of those who choose to leave care earlier, particularly given that these young people may be the most vulnerable and have the most complex needs.

While there has been limited research on the effectiveness of aftercare support programmes, evaluations in the UK and the USA indicate that such programmes do lead to improved outcomes in the areas of housing stability, education, employment and health, enhanced social connections and a decrease in long-term use of services (Daining and DePanfilis 2007; Stein 2012). Research points to the importance of an integrated and holistic approach with support tailored to the individual needs of the young person (Hannon et al. 2010). Strong cross-agency linkages are critical, including a focus on ensuring that the young person has stable housing and linkages to specialist support to address mental health and drug and alcohol issues (Crane et al. 2014). Special attention should be given to young people who have experienced disrupted placements while in care to minimize instability after leaving care, including monitoring their housing situation (McDowall 2008).

In Australia, existing legislation provides a weak basis for provision of aftercare support. In most states and territories, legislative provisions are discretionary, and access to aftercare support is not viewed as an automatic entitlement. Western Australia is the only jurisdiction where there appears to be a clear statutory obligation to provide some aftercare support, although provision of financial assistance remains discretionary.

There is also some variation in the duration of support across states and territories. In NSW, the Northern Territory, Western Australia, South Australia and the ACT, young people are eligible for aftercare support until they turn 25 years old. Three states, Victoria, Queensland and Tasmania, only provide support to the age of 21. The nature and availability of aftercare support also varies widely across jurisdictions, and even within them. For example, in NSW, there are major gaps in provision of specialist aftercare services in rural and regional areas.

The challenges that young people face in accessing appropriate support are often exacerbated by fragmented responsibilities and lack of coordination across government departments. This issue has been raised in numerous independent reviews and inquiries. The Special Commission of Inquiry into Child Protection Services in NSW (Wood 2008), for example, emphasized the need for an interagency approach, including priority access to a range of Government services. The child protection inquiry in Victoria also highlighted the need to strengthen supports for young people after they leave state care, particularly ensuring stable housing (Cummins et al. 2012, p. 269).

Certainly, there are some examples of innovative policy and programme responses. South Australia and Western Australia have both implemented 'rapid response' cross-government frameworks, which prioritize services to children and young people in care or who are transitioning from care. Partnership initiatives have been developed to support young people transitioning from care, such as automatic eligibility for priority social housing from age 15 (Western Australia) and fee waivers for vocational education (Western Australia and South Australia). In South Australia, all young people transitioning from care also have access to a career advisor to support informed decision-making.

Over the past few years, the Victorian Government has also strengthened supports for young people transitioning from care. In 2014, the Government established the *Springboard* programme, a state-wide initiative, which provides intensive support to young people (aged 16–21) leaving residential care to access education and employment (Baldry et al. 2015). It has also introduced a state-wide initiative to provide culturally appropriate support for Aboriginal young people aged 16–21 who are transitioning from OHC (Baidawi et al. 2015).

Following the Queensland Child Protection Commission of Inquiry, the Queensland Government established the *Next Step Aftercare* service as a state-wide initiative for young people aged 15–21 who have already transitioned from care (prior to 2015, there were no dedicated aftercare services in Queensland). The initiative differs from models in other Australian jurisdictions in providing multiple ways for young people to access support and referrals, including social media, a website, a mobile phone application and a toll-free number (Next step aftercare service 2015).

However, overall, the pace of reform in Australia has been slow, and, too often, there is limited support available to young people once they have left care. One reason for this is that child protection and OHC systems across different states and territories are over-stretched, crisis-driven and struggling to respond to unsustainable demand pressures (Wood 2008; Senate Community Affairs Reference Committee 2015; Scott 2014). Political demands to respond to high profile cases of abuse have led to a risk-averse culture, which focuses heavily on coercive, rather than supportive, strategies, and child protection decisions that favour removal from potentially unsafe situations (Queensland Child Protection Commission of Inquiry 2013; Senate Community Affairs Reference Committee 2015). This has resulted in priority allocations and focus on younger children at risk of harm. Older children and adolescents have been regarded as less vulnerable, and, generally, there has been limited policy attention to addressing their needs (Wood 2008). Additionally, young people transitioning from OHC are largely invisible, and there is a lack of community and media awareness about the challenges they may face. Consequently, in a political environment where federal and state governments are seeking to curb spending on social welfare programmes, the issue has remained low on the policy agenda.

In the UK, there has been rapid policy development and a shift from permissive legislation to strong legal duties since the 1980s. This has been driven by belief in the value of investing in children, particularly vulnerable children, as citizens of the future (Wade and Munro 2008). Legislation and guidance are underpinned by the principle of 'corporate parenting' and emphasize that care leavers should receive the same level of support that their peers would expect from a reasonable parent (Department for Education 2010). The concept of corporate parenting also emphasizes cross-government responsibility to ensure that young people are supported to make the best possible transition from care. Alongside these changes, the (former British Labour) government introduced broader initiatives to address youth homelessness, education and training and young parenthood, and these were also intended to impact care leavers (Stein 2012).

The move to strong legal duties has led to improvements in the quality and level of support provided in the UK. There is now greater involvement of other agencies to address young people's needs, with a shift from informal interagency links to more formal agreements, for example, with housing, health and education (Wade and Munro 2008). There is also some evidence of improved outcomes resulting from these changes. The proportion of young people continuing their education beyond the age of 16 has increased, and there has been a reduction in the numbers, not in education, training or employment (Stein 2012). However, there is still considerable variation between local authorities in implementing legal requirements. As Munro (2013) notes, the extension of statutory duties has not been backed up with sufficient resources and is being implemented in an environment of fiscal restraint.

In the USA, the introduction of the *Foster Care Independence Act* in 1999 increased federal government funds and gave states greater flexibility in the types of support they could provide to eligible young people (aged 16–21). States must match 20 per cent of federal government funds. In the area of education and employment, some states have waived tuition fees for young people who have grown up in care to attend state colleges or universities, and at least one state (Illinois) has created a wage subsidy for young people under 21 who have aged out of foster care (Courtney 2008). However, as in Australia, the decentralized child welfare system hinders consistent service provision (Mendes et al. 2011a). Eligibility criteria and availability of services vary widely between states and even within counties (Courtney 2008; Dworsky and Havlicek 2009). There is also too much emphasis on the goal of rapid independence or self-sufficiency (Mendes 2011a; Schelbe 2011).

Support for Young Parents Who Have Grown Up in Care

One particular policy concern in Australia has been the limited development of policy and programmes to support young women who are pregnant and young parents, to prevent the intergenerational cycle of children coming into care. The relatively high proportion of young women in care, who have just left care, or who become parents in their teenage years is a consistent finding in studies conducted in Australia and internationally (Centre for Social Justice 2015; Mendes 2009). A study conducted by Cashmore and Paxman (1996) in NSW found that 31 per cent of the young women were pregnant or had a child within 12 months of leaving care. Young maternal age is significant because it is strongly linked with poor outcomes for both mothers and their children (Putnam-Hornstein et al. 2015).

While Australian research is limited, there is some evidence that young women who have been in care are at greater risk of coming to the attention of child protection authorities and of having their own child taken into care. A study of 60 care leavers in Victoria, for example, found that 17 (28 per cent) became a parent either in care or soon after leaving care. More than half of the children of the 17 parents in the survey group were in care under orders (Raman et al. 2005). Similarly, the NSW Ombudsman's recent review of leaving care (2013) found that of the seven young mothers in the review group, three had their children removed from their care before their own care order expired. Notably, the transition plan adequately considered early childhood education and care and other supports in only one of the seven cases.

In the USA, there has been a much stronger focus on providing support to young women who are pregnant and young parents who are transitioning from OHC. As previously outlined, many states now give young people the option to stay in care until age 21. This option is especially important for young women who are pregnant and young parents. As Putnam-Hornstein et al. (2015) suggest, extended care provides a window for intentional efforts to delay pregnancy and to provide targeted support to enhance parenting capacity. Policies that allow young people to stay in care longer can ensure continued support for young parents and their children, including access to transitional housing, opportunities for further education, support with parenting and early childhood education and care. Extended care settings may include helping young people return home to their family of origin, enabling them to live with a relative or other adult with whom they have a strong attachment, being placed in a foster home with staff who are specially trained to support young parents or being placed in a supervised independent living placement where parents and babies can be together (Gaughen 2014).

Data Collection and Oversight

Generally, in Australia, there is little monitoring of compliance with legal requirements for leaving care planning or outcomes of young people after they have left formal care. There is also a lack of transparency on fiscal allocations to transitional or aftercare support programmes (with funding allocations often subsumed under broader programme categories).

Western Australia is the only jurisdiction that sets clear criteria for determining when the transition process can be considered as finalized, including the goals set out in the leaving care plan have been achieved, the long-term placement arrangement is likely to be sustained or the young person turns 25 (Department of Child Protection 2011). Western Australia will also implement indicators for measuring outcomes for young people transitioning from care as part of broader development of an outcomes framework for OHC (Senate Community Affairs Reference Committee 2015).

Currently, there are no Australian data routinely collected at the national level on outcomes for young people once they have left care. In contrast, in the UK, the Department for Education maintains a national database, which tracks outcomes for all care leavers on a range of measures, including education, training, employment, accommodation and being in custody (Department for Education 2012). This enables the government and community to assess progress being made in improving outcomes of care leavers and to compare the performance of local authorities. Similarly, in the USA, the Department of Health and Human Services maintains a National Youth in Transition Database to assess states' performance in providing support to young people transitioning from care. States must provide data on support provided and measure outcomes across six domains, namely, financial self-sufficiency, experience with homelessness, educational attainment, positive connections with adults, high-risk behaviour and access to health insurance (US Department of Health and Human Services 2012).

Conclusions and Implications for Policy Development

In comparing legislative and policy frameworks, it is clear that Australia lags behind the UK and the USA in addressing the needs of young people who are transitioning from care. The UK and the USA have both moved towards giving young people the option to stay in care until the age of 21 (although this is not yet available for all care leavers, except in Scotland). The USA has moved further than Australia in creating national legislation and funding to support young people transitioning from care. However, as in Australia, there is still wide disparity in eligibility and availability of support across states and counties. In the UK, there has been a shift from discretionary legislation to strong legal duties, and an expectation of providing normative supports at least equivalent to what other young people would expect from a reasonable parent.

In Australia, policy debates on this issue have been disjointed due to the federation of states and territories, and this has made it difficult to achieve a national approach. In most Australian jurisdictions, the provision of aftercare support remains discretionary and inconsistent. The difficulties young people face in accessing appropriate support are also exacerbated by fragmented responsibilities and lack of coordination across government departments.

A sustained commitment is needed across all levels of government to improve outcomes for young people transitioning from care in Australia. Apart from the moral argument, there are good economic reasons for governments to invest in this area. By providing good support to young people as they transition from care, we can reduce their progression into prolonged use of high-cost, publicly-funded services. Economic research in Victoria found that the costs of supporting a young adult who has been in care are extremely high compared to the costs of providing a modest suite of integrated support services for care leavers at the time they transition from OHC (Raman et al. 2005). This was based on the direct costs to the state, which result from the poor outcomes experienced by young people leaving care, such as becoming homeless, being unemployed, requiring mental health and/or substance abuse services, entering the juvenile or adult justice system or having their own children removed from their care. The report provides a clear rationale for governments to invest in support for young people transitioning to adulthood.

The Commonwealth Government's recent report on welfare reform also highlights the value of targeting additional resources to groups at risk of long-term reliance on welfare and makes specific reference to young people who have transitioned from OHC (Reference Group on Welfare Reform 2015). As Stein (2012) argues, a twin-track approach is required, which provides access to both universal services and specialist support. Key proposals for Australian policy reform include the following:

- Giving all young people the option to stay in care until the age of 21, including those living in residential care; young people should also be able to re-enter care if they are experiencing difficulties until they turn 21;
- ensuring all transition plans identify stable, initial accommodation options and adopting a 'no discharge to homelessness or temporary and inappropriate accommodation' policy;
- strengthening state and territory legislative frameworks by introducing an explicit legal duty to provide ongoing support to young people transitioning from care until the age of 25; dedicated budget allocations are also required to support effective implementation of legal requirements;

- developing cross-government strategies, which explicitly recognize the vulnerability of care leavers, including priority access to social housing and health services; waiver of fees for post-secondary education; and clear protocols for joint work across government and non-government agencies;
- developing effective models of support for young women who are pregnant and young parents to prevent the intergenerational cycle of children coming into care;
- developing an agreed national data set on the characteristics and outcomes of young people transitioning from care, with consistent data definition and collection across state and territory governments; and
- research and evaluation on the impact and effectiveness of different forms of support for young people transitioning from care.

References

AIHW. (2015a). *Child protection Australia 2013–2014, Child welfare series no. 61., Cat. no. CWS 52*. Canberra: AIHW.

AIHW. (2015b). *National framework for protecting Australia's children*. http://www.aihw.gov.au/nfpac. Accessed 23 Oct 2015.

Australian Capital Territory Government. (2014). *A step up for our kids, one step can make a lifetime of difference, out of home care strategy 2015–2020*. Canberra: ACT Government.

Baidawi, S., Mendes, P., & Saunders, B. (2015). *Indigenous care leavers in Victoria: Interim report*. Melbourne: Department of Social Work, Monash University.

Baldry, E., Trofimovs, J., Brown, J., Brackertz, N., & Fotheringham, M. (2015). *Springboard evaluation report*. Sydney: UNSW Australia and Australian Housing and Urban Research Institute.

Bava, S., & Tapert, S. (2010). Adolescent brain development and the risk for alcohol and other drug problems. *Neuropsychology Review, 20*(4), 398–413.

Cashmore, J., & Paxman, M. (1996). *Longitudinal study of wards leaving care*. Sydney: Social Policy and Research Centre, University of NSW.

Centre for Social Justice. (2015). *Finding their feet: Equipping care leavers to reach their potential*. London: Centre for Social Justice.

Child Welfare Information Gateway. (2015). *Understanding the effects of maltreatment on brain development*. Washington, DC: Department of Health and Human Services, Children's Bureau.

Commissioner for Children Tasmania. (2012). *An uncertain road ahead – young people leaving care in Tasmania, Issues Paper No 3*.

Courtney, M. (2008). United States. In M. Stein & E. Munro (Eds.), *Young people's transitions from care to adulthood, international research and practice* (pp. 279–288). London/Philadelphia: Jessica Kingsley Publishers.

Courtney, M., Dworsky, A., Gretchen, R., Keller, T., & Havlicek, J. (2005). *Midwest evaluation of the adult functioning of former foster youth: Outcomes at age 19*. Chicago: Chapin Hall, University of Chicago.

Crane, P., Kaur, J., & Burton, J. (2014). *Homelessness and leaving care: The experiences of young adults in Queensland and Victoria, and implications for practice*. Canberra: Department of Families, Housing, Community Services and Indigenous Affairs.

Cummins, P., Scott, D., & Scales, B. (2012). *Report of the protecting Victoria's vulnerable children inquiry*. Melbourne: Department of Premier and Cabinet.

Daining, C., & DePanfilis, D. (2007). Resilience of youth in transition from out-of-home care to adulthood. *Children and Youth Services Review, 29*, 1158–1178.

Department for Education. (2010). *The Children Act 1989 guidance and regulations, Vol 3: Planning transitions to adulthood*. http://media.education.gov.uk/assets/files/pdf/p/dfe-00554-2010.pdf. Accessed 27 Sept 2015.

Department for Education. (2012). *Care leavers in England data pack*. London: Department for Education.

Department of Child Protection. (2011). *Leaving care policy*. Perth: Western Australian Government.

Department of Families, Housing, Community Services and Indigenous Affairs. (2011). *An outline of national standards for out-of-home care: A priority project under the national framework for protecting Australia's children 2009–2020*. Canberra: Commonwealth of Australia.

Department of Social Services. (2015). *Driving change: Intervening early, third three year action plan 2015–2018, national framework for protecting Australia's children 2009–2020*. Canberra: Commonwealth of Australia.

Dworsky, A., & Courtney, M. (2010). The risk of teenage pregnancy among transitioning foster youth: Implications for extending state care beyond age 18. *Children and Youth Services Review, 32*(10), 1351–1356.

Dworsky, A., & Havlicek, J. (2009). *Review of state policies and programs to support young people transitioning out of foster care*. Chicago: Chapin Hall, University of Chicago.

Family and Community Services. (2015). New post care education financial support for carers. http://www.community.nsw.gov.au/welcome_to_docs_website. Accessed 6 Oct 2015.

Flatau, P., Thielking, M., MacKenzie, D., & Steen, A. (2015). *The cost of youth homelessness in Australia study, snapshot report 1*. Melbourne: Swinburne Institute for Social Research, Salvation Army Australia, Mission Australia and Anglicare Australia.

Gaughen, K. (2014). *Success beyond 18: Extending foster care beyond 18: Housing options for young adults, issue brief*. St Louis: Jim Casey Youth Opportunities Initiative.

Hannon, C., Wood, C., & Bazalgette, L. (2010). *In locos parentis*. London: Demos.

Harvey, A., McNamara, P., Andrewatha, L., & Luckman, M. (2015). *Out of care, into university: Raising higher education access and achievement of care leavers*. Melbourne: La Trobe University.

Höjer, I., & Sjöblom, S. (2014). Voices of 65 young people leaving care in Sweden: There is so much I need to know. *Australian Social Work, 67*(1), 71–87.

McDowall, J. (2008). *Report card, transitioning from care*. Sydney: Create Foundation.

McDowall, J. (2009). *Create report card 2009, transitioning from care: Tracking progress*. Sydney: CREATE Foundation.

McDowall, J. (2011). *Transitioning from care in Australia, an evaluation of CREATE's what's the plan campaign*. Sydney: CREATE Foundation.

McDowall, J. (2013). *Experiencing out-of-home care in Australia: The views of children and young people (CREATE Report Card 2013)*. Sydney: CREATE Foundation.

Mendes, P. (2009). Improving outcomes for teenage pregnancy and early parenthood for young people in out-of-home care: A review of the literature. *Youth Studies Australia, 2*(4), 11–18.

Mendes, P., Johnson, G., & Moslehuddin, B. (2011a). *Young people leaving state out-of-home care*. Melbourne: Australian Scholarly Publishing Press.

Mendes, P., Johnson, G., & Moslehuddin, B. (2011b). Effectively preparing young people to transition from out-of-home care, an examination of three recent Australian studies. *Family Matters, 89*, 61–70.

Munro, E. (2013). *Transitions from care to adulthood: English research, policy and practice*, presentation to CREATE Foundation forum, 27 Nov 2013.

Munro, E., Lushey, C., National Care Advisory Service, Makell-Graham, D., Ward, H., & Holmes, L. (2012). *Evaluation of the staying put: 18 plus family placement programme: Final report*. London: Department for Education.

Next step aftercare service. (2015). http://nextstepaftercare.com.au/. Accessed 11 Nov 2015.

NSW Ombudsman. (2013). *The continuing need to better support young people leaving care, Report under Section 13 of the Community Services (Complaints, Reviews and Monitoring) Act 1993*.

Peters, C., Dworsky, A., Courtney, M., & Pollack, H. (2009). *Extending foster care to age 21: Weighing the costs to Government against the benefits of youth, Chapin Hall issues brief*. Chicago: Chapin Hall, University of Chicago.

Putnam-Hornstein, E., Hammond, I., Eastman, A., McCroskey, J., & Webster, D. (2015). *California's extension of foster care through age 21: An opportunity for pregnancy prevention and parenting support* (Vol. 4–1). California: Children's Data Network.

Queensland Child Protection Commission of Inquiry. (2013). *Taking responsibility: A roadmap for Queensland child protection*. Brisbane: State of Queensland.

Raman, S., Inder, B., & Forbes, C. (2005). *Investing for success: The economics of supporting young people leaving care*. Melbourne: Centre for Excellence in Child and Family Welfare.

Reference group on Welfare Reform. (2015). *A new system for better employment and social outcomes: Final report*. Canberra: Commonwealth of Australia.

Rogers, J. (2015). *Leaving care is hard enough without the system favouring those who are fostered*. The Conversation. http://theconversation.com/leaving-care-is-hard-enough-without-the-system-favouring-those-who-are-fostered-36569. Accessed 6 Oct 2015.

Schelbe, L. (2011). Policy analysis of Fostering Connections to Success and Increasing Adoptions Act of 2008. *Journal of Human Behaviour in the Social Environment, 22*, 555–576.

Scott, D. (2014). *Children in Australia: Harms and hopes*. Family Matters. 96, 14–22. Australian Institute of Family Services.

Scottish Government. (2013). *Staying put Scotland providing care leavers with connectedness and belonging Guidance for local authorities and other corporate parents*. Edinburgh: The Scottish Government.

Scottish Government. (2014). *Greater rights for young people in care*. http://news.scotland.gov.uk/News/Greater-rights-for-young-people-in-care-818.aspx. Accessed 27 Sept 2015.

Senate Community Affairs Reference Committee. (2015). *Out of home care.* Canberra: Commonwealth of Australia.

Smyth, C., & Eardley, T. (2008). *Out-of-home care for children in Australia: A review of literature and policy, SPRC report no 3/08.* Sydney: Social Policy and Research Centre.

Stein, M. (2008). Transitions from care to adulthood: Messages from research for policy and practice. In M. Stein & E. Munro (Eds.), *Young people's transitions from care to adulthood, international research and practice.* London/Philadelphia: Jessica Kingsley Publishers.

Stein, M. (2012). *Young yeople leaving care, supporting pathways to adulthood.* London: Jessica Kingsley Publishers.

Stein, M., & Munro, E. (2008). *Young people's transitions from care to adulthood, international research and practice.* London: Jessica Kingsley Publishers.

US Department of Health and Human Services. (2012). *About NYTD.* http://www.acf.hhs.gov/programs/cb/resource/about-nytd?page=all. Accessed 18 Aug 2015.

Wade, J., & Dixon, J. (2006). Making a home, finding a job: Investigating early housing and employment outcomes for young people leaving care. *Child and Family Social Work, 11*(3), 199–208.

Wade, J., & Munro, E. (2008). United Kingdom. In M. Stein & E. Munro (Eds.), *Young people's transitions from care to adulthood, international research and practice.* London/Philadelphia: Jessica Kingsley Publishers.

Wilkins, R. (2015). *The household, income and labour dynamics in Australia survey: Selected findings from waves 1 to 12.* Melbourne: Melbourne Institute of Applied Economic and Social Research, University of Melbourne.

Wood, J. (2008). *Special commission of inquiry into child protection services in NSW* (Vol. 3). Sydney: NSW.

14

CREATE's Advocacy for Young People Transitioning from Care in Australia

Joseph J. McDowall

CREATE's Origins

This chapter will present a brief history, and discuss the operation and impact of the CREATE Foundation (CREATE), the peak consumer body in Australia representing the voices of children and young people with an out-of-home care (OOHC) experience. Its forerunner, the Australian Association of Young People in Care (AAYPIC), was formed in 1993 by Jan Owen AM, who guided its development for the first nine years. Summaries of its early activities can be found in the Annual Report of the New South Wales Association of Children's Welfare Agencies 1995–96 (ACWA 1996), under whose auspices it operated for six years. AAYPIC was established with seed funding of $46,000 from the Charles and Sylvia Viertel Charitable Foundation. By 1996, this group was attracting around $150,000 in financial assistance from governments and various corporate supporters, and had produced a major child welfare policy platform for

---

J.J. McDowall (✉)
CREATE Foundation, Brisbane, QLD, Australia

© The Author(s) 2016
P. Mendes, P. Snow (eds.), *Young People Transitioning from Out-of-Home Care*, DOI 10.1057/978-1-137-55639-4_14

reforms, including 'uniform child welfare legislation, national standards of care, accreditation of service providers and the appointment of a Federal Children's Commissioner' (ACWA: AAYPIC 1996). Interestingly, these are issues that are only now (2015) being addressed in Australia.

The early work of AAYPIC entailed establishing state networks, which by 1996 included all jurisdictions except for the Australian Capital Territory (ACT). State governments in most cases provided the funding to facilitate regional AAYPIC activities. The groups embarked on an ambitious programme of fundraising and advocacy, which, in 1996, led to the 'Share Our Future' campaign, culminating in the launch of a notable publication entitled *Every childhood lasts a lifetime* (Owen 1996).[1] This book epitomized the aims of AAYPIC by presenting, in their own words, the personal stories of young people who had been in the care system.

In 1997, Andrew O'Brien, the then AAYPIC State Coordinator for New South Wales, clearly articulated the issues that needed to be tackled in achieving consumer participation by children and young people in care. He noted that just having a voice was different from the two-way process of real participation, and identified three steps that AAYPIC adopted to encourage involvement by young people: (a) '(creating) regular opportunities for children and young people to come together to identify, discuss and resolve issues of concern to them and the service provider'; (b) 'providing young people with the skills and facilities needed to support their actions'; and (c) 'creating a structure by which children and young people in care can participate in an ongoing capacity' (1997, p. 57–58). These processes formed the basis for CREATE's current mantra: *Connect* to *Empower* to *Change*.

In a review of the emerging consumer groups supporting young people in care in the 1990s, Mendes (1998) presented a valuable evaluation of AAYPIC in which he acknowledged the significant achievements of the fledgling group, but emphasized that the organization would need to be tested over time to determine how well it was able to represent all of those

---

[1] The publication of this book represented a marker at the beginning of Jan Owen's career that has focused on child welfare issues, the significance of which was recognized by the awarding to her of an honorary Doctor of Letters degree by the University of Sydney in 2014.

in care, both the younger children and the older cohort and care leavers, and also how well it could address the issue of accountability within child protection as a response to possible 'systems abuse'.

By 1999, AAYPIC and the state branches had achieved sufficient recognition in the child protection sector to become an incorporated body independent of ACWA. Young people in care were consulted to decide on an appropriate name for the new body. As a result, the CREATE Foundation came into existence on 1 July 1999, with separation funding of AUD$12,000 from ACWA. While the New South Wales state government gave the newly formed organization credibility by incorporating information it provided into various discussion papers, questions were raised regarding CREATE's capacity, while operating as an 'insider' interest group, to effect policy change by engaging in 'cooperative rather than confrontational strategies' (Mendes 2002, p. 55). Parallels were drawn between CREATE and the more established Children's Welfare Association of Victoria, with the observation that when an interest group is dependent on substantial government funding, there is a low likelihood that it will issue harsh criticism of authorities. Current leadership at CREATE has been mindful of this tension, and while purposefully choosing to work within the system, has developed advocacy strategies more in keeping with the 'high profile insiders' identified by McKinney and Halpin (2007). These strategies will be discussed in more detail in a later section.

CREATE's Mission

As with many contemporary organizations, CREATE clearly articulates its vision, mission and core principles. It aims to do all it can to create 'a better life for children and young people in care' (CREATE 2015a, p. 2). This mission is achieved by a tripartite process (*Connect* to *Empower* to *Change*) representing a continuum of activities designed to (a) engage children and young people, and through their participation, link them with their peers and decision-makers; (b) provide them with training to develop their skills and capacity to express their views, and give them opportunities to use those skills to build self-confidence; and (c) listen to what the children and young people have to say, collect their wisdom, and share it with decision-makers to show where change for the better could occur in the care system.

CREATE follows a number of principles in striving for these goals, the main ones being that 'Children and young people are at the centre of the work we do', 'meaningful participation is essential for engaging children and young people' and 'our advocacy is independent, non-partisan and evidence based' (CREATE 2015a, p. 2). It is important to note that while CREATE's successful connection activities have resulted in 12,728 children and young people currently being active members of *clubCREATE*, and, over the past 12 months, *Speak Up* and *CREATE Your Future* have empowered over 1200 participants (CREATE 2015a), the organization's main focus is on systemic advocacy to improve the care system for all.

CREATE's Organizational Structure and Funding

From its humble beginnings, over the past 16 years, CREATE has developed into a not-for-profit company playing a significant role in the OOHC sector by ensuring that the voices of children and young people are heard loud and clear. This longevity and level of influence have been achieved through sound governance and effective management. Under its Constitution, CREATE's strategic direction is determined by a Board of Directors, the members of which are drawn from both the corporate and child protection sectors (see http://create.org.au/who-we-are/our-people/ for biographies of current incumbents). A copy of the current *Strategic Plan 2015–17* is available at http://create.org.au/publications/strategic-plan/. It is Board policy that at least two Directors have a care experience; at present, three satisfy this criterion (including the Chairperson who spent part of his childhood at Fairbridge Farm,[2] and a relatively new Director who herself has recently completed a PhD researching pathways

---

[2] Fairbridge Farm School was an institution that operated in western NSW between 1938 and 1974, which was intended to provide opportunities for children who had been living in poverty in Britain before migrating to Australia. The abuse experienced by many of these children is documented in David Hill's 2008 book 'The forgotten children: Fairbridge Farm School and its betrayal

14 CREATE's Advocacy for Young People Transitioning...

CREATE Organisational Chart 2015

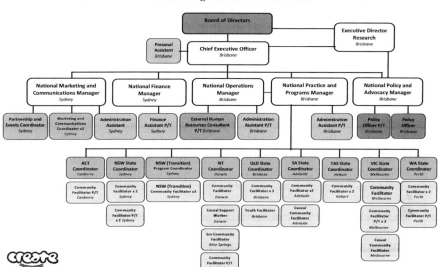

Fig. 14.1 Organizational structure of the CREATE Foundation as on October 2015

to higher education from out-of-home care). Governance and management are connected through having the Chief Executive Officer included as a voting Board member.

CREATE's current organizational structure, management role responsibilities, and staffing levels are shown in Fig. 14.1. A Leadership Committee comprising managers from the areas of Operations, Policy and Advocacy, Practice and Programs, Finance, and Marketing and Communications supports the CEO at the national level. In addition, each state and territory has its own Coordinator assisted by Community Facilitators, who work directly with the children and young people. In total, CREATE now employs 38 full-time equivalent staff throughout Australia, a relatively low number for a national organization.

As indicated in its 2014 Annual Review, CREATE obtains 67 per cent of its funding from state and federal government grants and service agreements.

---

of Britain's child migrants to Australia'. David was the first chairman of the CREATE Board, and currently is the organization's patron.

The remainder of the approximately AUD $6M budget is derived from corporate sponsorship, donations, fee for service, and consultancies. This split enables CREATE to use the government support to conduct its connection activities and empowerment programmes, while using the non-government funding (particularly the long-term investment of supporters such as AMP Limited) to enable its research and advocacy to remain independent when presenting the views of children and young people.

CREATE in the Global Advocacy Scene

Throughout the world, many non-government organizations and groups seek to meet the particular needs of vulnerable children and young people who cannot live with their birth parents. In a chapter of this limited length, it would be impossible to discuss all groups, even if their activities were well known. However, it is possible to broadly categorize these organizations, and identify characteristics that may help differentiate CREATE from similar groups supporting young people.

The development of advocacy groups for children and young people with a care background in the UK has been well documented by Stein (2011). He presents the highs and lows of the struggle in which young people from care were engaged, beginning in 1973 when *Ad-Lib* was formed, through *Who Cares?* followed by the *National Association of Young People in Care* (*NAYPIC*), until the current incarnation as *A National Voice* (*ANV*), a body formed in the same year that CREATE was incorporated (1999). When this group became fully independent in 2006, as Stein observed (p. 170), 'For the first time in the history of the rights movement, an organization existed that not only represented and campaigned for young people in care, but also controlled its own administration and funding'. This fact places *ANV* at one pole of the advocacy continuum in being run by, and for, young people from care themselves. However, it is still dependent on government for financial support.

Other interest groups in the UK operate with professional Boards supported by young people. For example, the *National Leaving Care Benchmarking Forum* (*NLCBF*), a consortium of 81 services from local authorities designed to assist young people making the transition from care to adulthood (Catch22 2015), is supported by the *Young People's Benchmarking Forum* (members aged over 16 years) that reports to the NLCBF and works to raise awareness of, and prioritize, issues affecting care leavers. This type of approach exemplifies a less direct model of young persons' participation. Organizations with similar structures exist in Scotland (*Who Cares? Scotland* where at least four Board members must have a care experience) and Ireland (*Voice of Young People in Care* [*VOYPIC*] in Northern Ireland incorporating 'Young Reps'; and *Empowering People in Care* (*EPIC*) in the Republic of Ireland that has a separate Youth Board).

The situation in the USA and Europe regarding advocacy groups for children and young people in care is less well documented, perhaps because of the greater diversity of regional jurisdictions comprising the larger entities and the plethora of local support groups and agencies. Discussions of the child welfare system (see for example, Pecora et al. 2011) tend to focus on the protections afforded to the child rather than on exploring how a young person's involvement can be harnessed to help improve the system. Large established organizations (such as the Child Welfare League of America) are influential in setting the national policy agenda concerning the welfare of all children; but the voices of children and young people can be heard only indirectly through the member agencies. However, other groups such as the *Children's Action Network*, the *National Foster Care Coalition*, and the *Foster Care Alumni of America* aim to provide opportunities for children and young people to be involved personally in advocacy and decision-making within the care system.

In Europe, a similar pattern emerges, with large organizations concerned with children's rights functioning to consolidate the actions of many smaller groups. For example, the Council of Europe in conjunction with the SOS Children's Villages International (2013) has produced guidelines for professionals to help them secure children's rights in an attempt to 'build a Europe for and with children'. Similarly, the Eurochild network strives to ensure that 'children's rights and well-being are at the heart of policymaking' (2014). Supporting such systemic advocates are the networks of *Independent Human Rights Institutions for Children* (*IHRICs*) and the *European Network of Ombudspersons for Children* (*ENOC*) (Thomas et al. 2011).

Recently, *Family for Every Child* (2015), a global alliance of members from 18 countries including Africa, South America, India, Indonesia, Russia, Middle East, and the UK, published the first international manifesto for delivering safe foster care, largely in developing countries, as part of its advocacy strategy. This included a major section on supporting children and young adults leaving foster care, in which it was suggested that 'low and middle income countries can learn from failures in high income countries by ensuring that support and follow-up services are in place and children are linked with their family of origin where appropriate' (p. 29).

It is difficult to compare CREATE's advocacy with the international groups because of the geographically large size of Australia and its relatively small population. However, following the previous discussion of activities of other organizations, a number of observations can be made.

The first concerns the role of children and young people. As with many groups, CREATE exists to access the voices of children and young people in the care system and ensure they are heard by decision-makers. At first, CREATE experimented with involving young people in the governance of the organization, expecting them to function in a highly structured 'corporate' environment. It soon became obvious, however, that the greatest contribution the young people could make required the free flow of ideas leading to issue identification in contexts they could control, rather than being constrained by adhering to a committee structure and process. This led to the current model of a formal governing Board acting on information and advice from young people provided through their monthly Youth Advisory Group meetings in each state and territory.

A second point concerns the type of advocacy CREATE can provide. Because of the small size of the organization, it is clear that it would not be possible for staff to undertake representation on behalf of individual children and young people regarding their specific treatment in the care system. Occasionally, young people may make a disclosure that requires an individual course of action; wherever possible, staff will refer these young people to bodies such as Children's Commissioners and Ombudspersons, which may have the capacity to deal with individual cases. Generally, CREATE attempts to gather the views of many young people to try to determine larger scale issues within jurisdictions. This is referred to as 'systemic advocacy'. CREATE staff attempt to provide a supportive environment (through connection and empowerment) that will enable children and young people across Australia to share their stories. The collected voices can have great impact, as is evidenced by CREATE's work on leaving care.

The third area for comparison relates to funding. One of CREATE's core principles concerns 'independence', a need for the organization to be able to address issues young people raise, without fear or favour, particularly being free of government or other third-party influence. This can be achieved only by devoting considerable effort to obtaining unattached funding, largely through the generosity of corporate supporters. As indicated previously, CREATE currently obtains approximately one-third of its funding in this way, allowing it to produce valuable independent research to guide system improvement.

CREATE and the Young People Leaving Care

CREATE provides young people in OOHC with two programmes to help prepare them for a successful life after care. *Speak Up* was designed as an empowerment experience comprising three levels from Introductory to Advanced that produces Young Consultants with the confidence and ability to share their views of the care system in public forums. The second programme, *CREATE Your Future*, is intended for young people aged 15–25 who are contemplating independent living. It provides a series of 14 workshops in which participants can acquire a range of life skills ranging from finding somewhere to live (familiarity with the rental market and its requirements) and obtaining a job (including self-presentation and interview skills), to using transport (public system or acquiring a driver's license) and producing nutritious meals (involving shopping, food preparation, and cooking).

Young people who have completed the programmes, particularly *Speak Up*, are given as many opportunities as possible to practice their skills and share their unique experiences with others. CREATE supports young people with a care experience until they reach 25 years by maintaining, if they wish, their membership of the *clubCREATE* network (at which time, they are encouraged to join the newly formed CREATE alumni). *Speak Up* graduates tend to be influential at the monthly Youth Advisory Group (YAG) meetings held in each state and territory (although any child in care is entitled to attend these meetings, not just those who have completed programmes).

More importantly, young people are invited to participate at launches of CREATE's reports, and many are involved in caseworker training events where they are able to ensure that the young person's perspective is clearly articulated and understood within the system. The young people, when involved at this level, are paid a consultancy fee by CREATE to show that their contribution is valued by the organization.

CREATE's Advocacy Strategies

CREATE employs many and varied forms of advocacy to present the voices of young people to the sector and decision-makers. In this section, examples of the most common and effective approaches will be given, including collaborations with governments, child welfare agencies, and other peak bodies; conferences; engagement with media (print and broadcast); and submissions to Commissions and Inquiries. In the next section, attention will focus on the strategy that has the most continuing influence, that is, research. It is through its research projects that CREATE is able to employ the core principle of listening to young people to obtain an understanding of issues that need to be addressed, and then responding with recommendations for policy and practice change in the OOHC system.

Collaborations

It is well known that effective advocacy depends on the building of 'exchange relationships between organizational representatives and constituents, policymakers and the news media' (Berkhout 2013, p. 227). CREATE values having positive working relationships with governments, and agencies within the child protection sector. State governments assist by supporting connection and empowerment events, and by facilitating contact with young people in the care system. The Australian government, while having limited responsibilities within child protection (as this is a state/territory matter), has contributed funding to two significant advocacy projects CREATE has undertaken in recent years concerning leaving care and sibling placement (CREATE 2010; McDowall 2015). In the former consultation, a total of 37 young people from around Australia shared their ideas regarding what could be done to improve the preparation, transition, and after-care independence phases of the journey, from care to emerging autonomy. The final report, published under the auspices of the then Department of Families, Housing, Community Services and Indigenous Affairs (FaHCSIA), presents a considered, comprehensive set of suggestions by young people who played a part in the establishment of the National Standards in Out-of-Home Care (introduced by FaHCSIA 2011), and CREATE's involvement in the National Framework Implementation Working Group.

CREATE is also concerned with establishing and maintaining connections with non-governmental organizations in the sector. In addition to communicating with children and young people as part of their regular professional activities, CREATE staff spend considerable time building relationships with their colleagues in department offices and child protection agencies. Key workers who respond by offering support can become part of the designated CREATE Mates network and receive newsletters and other relevant targeted information. CREATE relies on the goodwill of these workers to recommend its programmes to the children and young people for whom they are responsible.

Conferences

A powerful way to achieve change in the system is to speak directly to decision-makers and stakeholders at conferences. Conferences represent a valuable vehicle for advocacy through information exchange during presentations as well as in out-of-session networking. Because of its national focus, notwithstanding a relatively small staff, CREATE attempts to have representatives either presenting the latest, most salient concerns of young people, or promoting the organization's activities at major national conferences and symposia. Young people are invited to participate in and/or co-facilitate workshop sessions whenever possible. For example, CREATE regularly presents at Families Australia's *Child Aware Conference*, ACWA's annual conference, the National Foster Care and Kinship Care Conference, and the Secretariat of National Aboriginal and Islander Child Care Conference (conducted by the peak Indigenous body in child welfare), as well as responding positively to invitations to attend specialist forums.

In addition, CREATE has recently established a tradition of holding its own international biennial conference, the second having been conducted in 2015. The composition of delegates at this meeting is unique in Australia. About 400 people can attend; by design, one-third of these are children and young people, accompanied, when required, because of age, by their carers (who comprise another third), and the final group includes caseworkers, other professionals, and researchers. Activities are provided for each group appealing to a range of interests; variety is necessary since it was realized that some of the more academic papers might test the patience of young people. However, young people have demonstrated that they value the opportunity to be involved by participating in a variety of sessions including keynotes and panel discussions. The adult delegates benefit from gaining a broader understanding of many issues by seeing them from the young persons' perspective.

Media

In addition to CREATE providing advocacy within the child protection sector, current management realizes that many decisions affecting the system require a certain political will, which is most likely to be influenced by an informed voting public. Clearly, harnessing the media in its many forms is an efficient way to connect with the general community. However, it is not sufficient to wait for the media to become interested in a story; work has to be done to ensure that, while information must be factual and accurate (not sensationalized), it is presented in a manner that will attract continued interest and hopefully lead to greater awareness and possibly a change of attitude in the recipient of the message. To achieve this outcome, CREATE employs a media consultant who utilizes traditional print and broadcast channels (both radio and television) as well as postings on contemporary social media to promulgate the young persons' message within a general audience as well as niche sectors that could effect change.

CREATE's 2015 Annual Report (CREATE 2015a, p. 28) summarized the media coverage that this relatively small organization achieved in its most recent year of operation. A total of 74 media interviews were conducted involving 40 children and young people. This resulted in a total of 125 published items, including six television segments (e.g. Australian Broadcasting Corporation (ABC) Lateline and News 24), 22 radio broadcasts (including ABC *AM*), 29 print articles (several in major metropolitan papers, e.g. *Sydney Morning Herald*), and 68 online reports.

Mendes (2016) identified CREATE as one non-government advocacy group that has played an active role in releasing research reports and recommending policy reform to the media. While he claims that 'media reports do not appear to have played any significant role in driving policy reform' in the examples he cited, this view may be a little pessimistic. For example, reports such as that by Powell and Scanlon (2014) point to the media's 'key role in the construction of child abuse as a major social problem'. Locally, the action of minor political parties (e.g. the Greens in New South Wales and the Australian Capital Territory) in using the media to draw attention to data provided in CREATE's reports on transitioning from care has been influential in effecting recent changes that have occurred to leaving care policy in those jurisdictions (Barham 2012; Dyett 2012).

CREATE continues to explore how social media can be utilized for more direct, immediate contact with young people. This is an area that poses particular problems in terms of privacy concerns (Trepte 2015), but it may have beneficial applications in child protection (Thompson 2015). Given the ubiquitous nature of smart phones and Internet access, it would seem that anyone serious about accessing the contemporary voice of young people would need to explore and harness the affordances of this new media. CREATE's first exploration in this field has involved a collaboration with Queensland's Department of Communities, Child Safety and Disability Services, and Telstra to produce a mobile app called SORTLI (an acronym from 'sorting your life out') that provides young people transitioning from care with useful information about employment, education, housing, life skills, and health (Queensland Government 2015).

Submissions

Unfortunately, a common characteristic of child protection systems around the world is a tendency to be in a constant state of inquiry, experienced as they lurch from one scandal to the next (Gainsborough 2010). This situation certainly is found in Australia. As an indicator, it was noted in *Child Protection Australia 2011–12* (AIHW 2013, Appendix I) that at least 16 commissions or inquiries into child protection issues have been held since 1999, a list published before the holding of the recent Queensland Child Protection Commission of Inquiry, two Senate Inquiries (Out-of-Home Care; Grandparents Raising their Grandchildren), and the two Royal Commissions being conducted at present (Institutional Responses to Child Sexual Abuse; Child Protection Systems, South Australia).

CREATE, through its Policy and Advocacy Unit, devotes much time and effort to producing submissions, representing the views of children and young people in care, for these various inquiries. On many occasions, this dedication is rewarded when it becomes clear that recommendations contained within the submissions are considered seriously. An indication of how CREATE's impact has increased over the past eight years can be found by comparing its input into the Wood Commission of Inquiry into child protection in New South Wales (2008) with the 2015 Senate (Community Affairs References Committee) Inquiry into out-of-home care. In the former, CREATE's *Education Report Card* (2006) was mentioned three times, and comments from two young consultants were included; in the more recent inquiry, evidence from CREATE's Policy and Advocacy Manager and four young consultants was cited extensively, covering a variety of issues in out-of-home care including the National Framework, stability and permanency, participation, complaints, planning, education, health, and family contact. CREATE's evidence featured significantly in three sections dealing specifically with transitioning from care (e.g., 4.94, 4.101, and 4.117).

Another prime example concerns CREATE's association with the Royal Commission into Institutional Responses to Sexual Abuse (2015). The level of involvement requested by the Commission would seem another appropriate indicator of CREATE's influence in the sector. The CEO, Executive Director, and Leadership members have been invited to participate in three roundtables and workshops; the CEO and two Young Consultants were called to give evidence at one hearing; and two Commissioners conducted sessions at CREATE's 2015 Youth-for-Change conference at which young people had the opportunity to tell their stories.

Major recognition of the effectiveness of CREATE's submissions on behalf of children and young people in care, and of the organization's relevance, was expressed in the Child Protection Systems Royal Commission Report (2016) released in August. In this report, Recommendation 165 requires the South Australian government specifically to:

> Reach an administrative arrangement with the CREATE Foundation to provide it with the names and contact details of children entering care and/or their carers (as appropriate).

CREATE's Research into Transitioning from Care

Since 2008, CREATE has concentrated its efforts on issues confronting those leaving care and embarking on their transition to independent (or more appropriately interdependent) living. The action-research strategy adopted incorporated a variety of methodologies to identify problems within the system, and then to attempt systemic change in areas where improvements were clearly needed. Initial studies (McDowall 2008, 2009) reviewed the international leaving care literature as well as government legislation and policies relating to transitioning from care across all jurisdictions in Australia. To determine the impact of these policy expectations, a total of 635 young people who were either approaching the age at which they would exit the care system or who were already trying to forge an independent existence were surveyed over the two studies. Important discrepancies were found between policy and practice.

It was recommended, following the first transitioning-from-care Report Card (McDowall 2008), that:

- National leaving care support standards be established;
- More integrated support systems be developed;
- Carers receive special training to address the stages of transition;
- Serious attention be directed to transition planning;
- Specialist Transition from Care officers be appointed;
- Outcomes of transition (costs and benefits) must be monitored more closely; and
- Particular attention must be directed to supporting indigenous care leavers.

Because only 164 young people were consulted in the 2008 study, it was decided to conduct a follow-up project in 2009, in which more young people from both in-care and post-care groups could participate, and government departments also would have the opportunity to discuss their policies regarding their provision of support for care leavers.

This second study (McDowall 2009) identified considerable variability in legislation and policies applying to the transitioning process across state and territory governments. Further, a number of findings from this survey mirrored concerns that had been reported internationally. Of the 196 in the post-care group, 35 per cent had completed Year 12, a total of 28 per cent were looking for work, 50 per cent had to leave their care placement on turning 18 years, 70 per cent were wholly or partially dependent on Centrelink (government) payments, 35 per cent were homeless (defined as being without safe or adequate housing for five consecutive nights) within the first year after leaving care, and 45 per cent (of males) had some connection with juvenile justice.

A major problem identified through this research concerns leaving care planning, with just over one-third (36 per cent) of those surveyed being aware of having any such plan that might help guide their future independent living (McDowall 2009). The few completed plans that some governments had presented for review could be classified as either comprehensive, but incomprehensible, or simple, but lacking accountability. Clearly, more young people need to leave care with a useful plan for their future.

In an effort to increase the numbers with meaningful plans, and promote greater engagement of the young people in the planning process, CREATE embarked on its 'What's the plan?' project, a social marketing campaign (McDermott et al. 2005) designed to raise awareness of the need for planning, and to change the attitudes and behaviour of the young people, carers, and caseworkers involved, which hopefully would lead to more useful plans being produced. This programme, which employed a variety of promotional mechanisms to highlight the issues, ran for 12 months, at which time it was evaluated (McDowall 2011, 2012) to determine overall impact and establish which marketing elements seemed most effective. Of the 605 young people (15–17 years) surveyed, 31 per cent reported knowing about a personal leaving care plan. Although the overall result suggested no change in the incidence of planning, significantly more 17-year-olds (44 per cent) claimed to know about having a leaving care plan, with over 50 per cent of those in ACT, Victoria, and South Australia reporting such awareness. A similar finding was observed in the transitioning section of CREATE's more recent out-of-home sector review (McDowall 2013), with a national average of 65 per cent of 325 respondents indicating that someone had spoken with them about leaving care. These results indicate more work needs to be done to improve planning; however, they do give some encouragement that interventions such as this may have some impact if maintained over a longer time span.

These approaches led to CREATE's current leaving care project. Research indicated that more tangible assistance was needed if any significant change in planning behaviour of caseworkers with young people was to be achieved. With the support of all state and territory governments, as a key action under the National Framework for Protecting Australia's Children 2009–2020, CREATE produced the nationally consistent *Go Your Own Way* (GYOW) kits in consultation with young people in care, and planned to distribute these to all 17-year-olds identified by governments as transitioning over the 12 months from March

2014. This resource includes a leaving care plan template to be completed by the young person together with the responsible caseworker. The effectiveness of the kits in facilitating planning was evaluated in 2016. Even though all 17-year-old care leavers in 2014 were eligible to receive a kit, only 52% received this resource because of the variable, uncontrolled, inconsistent kit distribution practices adopted by governments. However, significantly more of those who received a kit knew about their leaving care plan than did those who had to prepare for independence using other strategies (McDowall, 2016).

CREATE's Strengths and Limitations

Measuring the impact of an advocacy group such as CREATE can be difficult because, as Lowery (2013) observed, such research often produces null findings. He found from meta-analytic studies into the impact of advocacy organizations that they were likely to report significant findings only about 20 per cent of the time (p. 18). It is essential that the areas of influence being investigated are clearly identified. Pedersen (2013) suggested three measures that can be considered: (a) the group's activity; (b) agenda-setting influence; and (c) legislative influence. She noted strong correlations between measures in these areas, even though legislative influence appeared more difficult to measure consistently than did group activity.

Much of the literature on advocacy evaluation concerns the effectiveness of individual advocacy, and hence does not relate directly to CREATE's focus in systemic advocacy. However, the three overarching features of an effective independent child protection advocacy service, as articulated by the National Children's Bureau (2013) in the UK, still seem relevant for CREATE and highlight the organization's strengths:

- [The] advocacy is child-led and child-controlled;
- The independent advocate is able to take all necessary action to ensure the child's views are heard and their rights upheld; and
- The independent advocacy service makes a positive difference to children's lives (NCB 2013, p. 7).

CREATE's advocacy certainly is child-led—not by individuals, but by the collective voice. The model of seamless engagement from *connect to empower to change* ensures young people are given every chance to be heard and to influence decision-makers. Perhaps, the greatest protection CREATE affords young people with a care experience is that its advocacy is independent of governments and support agencies. Being national, CREATE can address differential treatment across jurisdictions and make a positive contribution to the lives of young care leavers throughout Australia.

Another strength of CREATE as an independent advocacy organization is that it has the flexibility to use a variety of methods to bring its positive message of the potential of young people to public awareness. In addition to its more traditional approaches that have been discussed, it also disseminates good news stories about the experiences of children and young people in care through its *clubCREATE* magazines. At its recent national conferences, it featured a photographic exhibition displaying portraits that young people with a care experience had taken (after receiving a little professional training in using cameras) of individuals who had achieved a level of personal success in various fields of endeavour (including business, sport, academia, and culture), and who had also been in care. This *Power Within* exhibition was designed to show that no stigma should be associated with a care experience, and that, with support, wonderful opportunities are available to anyone, from any background, with the drive to succeed. The work has been exhibited in Canberra, Melbourne, Hobart, and Brisbane to a broad-based audience. A copy of the publication accompanying this show that includes the images, biographies of the participants, and reflections on the process by the young person is available on CREATE's website (CREATE 2015b).

One of CREATE's greatest challenges is that although it receives financial support from governments to conduct its connect and empower programmes, particularly *CREATE Your Future* for care leavers, 'privacy constraints' are often invoked to limit access to young people who are entitled to, and would benefit from, the programmes. As an example, CREATE's recent campaign of supplying leaving care resources (GYOW Kits) to all 17-year-olds ageing out of the care system became problematic when state and territory governments would not enable CREATE to distribute the kits because of privacy issues concerning provision of the contact details for the young people entitled to receive them. Consequently, CREATE has no direct knowledge of who received a kit, and departments apparently have not kept accurate records of the distribution. Therefore, in conducting the planned follow-up evaluation of the resource, CREATE will have to search broadly for care leavers (rather than target those who received a kit), and then determine whether the young person's transition planning was facilitated through utilizing a GYOW Kit.

It would be ideal for all children and young people, on coming into care, to be registered as members of CREATE, and be entitled to the continuing support this Foundation provides. If they actively do not want to be connected with CREATE, they can opt out. However, at present, they are required to opt in. It has long been recognized (Samuelson and Zeckhauser 1988) that there is a *status quo* bias in decision-making; whatever the current situation is, it is likely to be maintained. It would be preferable to ensure that the *status quo* provides ongoing support to encourage young people to strive for their aspirations, rather than imposing isolation and exclusion.

Conclusion

In this chapter, I have attempted to illustrate aspects of CREATE's activities in supporting children and young people in out-of-home care, with special attention to those exiting the care system. Many strategies have been identified for assisting those in transition to achieve their aspirations; but more work needs to be done. CREATE envisions a situation in which children and young people in out-of-home care, irrespective of where they live in Australia, all have the same rights, levels of support, and opportunities. Its leading role promoting the leaving care strategy of the National Forum for Protecting Australia's Children is an important way of addressing this quest for consistency and fairness.

CREATE's model of Connect to Empower to Change has stood the test of time in terms of its effectiveness in meeting the needs of children and young people in, and leaving, care, as well as enhancing their capacity to be heard. Obviously, the degree of funding that can be obtained through the hard work of the organization's staff, and the generosity of governments and corporate supporters, is a key factor in determining the number of children and young people with whom CREATE can connect, and who consequently feel empowered and confident enough to speak out to change the system. However, another factor is government recognition; given CREATE's unique position in the out-of-home care sector in Australia, it would seem an appropriate time for authorities to re-examine the status of this organization in terms of establishing information-sharing protocols, at least for basic contact details, so that CREATE's vision that '*All* children and young people with a care experience have the chance to reach their full potential (italics added)' can be realized.

References

Association of Children's Welfare Agencies. (1996). *ACWA annual report 1995/96*. Sydney: ACWA.
Australian Institute of Health and Welfare (AIHW). (2013). *Child protection Australia 2011–12, Child welfare series no. 55 Cat. No. CWS 43*. Canberra: AIHW.
Barham, J. (2012). *Foster kids deserve support: Leaving care plans are vital.* http://www.janbarham.org.au/wp-content/uploads/2012/02/12.2.24-PDF-FOSTER-KIDS-DESERVE-SUPPORT-_J.Barham_.pdf. Accessed 20 Dec 2015.
Berkhout, J. (2013). Why interest organizations do what they do: Assessing the explanatory potential of 'Exchange' approaches. *Interest Groups & Advocacy, 2*(2), 227–250.
Catch22. (2015). *National leaving care benchmarking forum*. http://www.catch-22.org.uk/expertise/care-leavers/national-leaving-care-benchmarking-forum/. Accessed 10 Oct 2015.
Council of Europe and SOS Children Villages.. (2013). *Securing children's rights: A guide for professionals working in alternative care.* http://www.coe.int/t/dg3/children/publications/SecuringChildrensRights_GBR.pdf. Accessed 10 Oct 2015.
CREATE. (2006). *Report card on education 2006*. http://create.org.au/wp-content/uploads/2014/12/01.-CREATE-Report-Card_Education_2006.pdf. Accessed 4 Dec 2015.

CREATE. (2010). *'What's the answer?': Young people's solutions for improving transitioning to independence from out-of-home care*. Canberra: Department of Families, Housing, Community Services and Indigenous Affairs.

CREATE. (2015a). *2015 annual review*. http://create.org.au/wp-content/uploads/2014/12/CREATE_Annual-Review-2015-web.pdf. Accessed 30 Nov 2015.

CREATE. (2015b). *The power within*. http://create.org.au/publications/the-power-within/. Accessed 8 Dec 2015.

Child Protection Systems Royal Commission. (2016). *The life they deserve: Child Protection Systems Royal Commission Report. Volume 1: Summary and Report*. Adelaide: Government of South Australia.

Department of Families, Housing, Community Services, and Indigenous Affairs (FaHCSIA). (2011). *An outline of national standards for out-of-home care*. Canberra: Author.

Dyett, K. (2012). *Extra support for teens*. http://www.abc.net.au/news/2012-02-22/act-govt-foster-support/3844374. Accessed 20 Dec 2015.

Eurochild. (2014). *Annual report 2014*. http://www.eurochild.org/fileadmin/public/01_Communications/Annual_Reports/EUROCHILD_ANNUAL_online_R_pdf. Accessed 10 Oct 2015.

Family for Every Child. (2015). *Strategies for delivering safe and effective foster care: A review of the evidence for those designing and delivering foster care programmes*. http://www.familyforeverychild.org/report/strategies-for-delivering-safe-and-effective-foster-care/. Accessed 11 Oct 2015.

Gainsborough, J. F. (2010). *Scandalous politics: Child welfare policy in the states*. Washington, DC: Georgetown University Press.

Lowery, D. (2013). Lobbying influence: Meaning, measurement and missing. *Interest Groups and Advocacy, 2*(1), 1–26.

McDermott, L., Stead, M., & Hastings, G. (2005). What is and what is not social marketing: The challenge of reviewing the evidence. *Journal of Marketing Management, 21*, 545–553.

McDowall, J. J. (2008). *Transitioning from care in Australia: The CREATE report card 2008*. Sydney: CREATE Foundation.

McDowall, J. J. (2009). *Transitioning from care: Tracking progress: CREATE report card 2009*. Sydney: CREATE Foundation.

McDowall, J. J. (2011). *Transitioning from care in Australia: An evaluation of CREATE's 'What's the plan?' campaign*. Sydney: CREATE Foundation.

McDowall, J. J. (2012). Factors influencing transition-from-care planning in Australia. *Developing Practice, 33*, 69–80.

McDowall, J. J. (2013). *Experiencing out-of-home care in Australia: The views of children and young people.* Sydney: CREATE Foundation.

McDowall, J. J. (2015). *Sibling placement and contact in out-of-home care.* Sydney: CREATE Foundation.

McDowall, J. J. (2016). *CREATE's Go Your Own Way resource for young people transitioning from care in Australia: An evaluation.* Sydney: CREATE Foundation.

McKinney, B., & Halpin, D. (2007). Talking about Australian pressure groups: Adding value to the insider/outsider distinction in combating homelessness in Western Australia. *Australian Journal of Public Administration, 66*(3), 342–352. doi:10.1111/j.1467-8500.2007.00532.x.

Mendes, P. (1998). Consumer groups in child protection: Enhancing the accountability of the system. *Children Australia, 23*(2), 33–38.

Mendes, P. (2002). Leaving care services in Victoria: A case study of a policy debate. *Developing Practice, 3,* 51–59.

Mendes, P. (2016). Young people transitioning from out-of-home care: A case study of Australian media reporting 2004–2015. *Developing Practice, 43,* 5–16.

National Children's Bureau. (2013). *Independent advocacy in child protection: Guidance for policy makers.* https://secure.toolkitfiles.co.uk/clients/22965/sitedata/files/Advocacy_in_CP_-_Policy_Ma.pdf. Accessed 12 Oct 2015.

O'Brien, A. (1997). Consumer participation for young people in care. *Family Matters, 46,* 56–58.

Owen, J. (1996). *Every childhood lasts a lifetime.* Brisbane: Australian Association of Children and Young People in Care.

Pecora, P. J., Whittaker, J. K., Maluccio, A. N., Barth, R. P., & DePanfilis, D. (2011). In R. D. Plotnick (Ed.), *The child welfare challenge: Policy, practice, and research* (3 ed.). New Brunswick: Aldine Transaction.

Pedersen, H. H. (2013). Is measuring interest group influence a mission impossible? The case of interest group influence in the Danish parliament. *Interest Groups and Advocacy, 2*(1), 27–47.

Powell, F., & Scanlon, M. (2014). *The media and child abuse.* http://discoversociety.org/2014/09/30/the-media-and-child-abuse/. Accessed 4 Dec 2015.

Queensland Government. (2015). *Youth: Apps and tools.* http://www.qld.gov.au/youth/apps-tools/. Accessed 12 Oct 2015.

Royal Commission into Institutional Responses to Child Sexual Abuse. (2015). *Issues papers and submissions.* https://www.childabuseroyalcommission.gov.au/research/issues-papers-submissions. Accessed 8 Dec 2015.

Samuelson, W., & Zeckhauser, R. (1988). Status quo bias in decision making. *Journal of Risk and Uncertainty, 1*, 7–59.

Senate Community Affairs References Committee. (2015). *Out-of-home care.* https://aifs.gov.au/cfca/2015/08/25/report-senate-inquiry-out-home-care. Accessed 4 Dec 2015.

Stein, M. (2011). *Care less lives.* London: Catch22.

Thomas, N., Gran, B., & Hanson, K. (2011). An independent voice for children's rights in Europe? The role of independent children's rights institutions in the EU. *International Journal of Children's Rights, 19*, 429–449.

Thompson, R. A. (2015). Social support and child protection: Lessons learned and learning. *Child Abuse & Neglect, 41*, 19–29. doi:10.1016/j.chiabu.2014.06.011.

Trepte, S. (2015). Social media, privacy, and self-disclosure: The turbulence caused by social media's affordances. *Social Media + Society, April–June*, 1–2. doi:10.1177/2056305115578681.

Wood, J. (2008). *Report of the special commission of inquiry into child protection services in NSW* (*Volume 2*). http://www.dpc.nsw.gov.au/__data/assets/pdf_file/0011/33797/Volume_2_-_Special_Commission_of_Inquiry_into_Child_Protection_Services_in_New_South_Wales.pdf. Accessed 4 Dec 2015.

15

Journeys of Exclusion: Unpacking the Experience of Adolescent Care Leavers in New Zealand

Nicola Atwool

Introduction

New Zealand has one of the youngest leaving care ages in the developed world (17th birthday) and has lagged behind other anglophone countries in the development of legislation and policy to support care leavers. Although this absence of legislative provision is a significant factor in our failure to meet their needs (Ashton 2014; Boshier and Wademan 2010), reviewing the literature from countries with more robust provisions demonstrates that legislation and policy are not the panacea (Broad 1999; Courtney et al. 2011; Mendes et al. 2011; Stott 2013). An overview of recent international developments sets the scene for an exploration of marginalization as a theoretical framework for understanding the experience of care leavers. The situation in New Zealand is then used as a case study to highlight the processes by which care leavers become

N. Atwool (✉)
Social Work Programme, University of Otago, Dunedin, New Zealand

marginalized. The chapter concludes with a discussion of policy reforms needed, and implications for policy and practice in other countries.

Global Perspective

A review of recent research indicates that abrupt transitions from care are continuing to create challenges (Dima and Skehill 2011; Geenan and Powers 2007; Goodkind et al. 2011; Höjer and Sjöblom 2014; McCoy et al. 2008; Mullan et al. 2007). Poor educational outcomes remain evident (Höjer and Sjöîblom 2014; Jackson and Cameron 2012; Pecora 2012; Ward 2011), compromising care leavers' ability to secure employment (Hook and Courtney 2011). Lack of resources hinder effective implementation of policy (Collins and Clay 2009; Geenan and Powers 2007; Hiles et al. 2014; Mendes et al. 2011; Stott 2013), and some policies have failed the most vulnerable by targeting only those who remain engaged with education or training (Courtney et al. 2011; Goodkind et al. 2011; Stott 2013). Assumptions that existing services will be sufficient to meet the needs of care leavers have also been identified as a barrier (Mendes et al. 2011; Höjer and Sjöblom 2011).

Policies based on a presumed readiness for the 'compressed and accelerated transition to adulthood' (Stein 2008, p. 39) do not seem to take account of the particular vulnerability of young people with a care history. Even those in Stein's (2008) 'moving on' category (see discussion in Introductory chapter) face the challenge of negotiating the transition to adulthood against a background of being different (Lee and Berrick 2014). Others are less fortunate, and attention has been drawn to the extreme vulnerability of some care leavers (Akister et al. 2010; Furnivall 2013; Hamilton et al. 2015; Samuels and Pryce 2008; Stein and Dumaret 2011). Lack of relational support is identified as a critical issue (Collins et al. 2006; Hiles et al. 2014; Hiles et al. 2013; Höjer and Sjöblom 2014; Mendes et al. 2012; Samuels and Pryce 2008; Stein and Dumaret 2011), and attention is drawn to our limited understanding of what counts as support (Cushing et al. 2014).

Negotiating identity is a key developmental task for young people, and research with care leavers highlights the particular challenges they face (Collins et al. 2010; Hiles et al. 2013, 2014; Höjer and Sjöblom 2014;

Mendes et al. 2012; Samuels and Pryce 2008; Stein and Dumaret 2011). It is readily apparent from young people's accounts that discontinuities and the stigma associated with being in care have an enduring impact. Some are clearly burdened by the past (Fransson and Storø 2011), but even those who take pride in their achievements do so at a cost. Samuels and Pryce (2008) identify a pattern whereby the combination of early entry to independence and awareness of difference shapes a staunchly survivalist identity. Although this can be seen as adaptive and evidence of resilience, such a stance may also serve to increase vulnerability by reducing the likelihood that these young people will reach out for, or accept, support.

Young people's accounts across different countries provide valuable information about their lack of engagement with the support offered, reporting lack of consultation and arbitrary rules that did not recognize their wish to have a say in deciding future pathways (Geenan and Powers 2007; Goodkind et al. 2011; Hiles et al. 2013; Höjer and Sjöblom 2014; McCoy et al. 2007; Mullen et al. 2007; Nybell 2013). Although they did not necessarily feel prepared, or have a good understanding of what lay ahead, they were keen to get away from a system that had failed to engage them. By the time they realized that support was needed, there were no obvious points of re-entry.

The emphasis on independence has been questioned, given the protracted nature of contemporary adolescence and the extension of transition to adulthood into the 20s and even 30s (Avery and Freundlich 2009; Goodkind et al. 2011; Samuels and Pryce 2008). Changes in social and economic circumstances have influenced this trend, but it is increasingly recognized that successful transition to adulthood relies on the capacity to relate to others. The notion of independence is being supplanted by one of interdependence, that is, a conceptualization of adulthood being attained within the context of social relationships that provide developmental scaffolding for youth (Avery and Freundlich 2009; Lee and Berrick 2014; Stott 2013).

Theory and Practice

Policy and practice seems driven by pragmatic responses to poor outcomes, and the lack of theory informing practice has been challenged (Pinkerton 2011; Stein 2006). Stein (2006) puts forward attachment, the focal model of adolescence (Coleman 1974), and resilience as relevant theoretical perspectives that may contribute to an increased understanding of the implications of empirical research. Recent developments in our understanding of neuropsychological changes during adolescence highlight opportunities for further gains to be made with appropriate support (Avery and Freundlich 2009).

Lee and Berrick (2014) focus on the role of social capital in the transition to adulthood, arguing that the accumulation of tangible (human and social capital such as education) and intangible (such as personal agency and adult identity) resources is critical in determining outcomes for care leavers. Rejecting services is one way in which disempowered youth may choose to exercise personal agency, thus reinforcing the importance of engaging with young people to negotiate pathways to adulthood that allow them to exercise personal agency within networks of support. These theoretical perspectives tend to focus on the individual, potentially overlooking the effect of the wider context on the care-leaving process. Mendes (2007) called for structural analysis to inform our understanding of the challenges faced, drawing attention to social processes of marginalization and exclusion.

Journeys of Exclusion

These processes operate at the micro level of intra- and interpersonal dynamics, but are mutually reinforced by meso- (organizational) and macro-level (social, political and economic) influences. Although marginalization occurs in a social context, the self is a social production, and the two are closely interrelated (Sibley 1995). Care leavers are located in multiple marginal spaces. Adolescents, in general, occupy the liminal space between childhood and adulthood, and may be perceived as threatening because of the ambiguity about the boundary between these states (Sibley 1995). Care leavers' combined adolescent status and lack of social capital amplify their marginalization, and any involvement in socially unacceptable behaviours exacerbates this. The process of marginalization begins much earlier, however, in the very circumstances that lead to their placement in care.

When the State intervenes, the primary focus is to return the child to an improved family or to place the child with another family. To secure such a family, social workers may seek to minimize the challenge of caring for a traumatized child (Atwool 2010). Kin carers and foster parents lack full awareness of the potential pitfalls, and are therefore ill-equipped to cope. When children's early experiences manifest as challenging behaviours, this is individualized, and the child becomes 'the problem'. Despite our knowledge of the impact of trauma, these children threaten our professional competence, calling accepted practices into question. Social workers and other professionals such as teachers may respond defensively, rather than addressing the underlying issues. Failure to ensure that children receive the level of support required to ensure positive outcomes is rationalized by social workers, citing the emotionally demanding nature of the work, workload pressure, lack of resources and the resulting burn-out (Hiles et al. 2014). These rationalizations protect social workers, carers and other professionals from confronting the fact that children in care become scapegoats, marginalized by the very circumstances that should evoke a compassionate response.

However, the marginalization arguably does not stop there. In New Zealand, indigenous children are over-represented in the care system (Office of the Children's Commissioner (OCC) 2015,) as they are in the USA (US Department of Health and Human Services 2011), Australia (Fernandez and Atwool 2013) and Canada (Blackstock and Trocmé 2005). In the USA and UK, the same is true for other non-white children. Their definition as racial 'other' increases the likelihood of entry to care, and once in care they are further marginalized through higher rates of admission to residential care, comprising 65 per cent of admissions in New Zealand (Child Youth and Family 2015). Their journey through care may result in the loss of cultural connections, exacerbating marginalization within their own culture as well as in relation to the dominant culture (Atwool 2008; McIntosh 2006). Other minority groups are also over-represented among those who age out of care, including those who identify as lesbian, gay, bisexual, transgender and queer (Stott 2013).

Perhaps, the most profound form of marginalization is the lack of voice experienced by children in care. As noted earlier, research undertaken with young people highlights the failure to engage with them during the transition phase (Atwool 2008, 2010; Geenan and Powers 2007; Goodkind et al. 2011; McCoy et al. 2007; Nybell 2013; OCC 2015; Stott 2013). To be denied the opportunity to exercise personal agency is arguably the most brutal form of exclusion amongst the many young care leavers' experience.

Similar processes at the meso level amplify micro-level experiences. In an analysis of practices in five European countries, lack of support from social workers and carers emerged as a critical factor in low educational attainment (Jackson and Cameron 2012). Interviews with policy and programme stakeholders in Massachusetts identified two system-oriented problems (Collins and Clay 2009). The most common was that the child welfare system focussed on children and child protection and was not, therefore, in a position to effectively serve transition-age youth. The second major problem was young people falling through cracks because the state systems designed to serve them were not well coordinated. Unrealistic expectations of independence, as discussed earlier, amplify these difficulties and become another means by which care leavers are marginalized.

Micro- and meso-level processes of marginalization originate from the macro level. Current policy in the USA and other anglophone nations has been constructed in the context of neoliberal politics. Individualism and competition are the hallmarks of this approach, underpinning social provision systems. Responsibility is devolved to the family to equip the next generation with the skills needed to achieve in a competitive world. A competitive world creates winners and losers, with losers defined as being in that position by virtue of their own failings, thus becoming convenient scapegoats for society's failure to ensure adequate social provision for all citizens. Even in social democratic nations, the family has prime responsibility, and those who come into care become the 'other' (Höjer and Sjöblom 2014).

The State as parent is a dismal failure. Collins and Clay (2009, p. 750) describe care leavers as 'a marginalized group (adolescents) within a marginalized policy sector (child welfare)'. At a global level, despite recognition of the vulnerability of children in care and the 2009 publication of guidelines outlining their expectations, an analysis of national reports to the United Nations Committee on the Rights of the Child reveals that policy relating to care leavers has a low profile in these reports and in the Concluding

Observations of the Committee (Munro et al. 2011). The continued failure of the State to provide for some of its most vulnerable citizens despite research evidence and theoretical perspectives suggests that something other than rationality underpins current responses. It is only when we consider the implications of defining children in care as 'other', thereby placing them outside the comfortable world of what is considered normal and acceptable, that we begin to comprehend what is happening. New Zealand provides a case study, highlighting these processes of marginalization.

Ageing Out of Care in New Zealand: A Case Study

In New Zealand (total population in 2015 of 4.5 million), the Child, Youth and Family (CYF) agency within the Ministry of Social Development provides care and protection and youth justice services under the auspices of the *Children, Young Persons and their Families (CYPF) Act, 1989*. Most children are placed in care through custody orders, which automatically expire when they turn 17. Despite provision for the Chief Executive to be appointed as an additional guardian with responsibility toward care leavers until they are 20 years old, in practice, most services and support orders expire at age 17 (Boshier and Wademan 2010).

Around 5000 children are in care, with another 2000 entering care each year (OCC 2015). As noted earlier, indigenous children are over-represented, 58 per cent compared to 15 per cent of the total population (OCC 2015), with Pasifika children making up a further 9 cent. Of the 1700 children who left care in 2014, a total of 400 moved to Home for Life placements,[1] 300 aged out of care and no information for the remaining 1000 was available (OCC 2015). In March 2015, a total 1078 young people aged 14–16 were in the custody of CYF, with 802 in out-of-home care.[2] Only 19 were aged over 17, demonstrating that most

---

[1] Home for Life is designed to secure permanency for children unable to return home. Adoption is not favoured as a permanency option and Home for Life allows foster parents to have custody. CYF withdraws but birth parents retain guardianship.

[2] The smaller number excludes those who are living at home or have moved into independent accommodation.

young people leave care at 17 (CYF 2015). The available data do not provide a breakdown of ethnicity for each age group, but it is likely that at least half are Māori.

Legislative and Policy Frameworks

Until recently, no legislative provision relating to care leavers existed, despite efforts to amend this. The recommendation in a Ministerial Review of CYF that consideration be given to 16-year-olds in care with insufficient support being placed under the guardianship of the Chief Executive and supported through their transition to adulthood until the age of 20 (Brown 2000) was never implemented. At that time, the primary focus appeared to be improving responses to new care and protection concerns, and children already in care were not accorded high priority (Atwool 1999). A legislative amendment introduced in 2006 to increase the care-leaving age to 18 and provide for transition support lapsed when the government changed.

Current CYF transition policy (n.d.-a, b) is divided into two parts: *Preparing for Independence* and *Towards Independence: Voices of Young People*. The former emphasizes the importance of a support network, and the sample plan identifies three goals: financial independence, ability to drive a car and completion of secondary school. Although longer-term plans may need to include accommodation, employment/education/training and family/whānau[3]/peer supports, the document warns that such a long list may be overwhelming. The plan assumes that the young person remains living with a caregiver despite the absence of provision for board payments to continue. To receive financial support, the young person must engage with a Youth Service programme (even if they are continuing at school) and meet many requirements, including provision of a letter from a social worker to confirm eligibility for the Youth Payment.

The second policy document opens with a statement that young people need to practice their independence before leaving care, and be

---

[3] The terms whānau, hapū and iwi are used to acknowledge Māori children's connection to wider social structures. Whānau is not restricted to nuclear family, hapū are extended family networks and iwi are tribes comprised of connected hapū.

supported to do so. The document notes the importance of fare-welling them with hopes and dreams for their future, having someone to guide them, making sure they are financially independent, are engaged in work or training and have somewhere supportive and secure to live. Transition from care to independence is described as a process, rather than a one-off event, that works best when the young person is encouraged to take the lead and be in control. Variability in development and maturity is noted, as is the need to begin early. Two years of planning and preparation is recommended on the basis of research evidence. A detailed checklist for transition planning for young people with disabilities is provided separately. The importance of coordinated planning with other agencies based on appropriate assessments is emphasized, and guardianship issues and the possible need for CYF to have a continuing role are discussed.

The CYF Auckland Regional office funds two transition programmes providing support to young people aged 15–20. In 2012, they delivered services to approximately 150 young people (Stevens et al. 2013). Demand is reportedly high, and an evaluation of one programme demonstrated that young people found the service valuable (Abbott 2010). One of the providers also runs Care Café (www.carecafe.co.nz), a website for young people in care with useful information for those in, and leaving, care. There are no transition programmes in other parts of the country. Both transition programmes are run by NGOs and were initially set up as pilot projects. It is likely that Auckland was chosen because of the availability of NGOs with relevant expertise and the large population-base. Despite the success of both programmes, the lack of expansion to other areas appears to be the result of financial constraints and failure to prioritize care leavers.

Outcomes for Care Leavers

Despite the dearth of research on outcomes for children in care (OCC 2015), a lack of longitudinal studies and a scarcity of funding for such research, the research that does exist indicates that outcomes are comparable to those reported in other countries. Ward (2000, 2001) reviewed 35 case records of 16-year-olds drawn from 177 children aged 15–16in statutory custody on 1 April 1997. Yates (2000) interviewed eight care leavers, and Fitzgerald, Mortlock and Jeffs (2006) seven. Coote (2007) interviewed five young people and conducted focus groups with the young people, family members and caregivers. Leoni (2007) focussed on the experience of Māori, interviewing eight people with care histories and ten professionals and community members who had been involved with young people leaving care. A 2010 OCC investigation into the quality of services for children in care included interviews with 47 young people, many of whom were approaching the age of 17 (Atwool 2010).

In all of these projects, the majority of participants experienced abrupt and unplanned departures from care and left with limited educational qualifications. A recent project focussing on the educational experiences of seven care leavers engaged in tertiary education found that their success was achieved despite the care system, rather than because of it (Matheson 2014). Most had experienced multiple placements and reported that foster parents did not provide educationally rich environments. The majority had birth families that valued education, and a key factor was feeling cared for, and cared about, by at least one adult. These young people experienced school as a place of belonging, saw education as a means of improving their situation and believed themselves to be resilient. The one unique finding was that most participants had experienced one or more serendipitous events without which it is unlikely that they would have gone to university, leading the researcher to conclude that current systems cannot be working well when such progression comes down largely to luck.

Many of the participants reported difficulties with accommodation and employment, ongoing challenges in their relationships with birth family, isolation and limited access to support. This was particularly significant for Māori participants who had lost contact with whānau, hapū and iwi, and struggled with their cultural identity as a consequence (Coote 2007; Leoni 2007). By way of contrast, a Māori participant in Matheson's (2014) study reported that an early whānau placement and later attendance at a Māori boarding school had an important and formative influence. Evidence of involvement with offending and challenges associated with substance abuse, mental health and early parenthood was also demonstrated.

The majority of the young people approaching the age of 17 in the OCC investigation reported anxiety and uncertainty about what would happen when they turned 17, the only exceptions being young people already engaged with a transition programme (Atwool 2010). A more recent report indicates that there has been no change because the young people consulted 'often report not being kept informed about their transition plans, or plans changing at the last minute and describe considerable fear and uncertainty about the future as they approach their 17th birthday and prepare to age out of the care system' (OCC 2015, p. 46). Earlier this year, the Minister for Social Development appointed an Independent Expert Panel to oversee the modernization of CYF. Their interim report notes that children and young people who have contact with CYF go on to experience 'dramatically worse outcomes as young adults' (Modernising CYF Expert Panel, 2015, p. 36). For example, outcome data at age 21 for a cohort born in the 12 months to June 1991[4] indicate that 80 per cent of children in state care leave school without National Certificates of Educational Achievement (NCEA) Level 2 (foundation skills for employment) compared to a national average achievement rate of 70 per cent. Nearly 90 per cent were on a benefit, and 25 per cent were on a benefit with child. More than 60 per cent of those with a custodial sentence had previously had contact with CYF.

Inadequate social provision exacerbates some of these difficulties. Young people are ineligible for state housing until age 18, and then only if they are a parent. Although there is some supervised accommodation for young people with disabilities, there is very little for youth who do not meet the criteria for such services. Young people cannot sign a lease for rental accommodation until they are 18 years old. Although a stable placement is a critical factor for scholastic success, this is threatened by the prospect of being discharged from care during their final high school year (Matheson 2014; Yates 2000).

As noted above, the Youth Payment is difficult to access, and once in receipt, there are specified obligations including engagement with school, training or employment and participation in budgeting (MSD n.d.). Non-compliance results in cancellation of payment, and no other

---

[4] This data is drawn from an unpublished report by the Ministry of Social Development (2014).

funding is available. Young people who return to family are not eligible for the Youth Payment.

Despite the challenges faced by all participants, the research provides evidence of optimism and hope for the future (Atwool 2010; Coote 2007; Fitzgerald et al. 2006; Leoni 2007; Matheson 2014; Yates 2000), indicating that increased support could enable care leavers to achieve their goals, avoiding the individual and societal costs associated with poor outcomes. Further supportive evidence can be found in the New Zealand Pathways to Resilience research (Munford, Sanders, Liebenberg, Ungar et al. 2013). Based on a cohort of 1477 participants comprising 605 matched pairs of multiservice users (the majority of whom were known to CYF) and a comparison group, data gathering techniques included a quantitive survey instrument, qualitative interviews and case file review. One of the findings is that challenged young people are able to make positive changes in their lives with appropriate and timely systemic support (Urry et al. 2014).

Recent Developments

The following provisions are mandated by a 2014 amendment to the *CYPF Act 1989*, applying to a person aged between 15 and 20, who has been in custody or care of CYF or an Iwi, cultural or family support social service for at least three months:

> The organization must consider what advice and assistance the person will need to become, and remain, independent after leaving care and provide, or arrange for the provision of, that advice and assistance to the extent that it reasonably relates to the period before the person leaves care or custody. A young person can request advice or assistance in the form of information, assistance with accommodation, education, training or employment, legal advice, counseling, and/or financial assistance in exceptional circumstances. *(CYPF Act 1989, s386)*

The amendment does not specify how these obligations will be met, given the failure to practice in accordance with current policy, and the limited availability of transition support services. This lack of clarity assumes even greater significance when viewed in the context of research from countries that have had more robust legislation for some time.

Pinkerton (2011) proposed a model to explain the globalized ecology of leaving care. National and international contexts and leaving and aftercare interventions are identified as factors impacting the local social ecology of support. This then impacts the care leavers' social capital and their resilience to determine coping capacity for youth transition. Despite a global perspective highlighting the challenges facing care leavers, the national framework in New Zealand has failed to ensure adequate provision of services for children and young people in, and after leaving, care. This creates a local social ecology characterized by lack of support, limiting access to social capital and failing to provide opportunities to develop resilience. This, in turn, reduces coping capacity for youth transitioning from care. Such a model challenges an individualize focus on care leavers, serving as a reminder of the multiple opportunities to influence outcomes in positive directions, and provides a framework for considering changes needed.

Implications for Policy and Practice

Improved service delivery to young people leaving care has to begin when they enter care. At micro, meso and macro levels, policy and practice need to be informed by an understanding of the processes of marginalization. Although legislative provision has not guaranteed an effective response to the challenges facing care leavers in other countries, it is an important place to start. It is very difficult to command resources without a legislative mandate, and current provisions in relation to both permanency and transition to adulthood are inadequate.

The expansion of responsibility for vulnerable children (including those in care) to the Ministries of Education and Health with the enactment of the *Vulnerable Children Act* 2014 is a significant step forward. It will, however, only make a difference if resources are available to ensure that all children in care are actively engaged with education and receive appropriate therapeutic intervention to address trauma. Significant improvement is needed to ensure that children in care experience stability and continuity during their time in care. Timely decision-making is critical, as is appropriate placement. Currently, approximately half the children in care are in kin placements, and although the rate is higher for Māori, more work is needed to ensure all children have access to their cultural networks. The current permanency legislation and policy is premised on the withdrawal of all support after three years, despite the fact that birth parents retain guardianship. The support provided is limited, and an urgent review is needed to ensure ongoing access to appropriate support when this is required.

In the meantime, it is imperative that young people leaving care are presented with opportunities to build the social capital necessary to reduce the marginalization created by less than satisfactory care experiences. This cannot be done unless the care-leaving age is raised to at least 18 years. Consideration should be given to the extension of board payments to foster parents willing to support young people in their transition to adulthood. Robust policy to ensure continuing coordinated support for care leavers is required. It is not appropriate that such support is the ongoing responsibility of the statutory care and protection service. Transition services funded by the government, but delivered in partnership with NGOs, are urgently needed. Such provision respects the expressed wish of young people to move away from the dependence associated with being in care, and towards independence with support. New and current transition services must be mandated to support involvement to age 25 if needed, and to allow re-engagement for those young people who exit at an earlier age but later recognize the need for support.

Such an arrangement also creates space for Iwi and other Māori and Pasifika providers to develop services specifically designed for their young people. Such services could facilitate re-connection with cultural networks for those who have lost these connections, and have the potential to enhance resilience by fostering positive cultural identity. In addition, Māori and Pasifika young people's higher rates of disengagement from the education system create barriers to engagement with mainstream providers of services for those not in education, training or employment, and alternatives are needed if they are to meet the requirements for the Youth Payment.

Transition services can only be effective in an environment that supports networking and inter-agency collaboration. Although New Zealand research demonstrates that services can make a difference, quality is variable, and inconsistent service delivery is as strongly associated with risk as poor quality service (Stevens et al. 2014).

At the micro level, the starting point has to be engagement that encourages personal agency. Every care leaver should have a relationship with at least one adult who is prepared to walk alongside him/her. Services need to have the flexibility to respond to the identified needs of the young person. For example, engaging with birth families to support re-connection, access to recreation and peer networks and support to access information to make sense of their care journey are all possibilities (over and above the more practical and obvious needs) that may be important for care leavers.

As noted earlier, young people are able to identify hopes and dreams, and despite their experiences, they often remain surprisingly optimistic. When confronted by resistance, despair, despondency or apathy, practitioners need to see this for what it is—the logical consequence of care leavers' journey of exclusion. Rather than allowing this to be an excuse for further marginalization, these are the young people who should be prioritized for more intensive service provision delivered in partnership with them.

Although New Zealand has lagged behind, the pathway forward outlined above has implications for other countries as well. A focus on processes of marginalization reduces the risk of piecemeal approaches and highlights the need to consider the whole care journey when developing services to support transition. Systemic responses need to have the flexibility to engage with children and young people to develop individualized plans at each stage of the journey. There are no one-size-fits-all solutions, but Pinkerton's model provides a framework that could facilitate the development of a shared language to support international exchange and comparison.

References

Abbott, D. (2010). *Do supported transitions from Foster Care achieve better outcomes for young people? An evaluation of young people's perspectives and experiences of Dingwall Trust's Launch Care to Independence Service.* A research report submitted in partial fulfilment of the Master of Social Work (Applied). Massey University, Albany campus.

Akister, J., Owens, M., & Goodyer, I. M. (2010). Leaving care and mental health: outcomes for children in out-of-home care during the transition to adulthood. *Health Research and Policy Systems, 8*(10), 10–19.

Ashton, S. (2014). The rights of children and young people in state care. *Educational Philosophy and Theory*. doi:10.1080/00131857.2014.9431432.

Atwool, N. R. (1999). Attachment and post-intervention decision-making. *Journal of Child Centred Practice, 6(1),* 39–55.

Atwool, N. R. (2008) *Who cares? The role of attachment assessments in decision-making for children in care.* Unpublished doctoral thesis. University of Otago, Dunedin.

Atwool, N. R. (2010) *Children in Care.* (Wellington: Office of the Children's Commissioner). http://www.occ.org.nz/publications

Avery, R. J., & Freundlich, M. (2009). You're all grown up now: Termination of foster care support at age 18. *Journal of Adolescence, 32,* 247–257.

Blackstock, C., & Trocmé, N. (2005). Community-based child welfare for aboriginal children: Supporting resilience through structural change. *Social Policy Journal of New Zealand, 24,* 12–33.

Boshier, P., & Wademan, J. (2010). Youth aging out of foster care – International perspectives'. *Family Court Review, 48*(2), 294–304.

Broad, B. (1999). Young people leaving care: Moving towards joined up solutions. *Children & Society, 13,* 81–93.

Brown, M. J. A. (2000). *Care and protection is about adult behaviour. Ministerial review of the Department of Child, Youth and Family Services.* Wellington: Department of Child Youth and Family Services.

Child, Youth and Family. (n.d.-a). *Preparing for independence.* http://www.practicecentrecyf.govt.nz. Accessed 24 Aug 2015.

Child, Youth and Family. (n.d.-b). *Towards independence: Voices of young people.* http://www.practicecentrecyf.govt.nz. Accessed 24 Aug 2015.

Child, Youth and Family. (2015). Key statistics. http://www.cyf.govt.nz. Accessed 24 Aug 2015.

Children, Young Persons and their Families Act (1989), Public act 1989 No. 24. www.legislation.govt.nz

Coleman, J. C. (1974). *Relationships in adolescence.* London: Routledge and Kegan Paul.

Collins, M. E., & Clay, C. (2009). Influencing policy for youth transitioning from care: Defining problems, crafting solutions, and assessing politics. *Children and Youth Services Review, 31,* 743–751.

Collins, M. E., Spencer, R., & Ward, R. (2006). Supporting youth in transition from foster care: Formal and informal connections. *Child Welfare, 89*(1), 125–143.

Coote, P. (2007). *Going home? The fate of children who leave care.* A thesis submitted for the degree of Master of Social Welfare. University of Otago, Dunedin.

Courtney, M. E., Lee, J., & Perez, A. (2011). Receipt of help acquiring life skills and predictors of help receipt among current and former foster youth. *Children and Youth Services Review, 33*, 2442–2451.

Cushing, G., Samuels, G. G., & Kerman, B. (2014). Profiles of relational permanence at 22: Variability in parental supports and outcomes among young adults with foster care histories. *Children and Youth Services Review, 39*, 73–83.

Dima, G., & Skehill, C. (2011). Making sense of leaving care: The contribution of Bridges model of transition to understanding the psycho-social process. *Children and Youth Services Review, 33*, 2532–2539.

Fernandez, E., & Atwool, N. (2013). Child protection and out of home care: Policy, practice, and research connections Australia and New Zealand. *Psychosocial Intervention, 22*, 175–184.

Fitzgerald, L., Mortlock, B. & Jeffs, L. (2006) *Finding out what we need to know: Developing a participatory research methodology with young people who have exited statutory care and protection.* (Unpublished report prepared by The Office of the Children's Commissioner and The Collaborative for Research and Training in Youth Health and Development).

Fransson, E., & Storø, J. (2011). Dealing with the past in the transition from care. A post-structural analysis of young people's accounts. *Children and Youth Services Review, 33*, 2519–2525.

Furnivall, J. (2013). *Understanding suicide and self-harm amongst children in care and care leavers.* Scotland: Institute for Research and Innovation in Social Services.

Geenan, S., & Powers, L. E. (2007). Tomorrow is another problem. The experiences of youth in foster care during their transition into adulthood. *Children and Youth Services Review, 29*, 1085–1101.

Goodkind, S., Schelbe, L. A., & Shook, J. J. (2011). Why youth leave care: Understandings of adulthood and transition successes and challenges among youth aging out of child welfare. *Children and Youth Services Review, 33*, 1039–1048.

Hamilton, D., Taylor, B., Killick, C., & Bickerstaff, D. (2015). Suicidal ideation and behaviour among young people leaving care: Case file survey. *Child Care in Practice, 21*(2), 160–176.

Hiles, D., Moss, D., Thorne, L., Wright, J., & Dallos, R. (2013). "So what am I?" – Multiple perspectives on young people's experience of leaving care. *Children and Youth Services Review, 41*, 1–15.

Hiles, D., Moss, D., Wright, J., & Dallos, R. (2014). Young people's experience of social support during the process of leaving care. *Children and Youth Services Review, 35*, 2059–2071.

Höjer, I., & Sjöblom, Y. (2011). Procedures when young people leave care – Views of 111 Swedish social services managers. *Children and Youth Services Review, 33*, 2452–2460.

Höjer, I., & Sjöblom, Y. (2014). Voices of 65 young people leaving care in Sweden: "There is so much I need to know!". *Australian Social Work, 67*(1), 71–87.

Hook, J. L., & Courtney, M. E. (2011). Employment outcomes of former foster youth as young adults: The importance of human, personal, and social capital. *Children and Youth Services Review, 33*, 1855–1865.

Jackson, S., & Cameron, C. (2012). Leaving care: Looking ahead and aiming higher. *Children and Youth Services Review, 34*, 1107–1114.

Lee, C., & Berrick, J. D. (2014). Experiences of youth who transition to adulthood out of care: Developing a theoretical framework. *Children and Youth Services Review, 46*, 78–84.

Leoni, K. (2007). *Ka Tipu Mai Nga Taiohi Māori: A Study of Taiohi Māori Leaving Care in New Zealand*. A thesis submitted for the degree of Master of Youth Development. Auckland University of Technology, Auckland.

Matheson, I. (2014) *Slipping down ladders and climbing up snakes: The educational experience of young adults who were in foster care*. A thesis submitted for the degree of Doctor of Education at the University of Otago, Dunedin.

McCoy, H., McMillen, J. C., & Spitznagel, E. L. (2008). Older youth leaving the foster care system: Who, what, when, where and why? *Children and Youth Services Review, 30*, 735–745.

McIntosh, T. (2006). Theorising marginality and the process of marginalisation. *Alternative, 2*(1), 45–65.

Mendes, P. (2007). A structural analysis of young people leaving state care. *Communities, Children and Families Australia, 3*(1), 69–79.

Mendes, P., Johnson, G., & Moslehuddin, B. (2011). *Young people leaving state out-of-home care*. Melbourne: Australian Scholarly Publishing.

Mendes, P., Johnson, G., & Moslehuddin, B. (2012). Young people transitioning from out-of-home care and relationships with family of origin: An examination of three recent Australian studies. *Child Care in Practice, 18*(4), 357–370.

Ministry of Social Development. (n.d.). *Youth payments and services.* http://www.msd.govt.nz/about-msd-and-our-work/newsroom/factsheets/budget/2012/youth-payments-and-services.html

Ministry of Social Development. (2014). *Insights. Outcomes for children in care: Initial data-match between CYF, the Ministry of Eduction and the Ministry of Health.* Unpublished report cited in Modernising Child Youth and Family Expert Panel. (2015) *Interim Report.* Wellington: Ministry of Social Development.

Modernising Child Youth and Family Expert Panel. (2015). *Interim report.* Wellington: Ministry of Social Development.

Mullan, C. S., McAlister, S., Rollock, F., & Fitzsimmons, L. (2007). "Care just changes your life": Factors impacting upon the mental health of children and young people with experiences in care in Northern Ireland. *Child Care in Practice, 13*(4), 417–434.

Munford, R., Sanders, J., Liebenberg, L., Ungar, M., Thisasarn-Anwar, T., Youthline, N. Z., et al. (2013). *Conceptual development of the pathways to resilience study. Technical report 1.* Palmerston North: Massey University Youth Transitions Research Programme.

Munro, E., Pinkerton, J., Mendes, P., Hyde-Dryden, G., Herczog, M., & Benbenishty, R. (2011). The contribution of the United Nations Rights of the child to understanding and promoting the interests of young people making the transition from care to adulthood. *Children and Youth Services Review, 33*, 2417–2423.

Nybell, L. M. (2013). Locating "youth voice:" Considering the contexts of speaking in foster care. *Children and Youth Services Review, 35*, 1227–1235.

Office of the Children's Commissioner. (2015). *State of care 2015.* Wellington: Office of the Children's Commissioner.

Pecora, P. J. (2012). Maximizing educational achievement of youth in foster care and alumni: Factors associated with success. *Child and Youth Services Review, 34*, 1121–1129.

Pinkerton, J. (2011). Constructing a global understanding of the social ecology of leaving out of home care. *Children and Youth Services Review, 33*, 2412–2416.

Samuels, G. M., & Pryce, J. M. (2008). "What doesn't kill you makes you stronger": Survivalist self-reliance as resilience and risk among young adults aging out of foster care. *Children and Youth Services Review, 30*, 1198–1210.

Sibley, D. (1995). *Geographies of exclusion.* New York: Routledge.

Stein, M. (2006). Young people aging out of care: The poverty of theory. *Children and Youth Services Review, 28*, 422–434.

Stein, M. (2008). Resilience and young people leaving care. *Child Care in Practice, 14*(1), 35–44.

Stein, M., & Dumaret, A.-C. (2011). The mental health of young people aging out of care and entering adulthood: Exploring the evidence from England and France. *Children and Youth Services Review, 33*, 2504–2511.

Stevens, K., Munford, R., Sanders, J., Dewhurst, K., Henaghan, M., Mirfin-Veitch, B., et al. (2013). *Services supporting youth transitions to adulthood: A review of policy and services in New Zealand.* Palmerston North: Massey University Youth Transitions Research Programme.

Stevens, K., Sanders, J., & Munford, R. (2014). *Review and analysis of case file summaries: Report on social service practice. Technical report 17.* Palmerston North: Massey University Youth Transitions Research Programme.

Stott, T. (2013). Transitioning youth: Policies and outcomes. *Children and Youth Services Review, 35*, 218–227.

Urry, Y., Sanders, J., Munford, R., & Dewhurst, K. (2014). *Turning points in the lives of vulnerable young people. Technical report 18.* Palmerston North: Massey University Youth Transitions Research Programme.

US Department of Health and Human Services. (2011). *Addressing racial disproportionality in child welfare.* Washington, DC: Child Welfare Information Gateway.

Ward, T. (2000). Happy birthday … goodbye! *Social Work Now, 17*, 21–27.

Ward, T. (2001). The tyranny of independent living. *Social Work Now, 18*, 19–27.

Ward, H. (2011). Continuities and discontinuities: Issues concerning the establishment of a persistent sense of self amongst care leavers. *Children and Youth Services Review, 33*, 2512–2518.

Yates, D. (2000). *Sink or swim: Leaving care in New Zealand.* A thesis submitted for the degree of Master of Arts in Social Policy. Massey University, Albany.

16

Youth Leaving Care in Developing Countries: Observations from Vietnam

Mary Elizabeth Collins and Bùi Thị Thanh Tuyền

Current knowledge of policy and practice regarding the transition from care is largely based on Western, primarily American and European, models. Yet, the problems related to leaving care and the needs of young people in this transition are global phenomena. Increasingly, scholarly attention recognizes leaving care as a transition occurring throughout the world. This chapter examines the appropriate adaptation of knowledge regarding ageing-out policy and intervention for non-Western developing contexts. Particular attention is focused on the Socialist Republic of Vietnam. Characteristics of Vietnam, including its location (Southeast Asia), political system (communist), and economy (developing, industrializing), offer a unique example to reflect on an international understanding of leaving care approaches. Vietnam has a complex history of colonization, conflict, and division, but, in

---

M.E. Collins (✉)
Boston University School of Social Work, Boston, MA, USA

B.T.T. Tuyền
School of Social Work, University of Illinois, Urbana, IL, USA

© The Author(s) 2016
P. Mendes, P. Snow (eds.), *Young People Transitioning from Out-of-Home Care*, DOI 10.1057/978-1-137-55639-4_16

recent years, has made substantial progress in raising standards of living and measures of well-being. In 2014, Vietnam's population was over 90 million; those of working age (15–64 years old) accounted for nearly 70 % of the population, and approximately 95 % (over age 15) are considered literate (General Statistics Office 2015). Recent data from the World Bank (2015) indicate that life expectancy was 76 years in 2013, and GNI per capita was US$1,890 in 2014. Child poverty and other problems related to child well-being remain a concern (UNICEF 2015), and will be discussed in terms of social context and the child protection system.

The Problem of Youth Leaving Care

Children and youth may live apart from their families for a variety of reasons. In the West, this may include parental abuse or neglect, youthful offending, or parents experiencing severe emotional or mental health problems. Young people may spend several years apart from their families in institutional settings or foster care because of these conditions. The 'problem' of leaving care occurs when the youth 'age out' as they attain the age of majority. At that point, services they received while in care may no longer be available. Historically, they have left care with little preparation and few resources, resulting in very poor outcomes in areas of education, employment, housing, and health (Collins 2015; Smith 2011). This understanding of the 'ageing out' problem is mostly documented and studied in Western industrialized countries that generally have a shared history of modern economic development, formal systems of child protection, and professional social work. Over decades, these countries have developed care systems that include out-of-home care for children who cannot live with their families. But how might this problem be understood in other countries that do not share this same history of an advanced industrial economy, a social work profession, and formal child care systems? To develop a global understanding of leaving care, inquiry must be extended to the many countries and cultures of the developing world (Pinkerton 2011).

Expanding an International Focus

With very few exceptions, the research on this topic and subsequent thinking regarding policy and practice have occurred in the USA, the UK, Australia, Western Europe, and Israel (Stein and Munro 2008; Stein et al. 2011). Despite this dominance, Pinkerton (2011) noted that wherever there are youth in out-of-home care, there will be young people who are experiencing the transition from care to young adulthood; yet, he found '…no readily available material on leaving care in Africa, China, India and South America' (p. 2412).

Outside of the countries and regions identified above, there have been some reports from Eastern Europe, specifically Romania (Anghel 2011), and Jordan (Ibrahim and Howe 2011). There are now a few studies coming from the African continent, including South Africa (Tanur 2012), Ghana (Frimpong-Manso 2012), and Ethiopia (Pryce et al. 2015). For example, Pryce et al. examined the experience of 54 young adults who aged out of institutional care in Ethiopia. These young adults reported numerous challenges related particularly to employment, basic life skills, and finding a support network. They also reported substantial feelings of stigma related to their history in care. There was some indication that the young adults remained connected to peers from the institutional setting; this was one source of social support after they left care. Studies such as these have begun to expand our understanding of the ageing-out experience in different parts of the globe; however, much more research is needed. At the time of our writing, we have not identified any studies from either Asian countries or current communist political systems. Our contribution is the first to consider some of the implications of leaving care for this region. We describe the policies and systems in place, and reflect on components of leaving care practice that we have observed.

International Guidelines

International guidelines can be particularly helpful to the many countries of the world that are in the process of building formal systems of care. The United Nations Committee on the Rights of the Child produced

Guidelines for the Alternative Care of Children (General Assembly of the United Nations 2009), which include expectations in regard to care leavers (Munro et al. 2011). The section of the guidelines relevant to transition from care is titled 'Support for aftercare'. Section 131 includes having a clear policy, procedures related to concluding the work with appropriate aftercare and follow-up and preparation while in care for later self-reliance and community integration, particularly through gaining life skills. Additional attention is paid to consideration of the child's 'gender, age, maturity and particular circumstances (p. 19)'; children with special needs are identified to require attention related to appropriate support and avoidance of institutionalization (Section 132). Other sections articulate key resources such as 'a specialized person' to facilitate independence after care (Section 133), educational and vocational opportunities (Section 135), and access to social, legal and health services, as well as financial support (Section 136). Guidelines also identify the importance of beginning preparation as early as possible (Section 134).

Despite these guidelines, '…the provision of leaving-care services is highly diverse, reflecting both varied political and cultural traditions and welfare regimes, and vast differences in the number of care leavers. But having the Guidelines as a statement of a global agenda in the field of leaving care usefully draws attention to the important role of global institutions in trying to manage and capitalize on the influence of global processes' (Mendes et al. 2014, p. 2). Moreover, it is well recognized that standards alone are insufficient to ensure appropriate legislation is enacted and implemented. Axford (2012) notes that countries with strong human rights records are as likely as countries with poor records to ratify treaties, but this does not necessarily translate into effective legislative action.

Social Ecology and Context

Pinkerton (2011) suggested that 'only through attention to the social ecology of care leaving, including its global dimension, can the needs of this group of young people be understood and appropriate services be developed... the questions that global exchange needs to illuminate concern the mechanisms of that social ecology' (p. 2412). Utilizing a social ecology approach fosters thinking about leaving care as an ongoing process of coping and adaptation with changing circumstances. Resilience and social capital are understood to be two key constructs. Pinkerton also suggests that a systemic perspective fosters 'vertical thinking' in regard to the '...nested nature of the social ecology of care leaving at the national and international levels' (p. 2414). Thus, leaving care policy and practice needs to be considered within the broader context of child welfare, which itself lies within a larger social welfare and political context (Collins and Pinkerton 2008). Overarching policy frameworks, service delivery systems, and organizational practices vary substantially internationally and require attention regarding the opportunities and barriers they provide care leavers. More developed and generous social welfare systems as well as child welfare systems that provide sufficient supportive services to families are likely to limit the number of youths leaving care and improve the prospects of those who do (Collins and Pinkerton 2008). Furthermore, Mendes et al. (2014) have also identified that attention to the political dimension of leaving care has been 'a notable absence'. A political dimension is linked to ideas of 'social investment'. Heretofore, dominant perspectives have focused on the development of 'human capital' through education and training to ensure worker productivity. Mendes et al. suggest an alternative to a politics of social investment is the politics of social justice and social inclusion. Care leavers are largely socially excluded, and some subgroups (e.g. those from minority ethnic communities; young people from rural and regional localities; young people with disabilities) face particular forms of exclusion. With a shift to social inclusion,

> ...leaving care ceases to be solely a technical program for social administration and becomes the political cause of championing the right of these young people to be included within every aspect of what it means to be a full citizen: access to the labour market, an income, housing, health education, transport, patterns of consumption, leisure and cultural activities, personal relationships, and participation in political and civic affairs. (Mendes 2014, p. 4)

The Vietnam Context

Since 1986, Vietnam has moved from a centrally planned economy to one with some characteristics of a market economy. Over the past two decades, economic growth has improved the well-being of many (The World Bank 2014). Vietnam has reached lower middle-income status (in 2010), and has achieved nearly all of the United Nations' Millennium Development Goals at the national level by the deadline year of 2015 (UNICEF 2010, 2015). However, poverty reduction among ethnic minorities has been slower than among the Kinh majority. In 2012, ethnic groups with the highest poverty rates were H're (63 %), Co Tu (62 %), and Mong (61 %). The Kh'mer and Kinh had the lowest poverty rates, 27 % and 30 %, respectively (Sub-PRPP Project, CEMA 2013).

Family plays an extremely important role in Vietnamese society; it is mentioned frequently in many documents that 'family is a basic unit of society' (Research Center for Gender – Family and Community Development 2015). Historically, traditional family values were attached to an agricultural economy and highlighted the male role and community relationships (Vietnam Culture 2015). Husbands and oldest sons were the heads of the family and were responsible for making important decisions. Wives were expected to manage domestic work and education of children (Centers for Disease Control and Prevention 2008; Vietnam Culture 2015). Partly influenced by Confucianism, extended multi-generational families were the norm, and grandparents helped with caring for, and educating, children (Centers for Disease Control and Prevention 2008; Vietnam Culture 2015). In addition, children and young adults are expected to obey parents and grandparents and to show their respect to the elderly (Vietnam Culture 2015).

The new economic reforms have also influenced the social culture of Vietnam. Many farmers lost land and became the working poor in cities (Social Watch 2015). Women have participated more in the workforce and have become financially independent, but male decision-making roles are still maintained. More nuclear and small-size families appear in urban areas; thus; children are less likely to be living with grandparents (Society and Culture Association 2015). Divorce is increasing;

more women expect equal rights when they share family financial contributions, but men want to preserve their position of authority in the family (Society and Culture Association 2015). In addition, although Vietnam enacted some laws to protect women (e.g. Law on Marriage and Family in 2000, Law on Gender Equality in 2006, Law on Domestic Violence Prevention and Control in 2007), Vietnamese men still have more advantages than women (Research Center for Gender – Family and Community Development 2015).

Rapid industrialization has led to new social problems. These problems are recognized as major concerns in Vietnamese social policy, and categorized as requiring 'social protection' of some groups (e.g. children, disabled, older people). As Nguyen describes, 'Vietnam is confronted with the whole range of problems connected with modernization, and they are developing faster than expected' (Nguyen 2002, p. 88). These problems include rural and urban poverty, rural–urban migration leading to problems of street children, exploitation of women in prostitution, national and international trafficking of women, substance and drug abuse, HIV/AIDS, and child neglect and abuse (Nguyen 2002). At the same time, social changes are negatively impacting traditional forms of social protection related to strong family and community ties.

International non-governmental organizations (NGOs) have been instrumental in identifying the lack of social workers as a major gap in providing social protection measures for vulnerable children. There has been increasing recognition that Vietnam must develop a social work workforce to achieve progress in child protection (Hugman et al. 2007). Consequently, in the early 1990s, a few university-based educational programmes began to open; the first one opened at Open University (Ho Chi Minh City [HCMC]) in 1992. After that, the College of Labor and Social Affairs offered some short-term training programmes on social work with technical supports from international NGOs. In 2010, the Vietnam government approved the Ministry of Labour, Invalids and Social Affairs (MOLISA) to officially classify social work as a profession, and allocated money to train thousands of social workers and develop a network of services. There are now over 50 Bachelor and Associate Degree programmes and three Masters' programmes in social work in Vietnam.

Child Protection Context

Children in need of protection are a recognized population and the focus of specific legislation as well as governmental and non-governmental efforts. A UNICEF report (2012) based on data from MOLISA identified that 9 per cent of Vietnamese children (2.6 million) were considered in need of special protection. This included: 1.2 million children with disabilities; 1.2 million living in poverty, 150,514 orphans, 283,667 affected by AIDS, 12,500 who were HIV+, 16,000 street children, 23,000 involved in child labour, 15,000 living in institutions, 14,000 in conflict with the law and 8500 misusing drugs. Acknowledged, but uncounted, were child victims of sexual exploitation and trafficking.

Since Vietnam ratified the United Nations Convention on the Rights of the Child (UNCRC) in 1990, there have been several legislative changes to develop child protection measures (UNICEF 2009). The Law on the Protection, Care, and Education for Children (the child protection law), enacted in 1991 and amended in 2004, covers the basic principles, identifies the roles and responsibilities of state agencies and reflects the critical aspects of the UNCRC. In addition to the child protection law, a variety of programmes have been introduced to address the needs of children with special circumstances, namely the National Program for Child Protection (2011–2015), the National Program of Action for Preventing and Tackling the Issues of Street Children, Sexual Abuse of Children and Child Labour for 2004–2010, the Decision No. 65 issued in 2005 by the Prime Minister approving the project on Community Based Care (for displaced orphans, disabled children, children who are victims of toxic chemicals and HIV/AIDS infected/affected children) from 2005 to 2010, the Education Law in 2005, and the Law on Gender Equality in 2006.

The child protection service system in Vietnam is organized to meet the needs of children at three levels: (1) primary level or prevention; (2) secondary level or early intervention; and (3) tertiary level or immediate intervention and protection (General Department for the Protection and Care of Children 2013; UNICEF 2009). At the prevention level, the services focus on raising awareness and building skills and capacity for community and societal protection of children. The early intervention level aims at special needs of the high-risk child population to prevent them from falling into the special circumstances. The protection level concentrates on helping those who were abused, exploited, and neglected. This level also aims to support children living in special circumstances recover and reintegrate into the community. The services include ensuring a safe environment; removing harmful factors; and providing health care, education, vocational training, and job placements for children and their families (General Department for the Protection and Care of Children 2013; UNICEF 2009). Currently, there are no specific governmental policies in place regarding care leaving in Vietnam, but tertiary-level interventions may address some leaving care needs.

In terms of organizational structures, the State plays the main role in organizing, managing, and coordinating the child protection services with the participation of governmental organizations, NGOs and mass organizations. The General Department for the Protection and Care of Children under MOLISA has the responsibility for administering all the programmes. Participating in the child welfare system of Vietnam are the People's Committees at all levels, including local communes, districts and provinces. At the commune level, one child protection officer works with village collaborators to provide direct services to children and families in the commune. Services at the commune level include mobilizing and coordinating resources; supervising law enforcement and programs for child protection; coordinating with relevant agencies to provide direct services for children in need; and investigating child abuse cases. Under the Government's decentralization, the People's Committees at all levels take the responsibility to execute the State's management over the protection, care, and education of children in localities (General Department for the Protection and Care of Children 2013).

The child protection structure consists of three main components: government (described above), non-government, and unofficial sectors (Phan 2013). In the legal framework of the child welfare system, the State affirms the critical roles of local and international NGOs. NGOs technically and financially contribute to the development of the child protection system. One study examining the situation of orphans and vulnerable children compiled a list of 22 organizations working with these children in Hanoi and HCMC. The majority of service providers (59 %) were international NGOs, 18 % were local NGOs, 18 % were government-based, and 5 % were faith-based (Boston University Center for Global Health and Development and Hanoi School of Public Health 2009).

There is also a tradition in Vietnam of an unofficial, informal response to the needs of children and families (extended family, neighbours, community). This includes a strong role for mass organizations that are part of the Communist party (Women's Union, Youth Union, and Fatherland Front) (UNICEF 2012).

Despite the recent legislative developments, according to UNICEF (2015), the problems for children in Vietnam are exacerbated by the absence of a strong and effective child protection system. This includes a lack of a professional social work and protective services system that can respond adequately to vulnerable children. In many areas, social work and protection services are provided by volunteers and untrained workers. There are numerous international NGOs working in Vietnam and some international funding to support programming; however, there is minimal coordination between governmental efforts, NGO activities, faith-based organizations, and volunteer activities. Although the government has promoted community-based care solutions versus institutional care, the number of alternative care models for at-risk and disadvantaged children is limited. There are no specialized agencies or procedures for investigation and assessment of child abuse complaints and a lack of reliable national data. Finally, the child protection system lacks unification and coordination because it employs a project- and issue-based approach, rather than a coordinated prevention and response system (UNICEF 2012).

Assessment of Leaving Care Strategies

To identify the approach to leaving care in Vietnam, we began with an identification of several common strategies used to assist care leavers in the USA. These strategies include (1) transition planning in the months or years leading up to age of adulthood; (2) life skills training (i.e., curriculum and experiential lessons regarding preparation for adulthood); (3) housing support such as stipend payments to help with rent; (4) access to education and employment (5) tuition support for college and access to job training programmes; (6) extension of time in care (i.e. flexibility in time of care leaving); (7) family reunification; and (8) youth development strategies (focus on relationships, social networks, opportunities) (Collins 2014). Our assessment reflects our knowledge of the care system, services, and programming based on practice experience (Bùi), engagement with the practice community during a ten-month fellowship (Collins), review of publically available information, and presentation and discussion of these issues at a Vietnamese social work conference (Collins and Bùi 2012). The focus is primarily HCMC.

Transition Planning

There is some effort at transition planning for those young people living in government centres, shelters, and orphanages. Most government shelters can support children until they are 16 years old; therefore, the shelters aim to prepare children for leaving care during their time in the shelter. Preparing for transition is included in the intervention plan for each child. The primary emphases are on life skills training within the programme and linkage to vocational training. These are discussed further below. This work aims at helping the child live independently when leaving care, and the solution is guiding the child to engage in vocational training and job placement before leaving care.

Life Skills Training

Nearly every centre or shelter has some type of life skills training. There is, however, no standardized curriculum, and therefore, the focus and activities are highly variable. Each setting develops their own approach to meet the youth needs within the specific programme. Common areas of training include the following: (1) self-awareness, (2) decision-making, (3) problem solving, (4) communication, and (5) interpersonal skills. These are considered soft skills in contrast to job skills. Life skills workshops include topics such as healthy living, personal hygiene, anger management, personal financial management, stress management, sex education, first aid, communication, teamwork, critical thinking, and interpersonal skills (YMCA Vietnam 2013). There are no reported evaluations regarding the effectiveness of any life skills training programmes in Vietnam.

Housing Support

Modest post-care housing support is provided by some programmes. All three shelters of the HCMC Child Welfare Association have a small stipend of about $15–$25/month to help the youth pay for the rent up to three months. This amount falls short of typical rent, usually about $40–50/month, but it helps reduce the financial burden when young people first live on their own income. This modest assistance is predicated on the belief that after three months, the youth's salary will be improved as he/she gains more experience in his/her work.

Education/Employment

Most homeless children and children with difficult circumstances have low levels of educational attainment; thus, they have to go to school when they live in the care setting. In some cases, workers may try to find scholarships to help the young people continue their education after leaving state care.

If a child comes into a shelter when they are almost 16, they can stay up to 12 months. The focus for these youth would be on employment, rather than education. Workers help them complete all the schedules for seeking jobs and gaining employment. For instance, Green Bamboo Shelter—a shelter for homeless boys—helps all the boys over 14 years to take part-time or full-time vocational training courses, although they are still in school, so that when they reach 16 they can find a job and continue their education. Vocational training courses typically last from six months to one year. Common areas of vocational training include motorbike repair, hair-cutting, cooking, house-keeping, and bartending.

Flexibility in Leaving Care

The Law on the Protection, Care, and Education of Children in Vietnam declares children to be persons under 16. Consequently, children living in public institutions leave these settings at age 16. Many agencies are flexible in making this decision, however. According to Mr. Nguyen Tri Linh, Manager of District 8 Shelter, the age for leaving care is not definite for all shelters. Each shelter sets up its own goals for leaving care (personal communication, November 21st 2013). If the youth have not fulfilled the goals in the intervention plan, the shelter may extend the time in care until the plan is accomplished. For non-governmental shelters that are not state-funded, the time in care can be extended to age 20 or 21.

Depending on the budget and policy of each agency, the post-leaving care support for the youth varies. Some agencies will stop all the support when the youth leaves the facility; others will provide follow-up until the youth has stable income. Orphanages tend to provide some continuing supports to youth leaving care, while public shelters/centres appear to offer more limited support after leaving care.

Family Reunification

Many young people in shelters and orphanages have family members. Because poverty and migration are leading causes of youth living in shelters and orphanages, family reunification can be a possibility in some cases. If applicable, family reunification is the ultimate goal of all the centres/shelters. During the intake process and while establishing initial contacts with the child, workers will try to collect information about his/her family. They will trace the child's origin and assess the possibility of reunifying the child with the family. Reunification can only occur if it will not be harmful to the youth and the family agrees with the reunification.

Youth Development

In addition to meeting the physical needs of children, shelters also pay attention to their psychosocial needs. Youth development strategies include recreational activities, sports, camping, forums, and networking. Green

Bamboo Shelter organizes the young people to play sports such as soccer, swimming, skating, and hiking every Sunday morning. Moreover, music and painting classes are organized frequently at Green Bamboo Shelter and Little Rose Shelter. Social workers usually bring the children to attend forums organized by other NGOs or foundations so that the children can enhance their social relationships and networking with other children.

Vietnam is a very youth-engaged culture, and YMCA Vietnam provides significant information related to child and youth health and well-being, including opportunities for life skills training and youth leadership development. In the US, European, and Australian contexts, youth development generally includes efforts at youth organizing and engagement for purposes of supporting the youth voice in advocacy and policy change. While a youth development strategy in Vietnam can be helpful in supporting youth to be socially engaged, the different political context does not allow youth voice for purposes of policy change. Communication and organizing for political purposes are constrained by the political system.

Access to Documents

One of the most important supports that shelters and orphanages can provide to youth before they leave care is helping them obtain personal papers such as their birth certificate and ID. Most homeless youth do not have these personal papers. According to the Vice-Chair of Department of Child Protection—HCMC, there are more than 6000 homeless children in HCMC who need personal papers (Voice of Vietnam 2014). Without such papers, individuals have difficulty accessing a wide variety of normative supports such as housing, health care, and education. This can consign individuals to a marginalized existence separate from mainstream society, and results in significant social exclusion.

Summary and Conclusions

Although care of children is recognized as a government priority in Vietnam, several factors limit the effectiveness of the governmental response. Economic resources remain a challenge. Visible improvements in the economy have led to an improved standard of living, but numerous economic challenges face the nation as a whole, and governmental investment in child protection remains limited.

Professional social work as known in the industrialized world is not well recognized in Vietnam. There is no professional and formal system of child welfare to respond to children and families in need. Both of these factors are strong influences on the type of care and transition experiences of young people. Informal kinship-based models of foster care are in place rather than formalized systems of foster care placements. This is consistent with the foster care approach in many developing countries (George et al. 2003). Because there is no formal child welfare system that oversees out-of-home care, there are few formal 'ageing out' programmes. Yet, clearly, young people do move from shelter settings and orphanages into independent adulthood. It is not known how many do so successfully.

In the USA and other industrialized, Western countries, enhanced assistance to youth leaving care recognizes governmental responsibility to support youth transitioning from care. In part, this reflects the fact that it was the government's action that removed the child from their family in the first place. Despite this acknowledgement, most child welfare systems remain under-resourced and are inadequate in their ability to prepare youth for a self-sufficient young adulthood. But, in much of the developing world, the child protection system is highly limited, and may not involve state intervention and child removal unless the circumstances are clearly extreme (e.g. orphans with no family, disabled children abandoned by families). In many of these countries, NGOs and voluntary systems are the primary assistance networks.

The reasons for entry into care are important. Without formal child welfare systems and systems for reporting and investigating child maltreatment, few children in Vietnam are in care due to reports of child abuse or neglect. Rather, poverty and migration are core underlying causes. This may have implications for the possibility of family reunification strategies. If the separation from family was primarily due to economic circumstances (i.e. migration related to work) rather than maltreatment, potentially economic supports or parental vocational opportunities might be used to reunify the family and move youths out of shelters or orphanages.

Shelters for street youth and orphanages constitute the bulk of the care system. Some are government-run, but many are operated by NGOs (some of which are international) or religious communities (in Vietnam, these are often Catholic or Buddhist). Thus, there is wide variation in the in-care and after-care experience. One potential upside of this is a certain amount of flexibility regarding care leaving. At least in some settings, there appears to be no formal time limit for transition and more flexibility in regard to returning to care. Another potential strength of the leaving care experience is that the level of social solidarity that exists is more communal than in the West, and young people from traditional cultures may fare relatively well in the transition process.

Our observations suggest that although little formal programming in regard to ageing-out exists, certain characteristics of ageing-out policies and practices well known in the literature do exist in some form in Vietnam (and likely in other developing countries as well). Life skills training, for example, was identified as a key strategy in the preparation of young people for adulthood. Vocational training was also identified as a core intervention for preparation for adulthood. The specifics of these interventions undoubtedly vary across countries, depending on local cultural (life skills) and economic (vocational skills) context, but the broad categories for preparing youth for adult life appear to have some universal relevance. Research evidence regarding effectiveness remains lacking, however.

Industrialization has clear impacts on societies that can lead to improvements in the health and well-being of populations (e.g. raising standards of living and life expectancy), but can also contribute to new social problems that tax existing systems of helping that are situated within family and community networks. Like the Vietnam example, this can lead to the recognition for new policies, practices, and programmes to address social problems. The rise of social work is part of the response. It is likely that there will be an increasingly formalized response to child protection in the years to come. There is already evidence that this is occurring in Vietnam.

There may be some strengths to informal systems of care. As noted, shelters and orphanages may have more flexibility in the transition from care, allowing gradual transitions and returns to care for some forms of assistance. Consequently, a specific demarcation point at which youth are cut off from assistance may not exist. Empirical research is needed to document the impacts of both formal and less formal methods of addressing the experience of transition from care. Informal responses supported by evidence of effectiveness might be preserved as more formal systems of care are developed.

The observations reported in this chapter should be viewed as tentative and require far more research in Vietnam and other developing countries. However, it must be noted that research can be more difficult to carry out in developing countries, compared to first-world nations. The necessary infrastructure is rarely available to carry out the type of sophisticated data collection and analysis, which are possible in first-world nations. Additionally, some types of political systems may be less open to allowing inquiry, particularly when policy and practice flaws may be exposed. These are only a few of the challenges to developing a global understanding of youth leaving care. In the interim, more modest reports from a greater number of countries will be useful to further identify the range of contextually appropriate strengths and challenges.

References

Anghel, R. (2011). Transition within transition: How young people learn to leave behind institutional care whilst their carers are stuck in neutral. *Children and Youth Services Review, 33*, 2526–2531.

Axford, N. (2012). Children and global social policy: Exploring the impact of international governmental organisations. *International Journal of Social Welfare, 21*, 53–65.

Boston University Center for Global Health and Development & Hanoi School of Public Health. (2009). *Vietnam research situation analysis on orphans and other vulnerable children: Country brief*. Boston: Boston University.

Centers for Diseases Control and Prevention. (2008). *Promoting cultural sensitivity: A practical guide for tuberculosis programs that provide services to persons from Vietnam*. Atlanta: U.S. Department of Health and Human Services.

Collins, M. E. (2014). Promoting youth development and transitional living services for youth moving from foster care to adulthood. In G. Mallon & P. Hess (Eds.), *Child welfare for the 21st century: A handbook of children, youth, and family services: Practices, policies, and programs* (2 ed., pp. 467–479). New York: Columbia University Press.

Collins, M. E. (2015). *Macro perspectives on youths aging out of foster care.* Washington, DC: NASW Press.

Collins, M.E., & Bùi Thị Thanh T. (2012). A global perspective on assisting youth leaving care: Implications for Vietnam. International conference on social work and social policy. Asian Pacific Islanders Social Work Educator's Association. Hanoi, Vietnam.

Collins, M. E., & Pinkerton, J. (2008). The policy context of leaving care services: A case study of Northern Ireland. *Children and Youth Services Review, 30*, 1279–1288.

Frimpong-Manso, K. (2012). Preparation for young people leaving care: The case of SOS Children's Village, Ghana. *Child Care in Practice, 18*(4), 341–356.

General Assembly of the United Nations. (2009). Guidelines for the alternative care of children. Resolution A/RES/64/142. Available online at: http:///www.un.org/ga/search/view_asp?symbol-A/RES/64/142. Accessed 19 Oct 2015.

General Department for the Protection and Care of Children, Ministry of Labors, Invalids, and Affairs. (2013). *Guidelines for child protection system: Using for the Steering Committee on child welfare at all levels.* Hanoi: MOLISA.

General Statistics Office (GSO). (2015). Vietnam population exceeded 90 million people in 2014. Available online at: http://www.gso.gov.vn/default_en.aspx?tabid=768&ItemID=15149. Accessed 5 Nov 2015.

George, S., Van Oudenhoven, N., & Wazir, R. (2003). Foster care beyond the crossroads: Lessons from an international comparative analysis. *Childhood, 10*(3), 343–361.

Hugman, R., Nguyen, T. T. L., & Nguyen, T. H. (2007). Developing social work in Vietnam. *International Social Work, 50*, 197–211.

Ibrahim, R. W., & Howe, D. (2011). The experience of Jordanian care leavers making the transition from residential care to adulthood: The influence of a patriarchal and collectivist culture. *Children and Youth Services Review, 33*, 2469–2474.

Law on the Protection, Care, and Education for Children. (2004). *Socialist Republic of Vietnam Government Portal.* Retrieved from www.chinhphu.vn

Mendes, P., Pinkerton, J., & Munro, E. (2014). Young people transitioning from out-of-home care: An issue of social justice. *Australian Social Work, 67*, 1–4.

Munro, E., Pinkerton, J., Mendes, P., Hyde-Dryden, G., Herczog, M., & Benbenishty, R. (2011). The contribution of the United Nations Convention on the Rights of the Child to understanding and promoting the interests of young people making the transition from care to adulthood. *Children and Youth Services Review, 33*(12), 2417–2423.

Nguyen, T. O. (2002). Historical development and characteristics of social work in today's Vietnam. *International Journal of Social Welfare, 11*(1), 84–91.

Nguyen, T. L. (2013). Manager of District 8th Shelter, personal communication, 21 November 2013.

Phan, T. M. (2013). *Child protection system and child protection services.* Proceedings of the Seminar on Child Protection System in the Family in Ho Chi Minh City. Ho Chi Minh City: Department of Culture, Sport, and Tourism.

Pinkerton, J. (2011). Constructing a global understanding of the social ecology of leaving out of home care. *Children and Youth Services Review, 33,* 2412–2416.

Pryce, J. M., Jones, S. L., Wildman, A., Thomas, A., Okrzesik, K., & Kaufka-Walts, K. (2015). Aging out of care in Ethiopia: Challenges and implications facing orphans and vulnerable youth. *Emerging Adulthood.* doi:10.1177/2167696815599095.

Research Center for Gender – Family and Community Development. (2015). Building Vietnamese family culture. Available online at: http://gfcd.org.vn/chi-tiet-tin/ve-xay-dung-gia-dinh-van-hoa-viet-nam.html. Accessed 7 Nov 2015.

Smith, W. (2011). *Youth leaving foster care: A developmental, relationship-based approach to practice.* New York: Oxford University Press.

Social Watch. (2015). The Doi Moi policy and its impacts on the poor. Available online at: http://www.socialwatch.org/node/10854. Accessed 7 Nov 2015.

Society and Culture Association. (2015). 'New spirits fear old ones': Change in the Vietnamese family. Available online at: http://scansw.com.au/pages/core/vietnam2.html. Accessed 7 Nov 2015.

Stein, M., & Munro, E. R. (Eds.) (2008). *Transitions from care to adulthood: International research and practice.* London: Jessica Kingsley Publishers.

Stein, M., Ward, H., & Courtney, M. (2011). Editorial: International perspectives on young people's transitions from care to adulthood. *Children and Youth Services Review, 33*(12), 2409–2411.

Sub-PRPP Project – CEMA. (2013). Poverty situation analysis of ethnic minorities in Vietnam 2007–2012: Key findings from quantitative study. Hanoi: United Nations Development Project. Available online at:http://www.vn.undp.org/content/dam/vietnam/docs/Publications/Summary%20KQdinhluongforCG2013_ENG%20and%20VIET.pdf. Accessed 25 Nov 2015.

Tanur, C. (2012). Project Lungisela: Supporting young people leaving state care in South Africa. *Child Care in Practice, 18*(4), 325–340.
UNICEF. (2009). *Creating a protective environment for children in Vietnam: An assessment of child protection laws and policies, especially children in special circumstances in Vietnam.* New York: UNICEF.
UNICEF. (2010). *An analysis of the situation of children in Viet Nam.* New York: UNICEF.
UNICEF. (2012). *Believe in zero: Protecting the vulnerable children of Vietnam.* New York: UNICEF.
UNICEF. (2015). Viet Nam overview. Available online at: http://www.unicef.org/vietnam/overview_20385.html. Accessed 30 July 2015.
Vietnam Culture. (2015). Vietnam traditional family values. Available online at: http://www.vietnam-culture.com/articles-53-6/Vietnamese-traditional-family-values.aspx. Accessed 5 Nov 2015.
Voice of Vietnam (VOV). (2014, March 17). Thousands homeless youth in Ho Chi Minh City needs personal papers.
The World Bank. (2014). Poverty reduction in Vietnam: Remarkable progress, emerging challenges. Available online at: http://www.worldbank.org/en/news/feature/2013/01/24/poverty-reduction-in-vietnam-remarkable-progress-emerging-challenges. Accessed 5 Nov 2015.
The World Bank. (2015). Vietnam. Available online at: http://data.worldbank.org/country/vietnam. Accessed 6 Nov 2015.
YMCA Vietnam. (2013). *Center for life skills and living values training.* Retrieved from www.hoptactre.com

17

Young People Transitioning from Residential Care in South Africa: Welfare Contexts, Resilience, Research and Practice

Adrian D van Breda and Lisa Dickens

South Africa has one of the most vulnerable youth populations in the world. It has the fourth highest rate of youth unemployment among 175 countries: 53.6 per cent among 15–24-year-olds in 2013 (World Data Bank 2015). This is compared with the global youth unemployment rate of 12.6 per cent, and rates of 11.5 per cent in Australia, 21.6 per cent in the UK, 16.3 per cent in the USA and 13.7 per cent in Brazil (International Labour Organization 2013). Similarly, the rate of 15–24-year-olds not in employment, education, or training (NEET) was 32.2 per cent in 2014 (StatsSA 2014a), compared with 11.8 per cent in Australia, 15.9 per cent in the UK, 16.1 per cent in the USA, and 19.6 per cent in Brazil (ILO 2013).

A.D. van Breda (✉)
Department of Social Work, University of Johannesburg, PO Box 524, Auckland Park, 2006 South Africa

L. Dickens
Girls & Boys Town South Africa & University of Johannesburg, Cape Town, South Africa

© The Author(s) 2016
P. Mendes, P. Snow (eds.), *Young People Transitioning from Out-of-Home Care*, DOI 10.1057/978-1-137-55639-4_17

Within the universally vulnerable population of young people in South Africa, those leaving residential care are especially at risk, resulting from various factors. The South African developmental social welfare approach, which emphasizes community-based rather than residential care, has tended to overlook the needs of young people in residential care (Meintjes et al. 2007). There is, in the South African legislation and policy, almost nothing specific to the provision of transitional support to those leaving alternative care. In addition, there had been only five published research reports on young people leaving residential care prior to our own research (Bond 2010; Mamelani 2013; Meyer 2008; Miller 2004; Muller et al. 2003). Collectively, these factors mean that those leaving care remain largely unseen by academics, researchers, policy makers and service providers, resulting in them being highly vulnerable within an already vulnerable context.

There are, nevertheless, many similarities between South Africa and the international community regarding the vulnerability of care-leavers in comparison with their peers living at home (Mendes et al. 2011). In most countries, youth are brought into residential care as a last resort, when all other options have been exhausted, including foster care. Youth are usually removed and placed in care as a result of challenging circumstances at home, often involving abuse and neglect. Occasionally, poor in-care experiences compound the vulnerability of care-leavers, as do experiences of being forced into adult-like roles before they are ready and the lack of ongoing support once they leave care (Mendes et al. 2011). It is unsurprising then that care-leavers across most countries have been shown to have consistently poorer outcomes than the general youth population, including higher levels of unemployment, lower levels of educational attainment and post-school qualifications, early parenthood, homelessness, engagement in criminal behaviour, proneness to substance abuse, and susceptibility to poorer physical and mental health (Cashmore and Paxman 2006; Courtney and Heuring 2005; Stein and Munro 2008; Van Breda 2015b).

Few studies on care-leavers have been conducted in African countries, but a small number are emerging from Ethiopia (Bailey et al. 2011; Pryce et al. 2016), Ghana (Frimpong-Manso 2012a, b, 2015), Kenya (Magoni et al. 2009; Roeber 2011), and Zimbabwe (Dziro and Rufurwokuda 2013).

The African situation regarding children in care and young people leaving care, in contrast with the situation in most developed countries (Stein and Munro 2008), appears to be characterized by a lack of legislation and policy, under-resourcing and an uneven suite of services. Notwithstanding this, the outcome challenges of African care-leavers bear striking similarities to those found in the developed world: inadequate preparation for independent living, poor access to education, unemployment, social exclusion, lack of social capital and cultural dislocation. A need for resilience also emerges in African studies, as young people have to rely on their own capacity, rather than on social welfare services, to create opportunities for themselves.

This chapter maps out the context within which South African youth transition from care. A review of the state of South African youth provides the social context within which to consider those leaving care. An overview is provided of the welfare context, which shows the move away from residential care as the preferred model of alternative care. South African research on care-leaving is described, with particular attention to the authors' own longitudinal study of resilience among care-leavers. Case studies of transitional support programmes serve to illustrate emerging practices. The chapter concludes with avenues for ongoing research, social activism, collaboration and policy development.

South African Youth

In 2014, the population of South Africa was estimated to be 54 million (StatsSA 2014b), comprising 80.2 per cent African, 8.8 per cent coloured (or mixed-race), 8.4 per cent white, and 2.5 per cent Indian or Asian people. South Africa has a high proportion of young people—those under 35 years constitute 66 per cent of the total population, including 19 per cent who are aged 15–24 years.

South Africa has a high prevalence of poverty and inequality. The Gini Coefficient (World Bank 2015), which measures economic inequality, shows South Africa has one of the highest levels of inequality in the world: 63.4 per cent in 2011, compared with 33.7 per cent in the UK, 41.1 per cent in the USA and 53.1 per cent in Brazil. StatsSA (2014c) reports that in South Africa in 2011, over half (55.7 per cent) of children were living below the poverty line, while 50.7 per cent of young people aged 18 to 24 were living in poverty. Many of these youth are supported through social grants, regarded as one of the country's most effective poverty alleviation strategies (Patel et al. 2008). The most widely accessed grant is the Child Support Grant (CSG), which is a cash transfer of R330 (approximately USD26) per month for children under 18 years if their caregivers meet the requirements of a means test. By March 2014, 11 million children were recipients of the CSG (Coetzee 2014).

While there is increasing State support for the care of young people, 20 years after the end of apartheid, South African youth continue to face many complex social problems. High unemployment rates, poor quality education, high HIV infection rates, race and gender issues, and child-headed households are some of the key challenges that affect social cohesion and stability.

The extraordinarily high rate of youth unemployment for 15–24-year-old South Africans, compared to youth elsewhere in the world, was noted in the opening paragraph. In addition, 60 per cent of currently unemployed youth below the age of 35 have never worked before (RSA 2015). Skills shortages, poor educational policies, a lack of experience, a lack of job supply and slow job creation are some of the reasons why the unemployment rate is so high (Van Breda and Dickens 2015).

Another major challenge is educational persistence and the quality of education in South Africa, resulting from the apartheid regime's institutionalized inequality (Van Breda and Dickens 2015). Only 40.7 per cent of the population aged 20 years and older have completed secondary schooling (StatsSA 2012). High unemployment rates and poor quality and inequitable education have resulted in extremely high NEET rates, which, in turn, increase young South Africans' engagement in risk-taking behaviours, including substance abuse, crime, violence and unsafe sexual practices (Graham 2012). Such is the time of youth in transition in South Africa that Crause and Booyens (2010) describe this as a period of 'waithood'—a period of waiting for education, for employment, for adulthood.

One of the biggest challenges South Africa faces is HIV. There are approximately 6.19 million people living with HIV, with a prevalence of 11.2 per cent of the total population (StatsSA 2015) and 8.7 per cent among 15–24-year-olds (StatsSA 2014b). The markedly high rate of AIDS-related deaths contributes significantly to orphanhood and child-headed households. Hall et al. (2014) report that in 2012, there were 3.54 million orphans in South Africa, equating to 19 per cent of all children. There are also an estimated 87,000 child-headed households in the country (Hall et al. 2014). It is unsurprising then that in 2009/2010, the Children's Court found a total of 88,600 children to be in need of alternative care and protection (South African Human Rights Commission/ UNICEF 2011).

South African Welfare Context

South Africa's welfare system has transitioned considerably, from an apartheid welfare system to a developmental state. Since the apartheid government came into power in 1948, South Africa's welfare policy was built on racial differentiation. As Patel et al. (2008) describe, this meant that welfare services were fragmented and largely inaccessible to people who were not white. Generally, the policies were consistent with a remedial social welfare approach, focusing on individual pathology, identifying social problems, making a diagnosis, and then treating clients for their problems. Statutory services and institutionalized care were the main types of interventions. Welfare services did not consider the circumstances of the indigenous people they were serving, resulting in inappropriate care (Patel 2015). This care system was costly and did not encourage personal growth or community-based empowerment, both vital to addressing the country's many social challenges. The apartheid regime's discriminatory policies and laws socially excluded the majority of the population, resulting in unmet needs, gross inequality and fragmented services, severely hampering the development of most citizens.

In 1994, the newly elected democratic government adopted a developmental approach to social welfare, as set out in the White Paper for Social Welfare (RSA 1997). This was seen as more appropriate to meet the needs of the people and address the deep-rooted challenges the country faced. The social development approach is defined by Midgley (2014, p. 13) as

'…a process of planned social change designed to promote the well-being of the population as a whole in conjunction with a dynamic multifaceted development process', with particular emphasis on the harmonization of social and economic growth. This construction of social development was augmented with uniquely South African themes, including a human rights approach and a commitment to democracy and participation.

While the social development approach has been effective in transforming South Africa's welfare policy (Patel 2015), it is not without criticism. Gray (2006) notes that its implementation has been slow, resulting in a massive backlog of unmet service needs. Greater capacity is still required in communities. Family and kinship care need to be further strengthened and supported, so that children can be properly nurtured and cared for in their homes. Capacity has to be increased, and more financial support is required in communities, where much of the care is provided by women. Poverty remains a major threat to the lives of many South Africans, including children.

South Africa's developmental approach advocates decentralizing care; therefore, care for youth was taken out of centralized institutions located in urban areas and brought back into the communities. As Patel and Selipsky (2009) explain, this improves the response time to problems and facilitates preventative and early intervention. It also complements informal African welfare practices already in place, including kinship care and communal living, with a focus on religion. There is far less reliance on government and institutions and greater focus on community-based support and community empowerment. The Isibindi project (Visser et al. 2015) is a good example of a community-based project for orphans and vulnerable children that recruits community members as child and youth care workers to provide a range of psychosocial, educational and economic support to vulnerable children within safe spaces in local communities.

The Children's Act No. 38 of 2005 provides principles to protect the rights of children and youth and ensures services are delivered in a manner that supports children and their families. Three types of alternative or out-of-home care are identified: foster care, child and youth care centres (CYCCs) and temporary 'safe' shelters. Two chapters of the Act deal with children's rights and responsibilities when placed in alternative care and regulate CYCCs, and another chapter provides standards for CYCCs (Mahery et al. 2011).

Despite the ideals of the White Paper (RSA 1997) and the Children's Act (RSA 2005) to keep children in their families or community, many young South Africans land in residential care. There are an estimated 354 registered CYCCs in the country, providing homes to a reported 13,250 youth (Mamelani 2013). Once in care, family reunification is the primary goal for permanent placement (Sauls 2015); however, it occurs in fewer than 50 per cent of cases. The reality is that many young people remain in care for longer than the recommended two years, often until they are 18 years old.

South Africa, in comparison with the UK, the USA and Australia, has a paucity of legislation and policy to facilitate successful care-leaving (Bond 2015). The White Paper (RSA 1997, 8§49.h) states, 'Appropriate strategies are needed to support young adults over 18 years of age who have been discharged from children's homes'. The Children's Amendment Act (RSA, 2007, 13§191.3) states, 'A child and youth care centre may in addition to its residential programmes, offer a programme to assist a person with the transition when leaving a child and youth care centre after reaching the age of 18.' While the Children's Act Norms and Standards (RSA, 2010, §75.1.a) are firmer about the need for children's homes to provide 'independent living [programmes] for children disengaging from the residential care programme', the legislation makes no tangible provision for transitional care beyond the age of 18. Support for care-leavers is optional and no state organ is mandated to provide it, resulting in increased vulnerability among all young people transitioning out of care.

South African Research on Care-Leaving

Prior to 2003, it appears that care-leaving was not a topic of research in South Africa. This may be a result of a skewed interest in children *in* care, rather than in children *after* care. It also points, perhaps, to a lack of research until fairly recently on the outcomes of social services. It is thus interesting that the increase in research on care-leaving has emerged within a welfare context that is moving away from residential care. In total, only five completed South African studies on care-leaving are available, outside of our own research. A summary of each of these is provided.

Muller et al. (2003) conducted a qualitative study of three young people who had previously been in the care of SOS Children's Village. Their research focused on their experience of 'success'—how they understood the term, how they had experienced success, and what SOS contributed to their success.

In 2004, Miller studied 20 young men who left the care of Girls and Boys Town (GBT) a year previously. Using a cross-sectional, predominantly quantitative design, Miller found that half the youth were working and a further quarter studying, leaving a quarter NEET. Most had returned to their families, three quarters were satisfied with their home life, just under a third had negative feelings about their lives, and a fifth displayed symptoms of depression. Miller concluded that half the youth had transitioned successfully out of care, a quarter had some difficulties and a quarter had not transitioned successfully.

Meyer (2008) conducted a phenomenological investigation with seven youth who had left residential care three or more years previously. Common experiences of the youth included discrimination because of having been in care, a lack of independent living and social skills, the abrupt ending of social support and structure, lack of trust, and feelings of loneliness.

Bond (2010) interviewed ten youth who had left residential care at least five years earlier, in order to understand how interventions in care could assist young people in transitioning successfully towards adult living. She found that few children received transitional support services, though, when they were received, they were appreciated. Most participants cited 'stability' as a key marker for successful post-care adjustment. Self-efficacy, hope or faith, and a range of coping mechanisms were found to assist in the transition.

Finally, Mamelani (2013), an NGO providing transitional support services to young people preparing to leave care (Tanur 2012), conducted a study on the experiences and challenges faced by young people leaving care in the Western Cape, using a survey of children's homes and focus groups with care workers, youth in care and youth who had left care. Youth reported considerable challenges with accessing employment, skills/education and accommodation, as well as ongoing family problems. Most felt unprepared to leave care. Organizations reported difficulties in providing after-care services.

Over the past five years, van Breda has, in partnership with GBT, built up a body of research on care-leaving in South Africa centred on resilience theory. This began with a grounded theory study with nine young men who had left GBT's care several years previously (Van Breda 2015a). This study yielded a model of the resilience processes young people engage in as they leave care: striving for authentic belonging, networking people for goal attainment, contextualized responsiveness, and building hopeful and tenacious self-confidence. Findings foregrounded the agency and resilience of young people carving out a life for themselves, often in depleted and adverse contexts.

GBT is currently in the fourth year of a longitudinal rolling cohort study of young people leaving care. All youth who are about to leave GBT are invited to enrol in the study, at which time they complete a narrative and quantitative assessment of their readiness to leave care, and a range of resilience factors are assessed (Van Breda 2014), together with a questionnaire completed by their social worker. Annually, thereafter, they are interviewed to elicit a narrative of the past year's journey, and a structured interview regarding a range of outcome measures is administered. By mid-2015, a total of 65 youth were actively enrolled in the study, 14 of whom will have their 36-month post-care interview towards the end of 2015.

Results of this ongoing longitudinal study are revealing poor post-care outcomes concerning self-supporting accommodation, educational attainment/engagement, employment status, NEET and financial security, but better outcomes regarding crime, substance use, relationships and well-being (Dickens et al. 2015). The negative outcomes are understood in relation to the high levels of vulnerability of all South African youth and the lack of transitional policy and after-care services. In addition, preliminary analysis shows the contribution of several resilience variables to better transitional outcomes, including a supportive relationship with an adult mentor, family financial security, teamwork and self-esteem. As the database grows, the results should become increasingly refined and robust. This is the first and only longitudinal care-leaving study in South Africa.

Van Breda is also currently conducting a situational analysis of care-leaving services provided by children's homes in Gauteng province. This mixed-methods study is the first investigation of these services and will shed light on gaps in service delivery, as well as promising practices. It is hoped that this study will begin to inform social welfare policy for care-leavers. He is also supervising several postgraduate students studying various aspects of care-leaving and resilience. One of his MA students, Mmusi (2013), conducted research on ten young men who had left the care of GBT two to five years previously to explore how they utilized the social skills they learned at GBT in their adult lives. She found that care-leavers did, in fact, remember and use many (though not all) of these skills, but that the skills often had to be adapted to fit 'real world' contexts.

In addition, six other students are currently busy with Masters and Doctoral research: Dickens is predicting transitional outcomes 12 months after leaving care, using a range of resilience factors; Bond is qualitatively exploring the resilience and possible selves of young people about to leave care and the ways care workers contribute to, or impede, these processes; Hlungwani is qualitatively testing the relevance of van Breda's (2015a) model of care-leaving resilience processes (developed with men) for women; Snyman is replicating part of Dickens' resilience-outcomes research with a sample of young people living at home transitioning out of secondary school in a suburban community; and Mkhonza and Makaula are replicating Snyman's study in township and rural communities.

Collectively, the findings from this body of research are expected to shed greater light on the kinds of resilience processes that enable more successful transitioning out of care, particularly in resource-constrained settings, common in the developing world. This results from the comprehensive utilization of an ecological-resilience theoretical framework, and from an evolution of research methods from exploratory-descriptive towards explanatory, and is expected to make a meaningful contribution to the international body of care-leaving research. However, this research is in its infancy, and there is still a need to address gender issues, disability, rural–urban comparisons, the role of culture, and programme evaluation, among others.

Emerging Practices

Transitional support for care-leavers is not regulated in South Africa. When transitional care is provided, it is typically done by CYCCs themselves. There are, however, a handful of organizations in South Africa that target youth in transition from care, either by providing transitional support services to CYCCs or by offering post-CYCC residential care. Two of those are discussed below.

Mamelani, based in the Western Cape, provides transitional support to youth exiting residential care. A key innovation of Mamelani is its argument that care-leaving is a transition to *interdependent* living, rather than the more familiar independent living (Tanur 2012). 'Interdependence' is a Western term for the African notion of *Ubuntu*, which is that people become human through relationships with other people. By placing this principle central in their programme, Mamelani has made significant strides in developing indigenous care-leaving practices in South Africa, which may be relevant in the developed world also.

Through their Project Lungisela (a Xhosa word meaning 'prepare'), Mamelani works closely with The Homestead, which helps street children build better lives for themselves. The programme focuses on three primary areas: personal and emotional support, work readiness (such as encouraging youth to find suitable employment) and accommodation support. They start their transitional programme with the youth one year before they leave The Homestead and continue to provide them with support once they have left. The programme has shown considerable achievements, highlighting the value of allowing time for the psychosocial process of transition, both before and after leaving care. Tanur (2012, p. 328) reports that fewer than ten per cent of the youth Mamelani works with go back to the streets. Further, since the inception of the programme, more than 50 per cent of youth in the internship programme have gained access to work.

Mamelani's ProSeed Programme was developed from the findings of its previous research (Tanur 2012). The aim of the 18-month programme is to provide youth exiting care with tools to increase their likelihood of better outcomes. They advocate a process-driven approach to care-leaving services, focusing on interdependence. ProSeed involves youth relying not only on themselves, but also on support networks and positive relationships to meet their needs as they journey out of care. It suggests a give-and-take system, where both parties offer value to, and benefit from, the other (Mamelani 2013). The programme is undergoing a three-year pilot evaluation, involving six CYCCs and 16 young people.

ProSeed is based on several components: the need for developmental and therapeutic support, including a focus on identity, relationships and resilience. It is also youth-centred, so the programme is driven by the youths' needs. Youth have access to a qualified mentor, with whom an Individual Development Plan is prepared, and youth are given specific support from one person. They are provided with ongoing support and have access to material support to meet their basic needs. Further, there is a reflective process throughout the project, where each youth's progress is regularly reviewed (Mamelani 2013).

Mentoring has been shown to promote positive outcomes for care-leavers as they receive extended support from positive role models (Stein 2008), especially when challenges exist with family relationships. South African Youth Education for Sustainability (SA-YES) is a mentoring programme for youth leaving care that is shown to have a positive impact on the youth (Pinkerton 2011).

SA-YES runs a Transition to Independent Living (TIL) programme, which is a one-on-one youth mentoring programme. Its aim is to support youth who leave care by providing them with positive mentors who guide them. SA-YES offers a three-phased programme: the first phase includes recruitment and training, matching, teambuilding, monitoring and support; the second phase includes closure and graduation; and the third includes post-programme support. Youth (mentees) are matched with mentors, who are trained volunteers. Both commit to meet once a week for a year to work together on what they deem important (Pinkerton 2011). Youth are provided with access to job opportunities through mentoring, training, and advice. Mentors help to develop skills, provide personal development, focus on education and community reintegration, and set goals with their mentees. Pinkerton (2011) reported that of the 15 mentees in the pilot programme, seven had gone on to attend university or college, and three remained in school. One of them had full time employment. Eight of the youth remained in their CYCCs, and four moved back to their communities. These initial results are positive, especially as education is so highly regarded in promoting positive outcomes for care-leavers.

Mapping the Way Forward

There is a growing recognition of the needs of young people leaving care among South African academics, researchers, practitioners and policy experts. There is, as always, a need for ongoing research. Particular attention should be given to expanding the database of outcome studies, especially comparative studies across residential programmes using the same or similar research tools and methods. There is also a need to compare the outcomes of various forms of alternative care, notably residential and foster care, to test the assumption that family or community-based care is inevitably better than residential care.

Research informs practice, and practice informs research. Our research on the contribution of resilience to positive transitional outcomes, for example, will inform practice, leading to the design of new, creative and indigenous practice models. These resilience-building interventions in turn need to be tested and evaluated. The partnership between academics, researchers and practitioners experienced over the past several years at GBT serves as a good model for the optimal use of the expertise and interest of a variety of role players. Overall, there is a need to move on from exploratory and descriptive research towards developmental and evaluation research, in order to identify and strengthen best practice models.

Greater collaboration and dialogue between organizations providing residential (and other forms of alternative) care will help to further raise the need for child and youth care workers and services to not only think about providing the best quality services to children in care, but also to prepare those children for life after care. Such collaboration will also lead to the identification of promising practices that can be further investigated and evaluated, leading to the organic development of the field of care-leaving and transitional support services.

Further engagement of youth who have left care is required in the design of interventions in preparation for care-leaving and after-care. Such a mobilization of care-leavers could contribute significantly to the development of services, the formulation of relevant policy and the direction of research. In addition, such youth could take up a meaningful role in mentorship programmes, which appears increasingly to be a powerful resilience process to strengthen young people during the transition out of care.

Given the high vulnerability of youth in general in South Africa, transitional support programmes for those leaving care require careful conceptualization, implementation and evaluation. The State has a responsibility to those in care, but also to all vulnerable children and youth. The State's key structural priorities for youth are raising the quality of education to prepare young people for employment and higher education, and the stimulation of the labour market to increase employment opportunities and entrepreneurship for young people. Within the universal provision of social development services to youth, specialized transitional support services need to be provided to those leaving care.

The development of policy relevant to those leaving care is required and needs to be a key focus area for the next few years. Policy for services to young people leaving care could include the provision of social welfare support services after leaving care, social security beyond the age of 18, the opportunity and encouragement to remain in care beyond the age of 18 and/or the completion of secondary education or a trade qualification, referral to skills development and employment agencies, the provision of transitional accommodation, and the psychosocial and economic strengthening of the families of young people in care. Such policies must be fit for purpose within the South African constraints of the massive numbers of vulnerable youth, limited financial resources, a history of problematic service delivery and the geographical inaccessibility of many parts of the country.

Lessons can and should be learned from first-world countries regarding support to young people leaving care, but the vast differences in socioeconomic and cultural contexts make it impossible to impose such lessons uncritically in the South African context. Indigenous models, aligned with the developmental social welfare paradigm, are required. With the recent growth in research and dialogue concerning care-leaving, South Africa, together with other African countries such as Ghana, appears well-positioned to initiate such a process.

References

Bailey, N., Loehrke, C., & French, S. (2011). *The transitions initiative: Youth aging out of alternative care*, from http://www.iofa.org/index.php?option=com_content&view=article&id=135&Itemid=128. Accessed 28 Nov 2015.

Bond, S. (2010). *Adult adjustment and independent functioning in individuals who were raised in a children's home*. Masters dissertation, Nelson Mandela Metropolitan University, RSA.

Bond, S. (2015). *Care-leaving legislation and policy: How does South Africa compare against the international arena?* Paper presented at the Social Work and Social Development conference, East London, RSA.

Cashmore, J., & Paxman, M. (2006). Predicting after-care outcomes: The importance of 'felt' security. *Child and Family Social Work, 11*, 232–241.

Coetzee, M. (2014). *Do poor children really benefit from the child support grant?*. http://www.econ3x3.org/article/do-poor-children-really-benefit-child-support-grant. Accessed 13 Aug 2015.

Courtney, M. E., & Heuring, D. H. (2005). The transition to adulthood for youth 'aging out' of the foster care system. In D. W. Osgood, M. E. Foster, C. Flanagan, & G. R. Ruth (Eds.), *On your own without a net: The transition to adulthood for vulnerable populations* (pp. 27–68). Chicago: University of Chicago Press.

Crause, E. J., & Booyens, M. G. (2010). Demographic tragedy or opportunity? Are micro-issues necessitating a new social contract with the youth in South Africa? *Commonwealth Youth and Development, 8*(2), 2–15.

Dickens, L. F., Van Breda, A. D., & Marx, P. (2015). *Growth beyond the town: A longitudinal study on youth leaving care: 30-month status report*. Cape Town: Girls & Boys Town South Africa and University of Johannesburg.

Dziro, C., & Rufurwokuda, A. (2013). Post-institutional integration challenges faced by children who were raised in children's homes in Zimbabwe: The case of "ex-girl" programme for one children's home in Harare, Zimbabwe. *Greener Journal of Social Sciences, 3*(5), 268–277.

Frimpong-Manso, K. A. (2012a). *Leaving and after-care in Ghana: The experience of young adults leaving a private children's home*. Doctoral thesis, Queen's University, Belfast.

Frimpong-Manso, K. A. (2012b). Preparation for young people leaving care: The case of SOS Children's Village, Ghana. *Child Care in Practice, 18*(4), 341–356.

Frimpong-Manso, K. A. (2015). The social support networks of care leavers from a children's village in Ghana: Formal and informal supports. *Child & Family Social Work*. doi:10.1111/cfs.12218.

Graham, L. (2012). *Understanding risk in the everyday identity-work of youth people on the East Rand*. Doctoral thesis, University of Johannesburg, RSA.

Gray, M. (2006). The progress of social development in South Africa. *International Journal of Social Welfare, 15*(Supplement 1), S53–S64.

Hall, K., Meintjes, K., & Sambu, W. (2014). *Demography of South Africa's children: South African Child Gauge 2014*. Cape Town: Children's Institute, University of Cape Town.

International Labour Organization. (2013). *Global employment trends for youth 2013*. Geneva: International Labour Organization.

Magoni, E., Bambini, A. D., & Ucembe, S. (2009). *Life as a care-leaver in Kenya*. Nairobi: International Network of Associations of Adoptive Parents and Care Leavers.

Mahery, P., Jamieson, L., & Scott, K. (2011). *Children's Act guide for child and youth care workers*. Cape Town: Children's Institute, University of Cape Town, & National Association of Child and Youth Care Workers.

Mamelani. (2013). *Transitional support: The experiences and challenges facing youth transitioning out of state care in the Western Cape*. Cape Town: Mamelani Projects.

Meintjes, H., Moses, S., Berry, L., & Mampane, R. (2007). *Home truths: The phenomenon of residential care for children in a time of AIDS*. Cape Town: Children's Institute, University of Cape Town & Centre for the Study of AIDS, University of Pretoria.

Mendes, P., Johnson, G., & Moslehuddin, B. (2011). *Young people leaving state out-of-home care*. Melbourne: Australian Scholarly Publishing.

Meyer, I. J. (2008). *The experience of a late adolescent state care leavers: A phenomenological study*. Masters dissertation, University of Johannesburg, RSA.

Midgley, J. (2014). *Social development: Theory and practice*. London: Sage.

Miller, B. (2004). *The adjustment of boys from Boys Town South Africa's programmes within the first year after disengagement*. Masters dissertation, University of Witwatersrand, RSA.

Mmusi, F. I. (2013). *Description and assessment of care leavers' application of social skills into independent living*. Masters dissertation, University of Johannesburg, RSA.

Muller, K. S., van Rensburg, M. S. J., & Makobe, M. (2003). The experience of successful transition from a children's home to independent living. *Social Work/Maatskaplike Werk, 39*(3), 199–211.

Patel, L. (2015). *Social welfare and social development* (2nd ed.). Cape Town: Oxford Press.

Patel, L., & Selipsky, L. (2009). Social welfare policy and legislation in South Africa. In L. Nicholas, M. Maistry, & J. Rautenbach (Eds.), *Introduction to social work* (pp. 48–74). Cape Town: Juta.

Patel, L., Hochfeld, T., Graham, L., & Selipsky, L. (2008). *The implementation of the white paper for social welfare in the NGO sector.* Johannesburg: Centre for Social Development in Africa, University of Johannesburg.

Pinkerton, J. (2011). Constructing a global understanding of the social ecology of leaving out of home care. *Children and Youth Services Review, 33*, 2412–2416.

Pryce, J. M., Jones, S. L., Wildman, A., Thomas, A., Okrzesik, K., & Kaufka-Walts, K. (2016). Aging out of care in Ethiopia: Challenges and implications facing orphans and vulnerable youth. *Emerging Adulthood, 4*(2), 119–130.

Roeber, E. (2011). *A fair chance to life: Young care-leavers in Kenya.* Nairobi: Kenya Network of Care Leavers.

RSA. (1997). *White paper for social welfare.* Pretoria: Government Printer.

RSA. (2005). *Children's Act (Act 38 of 2005).* Pretoria: Government Printer.

RSA. (2007). *Children's Amendment Act (Act 41 of 2007),* Pretoria: Government Printer.

RSA. (2010). *General relations regarding the Children's Act, 2005*, Pretoria: Government Printer.

RSA. (2015). *National Youth Policy 2015–2020.* Pretoria: Government Printer.

Sauls, H. (2015). *Proposal for an evaluation of family reunification services: Exploring children, families and social workers' experiences of the family reunification services within the first 12 months of being reunified.* Cape Town: Department of Social Development.

South African Human Rights Commission/UNICEF. (2011). *South Africa's children: A review of equity and child rights.* Pretoria: South African Human Rights Commission/UNICEF.

StatsSA. (2012). *Census 2011.* Pretoria: Statistics South Africa.

StatsSA. (2014a). *National and provincial labour market: Youth (Q1: 2008–Q1: 2014).* Pretoria: Statistics South Africa.

StatsSA. (2014b). *Mid-year population estimates 2014.* Pretoria: Statistics South Africa.

StatsSA. (2014c). *Poverty trends in South Africa: An examination of absolute poverty between 2006 and 2011.* Pretoria: Statistics South Africa.

StatsSA. (2015). *Mid-year population estimates 2015.* Pretoria: Statistics South Africa.

Stein, M. (2008). Resilience and young people leaving care. *Child Care in Practice, 14*(1), 35–44.

Stein, M., & Munro, E. R. (Eds.) (2008). *Young people's transitions from care to adulthood: International research and practice.* London: Jessica Kingsley Publishers.

Tanur, C. (2012). Project Lungisela: Supporting young people leaving state care in South Africa. *Child Care in Practice, 18*(4), 325–340.

Van Breda, A. D. (2014). A comparison of youth resilience across seven South African sites. *Child & Family Social Work*. doi:10.1111/cfs.12222.

Van Breda, A. D. (2015a). Journey towards independent living: A grounded theory investigation of leaving the care of Girls & Boys Town South Africa. *Journal of Youth Studies, 18*(3), 322–337.

Van Breda, A. D. (2015b). *Young people leaving residential care in South Africa: Risk and resilience at 12 and 24 months after leaving care.* Paper presented at the Journal of Youth Studies Conference, Copenhagen.

Van Breda, A. D., & Dickens, L. (2015). Educational persistence and social exclusion among youth leaving residential care in South Africa. *Nuances: Estudos sobreEducação, 26*(1), 22–41.

Visser, M., Zungu, N., & Ndala-Magoro, N. (2015). Isibindi, creating circles of care for orphans and vulnerable children in South Africa: Post-programme outcomes. *AIDS Care, 27*(8), 1014–1019.

World Data Bank. (2015). *World development indicators: Unemployment, youth total (% of total labor force aged 15–24 years) (modeled ILO estimate).* http://databank.worldbank.org/data//reports.aspx?source=2&country=&series=SL.UEM.1524.ZS&period=. Accessed 13 Aug 2015.

18

Improving Institutional Care to Enhance Outcomes for Care Leavers in Russia

Evgenia Stepanova and Simon Hackett

There is a considerable body of research that associates successful outcomes for care leavers with the skills and experiences they developed while residing in out-of-home care (OHC; Courtney 2008; Dixon 2008). In Russia, however, the nature of existing institutional care provision makes it challenging, and in some cases impossible, to ensure good life chances for care leavers.

This chapter examines the views of 15 Russian caregivers and 45 Russian care leavers regarding their institutional experiences, and explores a range of critical factors associated with care leavers' transition to adulthood. This survey-based account explores caregivers' experiences of looking after children and young people, with a focus on young people's preparation for independent living. Furthermore, young people's reflections on how institutional care can be improved are presented.

E. Stepanova • S. Hackett (✉)
School of Applied Social Sciences, Durham University, Gateshead, UK

© The Author(s) 2016
P. Mendes, P. Snow (eds.), *Young People Transitioning from Out-of-Home Care*, DOI 10.1057/978-1-137-55639-4_18

The majority of young people in care in Russia, who are given a status of 'ready for independent living', leave institutional settings between the ages of 16 and 23 (Dzugaeva 2013; Lerch and Stein 2010). The status of being 'independent' is usually seen as a step to an instant adulthood, followed by complete or partial discharge from institutional settings and the removal of legal supervision by the State. The publicly stated position in Russia is that care leavers receive all the support and help required for successful well-being in independent life. However, in reality, 'the State has lost more than one generation of care leavers', with an estimated ten per cent of young people committing suicide, 40 per cent becoming criminals and 40 per cent experiencing problems with alcohol and drug misuse (Philanthropy 2015). Annually, only 4000 out of 40,000 care leavers manage to live independently and do not put their lives at risk (Lerch and Stein 2010; Philanthropy 2015), and this demonstrates that care leavers very often do not receive the in-care and after care support necessary to enhance their life chances in adulthood. Despite ongoing international research and practices that emphasize the importance of preparation for aftercare independent living, Russian care support primarily focuses on the provision of material resources. Indeed, young people may leave care equipped with the latest electronic devices, but hardly know how to look after themselves (Philanthropy 2015). Furthermore, the process of leaving care makes it difficult, and often impossible, to provide smooth transition into adult life (Prisyazhnaya 2007). Factors such as separation from house parents, the search for a new home and the return to birth parents often act as challenging milestones in their independent life (Philanthropy 2015; Prisyazhnaya 2007). Care leavers may also be psychologically and emotionally unready to fit into a different social structure after care, where they are no longer perceived as 'poor orphans', but rather seen as mature and independent adults (Mensitova 2012).

The existing body of research argues that in order to ensure the smooth transition of care leavers to independent life, it is important to focus on the skills, knowledge and experiences they gain whilst in care (Courtney 2008; Dixon 2008; English et al. 1994 in Stepanova and Hackett 2014; Philanthropy 2015). That said, despite recent welfare policy debates about reducing the number of children entering care (Dzugaeva 2013), institutional care in Russia has rarely been the focus of research aiming to explore and potentially improve the existing infrastructure of the institutional system. This chapter aims to address this gap by presenting findings from a survey conducted with a group of Russian caregivers and care leavers, focusing on their institutional experiences and how these experiences shape and define life after care.

OHC in the Russian Federation

In Russia, there were 731,000 children and young people in OHC in 2010, with 260,236 children and young people placed in varying types of institutional care (Philanthropy 2011). The remaining 65 per cent of children were admitted to family placements where the predominant type of care is kinship care incorporating 87.6 per cent out of all family placements (Schmidt 2009). According to a member of the Public Chamber of the Russian Parliament (Altshuler 2010, 2013), each day, 250 Russian children become 'social orphans'. The term 'social orphans' ('*socialnie siroti*') includes individuals whose parents cannot raise their child due to incarceration, poverty, physical/sexual abuse, abandonment and neglect (Safonova 2005; Mulheir et al. 2004). Of the total number of children in OHC, 95 per cent are social orphans, who have at least one living parent (Yarskaya-Smirnova and Antonova 2009).

The child's placement process in the Russian context may be unpredictable and chaotic, and is often subject to local authority practices that vary widely in quality, rather than through a legal and formal procedure that follows a predetermined protocol (Philanthropy 2011). Institutional care is widespread, with this type of placement representing 98 per cent of all OHC facilities for children after kinship care (Groark et al. 2008; Human Rights Watch 1998). The remaining 2 per cent belong to *patronat* care[1] and adoptive families; however, with a lack of other available options, institutional care often

---

[1] In a patronat family, the responsibility for guardianship is shared between an institution and a family, (Schmidt 2009).

remains the only alternative for child placement in Russia. There are 5186 institutional childcare settings for children and young people in Russia (Philanthropy 2011), though the number of children requiring placement is three times higher than the capacity of these institutions (Yarskaya-Smirnova and Antonova 2009). There has been an ongoing debate around the effectiveness of contemporary institutional care in the Russian context (e.g. Sellick 1998; Astoyanc 2005; Groark et al. 2008; Schmidt 2009). The wide body of international research considers institutional care to be inferior to other models of OHC placement such as foster care, adoption or kinship care, and it is often viewed as a measure of 'last resort' for children (Schofield 2005; Forrester 2008; Little et al. 2005; Sellick 1998).

Perceptions of institutional care both internationally and in Russia continually associate children and young people in care with trouble, risk, abuse and danger (Emond 2003; Schmidt 2009; Taylor 2006; Prisyazhnaya 2007; Yarskaya-Smirnova and Antonova 2009; Zhuravleva 2013). In addition, financial arguments that institutional care is inferior influenced the widespread closure of State care in a significant part of Western Europe and in some states of the USA (Hellinckx 2002). Overall, the widespread stigma and status of marginalization attached to both institutionalization and children in care represent fundamental barriers to thorough research on institutional care as well as on development of new policies and practices to improve it.

Care Leavers' Profiles in Russia

In Russia, there is no federal monitoring system that tracks the pathways and life trajectories of children and young people after the point of their admission into institutional care. Information about each child in care can be found only in reports relating to their initial placement (Cinduk 2012). However, some small-scale and often unsystematic studies provide a degree of insight into the independent life trajectories of care leavers across the country. Several Russian studies demonstrate that there is only a small proportion of care leavers who manage to achieve successful independent living (Dovzhik and Archakova 2015; Philanthropy 2015). In the year 2000, from a total of 15,000 care leavers, 5000 were involved in criminal activities, 3000 became homeless and 1500 committed suicide (Philanthropy 2011). In the Kaluga region, only 10 per cent of young care leavers were reported to be 'fitting' into Russian society, whereas 90 per cent were socially excluded (Podolskaya and Vendina 2008). In contrast, the Vice-President of the Department of Social Care in the Moscow region argued that in 2013, of 3000 young people transitioning from care, 1200 received both vocational and higher education, 1000 had temporary or permanent jobs and only 52 had a history of criminal offending (Dzugaeva 2013).

Prisyazhnaya (2007) and Podolskaya and Vendina (2008) argue that the institutional care settings in Russia hinder positive outcomes when leaving care. In particular, Podolskaya and Vendina state that young people feel lost and scared of independence at the point of leaving institutional care. There is a considerable body of research, which associates successful independent living in care leavers with the skills and experiences they developed and gained whilst in care (Courtney 2008; Dixon 2008; English et al. 1994). Furthermore, Nazarova (2000) and Anghel (2011) argue that long-term institutional placements have a significant detrimental impact on the development of young people's identities and their behaviour. Nevertheless, some existing research suggests that the institutional experiences of children and young people can positively contribute to the development of a number of characteristics and skills critical to independent living, such as good communication skills (Astoyanc 2006), high levels of responsibility for individual actions, and careful consideration of health and well-being issues (Podolskaya and Vendina 2008). Conversely, institutional care may reduce care leavers' basic skills (Stein 2004), including financial responsibilities and budgeting, housekeeping and making food (Dovzhik and Archakova 2015). Podolskaya and Vendina (2008) argued that the most challenging characteristics to develop among children in care are adequate self-perception, independence, social responsibility and emotional stability. With these factors in mind, it has been argued that additional support for care leavers often inadvertently teaches them how to 'manipulate', rather than how to be responsible adults (Dovzhik and Archakova 2013).

Staff in Institutional Care

Prisyazhanya (2007) argued that caregivers working in institutional care play a central role in ensuring the well-being of children in their care, as well as of care leavers. Although there is evidence that in Russia the levels of caregivers' qualifications are relatively poor (Groark et al. 2008), some studies suggest that the personal characteristics of staff are far more important (Astoyanc 2005; Prisyazhnaya 2007). As such, the well-being of both children in care and care leavers depends on caregivers' levels of emotional attunement and individual character traits (Prisyazhnaya 2007). The qualifications of caregivers also depend significantly on the profile of an institution. In baby homes, caregivers are mostly qualified nurses and paediatricians (Groark et al. 2008). Most of the training received by staff is on issues associated with children's health and safety, with little focus on psychological issues or pedagogical training. Institutional units for older children such as children's homes and boarding schools most frequently employ unqualified staff (Philanthropy 2011). Here, all categories of specialists, including social workers, caregivers, nurses and teachers, often have low levels of qualification (Philanthropy 2011). There is also no evidence that there is any psychological or psychosocial training received by these personnel (Groark et al. 2008; Philanthropy 2011). Caregivers' lack of awareness about children's in-care needs and their vulnerability status can create severe disruptions in communication between caregivers and children, and subsequently lead to a long-term negative impact on children's well-being (Groark et al. 2008). Similarly, specialists such as medical staff in maternity and general hospitals have very poor recognition about children in care and their needs. It is often the case that medical doctors in maternity units convince any mother to give up children born with special needs immediately after giving birth (Philanthropy 2011). For example, the study conducted in Moscow by a non-governmental organization, entitled 'Downside Up', interviewed 40 women who gave birth to children with Down syndrome. According to them, the medical staff in maternity hospitals tried to persuade women to give up their child to a baby home (Downside Up 2008).

Study Aims and Methodology

The aims of this study were to explore both caregivers' reflections on young people's perceived readiness for independent living and also young people's own reflections following their transition to independence. In particular, the study sought to give voice to care leavers' suggestions and recommendations regarding what needs to be done to make institutional care more effective for other young people in the institutional care system in Russia.

Method

We undertook a cross-sectional survey to gather the views of different groups of people involved in institutional care. In an effort to 'give voice' to young people as the key informants about their experiences, the research was conducted with care leavers as well as with staff (Ireland and Holloway 1996; Oakley 2000; Ridley and McCluskey 2003). As we were conducting research with a vulnerable group of individuals and touching on sensitive topics, one of the goals was the development of a 'user-friendly' questionnaire, which would be self-completed, as this has been seen to be a useful technique in data collection in sensitive topics with young people (Ridley and McCluskey 2003; Ward et al. 2005). The survey design allowed care leavers to feel more comfortable when responding than might have been the case in a face-to-face interview, which can entail 'age and power differences between adults and children' (Ward et al. 2005, p. 11). Bowling (2005) reports that participants' willingness to disclose sensitive information reaches a very high level when the data are collected via a questionnaire, and this method is commonly used in care leaver research (Aldridge and Levine 2001; Holland 2009).

Two questionnaires were designed. The questionnaire for care leavers aimed at exploring their views on, and experiences of, institutional care. The second questionnaire focused on the perceptions of staff and their experiences of children in care in institutional settings. The questionnaires included both closed and open multiple-option responses as well as statements on which agreement was indicated using Likert scales. Those findings drawing on data, which explored young people's individual perceptions of institutionalization and identified in-care factors of significance to care leavers, are presented elsewhere (please see Stepanova and Hackett 2014, which provides a hitherto overlooked insight into the lives of Russian care leavers). In the context of this chapter, we focus on findings that relate to staff reflections on young people's institutional experiences, and we compare these to care leavers' recommendations. Ethical approval was gained from the School of Applied Social Sciences Ethics Committee at Durham University.

Participants

All of the participants were recruited with assistance from a non-governmental centre for care leavers in Moscow, which provides educational and socioemotional support to young people who have been in care. Participants comprised 45 care leavers from Russian institutional care settings and 15 members of staff. They came from various backgrounds and had a wide range of institutional experiences (Stepanova and Hackett 2014). All participants from the care leavers' sample were aged between 16 and 30.[2] Both female and male respondents took part in the study. At the point of completing the questionnaire, all care leavers had been living independently for at least one year. Here, the term 'independent living' refers to discharge or partial discharge (e.g. when a care leaver lives in accommodation provided by the vocational education system) from institutional care in Russia, followed by the withdrawal of legal supervision by the local authorities. Having an after care experience of educational and social provision offered by the centre enables participants to reconsider their in-care experiences, contrasting them with their current conditions (Ward et al. 2005; Stein and Verweijen-Slamnescu 2012).

Information about the study was provided to staff members of the non-governmental centre at a video conference prior to commencing any

---

[2] Some of the participants became independent before they reached the age of 16 to go to vocational education.

research activities in the centre. Subsequently, staff of the centre presented the research overview to care leavers, where the invitation to take part was announced. Where potential respondents demonstrated their willingness to take part in the research, they were individually approached and consulted by a General Manager of the supporting organization. This practice provided participants with a comfortable and trusting environment where they were able to ask questions about the research and make a decision about their participation. During the process and after completion of the questionnaire, all care leaver participants were supported by a psychologist permanently working in the centre.

The second group of participants included 15 caregivers who had been working with children in care and/or care leavers for minimum of two years. Caregivers' ages ranged from 21 to 50. The sample was a heterogeneous group of professionals working with care leavers in several areas including education, mental health, social well-being and practical preparation for independent living.

For all participants, Russian was their first language, so all questionnaires were translated and completed in their native language. Each participant was provided an information sheet, and they completed an informed consent form indicating their willingness to take part in the study. Participation was entirely voluntary and independent of any support being offered to care leavers. Responses to questionnaires were anonymous.

Findings

Profiles of Members of Staff

All 15 members of staff were female, and their average age was 28. This gender bias is representative of the existing population of those involved in social work and institutional care, in particular, in Russia (Philanthropy 2011). Not surprisingly, there was a relationship between staff age and their work experience in care settings. Nine respondents who were aged under 34 had less than seven years' experience in the care sector, whereas three of the participants aged over 38 had 13 or more years' work experience. Table 18.1 shows the personal characteristics and profiles of staff members.

Table 18.1 Personal characteristics and institutional experiences of members of staff

Characteristics, placement and current status	Total (N = 15)
Work experience (years)	
2–4	4
5–7	6
8–10	1
11–13	2
Over 13	2
Types of institutional settings worked in	
Army	1
Boarding school	2
Children's home	14
Rehabilitation centre for care leavers	15
Qualification/degree	
Art	1
Journalism	1
Law	1
Linguistics	1
Medicine	1
Pedagogy	1
Photography	1
Psychology	2
School Teacher	2
Finance	4
Types of institutional settings resided	
Shelter	39
Baby home	11
Children's home	28
Boarding school	30
Specialist boarding school	29
Role in current post	
Caregiver	5
Manager of social projects	1
Manager of social work department	1
Psychologist	1
Teacher	7
Gender	
Female	15
Male	0

Specialist boarding school is the translated term for "psychonevrologicheskij internat" previously used by Human Rights Watch (1998).

Overall, staff respondents' experiences ranged from working in children's homes and boarding schools to providing care leavers with social support. Ten members of staff had between two to seven years of work experience with children and young people in care. However, those who had worked less than seven years had not received any relevant qualification or professional training. Although not necessarily representative of all professionals working in institutional care in Russia, the lack of professional social work or social pedagogy qualifications for both managers and staff is a concerning finding.

Research suggests that the area of childcare is occasionally perceived as a sensitive and intuitive job, which requires more in the way of personal characteristics rather than professional qualification (Millham et al. 1986; Philanthropy 2012). This approach was largely criticized by Millham et al. (1986), suggesting that appropriate professional training helps to boost existing effective personal characteristics and improve practice around looking after children. Nine respondents in the current study highlighted that they would have liked to receive additional training. Although additional professional training opportunities may often be beneficial for staff, caregivers often lacked basic knowledge in working with children such as an understanding of child development. One specialist in children psychology argued that it would 'improve the knowledge about child development' (female caregivers aged 30), and another stated that it would 'give insight into difficulties around children behaviour' (female teacher aged 26). Similarly, training may play a positive role in teaching staff how to react to crisis situations such as burnout or secondary traumatic stress (ACS-NYU Children's Trauma Institute's 2012). Furthermore, the need for training around work with children and young people with disabilities was rated as the second most important professional development need among four respondents.

Staff Experiences

The majority of staff 'disagreed' or 'strongly disagreed' that the staffing ratios were high, arguing that children did not have too many different caregivers during institutionalization. This finding stands in contrast with the existing body of research claiming lack of staff as one of the key deficiencies in young people's in-care and after care experiences (Groark et al. 2008).

Eight caregivers reported that they established good relationships with residents, including the statement that 'relationships between a housemother and a child are at the core of institutional well-being' (female teacher aged 23). For half of the staff, particularly those with over seven years' experience of work with children in care, these relationships tended to continue even after young people had left care. This suggests that the enduring bond between staff and care leavers might be a relatively common feature in relationships between care leavers and staff. Eleven of the staff 'strongly agreed' that it is necessary to establish 'family-like' relationships between residents and caregivers. Only three respondents disagreed with this arrangement, arguing, for example, that 'it can be unpleasant to children' (female caregiver aged 50). This statement is consistent with the work of Little et al. (2005) who reported that staff barriers to establishing close family relationships with young people in care might be the existence of 'intact families' of residents. One of the key attributes regarding relationships with children in care is physical contact; however, none of the respondents in the current study said that they found that physical contact was of any importance for children and young people. Berridge and Brodie (1998) found that in contexts where a policy of control and order was emphasized within institutional care, physical contact, including public displays of affection, between staff and residents may be limited. According to participants' responses in our Russian study, staff believed that establishing close relationships was not associated with a strong positive impact on residents' well-being. Indeed, nine professionals 'strongly disagreed' with the statement that close relationships would enhance the quality and experiences of institutional care among residents. These findings, therefore, demonstrate mixed attitudes towards close relationships between staff and residents in care. Respondents highlighted the importance of family-type relationships and the continuation of such relationships for care leavers; nevertheless, close relationships were not seen as critical to positive well-being. Physical contact, which is often viewed as a traditional form of care, support and reassurance (Berridge and Brodie 1998), was not emphasized.

Institutional care in Russia is often associated with regulations, discipline, power and control. The discipline may include different types of punishment following perceived misbehaviour of a child (Human Rights Watch 1998). Among the most extreme punishments are 'warehousing them [children] in barren and windowless rooms', 'denying them available food' or 'keeping them [children] in unsanitary accommodations or in inadequate clothing' (Human Rights Watch 1998: 45). All 15 participants 'agreed' and 'strongly agreed' that the existing measures of control and management of children and young people in care are adequate, indicating that staff did not find the levels of control used abusive or in violation of residents' rights. Twelve respondents 'strongly disagreed' with the statement that caregivers punished residents too much, suggesting that 'every child is different, so we need to use different approaches' (female caregiver aged 50). Three professionals, all of whom had more than ten years' experience, stated that they 'strongly disagreed' with the statement.

Care Leavers' Perspectives

Profiles of Care Leavers

Most respondents were male (n = 27, i.e. 60 per cent), and 18 were female (40 per cent). This ratio is representative of the existing gender population in institutional care in Russia (Astoyanc 2005; Stepanova and Hackett 2014). All, but one, of the care leavers were single at the point of their participation in the study. Thirty-four care leavers (75.5 per cent) were admitted to OHC from a family environment after the age of five. Thirty-five out of 45 care leavers experienced more than one institutional placement (77.8 per cent). The age of the sample varied between 16 years old (n = 12, 26.6 per cent) and those over 17 (n = 33, i.e. 73.4 per cent). A more detailed profile on care leavers, including their history of institutional placements, is provided elsewhere (see Stepanova and Hackett 2014).

Care Leavers' Recommendations

The most common recommendation from care leavers on how institutional care could be improved to enhance their independent living outcomes focused around relationships with staff. Twelve care leavers emphasized that improvement in personal relationships between residents and caregivers would have a direct influence on young people's quality of life in institutions and after care. Some of the care leavers felt that they had negative experiences of relationships, for example, 'we tend to have the same kind of attitude towards staff as they do towards us, and it is not the positive one' (female care leaver aged 19), or 'it is important to employ caregivers who have at least some humanity' (female caregiver aged 20). Conversely, six care leavers recommended that young people in care should 'listen to staff and respect them' (female care leaver aged 16) and 'do your best to establish good relationships with your houseparents' (female care leaver aged 16).

Another recommendation from care leavers was to focus on education and to 'spend all your time in care studying as it will benefit your future life after care' (male care leaver aged 22), and 'to read more books and to study hard' (female care leaver aged 20). Here respondents encouraged children and young people in care to 'look for ways and opportunities of self-development' (female care leaver aged 22). The findings demonstrate that an emphasis on the value of education might be influenced by care leavers' independent living conditions and priorities. Often the quality of education is neglected in Russian institutional care, making it extremely difficult for young people to achieve successful independent living (Stepanova and Hackett 2014).

Discussion

Russian institutional care conforms to the definition of institutions in research on care provision in Eastern and Central Europe. Being often over-populated and understaffed, institutional life is organized around the principles of collective upbringing widely promoted during the earlier socialist regime (Khlinovskaya Rockhill 2010). Regardless of environments and some macro factors, the central element of institutional life is always shaped and defined by the established relationships between caregivers and residents.

The findings reported here provide insight into caregivers' experiences of institutional life. The caregivers in this study were an experienced group, often working in institutional settings for many years. Staff experiences of institutional care are often shaped and formed by individual practices, beliefs, relationships, values and emotions, rather than by professional qualifications and knowledge. Indeed, the majority of caregivers highlighted that their professional backgrounds are irrelevant to social pedagogy and care despite the international emphasis on the quality and levels of professional qualification (Groark et al. 2008; Sellick 1998; Taylor 2006). The majority of caregivers are convinced that child–caregiver relationships are of major importance to children and their well-being in care. Feelings such as love, altruism, responsibility and sympathy may contribute to caregivers' attempts to develop warm and reciprocal relationships with children (Dzugaeva 2013). Caregivers reported wanting to build a sense of good relationships, aiming to create family-type care followed by long-term bonding between staff and young people even after leaving care. Here, the practice of permanence and relationships beyond institutional formal responsibilities play critical roles in the lives of children. That said, such obvious attributes of family-type relationships as physical contact are often rejected by staff. The inconsistency in family-type relationships continues when some staff members demonstrate positive attitudes towards punishment, which may often constitute physical abuse (Human Rights Watch 1998). Overall, most caregivers show a tendency to promote and develop the notion of family in care. Driven by support and care, adults often create a sense of extended family in institutions where caregivers play the roles of parents. This voluntary practice of caregivers of building family-type relationships is in line with the Soviet ideology of creating 'one big public family' (Khlinovskaya Rockhill 2010, p. 14). However, whereas in Soviet times the practice was driven by control, surveillance and structure, the contemporary practice introduces more individual and intimate approaches to care, mixed together with Soviet practice. As a result, the family-type relationships still include a number of inconsistencies and contradictory experiences such as the absence of physical affection and the use of punishment.

Care leavers' recommendations on how to improve institutional care are consistent with caregivers' views on the importance of relationships. When entering care, most children experience long-term institutional placements followed by frequent moves between the settings (Stepanova and Hackett 2014). Given the paucity of contact with parents, institutional life often becomes a substitute for children's families. A significant number of young people highlighted the importance of establishing good and trusting relationships with 'house parents' to ensure positive experience in institutions. Having stable, meaningful and positive relationships with a caregiver contributes to children's development of a role model, secure attachments with an adult and subsequent success in care. Furthermore, reciprocal and quality relationships enable children to have a positive image about institutional life as well as about themselves. In turn, Berridge et al. (2010) show that positive child–caregiver experiences may contribute to children's development of resilience in care and after leaving care. The findings reported by Stepanova and Hackett (2014) also demonstrate positive outcomes among care leavers where young people had established strong attachments and had a sense of belonging with their house parents. Finally, care leavers emphasize the importance of focusing on receiving education in care. It is argued that low levels of education may have a negative impact on care leavers' success in independent life (Dixon and Stein 2003; Prisyazhnaya 2007; Stepanova and Hackett 2014).

Overall, the findings from both staff and care leavers' views are in line with the international research highlighting the significance of a family-like environment in care, enduring relationships between residents and staff and the importance of education. That said, some caregivers did not regard warm, family relationships between residents and staff as a critical factor in positive outcomes among young people, which contradicts some findings from international research (e.g. Berridge and Brodie 1998). Overall, the current research suggests a warm family-type environment, and strong bonds might be created in institutional settings provided there is individual openness and willingness to do so. However, such essential attributes of Russian institutions as placement instability, isolation in institutions and high staff and child ratios often hinder the relationships between staff and residents (Stepanova and Hackett 2014).

Conclusion

The research findings suggest a number of key recommendations for policy and practice reform. First of all, the current practice of looking after children in Russia is strongly influenced by the intuition and experience of caregivers rather than by empirically derived knowledge. This detachment of a professional body of knowledge from practice reflects the nature of care and children's experiences as well as relationships between caregivers, volunteers and early career professionals. In this respect, relevant training programmes should be designed and embedded into care in Russia, which would be available to all members of staff. The proposed training would professionalize practice in the area of care provision for the first time.

Next, evidence from this study shows that relationships in care may reflect complex factors. Ignoring the importance of secure attachment and emotional closeness may be a critical barrier to improving young people's lives. Such factors as caregivers' distance in relationships and collective upbringing might militate against continuous and secure relationships with house parents. In the first instance, Russian care providers need to consider and reflect on the importance of relationships in care. There is a need to develop a series of creative practices and approaches, which would enhance and sustain the opportunities for permanent, trusting, warm and reciprocal relationships. Both care leavers and staff demonstrated attachment to, and dependency on, the relationships with caregivers. Policy makers and practitioners in Russia need to introduce a clear and stable scheme of maintaining contact between residents and caregivers across different institutional settings. The opportunities for permanent contact need to become part of the routine available in care and after leaving care. Although continuity of care may be a more realistic goal in smaller institutional settings, each unit needs to promote the value of permanence in relationships. Furthermore, the study demonstrated that limited or non-existing professional qualifications among staff are common attributes of care provision practice across various institutions. This is likely to impact negatively on the nature of the care young people experience. Some staff members recognized and admitted the value of improving the level of professionalism through training. In this respect, relevant training programmes should be designed and embedded into care. These recommendations are developed to improve and change the everyday practice of children in care in Russia, and to promote the successful transition of young people into independent living. Although the Russian Government has demonstrated a general intention to enhance care provision for children in care and care leavers, this study identifies a number of specific approaches, which could further enhance their well-being.

It is important to stress the limitations of this study. Only a small number of participants and institutional units (drawn from only one geographic location, namely, Moscow) were included. This small sample cannot be assumed to be representative of care leavers and caregivers or institutional facilities across Russia. Russia consists of 83 Federal subjects (The Article 65 §1, 2007), where Moscow represents only one province. The region explored in this study differs from other districts due to different cultural and geographical location, socioeconomic status, government financial support, availability of professional and educational opportunities and levels of non-governmental support.

Furthermore, due to the complexity of experiences and events in institutional care, as well as the heterogeneity of the care leaving population, any generalizations could be premature and/or misleading. Further, it is important to acknowledge that the research did not include care leavers with severe learning disabilities. Although the study did include young people who had experience of residing in specialized boarding schools due to possible learning difficulties, the wards housing individuals with severe disabilities were closed to public or volunteers.

Lastly, the context of institutional care in Russia had a strong influence on the research findings. In this respect, the outcomes of this study may not necessarily apply to population groups elsewhere in Russia or in other countries. However, despite the aforementioned limitations of the study, the experiences of institutionalization resonate with other studies internationally, suggesting that institutionalized individuals may have experienced similar events. In this respect, the findings from this research can be used by practitioners, policy-makers and researchers in order to apply them to a specific population or as a starting point for further studies.

References

ACS-NYU Children's Trauma Institute. (2012). *Addressing secondary traumatic stress among child welfare staff: A practice brief.* New York: NYU Langone Medical Center.

Aldridge, A., & Levine, K. (2001). *Surveying the social world. Principles and practice is survey research.* Buckingham: Open University Press.

Altshuler, B. (2010). Children in care: The Russian orphan industry. *Open democracy Russia.* Available at: http://www.opendemocracy.net/od-russia/boris-altshuler/children-in-care-russian-orphan-industry. Accessed 11 July 2012.

Altshuler, B. (2013). Russian orphans are the means of business for local authorities [Rossijskie siroti–eto bizness dlya sistemi opeki]. Gazeta.ru. Available at: http://www.gazeta.ru/video/predmetnyi_razgovor/altshuler.shtml. Accessed 14 May 2012.

Anghel, R. (2011). Transition within transition: How young people learn to leave behind institutional care whilst their careers are stuck in neutral. *Children and Youth Services Review, 33*, 2526–2531.

Astoyanc, M. (2005). Analysis of living experiences in the institutional environment [Analiz zhiznennix praktik v usloviyax internatnogo uchezhdenija]. *Sociologicheskie Issledovanija, 3*, 54–63.

Astoyanc, M. (2006). Social orphanhood. [Social'noe sirotstvo: usloviya, mexanizmy i dinami-ka e'ksklyuzii (sociokul'turnaya interpretaciya)]. Rostov-na-Donu.

Berridge, D., & Brodie, I. (1998). *Children's homes revisited.* London: Jessica Kingsley Publishers.

Berridge, D., Biehal, N., & Henry, L. (2010). *Living in children's residential homes.* London: Department for Education.

Bowling, A. (2005). Mode of questionnaire administration can have serious effects on data quality. *Journal of Public Health, 27*(3), 281–291.

Cinduk, E. (2012). *Establishment of military classes within boarding schools as a after care support service of social adaptation for care leavers* [Sozdanie kadetskix klassov v internatnom uchrezhdenii, kak sposob socialnok adpatacii vipusknikov]. Available at: http://www.zavuch.info/methodlib/53/78706/. Accessed 12 Feb 2015.

Courtney, M. (2008). Use of secondary data to understand the experiences of care leavers. In M. Stein & E. Munro (Eds.), *Young people's transitions from care to adulthood: International comparisons and perspectives* (pp. 279–288). London: Jessica Kingsley Publishers.

Dixon, J. (2008). Young people leaving care: Health, well-being and outcomes. *Child and Family Social Work, 13*, 207–217.

Dixon, J., & Stein, M. (2003). Leaving care in Scotland: The residential experience. *Scottish Journal of Residential Child, 2*(2), 7–17.

Dovzhik, L. & Archakova, T. (2015). Socialization of care leavers from children's homes [*Socializacija vipusknikov detskix domov*]. Available at: http://psypress.ru/articles/25184.shtml. Accessed 22 Oct 2015.

Downside Up. (2008). Change life of people with Down syndrome to the better [*Menjaem k luchshemu zhizn ludej s sindromom dauna v Rossii*]. Available at: http://www.downsideup.org/. Accessed 10 Oct 2015.

Dzugaeva, A. (2013). *Press-conference 'Supporting the social orphans and developing the family-based model care' [Realisacija modeli profilaktiki socialnogo sirotstva I razvitie semejnogo ustrojstva detej, ostavshixsja bex popechenija roditelej']*. Moscow: Russian Ministry for Education.

Emond, R. (2003). Putting the care into residential care. The role of young people. *Journal of Social Work, 3*, 321–337.

English, D., Kouidou-Giles, S., & Plocke, M. (1994). Readiness for independence: A study of youth in foster care. *Children and Youth Services Review, 16*(3/4), 147–158.

Forrester, D. (2008). Is the care system failing children? *The Political Quarterly, 79*(2), 206–211.

Groark, C., Muhamedrahimov, R., Palmov, O., Nikiforova, N., & McCall, R. (2008). *The effects of early social-emotional and relationship experience on the development of young orphanage children, Author manuscript, Monograph social research child development*. New York: Wiley-Blackwell.

Hellinckx, W. (2002). Residential care: Last resort or vital link in child welfare? *International Journal of Child and Family Welfare, 3*, 75–83.

Holland, S. (2009). Listening to children in care: A review of methodological and theoretical approaches to understanding looked after children's perspectives. *Children and Society, 23*, 226–235.

Human Rights Watch. (1998). *Abandoned to the state: Cruelty and neglect in Russian orphanages*. New York: Human Rights Watch.

Ireland, L., & Holloway, I. (1996). Qualitative health research with children. *Children and Society, 10*, 155–164.

Khlinovskaya Rockhill, E. (2010). *Lost to the state: Family discontinuity, social orphanhood and residential care in the Russian Far East*. Oxford: Berghahn Books.

Lerch, V., & Stein, M. (2010). *Aging out of care. From care to adulthood in European and Central Asian societies*. Innsbruck: SOS Children's Villages International.

Little, M., Kohm, A., & Thompson, R. (2005). The impact of residential placement on child development: Research and policy implications. *International Journal of Social Welfare, 14*, 200–209.

Mensitova, V. (2012). Characteristics of a children's home as an educational and residential facility *[Xarakteristika detskogo doma, kak obrazovatelno-vospitatel'nogo uchrezhdenija]*. *Psihologicheskie nauki: teorija i praktika. Moscow:Buki-Vedi, 2*, 111–113.

Millham, S., Bullock, R., Hosie, K., & Haak, M. (1986). *Lost in care: The problems of maintaining links between children in care and their families*. Aldershot: Gower.

Mulheir, G., Browne, K., Darabus, S., Misca, G., Pop, D., & Wilson, B. (2004). *De-institutionalisation of children's services in Romanian: A good practice guide*. Bucharest: High Level Group for Romanian Children/UNICEF Romania office.

Nazarova, I. B. (2000). *Adaptation and possible models of orphans welfare*. Moscow: Moscow Scientific Fund.

Oakley, M. (2000). Children and young people and care proceedings. In A. Lewis & G. Lindsay (Eds.), *Researching children's perspectives* (pp. 73–85). Buckingham: Open University Press.

Philanthropy. (2011). *Orphans in Russia: Problems and suggested ways for improvement [Sirotstvo v Rossii: problemi i puti ix reshenija]*. Moscow: Philanthropy.

Philanthropy. (2012). Houseparents in children's homes: Charities never consult caregivers. *[Vospitatel' detdoma: Blagotvoritel' nikogda ne sovetuetsja s vospitateljami]*. Moscow: Philanthropy. Available at: http://philanthropy.ru/intervyu/2012/05/12/7692/#.VlQ8XF7MBtQ. Accessed on 24 Nov 15.

Philanthropy. (2015). A children's home is an amputation of future. *[Detskij dom-amputacija budushego]*. Moscow: Philanthropy. Available at: http://philanthropy.ru/news/2015/11/09/30667/#.VlRptl7MBtR. Accessed on 20 Nov 15.

Podolskaya, N., & Vendina, O. (2008). Social adaptation of care leavers [Socialnaya adaptacija vipusknikov]. *Kompleksnoe izuchnie cheloveka. Sbornik statey, 94*, 397–406.

Prisyazhnaya, N. (2007). *Orphans as a social group of Russian society*. Conference paper, Moscow State University of Sociology, Moscow.

Ridley, J., & McCluskey, S. (2003). Exploring the perception of young people in care and care leavers of their health needs. *Scottish Journal of Residential Child Care, 2*, 55–65.

Safonova, T. (2005). *Rehabilitation of children in children's homes*. Moscow: Nauka.

Sellick, C. (1998). The use of institutional care for children across Europe. *European Journal of Social Work, 1*(3), 301–310.

Schmidt, V. (2009). Orphan care in Russia. *Social Work and Society, 7*(1), 58–69.

Schofield, G. (2005). The voice of the child in family placement decision-making: A developmental model. *Adoption and Fostering, 19*(1), 29–44.

Stein, M. (2004). *What works for young people leaving care?* Barkingside: Barnardo's.

Stein, M., & Verweijen-Slamnescu, R. (Eds.) (2012). *When care ends: Lessons from peer research insights from young people on leaving care in Albania, The Czech Republic, Finland and Poland.* Innsbruck: SOS Children's Villages International.

Stepanova, E., & Hackett, S. (2014). Understanding care leavers in Russia: Young people's experiences of institutionalisation. *Australian Social Work, 67*(1), 118–134.

Taylor, C. (2006). *Young people in care and criminal behaviour.* London: Jessica Kingsley Publishers.

Ward, H., Skuse, T., & Munro, E. R. (2005). The best of times, the worst of times' young people's views of care and accommodation. *Adoption and Fostering, 29*(1), 8–17.

Yarskaya-Smirnova, E., & Antonova, E. (2009). *Social policy and childhood world in contemporary Russia, [Socialnaya politika I mir detstva v sovremennoj Rossii].* Moscow: Variant.

Zhuravleva, M. (2013). Girls physically abuse younger residents of a boarding school. *Dozhd*, from 19.05.2013. Available at: http://tvrain.ru. Accessed 25 May 2013.

19

Cast Out and Punished: The Experiences of Care Leavers in Jordan

Rawan W. Ibrahim

Introduction

International awareness of the plight of care leavers is increasing, including in Jordan, but, despite the increasing knowledge and responses, little is known about how local culture may create or contribute to their vulnerability. Similar to their international peers, many Jordanian care leavers face material and psychosocial challenges in and post-care. A specific finding in Jordan is that the social disadvantage of being stigmatized as a care leaver exacerbates the challenges inherent in their transitional journey, as the prevailing patriarchal and collectivist culture values family affiliation as a source of self-worth and support. This chapter draws on the findings of a qualitative study of 42 Jordanian care leavers. Stigmatization influenced all areas of their lives, including their accommodation, employment and everyday relationships. They had come to

R.W. Ibrahim (✉)
Consultant and Researcher in Alternative Care Systems, UNICEF Jordan Country Office, Amman, Jordan

© The Author(s) 2016
P. Mendes, P. Snow (eds.), *Young People Transitioning from Out-of-Home Care*, DOI 10.1057/978-1-137-55639-4_19

expect it, and had developed coping strategies to prevent potential risks and implications and learnt to navigate a way through it. Implications for policy and practice are addressed here; however, structures that produce discrimination and perpetuate the cycle of vulnerability must be addressed for change to occur. The consequences of such stigmatization warrant the inclusion of a cultural perspective in frameworks used to address leaving care. The problems of young people transitioning to adulthood from foster and residential care are increasingly internationally known through the growing body of original research examining their experiences in various regions, including Europe, the Middle East, Australia and North America (Stein and Munro 2008). While there are various types of research and degrees of responsiveness to the needs of care leavers in different countries, it is now widely recognized that this group of young people is among the most socially excluded in their respective societies (Stein and Munro 2008).

Research on youth involved in the Jordanian child welfare system is sparse. However, the existing findings suggest that like their peers in other countries, Jordanian care leavers are at increased risk of persistent vulnerability and challenges whilst transitioning to adulthood (Ibrahim and Howe 2011). This continued vulnerability is often due to compounded risk factors along a continuum encompassing their experiences prior to admission into care, in care and post-care (Stein and Munro 2008).

Particular challenges that Jordanian care leavers share with their international peers include difficult care histories involving multiple placement and school changes. Some experience abuse while in care and leave abruptly, unprepared to handle adult responsibilities. Many leave care without qualifications and struggle to re-engage with education, find accommodation and secure employment and cope financially (Ibrahim and Howe 2011; Stein and Munro 2008).

The benefits and challenges of Jordan's cultural context have been found to have a profound impact on the transitional journey of children in care as they become adults. Ibrahim and Howe (2011) called for a cultural dimension to be included in frameworks pertaining to the care-leaving experience. For example, despite the absence of formal support during the first wave of interviews for the current study, approximately 87 per cent of participants had received some form of support in various life areas. Examples included help with finding and sponsorship of accommodation, being invited to live with families, subsiding costs for qualifications, employment opportunities despite their lack of qualifications, mentoring and support in emergencies. The implications of such support varied. For some young people, it provided only temporary relief, preventing further immediate deterioration in their circumstances. For others, however, it resulted in a positive turning point that greatly improved their life chances and career (Ibrahim and Gilligan unpublished; Johnson and Mendes 2014).

The stigma attached to being a young person with a care history in Jordan, particularly where the family is not known, only exacerbated participants' already difficult journeys and increased their risk of vulnerability and social exclusion. The focus of this chapter is on the influence of stigmatization on various areas of the young people's lives, not only due to its pervasiveness, but also as a result of the limited initiatives to challenge this harmful *status quo*.

The Care Context

Residential homes remain the predominant model for out-of-home care provision in Jordan. At any time, there may be 800–1100 children in each of the nation's 32 homes. Children from the minority Christian community are placed in one of two church-based care homes. Some are placed in a Christian-based vocational and academic boarding school, which also serves young men from the Muslim community. On the whole, children are admitted to care for various reasons besides their protection, including their birth being the result of out-of-wedlock pregnancy. Challenges in the dominant care system include a lack of minimum-care standards and *ad hoc* or absent psychosocial interventions for children and their families (Allayan 2006; Ibrahim and Howe 2011). A typical trajectory for a child in the care system involves an average of three or four age-triggered placement changes as they transition to adolescence. Preparations to help youth transition out of care have also been found to be patchy and weak (Allayan 2006; Ibrahim and Howe 2011). Additional challenges in the wider Jordanian context include a severely under-developed social work education and training system contributing to the shortage of adequately trained and specialist staff.

Recently, policymakers have been seeking to improve practice in this field, including mandating preparations for leaving care, the provision of follow-up support for care leavers reunited with their family and support for youth discharged on reaching the age of majority (18 years). Political will and momentum towards the de-institutionalization of children have resulted in the development of a foster-care programme, although this is still nascent. Furthermore, the Jordanian Government developed a post-care unit and budding NGOs support care leavers with university scholarships, vocational training and employment, housing and other psychosocial needs.

The Cultural Context

The most salient elements of the cultural context and their implications, discussed below, contextualize the roots of stigma in the Jordanian and Arab setting. These elements are patriarchy, patrilineality and collectivism, with deep-rooted values based on notions of honour. Indeed, there is wide variation in how patriarchy manifests; however, the discussion here focuses on the Jordanian context.

The nature of patriarchy prioritizes the dominance and rights of males and older women (Joseph 1999). Patrilineality is patriarchy based on kinship, because it is based on 'kinship descent through the father's lineage' (Joseph 1999, p.2). Barakat (1993, p.23) argues that because the family remains the basic unit of society, this patriarchal system and its inherent hierarchical and authoritative relationships and values persist not only within the family, but also at work, at school and in religious, political and social associations.

The second key cultural characteristic is that Jordanian society is collectivist. This has several implications. First, unlike Western societies' emphasis on the individual and individualism, the intrinsic value of the individual in collectivist societies lies in being part of a kin group (Cinthio and Ericsson 2006, p.37). In Arab societies, the family, not the state, is the principal welfare safety net for the individual and the basis of emotional, economical and even political support (Joseph 1996). The interdependent nature of the Arab family allows individuals to rely on their family throughout their life course for multiple functions, from social security to childcare. Generations within families are expected to reciprocate care, and this can be a source of great pride. Transitioning out of the parental home typically occurs for three reasons: to continue education, to pursue employment or to marry. Moving out of the parental home in pursuit of independence, as occurs in the West, is unusual; women of more conservative families and communities can only leave their parental home when married, and even then, male kin may continue to play a protective role in their lives. Despite the subordination of women in the patriarchal system, this continued attachment within families means that when young adults of both genders transition from the parental home, they do so for positive reasons and with social capital, and continue to be provided with a form of care. The combination of religious prescriptions and the characteristics of the collective society endorses affiliation to the extended family, and support for those without their own safety net (i.e. family), especially those considered to be orphans. This can be a precarious source of support, since the treatment of less fortunate extended family members, including orphans, depends on the empathy and economic means of their family, and therefore even with this support system, orphans are vulnerable.

Collectivist societies see accomplishments and transgressions not as individuals' issues but as reflecting on the family. Members of the kin group are required to uphold society's expectations of families, which are that they are honourable, honest and generous (Kulwicki 2002). Men are expected to control the sexuality of the women in their families, as this can pose the greatest threat to family honour (Kawar 2000). The family is the main support network for its members, yet it can also be the main threat for those who transgress and are considered to have dishonoured it. The repercussions for transgressions vary and depend on how conservative the family and community is. Some may conceal the misdeed, disown the individual or withdraw support. *In extremis*, women particularly may be murdered in so-called honour killings. As a reflection of how deeply rooted these notions are, men receive more lenient sentences for murdering female kin in the name of honour than for other types of murder, which can result in a life sentence or capital punishment (Husseini 2009).

A more specific example of attachment to cultural notions is manifest in a legal system that affords power to men at a cost to women and their offspring: women who become pregnant outside marriage may abandon their children because their partners refuse to marry them. If discovered by the authorities, such women may be imprisoned. An unwed pregnancy is a family catastrophe; such women are at risk of being murdered for dishonouring the family. Men may pressure or coax women into sexual activity, but leave them to shoulder the blame and the responsibility for any offspring. Moreover, in the patriarchal and patrilineal system, the father's legal acknowledgement of his offspring separates legitimate from illegitimate children. The separation of children deemed 'illegitimate' is institutionalized due to the patrilineal system and the need to conceal 'dishonour'. The name of the birth family is concealed, and children are given ambiguous family names and placed in care homes that separate them from society, which further stigmatizes them.

This practice is problematic in itself because in the patrilineal and patriarchal system in Jordan, the name of any individual consists of four parts: the given name, followed by the father's name, the paternal grandfather's name and of course the paternal family name. As Farahat (2013) points out, family names in Arabic have suffixes or prefixes meaning 'house of' or 'tribe of'. Family names are rarely in the form of first names, as are those of young people without 'lawful lineage', whose distinguishable names place the young people at a disadvantage (Farahat, p.17), as it increases their difference from the rest of society. Moreover, based on Davies (2011) and Joseph (1999), Farahat (2013) reminds us that affiliation by means of family names in this context 'not only create boundaries of who belongs, but also carry the legacy of being part of a certain kin group. A surname is not an individual form of identity, but as all constructions of identity in Arab societies, it is embedded in collective understandings of the self, as well as ascribed power, access and belonging' (Farahat 2013, p.15), all of which care leavers are deprived of.

Moreover, in 2000, it was discovered that many such children in care were not registered at birth due to absent legal acknowledgement on behalf of fathers. These children were admitted to care during a period when all Jordanian citizens were required to obtain specific national identification cards and national numbers. This group of children and youth missed out on the given serial numbers. When their lack of registration was identified, they were treated as returning Jordanian expats reclaiming citizenship. The national numbers given to young people from unknown/withheld families are very different from the norm (in relation to their age), further emphasizing difference. As a result of reversing the neglect of not formally registering young people born to 'unknown/withheld families', it is anticipated that future generations (i.e. those born in the year 2000 and beyond) will have national ID numbers that are not stigmatizing.

Methodology

The aim of this qualitative study was to examine the pathways of young Jordanian adults transitioning from residential care to independent living (Ibrahim and Howe 2011). Against the lack of research concerning youth ageing out of residential care in Jordan, the study sought in-depth knowledge about this stigmatized population's experiences and self-supporting strategies. The objectives of the study were explored through several research questions. Amongst the questions were 'what are the most salient features impacting the transitional journeys of young Jordanians exiting residential care?' and 'what factors contribute to the vulnerability of those who do not fit within the patriarchal structure of Jordanian society?'

The first wave of semi-structured interviews took place in 2007, with 21 female and 21 male Jordanian care leavers. Recognizing the need for longitudinal research with care leavers, a follow-up study exploring longer-term developments in the lives of the same cohort since the first interview is now in its final stages, with a particular focus on coping with forced individuality in a collective culture.

The structure of the first wave of interviews was based on the chronology of the care-leaving experience, beginning with a focus on the final phase in care and the transition from the residential facility. This was followed by an exploration of a number of post-care life domains, including experiences with employment, accommodation, finances, relationships, types of support, identity and coping with stigma. In addition to individual interviews, 13 participants engaged in focus groups. Owing to the lack of records on Jordanian care leavers, the maximum number of access points were used: residential homes that may have been in contact with care leavers; women's rights NGOs; the Ministry of Social Development and personal contacts. These provided a small number of respondents. To increase the sample size, and to ensure both a more representative sample of the care-leaving population and the transparency of data collected, and the anonymity of participants, snowballing sampling was adopted.

Participants during the first wave were interviewed as they came along, as they are a difficult-to-reach population. However, the criteria for purposive sampling remained. The selection criteria included a minimum of two years in-care experience as a teenager, an equal number of each sex and a range of times since the individual had left care. The first wave of interviews was conducted as part of a doctoral study, and therefore in accordance with the Ethical Guidelines of the School of Social Work and Psychology at the University of East Anglia (Norwich, UK), which follow the British Psychological Society's *Code of Conduct, Ethical Principles and Guidelines* (2007). Owing to the absence of ethical review boards for the social sciences in Jordan, a research ethics committee was developed for the second wave of interviews. The ethical considerations required by the noted guidelines were approved by the committee and were adhered to.

All interviews and focus groups were conducted by the author in Arabic, and, on average, lasted one and a half to two hours. The interviews were analysed using a grounded theory analytical framework (Corbin and Strauss 2008). This inductive approach has been widely used as an analytical tool in areas that are relatively under-researched. Its use of implicit knowledge allows it to remain open to the data. The method requires gathering rich data in order to answer the research question. It allows for representing diverse experiences and for constant comparison of cases and experiences (Corbin and Strauss 2008). A grounded theory analytical framework was also favoured because it provides a systemic way of analyzing data. It has clearly defined stages, yet they are not entirely fixed. Thematic analysis was utilized for the analysis of focus group data. Analysis of interviews and focus groups was facilitated by the use of NVivo software.

The age range during the first wave was 17–28 years. Nearly half (43 per cent) of the respondents did not know their birth families and were categorized as of unknown/withheld family origin. The commonest cause of institutionalization was abandonment or separation from family due to culturally unacceptable practices by parents, including sexual abuse; incest; pre- and extramarital pregnancy and single parenthood (with one parent sent to prison); mental illness; denial of paternity or disowning the child. Age at admission to care ranged from infancy to 16, and 89 per cent were admitted before the age of 10. The mean amount of time spent in care was 14 years. On average, participants changed placement four times, with a similar number of school changes. Eighty-three per cent were aged 18 when they left care. Some preliminary findings from the follow-up study in relation to the focus of this chapter are shared with the aim of providing references to, and examples of, longer-term experiences.

Findings

Most of the young adults in this study disclosed that they had been subjected to various forms of stigmatization. As described by Ibrahim and Howe (2011), the most commonly experienced labels were 'children of sin' or illegitimate, warranting pity and feeling like easy prey. This chapter revisits these basic forms and definitions of stigmatization as reported by Ibrahim and Howe (2011). However, by way of explicating how vulnerability is perpetuated by stigmatization, this chapter details experiences of disadvantage in various life areas as a result.

Each of the noted faces of the stigma of having been in care has a cultural link or explanation, and resulted in stigmatizing treatment that the participants had learnt to expect. The term 'son/daughter of sin' is normally used to describe a person who is mean-spirited or cruel. When used for young people of unknown family, it is generally a way of saying that the person is a product of the practice of immorality and carries an 'evil seed' that can manifest at any time. On the basis of participants' accounts, these labels and views were seen to justify discrimination, as the object is seen as undeserving of, or beneath, equal treatment. The stigma attached to one who warrants pity is based on their not having a family and its support. The term denotes helplessness, as the young people are seen as weak. The third area of stigmatization is being regarded as easy prey, stemming from the view that no obvious formal or informal support network means no protection. Potential perpetrators would not be held accountable as they would be normally. According to the interviewees, disclosing their care history to the wrong person could weaken their position. The main gender difference was that the women spoke of their fear of being taken advantage of sexually or by their abusive husband, of lacking the normative benefit of male kin and of finding themselves in disadvantaged position *vis-à-vis* their abuser. The implications of these three forms of stigma were experienced in various life domains, as discussed below. Pseudonyms are used where direct quotes are included.

Life Areas of Disadvantage and Exclusion Resulting from Stigmatization

Participants described being stigmatized in three main areas: those of accommodation, employment and relationships. They experienced stigmatization in different areas simultaneously or just in a single area. Some were both stigmatized and supported in the same area (e.g. maltreatment and stigmatization by some colleagues at work in combination with support from others).

Accommodation

As described above, it is unusual for young adults in Jordan to move out of their family home solely because they want to be independent. Depending on their location and personal circumstances, young people who need or want to live alone may find it difficult to rent accommodation alone because landlords fear unruly behaviour, which could damage their own reputation as they may be perceived as wrongfully permissive.

Young single adults have an easier time living in affluent and therefore more liberal areas. The poorer the area, the more conservative it is. The participants' generally low incomes limited their housing options to poorer and more conservative locations. Females had to take extra measures compared to young men, for whom the rules are more lenient. For both, one of the main issues they faced was securing single accommodation. They had to explain why they were without family, and risk disclosing their care history without knowing what the reaction would be. Many anticipated a negative reaction and had various strategies for overcoming obstacles to accessing accommodation. Most used what they called 'legitimate lies', and fabricated culturally acceptable explanations of their single status (see the next section). Some, however, were honest with landlords, for example:

> …every time I spoke to a landlord and told him we were in orphanages he'd slam the door in our faces, because the only thing that occurs to them is 'What did his father do? And why did his mother do this?' He doesn't just think, 'Well it's a broken family'; he's got an idea in his head, and that's what goes! And isn't how to treat a person that's what causes friction between us and the people. (Najem)

According to some participants, the stigma related to single living resulted in their being mistrusted and made them easy targets for landlords. Some landlords took advantage of their lack of family or organizational backup. Some participants did not have legal tenancy agreements, which placed them at a disadvantage and made them feel that they had to beg for needed repairs, for example:

> … [the landlord] used to always insult us as orphans … For instance our house needed tiles for the stairs we waited for a year … we practically had to beg them to fix it. (Mukhtar)

Some females living in student halls were insulted or confronted with their care histories by fellow tenants or superintendents. One young woman left because the superintendent was overcharging her friends from care and called her a 'daughter of sin'; another's care history was exposed and denigrated by the superintendent:

> … Since I was living in halls I had to say I'm from the West Bank … that lie was quickly exposed because the superintendent spread the real story. So my lie was revealed! … When I first got into the halls I was in a really lousy state of mind … one day [the superintendent] said, 'Here! Iron my shirts!' Imagine! 'Here! Iron my shirts!' (Hanaya)

Employment

According to the participants, stigmatization in employment was evident in the change in their employers' or colleagues' attitudes, from treating them as equals to belittling them. A young man withdrew from his colleagues as a result of such treatment, began to get into fights and eventually quit:

> At first they saw me as a supervisor … when they got to understand the true nature of my situation they started looking at me in a totally different way; I was an orphan who had been brought up in care. I started sitting alone to eat … if I wanted to go out with them they'd tease me: 'You were in the centre!', and joked together and in front of the residents … I got into fights because of this; they wouldn't see me as a colleague. (Munir)

Besides this, Munir and other participants in the same situation were paid only meagre wages, or were not paid at all. They were supplied with room and board in exchange for services: generally menial jobs such as maintenance, working as a janitor or replacing anyone who was absent. When these young men, some of whom had worked in exchange for shelter for almost two years, demanded normal wages, they were abruptly asked to leave. They had no formal employment rights, although they had been working for their employers for years. This lack of equality in employment and treatment is an example of multi-level stigmatization; first by employers, and then by colleagues.

Stigmatization in employment also affected wages. A young woman's employer at first behaved as if he was doing her a favour by giving her her earned salary, and later stopped paying her altogether. Although he was aware of her circumstances and had known her since she was in care, she attributed this to him knowing she had no one to assert her rights for her and she left, feeling like 'garbage' and undervalued because she had no backup to make him accountable:

> Of course the first experience [of being taken advantage of] was while working for one of the neighbours of our girls' home. I worked for him for quite some time. Suddenly he stopped giving me my wages. When I'd ask

him about it he would act as if he was doing me a favour, as if I had no right to ask for my wages. He knew that [the care managers] didn't give a damn and they weren't going to run after him for what was my right. He didn't give me my wages – I, of course, was helpless ... I quit working for him. Of course that was accompanied by the feeling that people think of you and treat you like garbage ... they underestimate you because they know you have no one at your back. (Aida)

Relationships

A reflection of societal views and their impact on relationships with Jordanian care leavers was offered by a young woman who was approached by suitors for her hand in marriage, as any woman would be in Jordan. She was still living in care the first time she was approached. Nazek believed that the honest thing to do was to disclose her care history and where she was living. Although her suitor accepted the situation, his family objected without even meeting her. She believed that the stigma was attached to her place of residence rather than her care history. Nazek believed that it would end when she left care. However, she was rejected again:

> ... he approached me like any man would and asked if he could speak to my parents to ask for my hand ... So I told him [I was in care] ... he asked to visit [the home] ... he accepted the situation. I felt that there was still some good in the world ... Imagine, [his family] refused; they did not accept the idea at all. I was shocked. And I felt that the [home] and society had stood in my way again ... I don't want to always feel like I'm less… When I left care I imagined that that whole thing would be over, that society's attitude towards me would now end. So another man approached me ... and the same thing happened ... their point was, why I was there? And why were we now [single] girls living together? ... his family returned to the past, but not like the harshness of the first [guy's family, who] said ... 'her family only put her there because she's evil'. (Nazek)

Most male participants only wanted to marry fellow care leavers for fear of rejection by other partners' families and/or being denigrated by non-care partners for having a care history and no family, and thus no value.

They saw partners with a care history as better at understanding each other's background and needs:

> ... if I wanted to marry a girl with a family, if we quarrel the first thing she'll say is 'You don't have a family; it's good that I accepted you' ... her family will back her up; they'll say 'You have no parents and you're making problems for our daughter?' She'll use my status to put me down. But a girl from the centres, she'll know how we lived and were raised; we can give each other what we missed out on. (Ibrahim)

Unfortunately, societal views and the stigma attached to care are not limited to unrelated members of society, but were also found among extended family, grandparents and half-siblings. Very few participants had a continuous relationship with their family while in care. Many described feeling abandoned, and some clearly stated that their extended family wanted nothing to do with them. This is noted here because a likely factor in the lack of contact is the families' fear of the stigma being linked to them and a desire to keep their skeletons firmly in the closet. A clear example of how close to home stigmatization can come and how young people pay for their parents' transgressions is the case of a young woman who had been in care since infancy, having been born, according to her understanding, to parents who were not formally married.[1] Abla stated that her mother had been forced to give her up, and her father had always denied paternity, until he was forced to acknowledge her following a court-ordered paternity test when she had been in care for nearly 20 years. Abla's paternal half-siblings see her as a 'daughter of

---

[1] Common-law or customary marriage is a non-conventional form of marriage that is not an officially registered union (Zawaj Urfi). It is an unannounced clandestine arrangement between partners that provides (a very thin layer of) legitimacy to a sexual relationship. According to Rashadet al. (2005), some rural communities are said to opt for this form of marriage if the bride is under the legally permitted age to marry where formal registration of the union is differed until the young girl reaches the age of majority. Economic hardship and the high financial costs of marriage have said to increase this trend amongst urban communities in Egypt, for example. While it is religiously condoned (provided parents of the bride are aware), socially it is very much frowned upon, as it is seen as a cover for pre-marital sex. Rashad et al. (2005) point out that this form of marriage is a disadvantage to women because their rights and the terms of the marriage are not negotiated on their behalf by their family, as is the custom. As a result of Urfi marriages, and despite the scarcity of reporting and statistics, in 1998, Rashad et al. (2005) noted that there were approximately 10,000 contested paternity cases in Egyptian courts (ibid).

sin', even though it was their father who committed the 'sin'. Naturally, this affected her relationship with her family, and especially her father:

> Sometimes they say 'You were born out of sin' and sometimes they say, 'You're our sister'. So this is what affects my relationship with my family, especially my dad. (Abla)

Coping with the Stigma

Almost all of the participants were concerned about stigmatization and had learned to anticipate it. They were generally sensitive to it, either from first-hand experience (usually while in care from important figures such as carers, teachers and school peers), or because they had witnessed or heard how friends from care had been subjected to it. Both genders developed similar overarching coping strategies. Depending on how sensitive they were about potential reactions and implications, there was a consistent degree of vigilance, ranging from being cautious and taking time to disclose their care history, to being constantly guarded and wary. Irrespective of how cautious they were, the stigma was a constant theme, adding yet another challenge to their already-burdened lives. The overarching strategies that they used to manage and cope with the stigma were usually planned and applied to different life areas, including keeping a low profile, limiting social interaction and telling legitimate lies.

Keeping a Low Profile and Limiting Social Interaction

In Jordan, family background is at the forefront of social interactions. For example, as an ice-breaker, it is normal to identify the kin group another belongs to by asking a series of questions, which could be considered friendly: 'What's your family name?' 'Where does your family come from?' 'Who is your father, and what does he do?' and 'How many siblings do you have?' These everyday questions were a source of great anxiety for many participants and contributed to their often self-imposed isolation. Limiting discussion is implemented through a perceived non-verbal understanding, whereby participants do not initiate personal questions on social occasions in order to avoid being asked the same questions. For many, the consequence of maintaining their distance was not being sociable:

> There aren't any social relationships … it's better for me … I don't want to discuss anything. If personal relationships develop, people are going to ask me things like 'Where's your mum? And where's so and so?' (Jad)

Many participants felt the need to remain silent about their care history with their neighbours, colleagues at work and in relationships in general. Maintaining secrecy prevented stigmatization and its consequences. A young woman remained highly guarded with employers and colleagues to ensure that they had no knowledge of her circumstances, to protect herself from the classic types of stigmatization and their implications:

> … [My employers and colleagues] didn't know that I was an orphan, they knew nothing! I didn't dare tell anybody … I don't like anybody feeling sorry for me, or giving me that condescending look … not all people are the same. And there are a lot of men – thank God I never experienced this myself – who would take advantage. They think you're an orphan and helpless, so they take advantage of you [sexually]. I was tough … I understood how things worked. (Jebbara)

Legitimate Lies

Legitimate lies were used as a strategy when justification was required. They are called 'legitimate' because the participants' lies were culturally acceptable fabricated stories. Although both males and females resorted to legitimate lying, the specific justifiable story tended to be gender-appropriate. Despite their poor social integration in care and living in restricted environments for extensive amounts of time, their lies were creative, exhibiting a high degree of street-smartness. The longer a person had been out of care, the more appropriate the lie, reflecting their increased knowledge of what works culturally. Some lies told by more recent care leavers reflected less cultural and gender awareness. The lack of preparation for coping with these issues increased their vulnerability. For example, one girl who had left care three months before her first interview used the employment and commuting lie. Because she was so young, she put herself at risk of being pitied or exploited. How her invented family would allow a young girl to take on a male role at that age and so far away from the protection of any family is questionable. During the second wave of interviews, Yasmeen was raped and repeatedly exploited sexually, and found herself pregnant. Her child was removed by the authorities (Ibrahim 2016).

Whether or not their stories were believed, many tended to stick to them in self-defense, not only to protect their image and themselves from stigma, but also to avoid having to go through the pain of discussing their personal circumstances. Owing to the sensitivity of the issue, they also maintained lies to ensure that their own interpretation of any situation arising, for example, with colleagues, remained objective. Nour, who was 12 years out of care at the time of the second wave of interviews, and had held the same job for ten years, maintained the same story throughout, from concern that she might be treated differently should the truth become known, and to avoid misreading her colleagues' intentions:

> No way I'll tell them. I don't want how I'm treated to change. ... Them not knowing is better for me ... whatever happens at work I know I'm treated the same way as everyone. If they knew [the truth] I'd interpret their behaviour towards me differently and probably be too sensitive. I wouldn't give them the benefit of the doubt as I do now.

Fabrications were also used to avoid barriers to needed employment or accommodation. The young people became increasingly aware of social expectations, and how these could affect access for both genders:

> Everybody wants to rent to families [rather than single people]. Both females and males suffer from [trying to get] accommodation. And you have to tell your story [justifying living alone], so you risk embarrassing yourself and they may not even accept. So you're obliged to fabricate stories and to lie. (Sara)

On the whole, practical, matter-of-fact lies were used to justify their need to be in the capital, Amman, for work or education, for instance, saying that their family homes were in cities too far away to commute.

Employment lies were told especially by males, and could earn them respect if they were seen to be fulfilling the man's duty towards his family.

Conclusion

Care leavers in Jordan are part of a family-based culture that has clear expectations and social parameters; through no fault of their own, care leavers have fallen foul of these. Dysfunctional family dynamics and social taboos lead to their admission to care, for which they are stigmatized, placing them at a great disadvantage in society. This chapter has described, from the perspective of young people themselves, the roots of the stigma attached to growing up in a care home and the implications and risks connected to its various forms. It has discussed the coping strategies that the young people use to protect themselves emotionally and from ill-treatment, and to access housing. These young people are already burdened by the challenges inherent in their transition from care to a hostile outside world. Stigmatization is an additional difficulty that affects all areas of their lives.

Jordan's care structures are underdeveloped, but are increasingly responding to some of the needs of this population. The system provides basic care that is not otherwise available. However, it fails its young residents most glaringly by producing an imperfect transition from care, which is hurried and fails to provide short- or long-term emotional and other resources to assist them in Arab society, where all adults rely on family support with a range of functions. Some had benefitted from care and overcome adversity. In general, however, care fails to alleviate the ongoing social disadvantage that is an unremitting force perpetuating their economic and social marginalization.

Improving the care system and the care-leaving process is crucial to meeting our obligations towards children and youth. The conscious creation of meaningful change and more lasting turning points in their lives are needed to break the cycles of disadvantage and vulnerability. In Jordan, such change should stem from a shift from a 'charitable' to a rights-based paradigm. To reduce the gap between care leavers transitioning to adulthood and their peers in mainstream society, the perspective of care must extend beyond reaching the age of majority. Preparation must include coping with the inevitable stigmatization, and transitioning to adulthood should be accompanied by the ongoing help of a mentor. This should be alongside the provision of financial support, as well as support in housing and career building, particularly for those discharged from care without secondary schooling qualifications, as they are at a greater risk of marginalization, despite an increase in formal support.

Even with improved practice and policy, cultural norms in wider society are slow to change. In parallel to initiatives targeting policy and practice, effort is needed to change the attitudes and structures that produce and perpetuate discrimination in the first place and serve to legitimize the normative Arab social order. As a start, currently a local non-governmental organization is spearheading a project to combat discrimination against care leavers, with a particular focus on those from unknown families. Part of the project entails developing an advocacy campaign in collaboration with sympathetic stakeholders, as well as religious figures or establishments that may endorse the cause.

While the international literature on leaving care does include the influence of stigmatization, little is known about its roots and its contribution to perpetuating cycles of vulnerability. This chapter exemplifies how transitioning into, and from, care does not take place in a cultural vacuum. To tackle the factors perpetuating vulnerability, the inclusion of a cultural dimension in our approach to leaving care is critical.

References

Allayan, K. (2006). *Follow up on the evaluation of child care institutions study of 2002*. Amman: Research Institute for Education and Psychology (unpublished).

Barakat, H. (1993). *The Arab world: Society, culture and state*. Berkeley: University of California Press.

British Psychological Society. (2007). *Code of ethics and conduct*. Leicester: British Psychological Society.

Corbin, J. M., & Strauss, A. L. (2008). *Basics of qualitative research* (3rd ed.). Thousand Oaks: Sage.

Cinthio, H., & Ericsson, M. (2006). *Beneath the surface of honour: A study on the interplay of Islam and tribal patriarchy in relation to crimes of honour in Jordan*. Lund: Lund University.

Davies, H. (2011). Sharing surnames: Children, family and kinship. *Sociology, 45*(4), 554–569.

Farahat, H. J. F. (2013). *Orphaned youth in Jordan: Constraints of patriarchal citizenship*. Unpublished MA thesis, International Institute of Social Studies, The Hague.

Husseini, R. (2009). *Murder in the name of honour*. Oxford: One World Publications.

Ibrahim, R. W. (2016). Paying for my father's sins: Daughters of 'unknown lineage'. In N. Yaqub & R. Qawwas (Eds.), *Bad girls of the Arab world*. Austin: University of Texas Press.

Ibrahim, R. W., & Howe, D. (2011). The experience of Jordanian care leavers making the transition from residential care to adulthood: The influence of a patriarchal and collectivist culture. Special issue: Transitions from care to adulthood. *Children and Youth Services Review, 33*(12), 2469–2474.

Ibrahim, R.W., & Gilligan, R. (unpublished). From educational failure to educational success: A case study of a care leaver in Jordan.

Joseph, S. (1996). Patriarchy and development in the Arab world. *Gender and Development, 4*(2), 14–19.

Joseph, S. (1999). Descent of the nation: Kinship and citizenship in Lebanon. *Citizenship Studies, 3*(3), 295–318.

Johnson, G., & Mendes, P. (2014). Taking control and 'moving on': How young people turn around problematic transitions from out-of-home care. *Social Work and Society, 12*(1), 1–15.

Kawar, M. (2000). *Gender, employment and the life course: The case of working daughters in Amman, Jordan*. Amman: Community Centers Association, Konrad Adenauer Stiftung.

Kulwicki, A. D. (2002). The practice of honour crimes: A glimpse of domestic violence in the Arab world. *Issues in Mental Health Nursing, 23*, 77–87.

Rashad, H., Osman, M., & Roudi-Fahimi, F. (2005). *Marriage in the Arab world* (pp. 1–8). Washington, DC: Population Reference Bureau.

Stein, M., & Munro, E. (Eds.) (2008). *Young people's transitions from care to adulthood*. London: Jessica Kingsley.

20

The Role of Informal Leaving Care Peer Support Networks in Romania

Gabriela Dima and John Pinkerton

> If he sees someone in trouble, he offers him a hand, 'cause he knows that person needs it, I mean he knows it in his heart, 'cause he's been through that and he's good-hearted and he wants to do something for that person. (Mircea – Romanian Care Leaver)

Introduction—Learning from Variation

In a growing number of countries, there is now significant interest and engagement in the process and experience of young people leaving state care. This is expressed in legislative reform, policy development, advances in practice and improvements in information and research. It has also included attention to knowledge exchange through international

J. Pinkerton (✉)
Queen's University, Belfast, Northern Ireland

G. Dima
'Spiru Haret' University, Brasov, Romania

© The Author(s) 2016
P. Mendes, P. Snow (eds.), *Young People Transitioning from Out-of-Home Care*, DOI 10.1057/978-1-137-55639-4_20

comparison. Such international attention is to be welcomed, but given the variations in experiences between countries and the very different paths leaving care can take even within one country, it is important not to rush to 'international' generalizations. These can too easily become narrow, 'given' assumptions that limit questioning and dialogue both within and across national boundaries. The role of international comparison should be to throw into relief, call into question and prompt debate over how leaving care is understood and responded to. The aim of this chapter is to do that in relation to social support. It will draw attention to the role of informal support in general, and peer support from other young people in care in particular. These aspects of leaving care have not received sufficient theoretical, policy or practice focus to date. This chapter will suggest that a fuller understanding of the informal support available to care leavers, including that provided by their care peers, would help in the development of more effective formal support.

Two conceptual models will be presented as framing the discussion: one to emphasize the importance of the process of transition and the other the social ecology of leaving care. Together, they locate peer support as a likely aspect of care leavers' psychosocial development as well as their personal and situational circumstances. To illustrate the discussion, case material is used from a study of care leavers in Romania (Dima 2012). The chapter will end with a call for raising the profile of informal support in general, and care peer support in particular, within leaving care research, policy and practice.

Social Support and Leaving Care

A systematic review, undertaken in the UK by the National Institute for Health and Clinical Excellence and the Social Care Institute for Excellence (NICE/SCIE 2010) addressed the question: 'What is the effectiveness of support services for transition to adulthood/leaving care for improving a range of adult outcomes for looked after young people, compared with no intervention or usual care?'. Of 171 potentially relevant papers, only seven were ultimately judged to be of sufficient methodological rigour and clarity to be included (six American and one British). The review concluded that there was a dearth of rigorous evaluations of leaving care and after care services. The existing data provided no conclusive evidence of effectiveness, only suggesting that support services focused on education, employment, parenthood, and accommodation might have some beneficial effect.

Notable by its absence in the review was any discussion of the informal supports that might help young people cope with leaving care either in conjunction with, or as the focus of, formal support. The research reviewed was exclusively focused on formal services. Given the aim of the review, this is understandable, but it is also symptomatic of a way of thinking that sees care-leaving as primarily about formal services to ensure that young people achieve measurable normative scores of attainment after demonstrating independence has been achieved.

This technocratic approach is at odds with the growing understanding in the child welfare field that it is ongoing relationships, not the accruing of individual attainment, that determine the quality of young people's lives in care and aftercare (Winter 2015). In youth studies, a one-directional transition from youth to adulthood is increasingly questioned for 'focusing narrowly on educational and employment encounters; [because it] prioritizes normative and policy focused assumptions and de-prioritizes the actual lived experiences of young people' (Shildick & MacDonald in Cieslik and Simpson 2013, p. 10–11). Youth transition is best understood as a reflexive process of coping with complex, unsynchronized, physical, psychological, and social changes. Change and the capacity to cope with it are linked to, but not determined by, chronological age. Transitioning is as much about interdependence as it is about independence. It is an expression of personal agency dependent on formal and informal support and structures of opportunity (Coleman 2011; Coleman and Hagell 2007; Henderson et al. 2007; Pinkerton and Dolan 2007).

From these child welfare, youth studies, and psychological perspectives, 'navigation' and 'negotiation' are as important for thinking about leaving care as 'development' and 'transition'. As the phased model of transition in Fig. 20.1 indicates, what is being navigated

Fig. 20.1 Psychosocial phases of transition adapted to leaving care (Adapted from Dima and Skehill 2011)

in leaving care is a complex set of social and psychological processes that are difficult to synchronize. New beginnings require effective endings to care and the space between the two of an 'in-between zone' to deal with separation and loss, instability and insecurity, and the exploration of new roles and identities (Dima and Skehill 2011). This is not work that care leavers should be expected to cope with on their own. The 'in-between zone' can be a very lonely place (Adley and Jupp Kina 2015).

Whilst it has been recognized that, in coping with leaving care, young people 'can benefit from informal support from families, former carers and friends', there is only 'limited available research evidence' of this (Stein 2012, p. 52–53). A systematic review of young people's experience of social support during their transition from care (Hiles et al. 2013) identified 87 potentially relevant pieces of work, of which 47 met the study criteria. Material was drawn primarily from the UK (15 items) and the USA (12 items), but also covered seven other countries. The review found that 'whilst there are cultural, contextual and policy differences … many of the young people's experiences of social support appeared common across multiple countries' (Hiles et al. 2013, p. 2063). Five common themes were identified: the influence of past experiences of social support on the present; supportive relationships during the transition from care; relationships with birth families; the crucial role of practical support; and the lived experience of leaving care.

The reviewers concluded that research demonstrated 'the crucial role of social support for young people during their transition from care across informational, instrumental, emotional and appraisal domains'

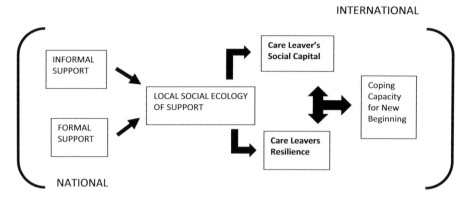

Fig. 20.2 Social ecology of leaving care (Adapted from Pinkerton 2011)

(Hiles et al. 2013, p. 2066). They also found that care leavers often found it difficult to ask for support even when they most needed it. Trust was crucial. 'Those offering support needed to demonstrate at least some genuine understanding of, and concern for the individual's current experiences, in order that they might be sufficiently trusted for the support to be accepted' (Hiles et al. 2013, p. 2066). Reliability and consistency of support were then required. Where friends and family were trusted, they were able to give support that covered all four domains. In addition, friends and partners played an important role in expanding care leavers' support networks by linking them to other families. However, the review also revealed that levels and quality of support to care leavers varied greatly: '[w]hilst some felt that they'd had sufficient, and that good support had made the difference between a successful and an unsuccessful transition for them, many felt completely unsupported or lacking in the specific types of support' (Hiles et al. 2013, p. 2067).

Social support is more than just the immediate network to which a young person belongs. It involves the entire social ecology in which they are located, including neighbourhood, school/work, social services, and the general political, economic, and cultural context at both national and international levels. The model (see Fig. 20.2 below) uses the concept of 'social capital' (Field 2003) to link the range of resources within a social ecology to an individual young person (Pinkerton 2011; Smith 2011; Collins 2015; Van Audenhove and Vander Laenen 2015). Social capital is understood here as 'the aggregate of the actual or potential resources which are linked to possession of a durable network of more or less institutionalized relationships of mutual acquaintance and recognition' (Bourdieu in Barry 2012, p. 57). A young person's capacity for coping with making a new beginning is resourced by the social capital that the model shows as complementary to their internal resources represented as resilience. Resilience is 'the quality that enables some young people to find fulfilment in their lives despite their disadvantaged backgrounds, the problems or adversity they may have undergone or the pressures they may experience' (Stein 2012, p. 165). The poor capacity for coping that international research to date has identified as characteristic of care leavers can be thought of as low resilience and limited social capital within an impoverished social ecology of support.

Learning from Romania

Romania is the largest Eastern European country, with a population of almost 20 million people. Of the 19 per cent of that population estimated to be children, about 1.5 per cent, numbering around 57,646, are involved with social services, just over two-thirds (65 per cent, or around 37,175) are cared for in family settings (professional foster care: 50.4 per cent; extended family: 37.8 per cent; other families: 11.8 per cent), and the other third in residential care (35.51 per cent, or around 20,471) (National Authority for the Protection of Children's Rights and Adoption's 2015). These figures represent a significant decrease from the infamous 100,000 institutionalized children of 1989. Since then, under pressure from the European Union to reform, notable progress has been made with the ratification of the United Nations Convention on the Rights of the Child in 1990, and the reforming of the childcare system in 1997, and then again in 2004. There has been a sustained policy of de-institutionalization and the development of family services—foster care, family reintegration, and prevention (Anghel 2011; Anghel and Beckett 2007; Anghel et al. 2013; Balica 2002; Baban et al. 2008; Marcovici and Dalu 2002; Marginean et al. 2004; Muga 2005; Roth 1999).

Care leavers were largely ignored by the first wave of reform, being considered as adults able to look after themselves. Young people had to leave care at age 18 unless they were in education, in which case they could remain until age 26 (Emergency Order 26/1997). Help with leaving care was non-existent except from some services provided by a few voluntary initiatives and non-governmental organizations (NGOs). An increased recognition of care leavers' needs and a clear political will to respond started in early 2000. The second childcare reform (Law 272/2004) accepted that the state's responsibility should not end on leaving care, and extended responsibilities for up to two years after leaving (Dima and Skehill 2011).

Although the current legislation for young people leaving care in Romania is a great improvement, many of the provisions are not implemented, and the financial crash of 2008 slowed down developments in service provision (Anghel and Dima 2008; Anghel et al. 2013). Since 2006, when the National Authority reported young people were leaving care at a rate of approximately 2000 per year, there has been no further publically available data. Care leavers are rarely prioritized for access to local resources, as required by the legislation. They encounter barriers such as lack of information about their rights, and discriminatory attitudes from some practitioners. Relationships between workers and young people determine who is and who is not provided with learning opportunities and access to community resources (Anghel and Dima 2008; Dima 2012).

In this context of underdeveloped formal provision for care leavers in Romania, it is not surprising that research there has drawn attention to the importance of informal support and specifically the mutual support between young people who leave care together. The study being drawn on here comprises three sets of data gathered by the same researcher, with appropriate university and agency ethical approval. The main mixed-methods study (Dima 2012) was carried out with a purposive sample of 34 care leavers (23 males, 11 females) aged 20–25 years who had left care for two to four years. Data collection by in-depth semi-structured interviews took place during 2004–2006. Qualitative analysis used the Interpretative Phenomenological Analysis (IPA) method. It was chosen for its potential to give voice to young people's lived experiences and provide in-depth understanding of the way they make sense of, and cope with, leaving care (Smith et al. 2009). The IPA analysis identified a set of seven themes: ending care; social transition to independent living; psychological transition to adulthood; identity; stigma; social support in transition; and coping with transition (Dima and Skehill 2011; Dima 2012).

That study was then supplemented 10 years later for the purpose of this chapter, with data from three of the young people from the initial sample (two males, one female); two through interview and one through file data from an NGO. They were selected to represent the three resilience groups described by Stein: 'moving-on', 'surviving', and 'struggling' (Stein 2005, 2012). The third set of data was gathered from a focus group in 2015. The six young people involved were accessed through a local NGO, which was supporting them, or had done so in the past, through an after-care programme. Thematic analysis was undertaken with the two sets of supplementary data focusing only on the theme of informal care peer support. There are clearly limitations to this approach, given the small numbers involved in the supplementary studies and the time lapse since the main study, but it did allow the insights of the original study to be refreshed and focused for the purposes of this discussion.

Informal Support and the Experience of Leaving Care

The young people in the study all became eligible for discharge from care as soon as they had finished education (18–26 years). Employment and accommodation were found for them by care staff. Two approaches tended to be used: discharge of young people singularly, and discharge of two or more in a small group. In the first case, a young person might go to a workplace with housing provision, or be transferred to an NGO with accommodation. In rare cases, a young person returned to family or was discharged with no planned destination (due to extent of challenging behaviours). The groups tended to go to a shared workplace, which either supplied housing, or the staff arranged shared rented accommodation.

The advantages of the second approach for providing mutual support when faced with having to cope with the outside world after years of growing up within a group were emphasized by the young people (pseudonyms are used throughout):

> Every child is afraid, I mean he's horrified…when he's got to leave. (Octavian)

> you can't get to know someone all of a sudden…you only know your friends after leaving the centre, that's your family and they are the ones who can help you, not the others. (Vasile)

> The day we left was so emotional…I went to the car and already felt fearful, such a fear…luckily that others were close to me and I looked at them, as if they were brothers, you know…as they pass the same you're going through. (Nicu)

By contrast, Elena was sent alone to an unknown village where she was going to work as a tailor (her profession) and be given accomodation. The day she arrived there she realized 'I was going to be alone and I hate being left alone', and immediately contacted her boyfriend with whom she went to live that very afternoon. Shortly afterwards, she became pregnant, but her boyfriend's family did not accept her. After many conflicts, they separated, and she was offered support in a mother–baby facility from the child protection board.

Once outside care, irrespective of their first destination, all young people in this study experienced crisis episodes, instability, and insecurity, and were challenged to deal with basic survival as well as social integration issues. More positive experiences were found: some form of aftercare support was received, either from statutory or private programmes or from foreign families known while in residential care. However, each young person at some point used the resource of a care peer network, regarded by some as a substitute for the absence of family:

> My conception is that…I grew up with them in the orphanage and put them first; if I would grew up with brothers, mother, father they would have been in the forefront. (Mihnea)

The care peer network was used to access various resources, namely, housing, money, employment, emotional, and moral support. Ionela moved with her boyfriend to the city, having left care from another county, and when she separated from him, she urgently needed accommodation. Elena, herself a young mother with a second newborn child, offered her accomodation:

> I had nowhere to stay and stayed with Elena one month or so… I felt the need to help her, when you have two kids and are alone it's hard and when you've got someone ,on the head' is even more dificult. (Ionela, focus group)

> It was hard when you have 2 kids…but in another way it's a relief…I mean, that's how I felt, I had an easy heart, because…I took into account that she had grown up in care, I knew what she had gone through. (Elena, focus group)

In some cases, care leavers took advantage of their friends and ended up staying for longer periods, without being motivated to get a job and find their own accomodation:

> …when I had a rented room I kept three guys; one guy stayed with me for one year, he asked me if I could keep him for a week or two he said, but I couldn't find it in my heart to tell him it's been a month and…it was mid winter, what should I have told him? Get out of here? (Victor)

Apart from short- and long-term housing support, many young people reported being helped with overnight stays, and saw the care peer network as a drop in resource. Money could also be a shared problem:

> We search through our pockets and sometimes we help each other out […] if I had money, I gave, if I didn't had some money, he had and I said 'hey lend me this sum 'cause I give you back'. He gave me. I gave him back. (Catalin)

However, as with housing, financial help could also be abused:

20 The Role of Informal Leaving Care Peer Support Networks…

Most times I gave and I got back; when I didn't got back, no problem, second time I remembered […] if they are my care friends…I couldn't care less if they don't' give me back'. (Dorian, focus group)

You know how it is when they see you have money 'let's go to give me a drink' stuff like that, and when you don't have and go to him 'well you see, I don't have…' [so other relationships were preferred] I get along well with those from outside…but I don't want 'centre persons. (Catalin)

Care peers proved to be a good source for food too:

There are days when we don't have anything (to eat) and we help each other, reciprocal; 'give me something to eat, 'cause I can't do it anymore!'… when he didn't have any, I had and so on. (Dumitru)

Financial security required employment and there too informal support was an important resource. When Elena separated from her partner and returned to the city looking for a job and a place to stay, she was lucky to meet a friend from care:

I say, 'do you work?'…'yes'", 'who is your boss'… I knew her from the shoes factory where I have worked before…"can you talk for me too?' … The next day I went there and talked to the boss, she told me the salary and the working hours. (Elena, 2nd interview, 10 years later)

It was quite usual for care leavers to be placed together for their first job or to search for jobs together. Whilst this was positive in that it helped them assume a worker's role and responsibilities, it had disadvantages. For example, Dumitru was discharged together with a group of care peers for whom work was found in construction. However, without any further support, the young people lost their jobs as a group and ended up homeless. Later, Dumitru managed to find another job with one of his best friends from care, but when he fell out with the employer, they both quit their jobs:

[The boss found out] that we are from the orphanage…since then both me and (friend) were treated differently to others…I said to the boss 'Hey you, what's your problem with us?' [he said]'Do you have something to say…

you don't like it, leave'. [So I say] 'I go, I quit. You think that if I am from the orphanage and come her to work it means I am a slave?' And I left; my friend came too'. (Dumitru)

In addition to practical help, care leavers need emotional support; yet, in the main study, fewer than half of the 34 young people interviewed mentioned the need for help to 'overcome tough times'(Rodica). One young man explained that even if the majority of care leavers need emotional support, they would not admit it. Findings from the focus group confirm that care leavers are more eager to offer emotional support than ask for it:

> First come the others, then ourselves; that's how we are. (Manuela, focus group)

> Yes, I'd sooner be of help, than ask something, I don't like asking. (Pamela, focus group)

Pamela offered a range of support to her friend Vera (focus group) with whom she shared four years of care. Vera was discharged to work and live in a guesthouse where she stayed for four months; then, feeling exploited, she decided to leave. Pamela let Vera live with her and her partner, taking her out to make her familiar with the city, helping her to make new friends, and advising her about life outside care:

> I feel very good…I helped her before and now open-heartedly…for now, she stays under my wing. (Pamela, focus group)

Another focus group member identified herself with Vera's shyness when she was younger: 'I really want to encourage her that she can do more…we all can, but I think we need to communicate more with each other. I have learned that if you do not ask no one can help you' (Manuela, focus group).

While care peers' support clearly had benefits, what was required from it and how it was used varied. In particular, there were differences between those care leavers staying mostly within the care peers network, and those moving on and extending their relational network. Calin is a young man whose experience fits the 'moving on' group (Stein 2005).

He was interviewed firstly at age 25, and then at age 35. At the second interview, he talked about his work as an area sales manager, progressing within the same company and being well paid. He is in a long-term stable partnership with a partner and step-son, aged 15 years. He perceived himself as a successful man, proud of his achievements. Calin was abandoned at birth and had no information on, or contact with, any family member. In care, he had the opportunity to build a significant attachment with a Dutch family, with whom he spent summer holidays as part of a programme for foreign families supporting Romanian children and young people in care. It proved to be a good aftercare support too. They became 'my family' and were supportive both in practical and in emotional matters: 'I always went to them [...] most of the times even late at night, and I've always had an answer from them'. When asked about his relationships with care peers, he said:

> Well, uh, I meet a lot of people who were with me in the home. Now, to be honest, I kind of put a lot behind me, because... I've learnt that it's better to avoid that which is not good for you [...] I don't disown my origins, I admit anytime where I grew up, whatever the position I will have on the social scale [...] Yet, uh, their influences are so negative, that I literally don't want to accept them...and so I prefer standing apart. (Calin, 2nd interview, 10 years later)

Despite that general distancing, Calin is offering help to 'my childhood friend' who is very sick and has been admitted to residential care:

> I've helped him before, I still do, until he's fated to live. Well, I see this, like...not necessarily obligation, rather like a mission of mine, by fate...as I have received, I have to pass on [...] I dare say, if there were at least, what do I know?!, Ten more like me, something better would happen. (Calin, 2nd interview, 10 years later)

Elena, whose experience fits with the 'survivors' category (Stein 2005), was first interviewed at age 20 when she was accomodated in a mother and child unit with her nine-month-old boy, and again at age 29 years, as an expectant mother. Motherhood helped Elena to let go of the 'care-identity': 'I feel like any adult from the moment my first child arrived, I became automatically another person'. Her social support network over the years consisted mostly of care peers, some work colleagues, and an NGO offering long-term support. Elena's life story of the past 10 years reveals periods of stability interspersed with instability and crises. A key one was when she gave up her full time job, gave up her rented apartment, and moved in with her boyfriend who was a care peer. He was given housing provision with other work colleagues by his employer, but children were not allowed to stay, so they both decided it would be better for the three-year-old boy to be placed in temporary foster care. This was a very tough time for Elena: 'I was crying, oh my God, crying and crying… poor (child's name) was crying too'. The initial three-month placement ended up to be two years, when she persuaded her partner to reunite the family and move together to his parents' house in a village. Although that relationship didn't last, when Elena and a new partner had a financial crises and were threatened with homelessness, she turned to her first partner as part of her informal network of support:

> We had appealed to friends of (name partner) some of those from care, but, well, uh… no one can keep you, especially the 3 persons […] willy-nilly, I had to appeal to him (ex partner) as I knew he could help me in that matter. (Elena, 2nd interview, 10 years later)

No one from the original sample whose life could be characterized as 'struggling' (Stein 2005) could be found for interviewing. However, Dumitru was followed-up through data accessed within an NGO. He was part of a larger group of care leavers who worked and lived together and also shared homelessness periods. He had previously emphasized the important positive functions of the care leavers' support network: 'Actually, our generation…none of us was in the situation to go to jail […] but, in other generations, this had happened […] they had never kept in touch the way we do' (Dumitru). Yet, the reality for care leavers like Dumitru seemed more like: 'if there's one who is better-off, then we all go to him' (Mircea). Some concluded, over time, that the peer group was holding them back by perpetuating negative behaviours when they were together in a larger group, and decided to put some distance between themselves and their peers: 'It is good too, but for now I prefer to stay away and not be part of the group anymore… just stay in touch' (Vasile).

Discussion

What is clear from this study is that, in line with the generally accepted international picture, emotional, relationship, accommodation, and employment instability and insecurity are salient markers of life after care for these Romanian care leavers. However, informal support in dealing with these challenges was also very apparent in the study in contrast to weak or non-existent formal support. Networks of informal support amongst the care leavers can be seen to have enriched the local social ecology from which they gleaned their social capital and emergent resilience. In particular, these relationships were there for them in the in-between zone as they made attempts to move into, and cope with, their new beginnings, having had the ending of care very much foisted on them. At the same time, the disadvantages of this informal support were also apparent. It can be very fluid, and perpetuate negative behaviours and a 'care identity', which hold the young people back from moving on in their lives as young adults. The networks and relationships were not necessarily strong enough or appropriate to meet the needs and aspirations of the care leavers.

Conclusion

If the emerging international agenda on leaving care (United Nations General Assembly 2009) is to be effectively addressed, the importance of informal support, not least the relationships between care leavers themselves, needs to recognized. Policy needs to take account of informal support without expecting too much from it, as is tempting in times of austerity (Briheim-Crookall 2011). Practice needs to develop ways to support this agenda through care alumni groups, peer mentoring, peer educators, and network group conferencing. Research needs to adopt methods such as biographical narrative accounts (Pinkerton and Rooney 2014) and network analysis (Blakeslee 2012) to advance understanding of the features and processes involved in these relationships and networks of support, not least its power dynamics and interface with formal services. Special attention needs to be given to learning from those countries where, in the absence of formal leaving and aftercare systems, informal support is highly visible (Frimpong-Manso 2015; McMahon and Curtis 2013; Van Breda and Dickens chapter in this volume). Informal support is no panacea, but it may be the richest resource available to those who have left care and those who work with them.

References

Adley, N., & Jupp Kina, V. (2015). Getting behind the closed door of care leavers: Understanding the role of emotional support for young people leaving care. *Child and Family Social Work*. doi:10.1111/cfs.12203.

Anghel, R. (2011). Transition within transition: How young people learn to leave public care behind while their carers are stuck in the neutral. *Children and Youth Services Review, 33*(12), 2526–2531.

Anghel, R., & Beckett, C. (2007). Skateboarding behind the EU lorry: The experience of Romanian professionals struggling to cope with transitions while assisting care leavers. *European Journal of Social Work, 10*(1), 3–19.

Anghel, R., & Dima, G. (2008). Romania. In M. Stein & E. Munro (Eds.), *Young people's transitions from care to adulthood: International research and practice* (pp. 158–172). London: Jessica Kingsley Publishers.

Anghel, R., Herzog, M., & Dima, G. (2013). The challenge of reforming child protection in Eastern Europe: The cases of Hungary and Romania. *Psyhosocial Intervention (Intervencion Psicosocial), 22*(3), 239–249.

Baban, A., Marcu, O., & Craciun, C. (2008). Romanian country report, In Ai.Bi. Report 2008, *Child abandonment: an emergency*, Milano: FrancoAngeli.

Balica, E. (2002). Tinerii din centrele de plasament intre integrare si marginalizare. *Revista de Asistenta Sociala, 6*.

Barry, M. (2012). Social capital in the lives of young carers. In J. Allan & R. Catts (Eds.), *Social capital, children and young people: Implications for practice, policy and research* (pp. 53–76). Bristol: Policy Press.

Blakeslee, J. (2012). Expanding the scope of research with transition-age foster youth: Application of the social network perspective. *Child and Family Social Work, 17,* 326–336.

Briheim-Crookall, L. (2011). *Making the cut: Planning transitions for care leavers in an age of austerity.* London: National Care Advisory Service.

Cieslik, M., & Simpson, D. (2013). *Key concepts in youth studies.* London: Sage.

Coleman, J. (2011). *The nature of adolescence* (4th ed.). London: Routledge.

Coleman, J., & Hagell, A. (Eds.) (2007). *Adolescence, risk and resilience: Against the odds.* Chichester: Wiley.

Collins, M. E. (2015). *Macro perspectives on youths aging out of foster care.* Washington, DC: NASW Press.

Dima, G. (2012). *Experiences of young people leaving care: A Romanian psychosocial study.* Saarbrucken: LAP Lambert Academic Publishing.

Dima, G., & Skehill, C. (2011). Making sense of leaving care: The contribution of Bridges model of transition to understanding the psycho-social process. *Children and Youth Services Review, 33,* 2532–2539.

Emergency Order 26. (1997). The protection of children in difficulty, published in Official Monitor, nr.276 on 24/07/1998.

Field, J. (2003). *Social capital.* London: Routledge.

Frimpong-Manso, K. (2015). The social support networks of care leavers from a children's village in Ghana. *Child and Family Social Work.* doi:10.1111/cfs.12218.

Henderson, S., Holland, J., McGrellis, S., Sharpe, S., & Thompson, R. (2007). *Inventing childhoods: A biographical approach to youth transitions.* London: Sage.

Hiles, D., Moss, D., Wright, J., & Dallos, R. (2013). Young people's experience of social support during the process of leaving care: A review of the literature. *Children and Youth Services Review, 35*(12), 2059–2071.

Law 272. (2004). *On the protection and promotion of children's rights.* Published in the Official Monitor, nr.557 on 23/06/2004.

Marcovici, O., & Dalu, A. M. (2002). *Youth transitions, youth policy and participation, workpackage 2 Report.* Bucharest: YOYO Project.

Marginean, I., Popescu, R., Arpinte, D., & Neagu, G. (2004). *Conditii Sociale ale Excluziunii Copilului.* Bucharest: Academia Romana, INCE, ICCV.

McMahon, C., & Curtis, C. (2013). The social networks of young people in Ireland with experience of long-term foster care: Some lessons for policy and practice. *Child and Family Social Work, 18,* 329–340.

Muga, M. (Ed.) (2005). *Studiu Privind Situatia Tinerilor care Parasesc Sistemul de Protectie a Copilului.* Bucharest: Institutul National de Cercetare Stiintifica in Domeniul Muncii si Protectie Sociale.

National Authority for the Protection of Children's Rights and Adoption (ANPDCA). (2015). Statistics. At http://www.mmuncii.ro/j33/images/buletin_statistic/copil_III2015.pdf. Accessed 25 Jan 2016.

National Institute for Health and Clinical Excellence and the Social Care Institute for Excellence (NICE/SCIE). (2010). *The effect of support services for transition to adulthood/leaving care on the adult outcomes of looked after young people*. Available online at www.nice.org.uk/guidance/

Pinkerton, J. (2011). Constructing a global understanding of the social ecology of leaving out of home care. *Children and Youth Services Review, 33*, 2412–2416.

Pinkerton, J., & Dolan, P. (2007). Family support, social capital, resilience and adolescent coping. *Child & Family Social Work, 12*(3), 219–228.

Pinkerton, J., & Rooney, C. (2014). Care Leavers' experiences of transition and turning points: Findings from a biographical narrative study. *Social Work and Society, 12*(1), 1–12.

Roth, M. (1999). Children's rights in Romania: Problems and progress. *Social Work in Europe, 6*(3), 30–37.

Smith, W. B. (2011). *Youth leaving foster care: A developmental, relationship-based approach to practice*. New York: Oxford University Press.

Smith, J. A., Flowers, P., & Larkin, M. (2009). *Interpretative phenomenological analysis: Theory, method and research*. London: Sage.

Stein, M. (2005). *Resilience and young people leaving care: Overcoming the odds*. York: Joseph Rowntree Foundation.

Stein, M. (2012). *Young people leaving care: Supporting pathways to adulthood*. London: Jessica Kingsley.

United Nations General Assembly. (2009). *Guidelines for the alternative care of children*. Adopted by the UN General Assembly 18 December 2009 (A/RES/64/142). http://www.iss-ssi.org/2009/assets/files/guidelines/Guidelines-English.pdf

Van Audenhove, S., & Vander Laenen, F. (2015). Future expectations of young people leaving youth care in Flanders: The role of personal and social capital in coping with expected challenges. *Child and Family Social Work*. doi:10.1111/cfs.12233.

Winter, K. (2015). Supporting positive relationships for children and young people who have experience of care. *IRISS Insights, 28*, 1–20.

Index

B

Buttle UK Quality Mark program, 102
By Degrees report, 96, 97

C

child maltreatment
    abuse, 26, 46
    and educational attainment, 175
    neglect, 30, 47, 63, 71, 72, 175, 335, 343
    parental mental health issues, 71
    reporting and monitoring systems, 343, 370
    risk for youth justice involvement, 32
CREATE Foundation, 24, 99, 101, 116, 120, 121, 266, 272, 285–304
cultural context of leaving care, 392–5

D

developmental disability
    and leaving care, xxxii, xxxvi

E

education
    disability, 40, 79, 80, 81, 82, 83, 84, 86, 87, 180, 227
    exclusion, 26, 34
    low attainment, 174, 314
    post-secondary, 174, 179, 192, 280
    school, 141, 182
    teachers, 34, 101, 121, 122, 123, 128, 129, 136, 137, 142, 143, 145, 146, 165, 167, 180, 182, 188, 189, 191, 314

© The Author(s) 2016
P. Mendes, P. Snow (eds.), *Young People Transitioning from Out-of-Home Care*, DOI 10.1057/978-1-137-55639-4

428 Index

employment, 10, 12, 13, 14, 27, 34, 51–2, 55, 57, 59, 60, 78, 79, 80, 82, 83, 84, 85, 94, 100, 101, 149, 178, 179, 192, 202, 203, 207, 223, 227, 229, 233, 234, 242, 271, 272, 274, 275, 278, 298, 310, 316, 318, 319, 320, 322, 330, 331, 339, 340, 349, 352, 357, 359, 360, 362, 389, 390, 391, 392, 393, 395, 398, 400–1, 405, 406, 411, 416, 418, 419, 423
ethics and care leaver research
  confidentiality, 245, 246
  consent, 48, 121, 246, 254
  ethics committees, 49
  safety, 27, 224, 235

F

families
  grandparents, 298, 334, 402
  kinship care, 32, 94, 96, 107, 129n2, 266, 269, 354, 369, 370
  parents/guardians, 6, 12, 14, 36, 40, 46, 47, 48, 52, 57, 64, 82, 99, 102, 105, 106, 107, 108, 116, 122, 123, 124, 125, 127, 128, 129n1, 138, 139, 140, 141, 142, 143, 146, 149, 158, 163, 166, 167, 176, 180, 186, 187, 191, 202, 206, 223, 224, 267, 269, 275, 276–7, 277, 278, 315, 319, 322, 330, 334, 369
  siblings, 58, 126, 137, 158, 403

H

housing and homelessness, 12, 27, 34, 35, 36, 38, 47, 51, 55, 62, 64, 71, 78, 79, 84, 85, 86, 100, 105, 106, 137, 146, 158, 207, 267, 269, 270, 272, 273, 275, 277, 278, 279, 280, 298, 300, 330, 333, 340, 342, 350, 384, 392, 398, 407, 416, 418, 422

I

indigenous children and young people, 108, 313, 315
informal systems of care, 344
institutional care, 136, 176, 331, 338, 367–84

M

media, 253, 274, 294, 296–8
mental health issues in leaving care populations, 26, 31, 33, 47, 61, 105
MidWest evaluation of the Adult Functioning of Former Foster Youth, 270

models of care
  kinship care, 32, 94, 96, 107, 129n2, 266, 269, 354, 369, 370
  out-of-home care (OHC), 3, 23–40, 45–66, 71–88, 94, 118, 135, 139, 149, 159, 174, 199, 229, 242, 245, 254, 255, 256, 259, 265, 267, 285, 289, 293–5, 298, 304, 315, 330, 331, 354, 367, 391
  residential care, 6, 12, 25, 31–5, 38, 78, 94, 121, 123, 155, 156, 161, 162, 175–8, 180, 181, 186, 189–91, 202, 204, 205, 207, 209, 244, 266, 270, 274, 279, 313, 349–62, 390, 395, 414, 417, 421
Models of leaving care, xxxix

N

National Framework for Protecting Australia's Children (Australia), 100, 267, 301
National Standards for out-of-home care (Australia), 118, 267

P

parents/guardians
  contact with, 382
  mental health issues, 26, 31, 33, 47, 61, 105
peer research methods, 221–39
Peer Support Networks, 409–24

policy, 4, 7, 15, 24, 27, 29, 38, 39, 45, 48, 61, 63–6, 72, 74, 78, 81, 86–8, 93–109, 119, 136, 141, 149, 150, 174, 178, 192, 199, 201, 202, 205, 208, 213, 234, 238, 256, 265–80, 285, 287–9, 291, 294, 297–9, 309–11, 314, 316, 317, 320, 321–3, 329–33, 335, 341, 342, 345, 350, 351, 353–5, 357, 358, 361, 362, 368, 378, 383, 384, 390, 392, 407, 409–12, 414, 423

R

research challenges with care leavers
  confidentiality, 245, 246
  consent, 48, 121, 127, 140, 246–8, 250, 254, 257, 375
  ethics committees, 49
  funding, 64, 78, 80, 107, 108, 143, 220, 243, 266, 268, 277, 278, 285–90, 293, 295, 304, 317, 338
  safety, 247

S

siblings. *See* families
social capital, 9, 312, 321, 322, 333, 351, 393, 413, 414, 423
social ecology model of leaving care, 410, 413
social marginalization, 406
Staying Put program, 119

stigma and leaving care, 14, 62, 63, 117, 120, 122, 126, 127, 129, 145, 148, 160, 245, 256, 289, 303, 311, 331, 370, 390–2, 394, 395, 397–407, 416
substance abuse, 26, 33, 34, 36, 38, 71, 80, 99, 269, 279, 318, 350, 352

T

teenage pregnancy, 276, 277
trauma-informed approaches, 36, 38

U

United Nations Committee on the Rights of the Child, 314, 331
United Nations Guidelines for the Alternative Care of Children, 208, 332

W

welfare regimes (varied), 199–213

Y

Young people from a public care background pathways to education in Europe (YiPPEE), 98, 137, 138, 149, 158, 192
young people transitioning from out-of-home care
country by country, 108, 118, 137, 205, 317, 352, 353, 355, 362, 370, 409, 414

Argentina, 221–39
Australia, 23–40, 265–80
China, 241–60
Denmark, 98, 137, 200, 202, 204, 207, 209, 210, 211, 212
England, 3, 7, 12, 97, 98, 100, 103, 137, 156, 158, 204, 205, 206, 207, 209, 211, 221–39
Germany, 173–92, 241–60
Hungary, 98, 137, 156
Israel, 155–7, 159–62, 165, 168, 169, 174, 180, 241–60, 331
Jordan, 331, 389–407
New Zealand, 138, 309, 313, 315–23
Northern Ireland, 3, 7, 71–88, 97, 205, 207, 221–39
Norway, 200, 202, 204, 207, 212
Romania, 409–24
Russia, 292, 367–84
Scotland, 97, 204, 205, 207, 270, 278, 291
South Africa, 331, 349–62
Spain, 98, 137, 156
Sweden, 98, 137, 200, 202, 204, 207, 208, 209, 211
Switzerland, 7, 241–60
United States of America, 46, 73, 138, 161, 229, 291, 292, 329, 331, 390, 410
Vietnam, 329–45
youth justice system and leaving care, 1, 7, 23, 24, 26, 27, 28, 31, 32, 35, 36, 37, 38, 267